**CENTRAL
CUBA – WEST**
Pages 150–173

**CENTRAL
CUBA – EAST**
Pages 174–203

CENTRAL CUBA - EAST

EASTERN CUBA

WESTERN CUBA
Pages 128–149

EASTERN CUBA
Pages 204–241

D0489845

CUBA

DK EYEWITNESS *TRAVEL GUIDES*

CUBA

DK

DORLING KINDERSLEY

LONDON • NEW YORK • MUNICH • MELBOURNE • DELHI
www.dk.com

LONDON, NEW YORK,
MELBOURNE, MUNICH AND DELHI
www.dk.com

PRODUCED BY Fabio Ratti Editoria Srl, Milan, Italy

PROJECT EDITOR Giorgia Conversi
ART EDITOR Paolo Gonzato

EDITORS Carla Beltrami, Barbara Cacciani,
Fernanda Incoronato, Alessandra Lombardi

MAIN CONTRIBUTOR
Irina Bajini

OTHER CONTRIBUTORS
Alejandro Alonso, Miguel A Castro Machado,
Andrea G Molinari, Marco Oliva, Francesca Piana

PHOTOGRAPHERS
Heidi Grassley, Lucio Rossi

CARTOGRAPHERS
Laura Belletti, Oriana Bianchetti, Roberto Capra

ILLUSTRATORS
Marta Fincato, Modi Artistici

ENGLISH TRANSLATION
Richard Pierce

Dorling Kindersley Limited
EDITOR Fiona Wild
CONSULTANT Emily Hatchwell
DTP DESIGNERS Jason Little, Conrad van Dyk
PRODUCTION Joanna Bull

Reproduced in Singapore by Colourscan
Printed and bound in China by South China Printing Co.Ltd.

First published in Great Britain in 2002
by Dorling Kindersley Limited,
80 Strand, London WC2R 0RL

Reprinted with revisions 2004

**The information in every
Dorling Kindersley Travel Guide is checked regularly.**
Every effort has been made to ensure that this book is as up-to-date
as possible at the time of going to press. Some details, however,
such as telephone numbers, opening hours, prices, gallery hanging
arrangements and travel information are liable to change. The
publishers cannot accept responsibility for any consequences arising
from the use of this book, nor for any material on third party
websites, and cannot guarantee that any website address in this
book will be a suitable source of travel information. We value the
views and suggestions of our readers very highly. Please write to:
The Publisher, DK Eyewitness Travel Guides,
Dorling Kindersley, 80 Strand, London WC2R 0RL.

CONTENTS

Ídolo de Tabaco, Museo
Montané, Havana *(see p101)*

INTRODUCING CUBA

**Primary school children in
Santiago de Cuba**

◁ **A house in Trinidad with characteristic iron grilles; in the insert, the bust of Hatuey at Baracoa**

The beach at Guardalavaca, one of the best-known resorts in Cuba

Grilled *camarones* (prawns)

Dancing at the Casa de la
Tradición in Santiago de Cuba

Museo de la
Revolución *(see pp88–9)*

HOW TO USE THIS GUIDE

THIS GUIDE will help you to get the most out of your visit to Cuba by providing detailed information and expert recommendations. *Introducing Cuba* maps the island and sets it in its historic, artistic, cultural and geographical context. *Havana* and the four regional sections describe the most important sights, with maps, floor plans, photographs and detailed illustrations. Hotels and restaurants, together with night spots and shops, are described in *Travellers' Needs*, while the *Survival Guide* offers tips on everything from transport to phones and local currency.

HAVANA
AREA BY AREA

The centre of the city is divided into three areas, each with its own chapter. The last chapter, *Further Afield*, covers peripheral sights. All the sights are numbered and plotted on the *Area Map*. The detailed information for each sight is easy to locate because it follows the numerical order on the map.

Sights at a Glance lists the sights in each chapter by category: Churches, Museums and Galleries, Streets and Squares, Historic Buildings, Parks and Gardens.

2 **Street-by-Street Map**
This gives a bird's-eye view of the most important areas in each chapter.

Stars indicate the sights no visitor should miss.

All pages relating to Havana have red thumb tabs.

A locator map shows where you are in relation to the other areas of the city.

1 **Area map**
All the major sights are numbered and located on this map. Those in the historic centre are also listed in the Havana Street Finder (see pp118–23).

Suggested routes are shown in red.

3 **Detailed Information**
The most important monuments and sights in Havana are described individually. Addresses, phone numbers, opening hours and information concerning guided tours and taking photos are also provided.

1 Introduction to the Region
The landscape, history and character of each region are described here, showing how the region has developed over the centuries and what it has to offer to visitors today.

CUBA REGION BY REGION

Apart from Havana, the island has been divided into four regions, each with a separate chapter: Western Cuba, Central Cuba – West, Central Cuba – East and Eastern Cuba.

2 Pictorial Map
This shows the road network and provides an illustrated overview of the whole region. All the interesting places to visit are numbered in the same order in which they are described, and there are also useful tips on getting around the region by car and by public transport.

Each region can easily be identified by its own colour coding.

3 Detailed Information on Each Sight
All the major cities and other top sights are described in detail. They are listed in order, following the numbering on the Pictorial Map. Within each town or city there is detailed information on important buildings and other sights.

The Visitors' Checklist
provides all the practical information you will need to plan your visit.

Boxes provide further information on the region: leading figures, legends, historical events, local flora and fauna, curiosities, and so on.

4 Cuba's Top Sights
These are given two or more full pages. Historic buildings are dissected to reveal their interiors, while museums have colour-coded floor plans to help you locate their most interesting features, which are shown in photographs with captions.

INTRODUCING CUBA

Putting Cuba on the Map

WASHED BY THE ATLANTIC OCEAN, the Caribbean Sea and the waters of the Gulf of Mexico, Cuba is the largest island in the Greater Antilles, situated just south of the Tropic of Cancer. It lies only 180 km (112 miles) from Florida and 210 km (130 miles) from Mexico, while Haiti and Jamaica are slightly less than 80 km (50 miles) and 140 km (87 miles) away, respectively. Cuba is not a single island, but a varied archipelago with a total surface area of 110,922 sq km (42,815 sq miles). Lying on an east-west axis, the main island, the elongated Isla Grande, is about 1,250 km (776 miles) long, and 100 km (62 miles) wide on average. Around it are five archipelagoes: Colorados, Sabana, Camagüey, Canarreos and Jardines de la Reina, consisting of thousands of *cayos* (keys and small islands). The largest minor island is Isla de la Juventud. Cuba has about 11 million inhabitants, 2,500,000 of whom live in Havana, the capital.

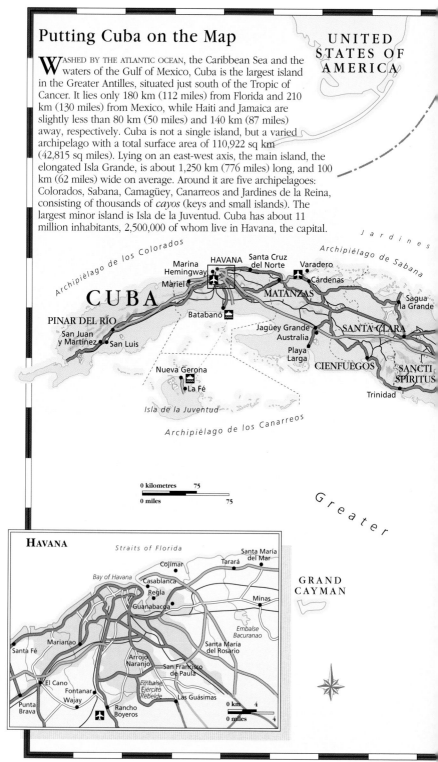

UNITED STATES OF AMERICA

Jardines
Archipiélago de Sabana

Archipiélago de los Colorados

Marina Hemingway
HAVANA
Santa Cruz del Norte
Varadero
Cárdenas

Mariel

CUBA

MATANZAS

Sagua la Grande

PINAR DEL RÍO

Batabanó

Jagüey Grande
Australia

SANTA CLARA

San Juan y Martínez
San Luis

Playa Larga

CIENFUEGOS

SANCTI SPÍRITUS

Nueva Gerona

La Fé

Trinidad

Isla de la Juventud

Archipiélago de los Canarreos

0 kilometres   75
0 miles   75

Greater

HAVANA

Straits of Florida

Santa María del Mar

Bay of Havana
Cojímar
Tarará

Casablanca
Regla

GRAND CAYMAN

Guanabacoa

Minas

Embalse Bacuranao

Marianao

Santa Fé

Arrojo Naranjo
San Francisco de Paula

Santa María del Rosario

El Cano
Fontanar
Wajay

Embalse Ejército Rebelde

Las Guásimas

Punta Brava

Rancho Boyeros

0 km   4
0 miles   4

◁ **Mural on the corner of Calle Heredia and Calle Clarín, Santiago de Cuba**

THE BAHAMAS

ANDROS

d e l   R e y

Archipiélago de Camagüey

THE BAHAMAS

UNITED STATES
OF AMERICA

*ATLANTIC
OCEAN*

MEXICO

BAHAMAS
Havana   ANDROS
CUBA
JAMAICA

DOMINICAN
HAITI REPUBLIC
PUERTO
RICO

*PACIFIC

OCEAN*

BELIZE
GUATEMALA HONDURAS
EL SALVADOR   NICARAGUA

COSTA RICA
PANAMA

VENEZUELA

COLOMBIA

ECUADOR

PERU

BRAZIL

0 kilometres 900

0 miles   900

*ATLANTIC

OCEAN*

Morón

atibonico

**CIEGO
DE ÁVILA**   Florida   Nuevitas

CAMAGÜEY   Sibanicú

Guáimaro   Gibara

LAS TUNAS   **HOLGUÍN**

Jardin s de la Reina   Mayarí

BAYAMO Contramaestre   Baracoa
Manzanillo   **GUANTÁNAMO**
Yara Palma Soriano   Imías
El Cobre   Caimanera
Pilón   **SANTIAGO**   San Antonio
DE CUBA   del Sur

A n t i l l e s

KEY

✈ International airport

⛴ Ferry

━ Motorway

━ Major road

─ Railway line

━ International border

---- Provincial border

JAMAICA

A PORTRAIT OF CUBA

I MAGES OF CUBA SHOW HOT SUN *and fields of sugar cane, tall palm trees and deep, clear blue sea. Cuba is indeed all these things, but it is also a country with a deep-rooted, complex culture in which old traditions and new intellectual developments co-exist. It is a young and vital island, a place of music and colour, which despite severe economic difficulties in recent years has held on to its unique identity.*

Cuba's identity owes a great deal to the fact that it is surrounded by sea as well as to its geographical position. It is sometimes called the "key to the gulf" because of its strategic location between North and South America at the entrance to the Gulf of Mexico, and the island has been a crossroads since the beginning of the Colonial period. As a result, the island's early population consisted of European settlers, a few native Indians who had survived struggles against the invaders, imported diseases and hard labour, and thousands of black slaves, brought over from Africa. Up to the abolition of slavery in 1886, the dominant culture was that of the

The crest of Cuba, "key of the gulf"

conquering Spanish, with some influence from the sailors and travellers who had stopped in Cuba. However, by surreptitious means, the African slaves managed to preserve their songs, musical instruments and dances, introduced new spices and tastes to the local cuisine, and continued to worship their Yoruba gods *(see pp20–21)*.

The result of this cross-fertilization is a surprising ethnic mosaic of whites, blacks, people of mixed race and Asians (a Chinese community grew in Havana in the 19th century). The same mosaic characterizes Cuban culture too: the bringing together of vastly different traditions has produced a unique blend.

Chatting outside the front door, a typically Cuban habit

◁ **Students outside their school, illustrating the diverse ethnic mix of the Cuban population**

Playing dominoes, a national game

THE LIFESTYLE

In general, Cubans are outgoing, talkative and sociable. The doors of their houses are always open, a glass of rum or a cup of coffee is there for anyone who passes by to say hello and chat. There is no clear-cut boundary between home and the street: people talk to one another from their balconies, or from the steps or pavement in front of their house.

The whole day can be spent outside, thanks to the perennial tropical summer. People spend a lot of time outdoors, chatting, playing dominoes, flirting, cycling around the streets buzzing with colour, voices and sounds, or simply sitting. Music is everywhere and is the soul of the island. Melodic thanks to the Spanish heritage, and dynamic due to the hypnotizing rhythm of Afro-Cuban percussion, religious and passionate at the same time, music is a vital part of daily life, like dance. Even the smallest Cuban town has a Casa de la Trova, now a Cuban institution,

A trio of musicians playing in the street

where local bands play and young and old alike go to dance. Indeed, there is no single designated venue for dancing in Cuba, and any excuse is good enough to improvise a party. One of the official celebrations is the debut in society of 15-year-old girls, who are dressed up like brides for the occasion. Besides this lively, fun-loving side, Cubans have an equally strong domestic one, and love to spend time at home with the family, in front of the television or chatting from the ever-present rocking chairs.

THE POLITICAL SYSTEM

The present Constitution of the Republic of Cuba, approved by 97.7 per cent of legal voters (in Cuba people can vote at the age of 16), was promulgated in 1976. In 1992 various amendments were introduced, including guarantees for foreign investments, some flexibility in foreign trade, more religious freedom, and the introduction of direct election by universal suffrage of deputies to the National Assembly. The Constitution states that Cuba is a socialist republic whose supreme governmental body is the

A 15-year-old girl preparing for her debut in society

Fidel Castro, the Líder Máximo, during a rally in Plaza de la Revolución

National Assembly of People's Power (the equivalent of Parliament), elected by universal suffrage every five years. The Assembly in turn elects the State Council, the Council of Ministers, and the president of the State Council, who is the head of state and of the government, as well as the judges of the Supreme Court. There are also the Provincial and Municipal Assemblies of the People's Power (Poder Popular), through which the population expresses its wishes. Since the only political party is the Cuban Communist Party, which by law cannot propose candidates, the citizens directly elect their candidates. Lastly, there are numerous social organizations, to which most of the citizens belong. These groups are for young people (UJC), children (UPCJM), women (FMC), students (FEU), trade unions (CTC), and small private farmers (ANAP). The largest of these groups consists of the numerous Committees for the Defence of the Revolution (CDR), founded in 1960 to watch over the country and tackle social issues.

Billboard with political propaganda along the Carretera Central

In spite of the severity of the Castro government, national pride is quite strong in Cuba, partly thanks to the continued embargo imposed by the US. Fidel Castro is still regarded as a charismatic figure by many, and there is general awareness and appreciation of the social reforms achieved since the revolution. It remains to be seen how the introduction of Western affluence will affect the country in the long term.

THE ECONOMY
The most important factor in the Cuban economy is tourism. Since 1980 the island has been open to foreign tourists, which has meant that the traditional flow of citizens from Eastern European countries has been replaced

Waving Cuban flags at a rally

Varadero, one of the most popular resorts for international tourism

by the arrival of tourists from western capitalist countries – the only people who can bring strong currencies into the country, particularly the US dollar. The decision to make more of the nation's rich natural and architectural heritage to produce some degree of wealth was crucial for the economy. However, it has also created major changes in the social relationships, habits and customs of millions of people, who after 30 years of semi-isolation have begun to measure themselves alongside Western Europeans, Canadians and even the occasional embargo-defying American. The uneasy dual economy of the Cuban

A popular toy made of wood and three wheels

peso and the American dollar, the result of the boom in tourism, is still a problem to be resolved. Another important item in the local economy is sugar cane: Cuba is still one of the world's leading exporters of sugar, with 156 extraction centres.

EDUCATION AND CHILDREN

José Martí, who was a poet and man of letters, and became a hero of national independence *(see p45)*, stated that the only way to be free was to be educated. The Cuban Revolution has not forgotten this motto and has staked much on fostering free public education. Thanks to the massive literacy campaign of 1961 *(see p52)*, illiteracy was almost completely eradicated within a short time. Today most of the island's people, half of whom are under 30 – that is, born since the Revolution – can read and write the official language, Spanish, and are also taught foreign languages.

Throughout the country Casas de la Cultura, or cultural centres, act as venues for exhibitions, performing arts and even dance evenings. Child care is an important component of the

Machines used to harvest sugar cane

nation's educational policy: the government has invested a great deal of effort and funds in the younger generations and is particularly keen on protecting children, who are safeguarded from the exploitation and sweatshop labour so common in many Latin American and Third World countries. Children are well looked after in Cuba: they have the right to attend nursery schools and day-care centres and to education, physical education and recreational activities. All these services are free for everyone and generally of good quality.

HEALTH

The achievements of the government in the field of health have raised the country to the level of the world's most industrialized nations. A great deal has been invested in providing hospitals and medical consultants throughout the island, in free medicine, and in concentrating on prevention (the nationwide vaccination of infants and children has virtually eliminated diseases common on the American continent) and medical research. Cuba has the lowest infant mortality rate and the highest life expectancy rate in Latin America. The health service, which is free for everyone, is excellent despite restrictions imposed by the economic crisis. The presence of highly trained Cuban doctors and the reduced costs of therapy and hospitalization have made the island a centre for "health tourism"; patients from many countries come here for specific treatments, especially for skin and stress problems.

Javier Sotomayor, the gold medallist in the high jump in the 1992 Olympics at Barcelona

SPORTS

Physical activity has always been encouraged by the government via a mass physical education programme and numerous specialist schools that offer talented youngsters the chance to make a name for themselves. As a result, sports standards are high, and Cuba has many Olympic champions. Baseball is the national sport (the Cuban team is one of the best in the world), and athletics, volleyball, basketball and boxing are also popular. Leading figures in sport include boxer Kid Chocolate (1910–88), successful in the US before the Revolution, high-jump champion Javier Sotomayor, Ana Fidelia Quirot, the 800m world champion in 1995 and 1997, and Ivan Pedroso, gold medallist in long-jump in Sydney 2000 and Edmonton 2001.

Boxing training in a Havana gym

Landscape, Flora and Fauna

A land crab, a marsh inhabitant

THE CUBAN POET Nicolás Guillén once likened his native island to a green crocodile with eyes of stone and water. An aerial view would show the island stretching out in the Caribbean Sea and indeed covered with vegetation and patterned with rivers. Small islands and coral reefs lie just offshore in the sparkling blue sea. In the interior, the landscape is very varied, from plains of red earth to the *mogotes* outcrops of Viñales, from desert cactus to tropical forest. Protected reserves make up 22 per cent of the national territory. There are numerous species found only on Cuba, but no poisonous creatures.

Coral reefs, with their own distinct ecosystem *(see p143)*

MOUNTAINS

The most important ranges are the Sierra de los Órganos to the west, the Sierra del Escambray in the centre and the Sierra Maestra to the southeast. The latter is Cuba's principal range and includes Pico Turquino (1,974 m/ 6,475 ft), the highest peak in the country. The slopes are covered with forests of deciduous trees, pines and tropical plants, and by coffee and cocoa plantations.

PLAINS

Areas of plain occur throughout the island, but are particularly prevalent in the central regions – the provinces of Matanzas, Sancti Spíritus and Camagüey – and in the Pinar del Río area. The land is fertile and planted with sugar cane, palm trees, mangoes and citrus fruit, or left as grazing land for cattle.

Carpintero *(carpenter) is the Cuban name for the woodpecker, which nests in tree trunks.*

The cartacuba *(Todus multicolor) is an endemic species only a few centimetres long. It has highly coloured plumage.*

The tiñosa, *or turkey vulture, with its unmistakable red head, flies the plains in search of carrion.*

The cattle egret *follows grazing cows and feeds on insects, both those disturbed by ploughing and others on the cows' hides.*

The tocororo *(Cuban trogon) is the national bird. The colours of the flag of Cuba were inspired by its feathers.*

The so-called gulf fritillary *is one of 190 species of butterfly in Cuba, about 30 of which are endemic to the island.*

FLORA

The Cuban landscape is characterized by the many varieties of palm tree *(see p169)*, together with the pine in the mountainous areas, and the ceibas in the plains. The *yagruma*, with large dark green and silvery leaves, is also widespread. Three important hardwoods are mahogany, cedar and *majagua*. Splashes of colour are added to the luxuriant green vegetation by flowering hibiscus, bougainvillea and *flamboyán* (royal poinciana). Numerous species of orchid grow here, as well as mariposa, Cuba's national flower.

A *flamboyán* (royal poinciana)

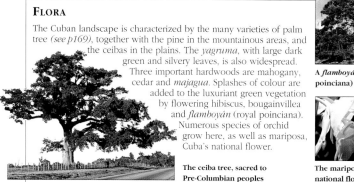

The ceiba tree, sacred to Pre-Columbian peoples

The mariposa, the national flower

MARSHLANDS

The southern part of the island in particular has many lagoons and marshlands, often distinguished by mangrove swamps, and is rich in birdlife. The most important area is the Ciénaga (swamp) de Zapata, in the province of Matanzas *(see p162)*.

Pink flamingoes *live in areas of brackish water from Cayo Coco to Zapata.*

Buteogallus anthracinus gundlachi *is an endemic hawk that feeds on crabs.*

Mangroves *develop an intricate root system under water. This habitat suits a diverse range of birds and fish.*

TROPICAL FOREST

The Sagua-Baracoa mountain range in Eastern Cuba, under the influence of northeast trade winds, is one of the most biologically diverse areas in the Caribbean. Here, the heavy rainfall produces thick vegetation.

The tiny zunzuncito, *the smallest humming-bird in the world, lives in protected or wooded areas like the Península de Zapata.*

The black anolis *lizard, a forest reptile, reacts to disturbance by inflating the white part under its throat.*

The Polymita picta, *an endemic species of snail that lives only in the Baracoa area, has a brightly coloured shell and feeds on plant parasites.*

Santería

DIFFERENT RELIGIONS CO-EXIST in Cuba as the result of its history. Both the Catholicism of the Spanish conquerors and the cults imported by the African slaves have survived. The most widespread of the African faiths is santería, also called Regla de Ocha. In order to be able to worship their gods despite the persecution of the Spaniards, Yoruba slaves, originally from Nigeria, merged their gods' identities with certain Catholic saints. Over the years the two religions have almost become blended. Pure Catholicism today is not a widespread religion in Cuba, while santería is so strongly felt that it is an important part of the national identity.

The batá, three conical drums of different sizes with two skins, accompany the most important santería ceremonies.

The crown of Changó, the king of the orishas

Rituals *are almost always performed in a domestic context (santería has no temples as such). Rites are inspired by animistic spirituality, although there are elements that share similarities or even merge with Catholicism.*

Fresh fruit, including bananas, Changó's favourite

Santeros *and* babalawos, *the santería priests, foretell the future, the former by means of seashells, the latter through a complex system of divination that makes use of stones, seashells, seeds and coconut shells.*

Agogó (traditional rattles), maracas and bells are played while greeting the gods.

AN ALTAR FOR CHANGÓ
Altars are set up by santería initiates on feast days, such as their "saint's birthday" (the initiation anniversary), and decorated with the attributes of the god to whom they are dedicated. They also contain elements belonging to other *orishas*, such as cloth, devotional objects, flowers, fruit and other special foods.

THE ORISHAS
The main santería god is Olofi, the creator divinity, similar to the God of Christianity but without contact with Earth. The gods who mediate between him and the faithful are the *orishas*, who listen to the latter's prayers. Each *orisha* has his own colour and symbols, as well as a ritual characterized by its type of dance, music and costumes: Ochún, for example, wears yellow clothes and loves honey, pale soft drinks and violins.

Obbatalá, *a hermaphrodite god, is the protector of the head as well as the chief intermediary between Olofi and humankind.*

Ochún, *the goddess of love, lives in rivers, and corresponds to the Virgen del Cobre (see p217).*

The aspiring priest (santero) *has to undergo a week of intense initiation ceremonies, and for an entire year has to dress in white and adhere to strict rules of behaviour.*

The axe and sword are Changó's two warlike attributes.

The batea is a wooden receptacle containing natural elements in which the spirit of the god resides. Only the *santero* may open it.

The pilón is the large wooden mortar on which the *santero* sits during the week of initiation, and it is preserved as an object of worship.

Various objects – *Christian, secular or even personal items* – *are set together on santería altars. Here, three Madonnas are placed alongside plastic horses.*

Elegguá is the first god to be greeted during ceremonies. He is represented by a stone made to look like a face, with two shells as eyes, and is usually placed behind a believer's front door.

Fresh flowers are always placed on the altars of the *orishas*: red ones for Changó, yellow ones for Ochún, and white ones for Obbatalá.

Candles

A basket of offerings is on display during ceremonies. The money is used to buy objects of worship.

OTHER AFRO-CUBAN RELIGIONS

Among the African cults practised in Cuba, two others are also significant: Palo Monte (or Regla Mayombé), in which herbs and other natural elements are used for magical purposes, and Abakuá, more of a mutual aid secret society, for men only. The former, introduced to Cuba by Bantu-speaking African slaves from the Congo, Zaire and Angola, is based on the cult of the dead. The faithful, called *paleros*, perform rites that are sometimes macabre and even verge on black magic. A region between Nigeria and Cameroon was the birthplace of the Abakuá cult. In celebrations the participants, disguised as little devils *(diablitos),* dance and play music. The *diablito* has become part of Cuban folklore.

An Abakuá diablito with his typical headdress

Yemayá, sea goddess and mother of orishas, *wears blue. Capable of great sweetness and great anger, she is linked with the Virgen de Regla (see p112).*

Changó is the virile and sensual god of fire and war who adores dancing and corresponds to St Barbara.

Architecture in Cuba

FORMAL ARCHITECTURE in Cuba began in the Colonial period. For the entire 16th century all efforts were concentrated on building an impressive network of fortresses; then came the first stone-built *mudéjar*-style houses, which replaced simple wooden dwellings with tiled roofs. The 18th century was a golden age of civic architecture, characterized by the Baroque style imported at a late stage from Europe, which in turn made way for Neo-Classical buildings in the 19th century. The mixture of styles typical of the *fin de siècle* was followed, in 1900–30, by Art Deco architecture, a forerunner of the 1950s skyscrapers. Ugly prefabricated buildings characterize the post-1959 era.

The courtyard *was a typical feature of Colonial architecture and the centre of domestic life. Above, the Conde de Jaruco's Havana residence (see p76).*

THE 17TH CENTURY

The tropical climate, with high temperatures and heavy rain, influenced the local architecture. Many private homes had thick walls, tiled roofs and windows protected by shutters.

A typical wooden ceiling at Calle Tacón 4, in Havana

Balconies with slender wooden columns

Sloping roof of terracotta tiles

The house at Calle Obispo 117–19 (p72), *with its characteristic central courtyard and wooden balconies, shows a clear Spanish influence in the structure itself and in the building techniques used.*

THE 18TH CENTURY

More rooms were added to houses with a central courtyard, more houses were built, and some wonderful examples of civic architecture were created. Three highlights of light Cuban Baroque in Havana are the Palacio de los Capitanes Generales *(pp70–71)*, Palacio del Segundo Cabo *(p66)* and Havana Cathedral *(p64)*. Trinidad also has many 18th-century Colonial buildings.

The mezzanine, a structural element introduced in the 1700s

The arcade on the ground floor, which was the external equivalent of the inner courtyard, was an 18th-century innovation. As trade increased, mansions like this housed growing numbers of servants, who lived in the lower part of the building.

Stained-glass windows

Arches supported by columns and pilasters distinguish 18th-century buildings.

Limestone façade

Palacio de los Capitanes Generales is a typical Cuban Baroque mansion, with thick stone walls, an abundance of arches, columns, porticoes and balconies, and a large central courtyard with dense vegetation.

An elegant arched *mediopunto* window

MEDIOPUNTO

These stained-glass windows were created in the mid-18th century to protect houses from the glare of the tropical sun. They became popular in the 1800s, when mansion windows were decorated with glass set into a wooden frame. The original geometric motifs were later replaced by others drawing inspiration from tropical flora and fauna.

THE 19TH CENTURY

The widespread use of porticoes with columns and lintels, wrought iron and decoration inspired by Classical antiquity or the Renaissance, is the distinguishing feature of 19th-century Cuban Neo-Classical architecture. Grilles across windows and shutters helped air to circulate inside (previously the central courtyard performed this function). Buildings that best represent Cuban Neo-Classicism are the Palacio de Aldama in Havana *(p84)* and the Teatro Sauto in Matanzas *(p154)*.

Wrought- or cast-iron grilles

Shutters and *mediopuntos* protected rooms from bright light.

Ionic pilasters

Palacio de Aldama, *designed by Manuel José Carrera in 1840 for the wealthy Don Domingo de Aldama, is the most important Neo-Classical building in Havana. Rejecting Baroque exuberance, it echoes the austerity and purity of line of Classical architecture.*

Doric columns

In the portico the arch is replaced by the lintel.

BRIDGING THE 19TH–20TH CENTURIES

The architectural value of many Cuban cities derives from the mixture of different styles. This is seen in buildings such as the Neo-Moorish Palacio de Valle in Cienfuegos *(p166)*, the Capitolio in Havana *(pp82–3)*, and at Paseo and Calle 17, Havana's so-called "millionaires' row", with splendid mansions such as the Casa de la Amistad, built in 1926 *(see p99)*.

Detail of the façade of the Palacio Guasch, Pinar del Río *(p136)*

Palacio de Valle *in Cienfuegos, designed by the Venetian architect Alfredo Colli in 1912 for Acisclo del Valle, combines Moorish and Venetian Gothic elements with references to Beaux Arts forms – a typical example of the eclectic style's use of a range of prevailing architectural motifs and elements.*

THE 20TH CENTURY

The early 20th century saw the construction of a few examples of Art Nouveau and Art Deco buildings, paving the way for the major urban development that took place in Havana in the 1950s. This period witnessed the building of some very tall, modern skyscrapers and hotels such as the Riviera and the Habana Libre (then called the Habana Hilton, *p98*). In parallel with this came the rise of a style that was reminiscent of Rationalist architecture.

Edificio Bacardí *(1930) in Havana, designed by E Rodríguez, R Fernández and J Menéndez, is a splendid example of Art Deco. It is clad in granite and limestone, with motifs in terracotta.*

Painting in Cuba

THE HISTORY OF CUBAN PAINTING can be divided into three basic stages. The first began in 1818 with the foundation of the San Alejandro Fine Arts Academy, run by Jean-Baptiste Vermay, a French Neo-Classical painter. The second began over a century later, in the 1930s, when, thanks to great artists such as Wifredo Lam, René Portocarrero and Amelia Peláez, a movement influenced by the European avant-garde created a universally comprehensible idiom that expressed the unique essence of Cuban identity. Thirdly, after 1959, as part of a programme of art education that promoted avant-garde artists, the National School of Art and the Institute for Advanced Art Studies were founded. Cuban painting has always brimmed with vitality and painters of recent generations have achieved international recognition, helped by shows like the Havana Biennial.

Víctor Manuel García, one of the fathers of modern Cuban art, created the archetypal Gitana Tropical *(1929).*

Wifredo Lam (1902–82), lived for a while in Europe and worked with Pablo Picasso in Paris. He developed a new pictorial language that went beyond national boundaries. He painted extraordinary pictures such as La Jungla *(The Jungle), now in the Museum of Modern Art, New York,* La Silla *(see p93), and* The Third World *(1966), seen here, which cast a dramatic light on the elements in Cuban religions.*

Amelia Peláez (1897–1968) blended still life motifs with the decorative elements in Cuban Colonial architecture such as stained glass and columns, as seen here in Interior with Columns *(1951).*

René Portocarrero (1912–86) expressed the essence of Cuba through a Baroque-like vision of the city, painting domestic interiors and figures of women, as in Interno del Cerro *(1943). He made use of bold colour and was influenced by the European avant-garde and Mexican mural painting.*

Raúl Martínez and Guido Llinás were leading exponents of the abstract art movement that came to the fore in the 1950s–60s and later adopted the Pop Art style in representions of current-day heroes, as exemplified by Island 70 *(1970) by Raúl Martínez, seen here.*

Alfredo Sosabravo (b.1930) – a painter, illustrator, engraver and potter – tackles the themes of nature, man and machines with an ironic twist. A leading figure, he has been active since the 1960s, together with Servando Cabrera Moreno, a Neo-Expressionist, Antonia Eiriz, a figurative artist, and Manuel Mendive, whose subject is Cuba's African heritage.

Flora Fong – along with Ever Fonseca, Nelson Domínguez, Pedro Pablo Oliva, Tomás Sánchez and Roberto Fabelo – represents a strand of 1970s painting, which tended towards abstraction without quite losing sight of objective reality. Her Dimensiones del Espejo *is seen here.*

GRAPHIC ART

Graphic design, which first flourished during the Colonial period, when it was used in the sugar and tobacco industries, with time became an independent art form, with the creation of prestigious periodicals such as *Social*. During the 20th century the growing importance of marketing produced different types of graphic art. In the 1960s, in the wake of the enthusiasm for the victorious revolution, well-designed graphic posters became a natural part of the main political and cultural campaigns, and designs became ever more sophisticated. Use of graphic art is still very visible in Cuba's towns and cities and at the roadside all over the island.

Poster by Alfonso Prieto for July 26 celebrations

CERAMICS

In 1950, the physician Juan Miguel Rodríguez de la Cruz brought together leading painters such as Wifredo Lam, René Portocarrero and Amelia Peláez in Santiago de las Vegas, near Havana, so that they could all work on ceramic designs. It marked the beginning of a new artistic genre in Cuba that today ranges from crockery to sculpture, and also includes installations and works for home interiors. Wonderful examples of Cuban ceramics can be found in the Museo Nacional de la Cerámica in the Castillo de la Real Fuerza *(p68)* and in the Hotel Habana Libre *(p98)*.

Decorated plate, Havana Ceramics Museum

Cuban Literature

A FREQUENT THEME IN THE LITERATURE OF CUBA has always been the question of national identity, and the genre has evolved with a marked interest in social problems and questions about reality. The works of the great 20th-century Cuban authors are regarded as classics, and younger authors are beginning to attract attention on the international scene. The Revolution was a golden era for publishing, because production costs for books were very low. However, the trade was plunged into sudden crisis in the early 1990s and many publishers are only now slowly regaining their former status. Every year Havana plays host to an International Book Fair, a major literary event involving authors and publishers from all over the world.

An expressive portrait of the great Cuban poet Nicolás Guillén

THE 19TH CENTURY

THE BIRTH of Cuban literature is usually dated from *Espejo de Paciencia*, an epic poem written in the early 1600s by Silvestre de Balboa, originally from the Canary Islands. However, truly national literature only began to emerge in the 19th century, with the call for an end to slavery and for Cuban independence from Spain.

Félix Varela, writer-philosopher

Among the literary figures of that time, various names stand out. Father Félix Varela (1787–1853) was an eclectic philosopher and patriot who wrote a pamphlet extolling the "need to stamp out the

***La Edad de Oro*, José Martí's children's periodical**

slavery of the blacks on the island of Cuba, which would also be in the interests of their owners". José María de Heredia (1803–39) was a romantic poet who introduced the American landscape into New World literature and was forced to live in the US and Mexico because of his nationalist stance. Gertrudis Gómez de Avellaneda (1814–73), another romantic, lived for a long time in Spain and defended the black population in her novel *Sab*. Cirilo Villaverde (1812–94) was a patriot and author of *Cecilia Valdés*, a famous abolitionist work which was made into a *zarzuela* (operetta) in the 20th century by the Cuban composer Ernesto Lecuona.

However, the towering figure in the 19th century was the great José Martí (1853–95), an intellectual, journalist and author who expressed his nationalist ideas in elegant literary form (*Ismaelillos* and *Versos Sencillos* are his best-known works), and became a leading exponent of Latin American modernism.

Another figure in this movement was Julián del Casal, a decadent, symbolist writer. The premature deaths of these two brought the development of innovative literature to a halt.

THE 20TH CENTURY

THE LEADING INTERPRETERS of 20th-century Cuban literature were the poet Nicolás Guillén (1902–89) and the novelist Alejo Carpentier (1904–80), both of whom were sent into exile because of their opposition to Gerardo Machado's regime and their fierce criticism of Batista's dictatorship.

Guillén, who was of mixed race, spoke for the black population, exposing among other things the brutal working conditions of the *macheteros*, the labourers who cut sugar cane on the plantations. After Castro's victory, Guillén was proclaimed as "national poet" and asked to head UNEAC, the Cuban writers' union. Taking as his starting point the rhythms of dance and traditional musical genres such as *son* (*see p28*), grafted onto the classical Spanish octosyllable, Guillén's stylistic studies gave rise to bold experiments as early as 1931 in works like *Songoro Cosongo, poemas mulatos*.

Alejo Carpentier, an architect, musicologist and writer acutely

José Lezama Lima

aware of the realities of Cuba's situation, was one of the most original and innovative authors in 20th-century world literature. Using a blend of irony and respect, he gave voice to the myths of his country, anticipating the destructuring of the post-modern novel. Among his major works are *The Kingdom of This World*, *The Lost Steps*, *Concierto Barroco* and *The Age of Enlightenment*.

Two other leading figures of the same period are the dramatist Virgilio Piñera (1912–79), a reformer, who had a marked taste for experimental theatre, and José Lezama Lima (1910–76), a poet of elegance, also a novelist and chief editor of the magazine *Orígenes*. From 1944 to 1956 this leading periodical printed works by the best Cuban writers and artists of the time. It became one of the key publications in Latin America. Lima is internationally known as the author of *Paradiso* (1966).

Alejo Carpentier
CONCIERTO BARROCO

A famous novel by Alejo Carpentier (1974)

In general, the literary scene in revolutionary Cuba has been characterized by creative fervour, in poetry and in novel-writing. Among the "veterans", people who lived through the experience from the outset, mention should be made of the poets Eliseo Diego (author of *Biography of the Fugitive Slave*), Cintio Vitier, Pablo Armando Fernández and Fina García Marruz; and the novelists Félix Pita Rodríguez, Mirta Aguirre, and Dulce María Loynaz. The works of Loynaz were not published in Cuba until the late 20th century, just before her death.

These authors were followed by the younger writers Miguel Barnet, Antón Arrufat, López Sacha and César López, committed writers in favour of the revolution.

Among the anti-Castro authors writing in exile, the leading name is Guillermo Cabrera Infante, whose works include *Havana for a Dead Infant*.

Author Dulce María Loynaz, pictured in her twenties

CONTEMPORARY WRITERS

PRESENT-DAY AUTHORS worthy of mention include Abel Prieto, the Minister of Culture, a brilliant and perceptive author of several novels, including *The Cat's Flight*. Another name is Abilio Estévez, a dramatist and novelist of extraordinarily expressive intensity, with a lyrical and visionary tone. Marylin Bobes and Mirta Yáñez both write from the feminist angle. Senel Paz wrote the story that inspired the film *Strawberry and Chocolate*; and detective-story writer Leonardo Padura is known abroad for a mystery trilogy set in Havana.

CUBAN CINEMA

The founding of the Instituto Cubano del Arte y la Industria Cinematográficos (ICAIC) in 1959 virtually marked the birth of cinema in Cuba. The aim of this institution was to disseminate motion picture culture throughout the country, and thus encourage the formation of Cuban directors, to work on documentary films in particular. Fostered by the revolutionary government, Cuban cinema experienced a golden age in the 1960s and has been evolving ever since. Today Havana is the capital of new Latin American cinema thanks to the annual film festival organized by ICAIC. Gabriel García Márquez, winner of the Nobel Prize for Literature, is president of the Fundación del Nuevo Cine Latinoamericano, which also runs the Escuela Internacional de Cine film school, based in San Antonio de los Baños. Among Cuba's many directors, who include Julio García Espinosa, Manuel Octavio Gómez and Pastor Vega, there are three particularly outstanding names: Santiago Alvarez, who has made fine documentaries; Humberto Solás, director of the classic *Lucía* and of *Cecilia*; and the late Tomás Gutiérrez Alea, who found fame abroad in 1993 thanks to *Fresa y Chocolate (Strawberry and Chocolate)*, which he made with Juan Carlos Tabío, which courageously dealt with the themes of homosexuality and dissent.

Symbol of the ICAIC

Poster for the film *Strawberry and Chocolate*

Music and Dance

ANYTHING CAN BE USED TO MAKE MUSIC IN CUBA: two pieces of wood, an empty box and a tyre rim are enough to trigger an irresistible rhythm, anywhere and at any time of day, on the bus, on the beach or in the street. There are top classical music composers and interpreters, but it is popular music, a fusion of Spanish melodies and African rhythm, that is the very essence of Cuba. The success enjoyed by mambo and cha-cha-cha in the 1950s was followed by the worldwide popularity of *son*, rumba and salsa. Dance, too, is an essential part of life here. No-one stays seated when the music starts: feet and hands start to move with the rhythm, and bodies sway and rock.

Compay Segundo, the famous *son* singer and songwriter

Salsa *is dance music which maintains the rhythmic structure of* son *while adding new sounds borrowed from jazz and other Latin American genres.*

The guitarist is often also the accompanying voice, while the solo singer plays a "minor" percussion instrument such as the maracas or *claves*.

Traditional maracas are made from the fruit (gourd) of the *güira* tropical tree.

Bongo

Double bass

Tres

SON

This genre is a type of country music that originated in Cuba in the 19th century, a blend of African rhythm and Spanish melody, which then greatly influenced Latin American music as a whole. In around 1920 *son* began to be played in towns in Eastern Cuba, where, along with other genres, it produced the *trova tradicional*, a ballad-style song with guitar.

THE MUSICIANS

Ernesto Lecuona

Three great 20th-century composers and musicians are pianist Ernesto Lecuona (1896–1963), Ignacio Villa (or "Bola de Nieve"), and Pérez Prado, in whose orchestra Benny Moré sang (*see p167*). In the 1920s there was the star Rita Montaner and the Trío Matamoros, the top *trova* band in Santiago. Others are Sindo Garay, a bolero writer, and César Portillo de la Luz, a founder of *feeling* music in the 1960s. Contemporaries include the *salsero* Issac Delgado and Afro-Cuban jazzman Chucho Valdés.

Bola de Nieve (*1911– 71*), *or "snowball", is the stage name that Rita Montaner gave to her pianist Ignacio Villa. This husky-voiced musician also wrote and sang very moving love songs.*

Damaso Pérez Prado (*b.1922), the king of mambo, became an international success with his orchestra in the 1950s.*

Guaguancó, a fast variation of rumba, enacts a breezy battle between a man and woman who tries to parry his insistent advances. In effect, this dance is a thinly disguised simulation of the sexual act.

The voice was the original element of the rumba, which began as song. The percussion instruments, the basis of this musical genre, were added at a later stage.

A *batá* covered with canvas and seashells

Tumbadora or conga

CUBAN MUSICAL INSTRUMENTS

Claves

Tres

Güiro

There are several exclusively Cuban musical instruments.

Among the stringed instruments are the *tres*, a small guitar, always used in *son* bands, with three pairs of metal strings, and the *requinto*, another small, high-pitched guitar that is used in trios to play melodic variations.

Typical Cuban percussion instruments are the *tumbadora*, a tall wooden and leather drum played with the hands, which is used in all musical forms, including jazz; the *bongo*, two small round drums; the *claves*, two wooden cylinders played by striking them against one another; the *güiro*, the gourd of the güira fruit which is stroked with a small stick; and the *marímbula*, a rarely used small piano.

RUMBA

The African soul of Cuban music, the rumba originated in poor neighbourhoods as a voice of rebellion against slavery and segregation. It then became a form of political satire and social criticism, as well as the poignant expression of an unhappy love affair. *Columbia* is country-style rumba, while *yambú* and *guaguancó* are the urban varieties, with a dance rhythm that can be sensual and dynamic, or sad and slow.

Los Van Van have dominated the Cuban musical scene for over 30 years and are world-famous for their new rhythms and sounds (they invented a new genre, the songo).

Silvio Rodríguez, a singer and songwriter who defends the ideals of the Cuban revolution, founded the Nueva Trova with Pablo Milanés (right) in the late 1960s, revitalizing the style and repertory of the trova, a rural musical genre.

Buena Vista Social Club, Wim Wenders' film (1998), brought into the limelight traditional son interpreters over 80 years old, such as the guitarist and singer Compay Segundo, the pianist Rubén González, and the singer Ibrahim Ferrer.

Cuban Cigars

T HE CIGAR IS AN INEXTRICABLE PART of Cuba's culture, history, and even, for some, its essence. It is known that cigars were used by the native Indians. After Columbus's voyage, tobacco, regarded in Europe as having therapeutic qualities, was imported to Spain. However the first smokers were imprisoned, because people believed that cigar smoke produced diabolical effects. Even so, tobacco grew in popularity and was later exported to other European nations, where government agencies were set up to maintain a monopoly over the product. After the revolution, the US embargo had a serious effect on the international sale of cigars *(puros)*, but since the 1990s the fashion for cigar smoking has given a boost to sales.

Tobacco (cohiba) *was used by Cuban Indians during religious rites to invoke the gods. They either inhaled the smoke through a tubed instrument called a tabaco, or smoked the rolled leaves.*

The *tripa* is the inside, the "core" of the cigar with the filler leaves. In hand-made cigars, the *tripa* consists of tobacco leaves which have been selected in order to obtain a particular flavour.

The *capa* is the wrapper leaf on the outside of the cigar. It gives it its smooth, velvety look as well as its colour.

The head (or top part of the cigar) is cut off before smoking.

Foot

THE PARTS OF A CIGAR
Cigars can be either hand-made or machine-made. With hand-made cigars, the inside consists of whole tobacco leaves, while machine-made cigars are made up of leaves that are blended and then shredded.

The *capote* is the binder leaf that holds the inner part together and keeps it compact.

BRAND NAMES

There are 32 brands of Cuban cigar on the market today. Below are four, each represented by a *marquilla*, or label, which is placed on the cigar box to identify the brand. Some designs have not changed since first marketed.

Montecristo (1935)

Cohiba (1966)

Cuaba (1996)

Vegas Robaina (1997)

The anilla, *the band that goes around the central part of the cigar and bears its brand name, has a curious history. It is said that in the 18th century, Catherine the Great of Russia, a heavy smoker, had her cigars wrapped with small bands of cloth so they would not leave stains on her fingers. Her eccentricity soon became fashionable. The first commercial cigar band was produced in 1830 by the manufacturers Aguila de Oro. Above is a band produced by the Cuban cigar-maker Romeo y Julieta in 1875.*

HOW CIGARS ARE MADE

Cigar manufacturing is a real skill that Cubans hand down from generation to generation. This sequence of photographs shows how Carlos Gassiot, a highly skilled *torcedor* (cigar roller), makes a cigar, from selecting the loose tobacco leaves to the final touches.

Chaveta (blade)

Cutter

Capote (wrapper)

Vegetable glue

1 Having placed the capote *(wrapper leaf) on the tablet, the* torcedor *chooses the filler leaves he wants to use for the core of the cigar: three leaves from different parts of the plant – seco, volado and ligero (see p135).*

2 He begins to roll (torcer *in Spanish, hence the term* torcedor) *the leaves. The* capote *is wrapped around the filler leaves selected for the* tripa, *which in turn is covered by the* capa, *which is smooth and regular. This determines the appearance of the cigar.*

3 Once the wrapping is complete, the final touches are added. First the wrapper leaf is worked until it is completely smooth. Then comes the trimming. The cigar tip is finished off by wrapping the end with a last tobacco leaf.

Chaveta

Tableta (tablet)

Gauge

4 Once the cigar is finished, the torcedor checks its diameter with a special gauge stamped with the various standard sizes established for every kind of cigar. The same instrument is also used to measure the pre-established length, after which the cigar is cut to this size using the cutting machine.

THE SHAPE AND SIZE

Cigars are made in different sizes (heavy, standard or slim ring gauge) and shapes (they may be regular or tapered, *figurado*). Fatter cigars tend to have a fuller flavour, which connoisseurs prefer. The best hand-rolled Cuban cigars benefit from ageing, like fine wine.

Cuaba Exclusivo, *figurado* cigar

Trinidad Fundador, regular-shaped cigar

Transport, Cuban style

SINCE THE ENERGY CRISIS of the late 1980s, when the Soviet Union and Eastern European countries stopped supplying Cuba with the petrol it needed, every possible means has been used to get around the island. As a result, bicycles and one-horse carriages rub shoulders with vintage American cars and Soviet vehicles made in the 1970s. Getting from one place to another is no easy matter for Cubans. Before the Periodo Especial, a bus network covered the whole island, but there are no longer enough buses, and those that do run are always crowded. Walking has become a common necessity, even if a considerable distance needs to be covered. See also pages 303–307.

Hitch-hiking is a normal everyday institution in Cuba: drivers with space to spare give lifts to hitch-hikers of all ages.

Ricksbaws were recently introduced to Cuba as another solution to the fuel shortage. They are used for short trips in towns and each can carry up to two people.

Sidecars from Eastern Europe are less popular than before. They are most common in rural areas.

The traditional carriage is a common means of transport, especially in the countryside.

Typical city traffic, including a yellow cocotaxi (see p307), bicycles, a 1950s American car, a bus, a modern van, and old cars made in the 1970s.

VINTAGE CARS

Image of Hatuey, seen on car bonnets

Because of the embargo and the shortage of petrol, the Cuban government prohibited the sale of vehicles to private citizens. Cars made in the 1940s and 1950s, mostly American makes, could not be replaced and owners have had to do their utmost to preserve and restore them and keep them running – not an easy task in the absence of spare parts. Cuban car mechanics have been forced to devise ingenious, creative solutions and have even been known to fit Lada engines in Chevrolets. It is quite common to see museum pieces on the streets.

The Cadillac is still a luxury car. This one is a 1959 sedan, with full chromium-plate trim, large wings, and a spacious and elegant interior.

__Lorries__ are a makeshift means of conveyance used to get around town or get from one city to another. Passengers stand more often than they sit. Both government lorries, normally used to transport freight, and other state vehicles are obliged to pick up hitch-hikers.

Bicycles made their appearance in Cuba in the early 1990s, when over a million were imported from China. Since then they have become the most common means of transport on the island.

__This cart__ is fitted with traces for a horse and wheels from a lorry, just another example of a serviceable vehicle made by assembling different parts.

ON THE ROAD

Methods of transport on the roads vary so much that everything moves at a different speed – and the speed of a vehicle is not always predictable – so extra attention is required by both drivers and pedestrians.

__Reproductions__ of the swan with outspread wings from Chevrolet bonnets are sold in the markets to replace the originals.

__Fords__ like this one, made in the 1930s, are real museum pieces. Lately, vintage cars like these, as well as being a necessary means of transport, have become fashionable in Cuba.

__The Bel Air__ is a popular Chevrolet model. It has a chromium-plated dashboard.

__The Chevrolet__ is the most commonly seen car in Cuba, appreciated for its durability and passenger space. There are many in circulation, often used as communal taxis.

CUBA THROUGH THE YEAR

BECAUSE OF ITS TROPICAL CLIMATE, Cuba does not really have a high or low season, although officially, peak season is from December to the end of March and in July and August, when hotel rates are higher and flights are packed. Except for the peak of summer, when temperatures can be searingly hot, and September and October, when hurricanes are likeliest, any month is suitable for a visit. It is warm at the beach even in winter, because the *frentes fríos* (cold fronts)

A Carnival outfit

generally last only a couple of days and even then the temperature hardly ever drops below 10°C (50°F). The cooler, drier months from November to March are the best for sightseeing. Thanks to the climate, and the Cubans' love of music and cultural events, there are open-air concerts, festivals, and religious and folk festivities all year round. However, the most interesting and eventful months are July, during Carnival, and December, when the festivities in Remedios and Havana's two famous cinema and ballet festivals take place.

SPRING

DURING THIS SEASON there is an escalation of dance and theatre performances. The beaches are crowded, but mainly with visitors – the Cubans usually go to the seaside only in summer.

MARCH

Festival de Monólogos y Unipersonales, Havana *(Mar)*. A competition for actors, authors, directors, dancers and choreographers from all over Cuba. It also features monologues by foreign performers.
Taller Internacional de Teatro de Títeres, Teatro Papalote, Matanzas, *(Mar–Apr)*. Performances by leading puppet theatres, with seminars, conferences and workshops.

APRIL

La Huella de España, Gran Teatro de la Habana and Castillo de La Real Fuerza, Havana *(Apr)*. A festival of Cuban culture of Spanish derivation: concerts, classical dance, flamenco and theatre.
Festival Internacional de Percusión, Havana *(Apr)*. Concerts, courses, conferences, lectures and documentary film screenings, all revolving around Cuban percussion instruments.
Bienal del Humor de San Antonio de Los Baños, Museo del Humor, San Antonio de los Baños *(1–15 Apr)*. Festival of Humour, with exhibits, lectures and performances.

The First of May Parade in Plaza de la Revolución, Havana

Festival de Arte Danzario, Havana and Camagüey *(Apr–May)*. Festival featuring all types of dance, from traditional to contemporary experimental. Also includes lectures, seminars, educational activities and workshops held by Cuban and visiting international dancers and scholars.

A batá player at the Percussion Festival

Los Días de la Danza *(Apr–May)*. Festival featuring Cuban dance groups. On 29 April, International Dance Day, the Premio Nacional de la Danza, a national prize, is awarded in Teatro Mella, Havana.

MAY

Primero de Mayo, Havana *(May 1)*. Rallies, marches and parades are held in every city in the country. The most important one takes place, of course, in Havana: the citizens gather in Plaza de la Revolución for speeches and patriotic songs.
Fiera Internacional del Disco Cubadisco (International Record Fair), Pabexpo, Havana *(mid-May)*. Records on display and for sale; conferences and concerts.
Fiesta Nacional de la Danza, Santa Clara *(Apr–May)*. The best local dancers perform in the towns of this province. The fiesta ends with a great celebration in Santa Clara.

AVERAGE DAILY HOURS OF SUNSHINE

Hours
10
8
6
4
2
0
Jan Feb Mar Apr May Jun Jul Aug Sep Oct Nov Dec

Sunshine
This chart shows the average daily hours of sunshine in Cuba. In the winter the days are short: at 6pm the sun has already set. In the summer the sun is strong and you should protect your skin and wear a hat and sunglasses, even if only taking a short stroll in town.

SUMMER

THERE ARE VARIOUS festivals and festivities during the summer months, especially in Havana and Santiago. Almost every evening there are open-air concerts along the Malecón in Havana, particularly in the square known as the Piragua, which is transformed into an open-air dance floor (free of charge). If you plan to include the Carnival in your visit, book accommodation well in advance in both cities.

JUNE

Festival Boleros de Oro, Santiago, Morón, Havana *(mid-Jun)*. String of concerts by the best Cuban and international performers of bolero songs, lectures.
Encuentro de Bandas de Concierto, Plaza de la Revolución, Bayamo *(Jun 1–15)*. Outdoor concerts by national and international bands. Lectures, workshops.

Walking on stilts in Morón during the Fiesta del Gallo

Fiesta del Gallo, Morón *(end of Jun)*. Parade through town based on theme of the cockerel, symbolic here.
Jornada Cucalambeana, Encuentro Festival Iberoamericano de la Décima, Las Tunas *(end of Jun, biennial)*. The most important festival of Cuban rural culture. Concerts and performances by poets, musicians and *repentistas* (improvisers). Lectures and literary meetings, exhibits of local handicrafts, theatre.
Havana Carnival *(Jun–Jul)*. A parade of floats in the city streets, going from the Hotel Nacional to Calle Belascoaín, and live music performances by *comparsas* (processional groups who prepare all year long) in various parts of the city. At weekends, free concerts are held at the Piragua. The parades can be viewed from a grandstand.

JULY

Fiesta del Títere, Havana *(first week of Jul)*. Puppet shows in different parts of the old town.
Fiesta del Fuego, Santiago de Cuba *(first half of Jul)*. Annual festival celebrating the music, poetry, figurative art, religions and history of the Caribbean nations. Meetings, shows, exhibits, round tables, concerts, poetry readings and festivities throughout the city.
Festival Internacional de Música Contemporánea de Camagüey, Camagüey *(Jul)*. A major contemporary music festival with concerts,

A group of dancers from a Havana *comparsa*

seminars and round table discussions on Cuban and foreign composers.
Santiago Carnival, Santiago de Cuba *(second half of Jul)*. Parade of floats along the city streets, live music performed by *comparsas*, and a show from the Tropicana in Santiago *(see p225)*. For the most important parades there is a grandstand for spectators.
"26 de julio" *(held every year in a different city)*. The official commemoration of the attack on the Moncada barracks *(see p226)*, with a speech by president Fidel Castro and other political leaders in the main square of a Cuban city, accompanied by children who recite poetry and by concerts.

AUGUST

Festival Internacional de Música Popular "Benny Moré", Cienfuegos, Lajas and Havana *(end of Aug, biennial)*. Survey of Cuban popular music and its most important figures, with lectures and meetings centred around the figure of Benny Moré *(see p167)*.

AVERAGE MONTHLY RAINFALL

mm		Inches
300		12
240		9
180		6
120		3
60		
0	Jan Feb Mar Apr May Jun Jul Aug Sep Oct Nov Dec	0

Rainfall
In Cuba, the dry season (from November to April) alternates with the rainy season, when brief but heavy showers fall. In the Baracoa and Moa area at the eastern tip of the island, rainfall is heavier because the mountains block the Atlantic winds.

AUTUMN

AFTER THE AUGUST HEAT, when everything to do with work seems to slow down, life starts to pick up again. In autumn the schools reopen and work returns to a normal rhythm. The number of tourists – Europeans in particular – decreases.

SEPTEMBER

Fiesta de la Virgen del Cobre, El Cobre, Santiago de Cuba *(8 Sep)*. On the feast-day of the Virgin there is a surge in the regular pilgrimage to this site from all parts of the island. The statue of the Virgin is borne in procession through the streets.

Festival de Teatro de La Habana, Havana *(second half of Sep)*. This biennial theatre festival features a wide range of performances, including opera, dance, puppet theatre, street shows and pantomime. The theoretical aspects of theatre are also discussed, and experts from all over the world participate.
Matamoros Son, Santiago *(Sep)*. A biennial festival given over to *son* (see p28).
Festival de Teatro de Camagüey, Camagüey *(Sep–Oct)*. A national theatre competition dedicated to

Alicia Alonso performing at the Teatro García Lorca

Gertrudis Gómez de Avellaneda *(see p26)*, with the added participation of various foreign companies. As well as productions there are seminars, discussions, lectures and conferences.

OCTOBER

Festival de La Habana de Música Contemporánea, Havana *(first half of Oct)*. Concerts with top conductors and soloists, world premières, lectures and meetings with contemporary Cuban and foreign composers.
Fiesta de la Cultura Iberoamericana, Holguín *(second half of Oct)*. A festival given over to Spanish culture, with concerts, exhibitions, festivities and lectures.
Festival Internacional de Ballet de La Habana, Teatro García Lorca, Havana *(second half of Oct)*. A wide-ranging survey of classical ballet, organized by the Ballet Nacional de Cuba headed by Alicia Alonso. Famous international artists take part as well.

NOVEMBER

Salón de Arte Cubano Contemporáneo, Centro Desarrollo de las Artes Visuales, Havana *(biennial)*. An expo-competition of contemporary art works, with prizes awarded at the end. Also conferences, lectures, round table discussions.

HURRICANES

Hurricanes form when masses of hot air with low central pressure move upwards in a spiral, pulling cold air in towards the centre from the surrounding atmosphere. In the Northern hemisphere (which includes Cuba) this air circulation moves counter-clockwise. Hurricanes cause high tides, extremely strong winds, and very heavy and persistent rainfall resulting in floods. The areas most vulnerable to these storms are the coasts, areas with little surface drainage, the valleys, the mountain areas and the cities. Most of the natural disasters in Cuba in the last 100 years have been caused by these storms. In 1993, a freak hurricane destroyed thousands of homes. September and October are the most likely months for Caribbean hurricanes to occur.

Satellite photograph of Hurricane Irene over Cuba

AVERAGE MONTHLY TEMPERATURE

Temperature
The chart covers the entire island. In practice, Eastern Cuba, especially the Santiago area (except for the mountainous zones) is hotter. On the cayos the annual temperature range varies little. The humidity level goes from 81 per cent in summer to 79 per cent in winter.

Dancing at the Festival de Raíces Africanas, Guanabacoa

Festejos de San Cristóbal de La Habana *(Nov).* Festivities and concerts to commemorate the foundation of Havana.
Festival Internacional de Coros, Sala Dolores, Teatro Heredia, Santiago de Cuba *(biennial).* Concerts by choral groups from all over the world.
Festival de Raíces Africanas "Wemilere", Guanabacoa *(second half of Nov).* A festival of folk events, with closing prize-awarding ceremony.
Festival Cubadanzón, Teatro Sauto, Matanzas *(second half of Nov).* Performances by *danzón* orchestras and dancers, courses and conferences.

WINTER

THE MOST ACTIVE SEASON of the year from a cultural point of view, with many top conferences and festivals, the majority held in the capital. The events calendar is not generally disrupted by the holiday season, because although Christmas has been an official holiday since 1997,

it is in fact little celebrated. New Year's Day is usually celebrated at home with the family or with close friends, rather than being the focus for public events.

DECEMBER

Festival Internacional del Nuevo Cine Latino-americano, ICAIC, Havana *(first half of Dec).* This is the most important cinema festival and competition of the year, attracting famous international guests. The main cinemas in the capital present screenings of the Latin American films in the competition, as well as retrospectives of Cuban and international filmmakers.
Fiesta a la Guantanamera, Guantánamo *(first half of Dec).* Performances of, and lectures on, Afro-Cuban religion. Visits to the French *cafetales* (old coffee plantations) and the stone zoo.

Festival Internacional del Nuevo Cine Latinoamericano poster

Día de San Lázaro, Santiago de Las Vegas, El Rincón *(17 Dec).* The faithful and the sick come on pilgrimage to the church of Rincón; many come from Havana on foot.
Parrandas di Remedios, Remedios *(8–24 Dec).* Cuba's most popular folk festival begins with a children's parade and ends with floats, fireworks and exuberance on Christmas Eve *(see p173).*

JANUARY

The Feria Internacional del Libro logo

Feria Internacional de Artesanías, Pabexpo, Havana *(Jan–Feb).* Handicrafts fair. Stands from different countries; meetings and lectures.

FEBRUARY

Feria Internacional del Libro, Fortaleza de San Carlos de La Cabaña *(first half of Feb).* Book fair featuring a different nation each year. New Cuban and foreign publishing initiatives presented and sold. Round tables, conferences, poetry readings, events and concerts.

NATIONAL HOLIDAYS

New Year's Day/Liberation Day (1 Jan)
Labour Day (1 May)
National Rebellion Day (26 July)
Start of First War of Independence (10 Oct)
Christmas Day (25 Dec)

THE HISTORY OF CUBA

FIRST INHABITED IN Pre-Columbian times, Cuba was later conquered by the Spanish, who ruled here for four centuries. The island gained independence in 1899, only to come under the virtual control of the US, with the help of dictators Machado and Batista. The Revolution headed by Fidel Castro and Che Guevara, who defeated Batista on 1 January 1959, was a turning point for the country. The new political system achieved major social results and Cuba is now finally emerging from decades of isolation.

Before the arrival of the Spanish, Cuba was inhabited by three Amerindian ethnic groups: the Guanajatabey, Siboney and Taíno. The first were gatherers who lived in caves. The Siboney, hunters and fishermen, left behind the most interesting Pre-Columbian rock paintings in the country, more than 200 pictures in the caves of Punta del Este on Isla de la Juventud *(see p147)*. The Taíno were farmers and hunters thought to be from present-day Venezuela, and their culture, the most advanced of the three, achieved a primitive form of social organization.

On 28 October 1492, Christopher Columbus landed in Cuba during his first voyage of discovery in the New World *(see p210)*. He named it "Juana" in honour of the king of Spain's son, but the natives continued to call it "Cuba". From 1510 to 1514 Diego Velázquez de Cuellar, upon commission from Columbus's son, set about annexing the island to Spain. This proved to be a straightforward enterprise, because the Indians put up little

Indo-Cuban find, Museo Bani *(see p211)*

resistance, with the exception of a few episodes. The chief Hatuey led a rebellion in 1511–12, but was taken prisoner and burnt at the stake *(see p215)*.

Diego Velázquez then turned to colonization. He founded the city of Baracoa, first capital of the island, in 1512; San Salvador (present-day Bayamo) in 1513; San Cristóbal (Havana), Santísima Trinidad (Trinidad) and Sancti Spíritus in 1514; and Santiago de Cuba and Santa María del Puerto del Príncipe (present-day Camagüey) in 1515. The native population was decimated despite vigorous defence by Friar Bartolomé de las Casas, so-called "Protector of the Indians", and the Spanish soon had to import slaves from the western coasts of Africa to fulfil the need for labourers. Later, dissatisfied with the lack of gold in Cuba, the Spanish began to use the island both as a base from which they set out to conquer other American territory, as well as a port of call for ships taking the riches of the New World back to Spain.

TIMELINE

Before 1492 Cuba inhabited by Guanajatabey, Siboney and Taíno Indians

Diego Velázquez de Cuellar

1511 Indian resistance led by Hatuey, who is killed by the Spanish

1514 San Cristóbal (present-day Havana), Santísima Trinidad (Trinidad) and Sancti Spíritus founded

Pre-Columbian age	1490	1500	1510

Bust of Columbus, Museo de la Revolución, Havana

28 October 1492 Christopher Columbus lands on the island

1510 Diego Velázquez de Cuellar conquest of Cuba

1512 Foundation of Baracoa, first city in Cuba

1515 Foundation of Santiago de Cuba and Santa María del Puerto del Príncipe (Camagüey)

◁ **Detail from the painting *Siempre Che* (Che Forever) by Raúl Martínez**

PIRATES AND BUCCANEERS

By the mid-1500s the population of Cuba had dwindled considerably because the native Indians had been virtually annihilated by forced labour and diseases, and the Spanish had left for other parts of the New World in search of gold. However, the island was still important strategically as one of the defensive bastions of the Spanish colonies in America against the expansionist policies of France, Britain and the Netherlands.

Havana, the chief dock for vessels transporting treasure from America to Spain, soon drew the attention of pirates, who were plying the Caribbean Sea by the second half of the 16th century. In 1555, the French buccaneer

Henry Morgan, the British buccaneer

Jacques de Sores sacked and burned Havana, triggering the construction of an impressive fortification system. Pirate raids became more and more frequent in the 17th century. The first buccaneers were French, then came the turn of the British (including Francis Drake and Henry Morgan) and

The French buccaneers led by Jacques de Sores sacking the city of Havana

the Dutch, who attacked Spanish galleons loaded with treasure as well as the Cuban ports.

In order to deprive Spain of her colonies, France, Britain and the Netherlands joined in the "corsair war" – essentially state-sanctioned piracy – by financing attacks on Spanish merchant ships. The Spanish crown took several measures to defend its possessions, but to no avail. In 1697 the Ryswyk Treaty signed by Spain, France and Britain finally put an end to this unusual war in the West Indies.

In the meantime Havana had become the new capital of Cuba, thanks to its well-protected bay, and the constant ebb and flow of men and precious cargo imparted a vitality unknown to most of the other cities in the New World. However, the rest of the island was isolated from this ferment, even though agriculture was developing rapidly as the Spanish encouraged the large-scale cultivation of sugar cane and tobacco, which soon became desirable commodities in Europe (see p30). Cuba, a major hub of maritime traffic, was compelled to trade only with the parent country, Spain. Within a short time the island became a haven for smuggling, which was a boost for the island's economy, stimulating the exchange of Cuban sugar and tobacco for the products of the Old World.

THE BRIEF BRITISH DOMINION

Although in the 17th century the Cuban population, concentrated around Havana, had increased with the arrival of Spanish settlers and African slaves, in the early 18th century the island was

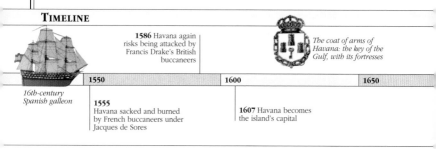

TIMELINE

1586 Havana again risks being attacked by Francis Drake's British buccaneers

The coat of arms of Havana: the key of the Gulf, with its fortresses

1550 | **1600** | **1650**

16th-century Spanish galleon

1555 Havana sacked and burned by French buccaneers under Jacques de Sores

1607 Havana becomes the island's capital

The British fleet attacking Havana in the summer of 1762

still a minor colony. In the summer of 1762 Havana was conquered by the British under the leadership of George Pocock and Lord Albemarle, who ruled for about a year. However, even in this short period the British occupation changed the economic and social organization of the island. The trade restrictions imposed by Spain were abolished, and Cuba began to trade openly with British colonies in North America. The slave trade intensified with Africans being used as labourers on the sugar cane plantations. As a result of the Treaty of Paris, drawn up in 1763, Havana was returned to the Spanish in exchange for Florida.

THE RISE OF NATIONAL IDENTITY

The 18th century marked the birth of a Creole aristocracy. These people, Cuban-born of Spanish descent, commissioned the fine buildings which can still be seen today, and led a Colonial lifestyle based on a combination of local, Indian and African traditions. At the end of the century, a cultural movement promoted by the intellectuals De Heredia, Varela and Villaverde (*see p26*) aimed at establishing a Cuban national identity. In the early 19th century, Spain, forced to recognize the independence of other American colonies, granted some freedom to Cuba, but then gave the island's governors dictatorial powers. Years of revolts, which the Spanish subdued mercilessly, then ensued. However, the new Creole middle class no longer had vested interests in the Spanish crown, and was determined to gain independence for the island.

The new Havana middle class taking a carriage ride

1697 The Treaty of Ryswyk ends the "corsair war" in the West Indies

1762 The British attack and occupy Havana

1830 Cuba replaces Haiti as the world's leading producer of sugar

1700 | **1750** | **1800**

1763 The Treaty of Paris marks the end of British occupation and Havana is given back to the Spanish

Captain General Luis de las Casas, governor of Cuba 1790–96

1837 First Cuban railway line opens, beginning at the port of Havana

Sugar, Slaves and Plantations

At the beginning of the 19th century the Cuban sugar industry was booming, thanks to the growing demand for sugar in Europe and America. The growth of the industry was made possible by the labour of slaves brought from Africa in their greatest numbers from the late 18th to the early 19th centuries. About one million men and women were brought to Cuba, and by around 1830 black Africans, including slaves and legally freed slaves, made up more than half the population of Cuba. The island became the world's leading sugar manufacturer, overtaking Haiti, and the industry continued to thrive after the abolition of slavery. Life on the sugar plantations therefore became a key feature of the island's history and life.

Bells *marked the daily routine of life in the* ingenio: *at 4:30am the* Ave Maria *was played to wake the workers; at 6am the assembly marked the beginning of work proper. At 8:30pm the last bell sounded to announce bedtime.*

Cimarrones *were runaway slaves who hid in the mountains or forests to avoid the* rancheadores, *whose job it was to find and capture them, dead or alive. These fugitives organized frequent revolts, which were almost inevitably suppressed with bloodshed.*

Storehouses, stables and cattle sheds were built around the *ingenio* area.

The sugar refining area stood in the original core of the sugar factory, the *trapiche* or mill.

The first stretch of railway on the island, which actually preceded the introduction of trains in Spain, was inaugurated in 1837 to transport sugar cane to the port of Havana.

Slaves were used *in all phases of sugar manufacture, and not only as field labourers. This old illustration shows the* sala de las calderas, *where the cane juice was boiled before being refined.*

Carlos Manuel de Céspedes, the owner of an estate near Manzanillo, freed his slaves on 10 October 1868, thus triggering the Cuban wars of independence. In his manifesto he asked for the abolition of slavery.

The dances and music that are thought to have given rise to the rumba (see p29) were performed in the ingenio, accompanied by the drumming of cajones, wooden boxes used to transport goods. Every year on 6 February the plantation owners allowed their slaves to celebrate their origins by dancing in the streets dressed in traditional costumes.

The barracones (the slaves' dormitories) were rectangular buildings divided into small rooms and with only one grilled door.

THE *INGENIO*

The sugar factory *(ingenio)* was in reality an agro-industrial complex, in the middle of which stood the owner's house. This was usually an elegant building, often embellished with arches and wrought-iron grilles. The sugar factory owner would stay here during the long inspection periods. The *batey*, an Amer-indian term used to describe collectively all the buildings on an *ingenio*, included a sugar cane mill, refinery rooms, a distillery, an infirmary, stables and cow sheds, vegetable gardens, storehouses, and the slaves' *barracones*, or sleeping quarters.

los negros esclavos

Fernando Ortiz

The ethnologist Fernando Ortiz (1881–1969) was the first person to seriously analyze the social condition of the blacks in Cuba, emphasizing the cultural bonds with African traditions.

A CULTURAL MELTING POT

Symbol of the Abakuá religion

The *ingenio* was a place where landowners, farmers and slaves, white and black, men and women, had to live and work together. The African slaves came from different ethnic groups and spoke different languages, but they managed to keep their religious practices alive by meeting in the *cabildos* (mutual aid associations), where they continued to pray to their gods, "concealing" them in the guise of Catholic saints *(see pp20–21)*. The Spanish themselves ended up assimilating elements of the very traditions they had been trying to suppress. Present-day Cuban music and dances were widespread in the *batey*, and the original songs and literature constantly refer to the *ingenio*, since it was here that the cultural crossover typical of Cuba evolved.

THE TEN YEARS' WAR AND THE ABOLITION OF SLAVERY

On 10 October 1868, at his La Demajagua estate *(see p215)*, the landowner Carlos Manuel de Céspedes launched the *grito de Yara* (war-cry from Yara), calling upon his fellow Cubans to rebel against Spanish rule. After conquering Bayamo, the rebels set up a revolutionary government and chose Céspedes as President of the Republic. On that occasion, the Cuban national anthem was sung for the first time. The new republic, however, was short-lived. The Spanish came back with a vengeance and the rebels – known as *mambises* (villains) – responded with the famous "machete assaults". In the meantime, the struggle had spread to other provinces, but differences among the rebels certainly did not help the cause.

The Ten Years' War – during which the first Cuban constitution was written (1869) – ended in 1878 with the Treaty of Zanjón, at which the rebels capitulated. Some revolutionaries rejected this agreement; one was General Antonio Maceo, who was forced into exile. There followed the so-called *"guerra chica"*, a brief conflict that resulted in the official abolition of slavery in 1886 (slave trade had in practice been prohibited since 1880). Cuba was the last American colony to abolish slavery. It was in this period that trade relations with the US developed.

Máximo Gómez

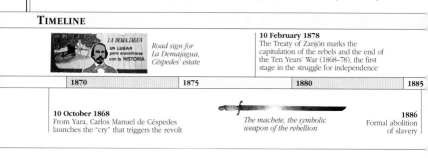

General Maceo, who was exiled in 1878

RESUMPTION OF HOSTILITIES AND THE END OF THE WAR

Towards the end of the 1800s, despite the rebellions, living conditions on the island had remained basically the same and none of the promised reforms had been enacted. In 1892, the Cuban intellectual José Martí (1853–95), in exile in the US, made a major contribution to the struggles that would follow: he founded the Partido Revolucionario Cubano, which united the Cuban forces in favour of independence.

The war against Spanish repression resumed on 24 February 1895. The leading figures were Martí – the real author and coordinator of Cuba's struggle for independence, who died in battle on 19 May, Máximo Gómez (recruited by Martí himself, who went to Santo Domingo to meet him) and Antonio Maceo. These last two had already distinguished themselves in the Ten Years' War. There was an escalation in the war and Spain sent reinforcements, but the situation was already out of control. Gómez and Maceo extended the war from the east to the west, gradually liberating the island. Not even the arrival of the Spanish general Valeriano Weyler, who was granted extraordinary powers, did any good: the war had taken a decided turn for the worse for the Spanish.

On 15 February 1898, when the Cubans had practically won, the American cruiser *Maine*, officially sent to the bay of Havana to protect US citizens and property in Cuban territory, exploded mysteriously, causing the death of about 250 marines. The US accused Spain of being responsible for the tragedy and, with public opinion

TIMELINE

LA DEMAJAGUA — Road sign for La Demajagua, Céspedes' estate

10 February 1878
The Treaty of Zanjón marks the capitulation of the rebels and the end of the Ten Years' War (1868–78), the first stage in the struggle for independence

| 1870 | 1875 | 1880 | 1885 |

10 October 1868
From Yara, Carlos Manuel de Céspedes launches the "cry" that triggers the revolt

The machete, the symbolic weapon of the rebellion

1886
Formal abolition of slavery

The US battlecruiser *Maine* in Havana Bay in 1898, with the Castillo del Morro on the right

on their side at home, intervened in the war. On 3 July the US Navy defeated the Spanish fleet, with the obvious intent of taking part in the peace treaty. On 10 December the Treaty of Paris – which involved Spain and the US, but not Cuba – marked the end of Spanish Colonial dominion in America. On 1 January 1899 the last Spanish governor, Jímenez y Castellanos, officially handed the keys of Havana to US general John Brooke. From this point onwards, Cuba became inextricably linked with the United States.

US SUPERVISION

In February 1901 the Constituent Assembly approved the first Cuban constitution and Tomás Estrada Palma was elected president. However, the delegates were forced to accept the Platt Amendment, formulated by US senator Orville Platt and added to a bill in Congress. Officially this provision aimed at safeguarding peace on the island, but its underlying purpose was to sanction the right of the US to intervene in Cuban affairs and to supervise trade relations between Cuba and other nations. In addition, the US was granted the right to establish naval bases on the island, including the one at Guantánamo in Eastern Cuba, which it still maintains *(see p235)*.

Although formal independence was granted to Cuba on 20 May 1902, in the years that followed American involvement in the local economy increased and, on the pretext of safeguarding their citizens and investments, the US sent marines to the island on many occasions.

JOSÉ MARTÍ

In 1895, when he died in battle at Boca de dos Ríos, José Martí was only 42. Despite this, he had had years of experience of living in exile and revolutionary struggle, besides writing a number of poems, articles and essays that would be the envy of a veteran author. Martí was born in Havana in 1853 to Spanish parents. By the time he went to secondary school he was already participating in anti-Spanish conspiracies. This activity led to his being deported in 1868, and exiled in 1878, after which he lived in the US, Spain, Mexico, Guatemala and Venezuela. As an essayist and journalist, Martí was known for his vigorous style. He was also a modernist poet *(see p26)*. He was an activist, a great politician and a sensitive interpreter of the impulses of the human soul.

José Martí, a national hero

The Early Period of the Republic

In its first 25 years, the Cuban Republic was headed by various presidents who did relatively little for the country. The second incumbent, José Miguel Gómez, who was nicknamed *tiburón* (shark), is at least to be credited for having introduced free public education and freedom of association and speech, as well as the separation of Church and State, and laws regarding divorce. In the early 1900s, sugar cane production increased to the point where sugar became virtually the only crop grown, and several new sugar factories were built. Havana, especially in the 1920s, saw the development of entire urban areas.

However, in general, independence had not really benefited the population at large, and protest demonstrations, repressed with force, began to increase. The first trade and student unions were set up, and in 1925 the Cuban Communist Party was founded. The leading figure in the party was the Marxist intellectual Julio Antonio Mella, leader of the Havana student movement and key to Latin American left-wing politics. Mella was arrested in Cuba but then freed because of the massive demonstrations that took place after he went on hunger strike; he was then sent into exile in Mexico. However, on 10 January 1929, Mella was assassinated in Mexico City by hired killers in the pay of the dictator Gerardo Machado. He became a national hero.

A popular uprising against the corrupt, inefficient government of Gerardo Machado

The Marxist intellectual Julio Antonio Mella

Gerardo Machado's Regime

In 1925 Gerardo Machado became president of Cuba, later changing the Constitution so he could rule for a further term, which he did with iron force until 1933. This period was marked by violence and tyranny; the people demonstrated their discontent by means of continual strikes, and the situation worsened with the Great Depression. A long general strike and the loss of the support of the army forced Machado to flee to the Bahamas on 12 August 1933.

After a brief period of progressive government, from early 1934 onwards there were various presidents who were little more than puppets, placed there by Sergeant Fulgencio Batista – who himself became president from 1940 to 1944. From 1934 to 1940 various social reforms came into being: the Platt amendment was revoked, women were allowed to vote, an eight-hour working day was instituted, and a new constitution was enacted.

BATISTA'S DICTATORSHIP

After World War II the Orthodox Party led by Eduardo Chibás became popular, supported by the more progressive members of the middle class. This party might have won the election that was to take place on 1 June 1952, but on 10 March Fulgencio Batista staged a coup. Protest demonstrations followed, consisting mostly of students, which were ruthlessly repressed. The university was then closed. Batista's government, having the official support of the US, abandoned its initial populist stance and became an out-and-out, violent dictatorship indifferent to the needs of the Cuban people. In fact, vast areas of land were sold to American and British firms, and the money was pocketed. As the dictator's cronies became rich, the population became poorer, and the country more and more backward. Cuba was becoming a "pleasure island" which held an overpowering fascination, especially for Americans.

By the 1950s Cuba was famous for glamour – its music and cocktails, its splendid prostitutes, cigars, drinking and gambling, and the sensual tropical life attracted mafiosi and film stars, tourists and businessmen, in equal

Fulgencio Batista (left) with American vice-president Richard Nixon

measure. However, there was a high price to pay: Cuba had not only become a land of casinos and drugs, it had also fallen into the hands of the American underworld, which ran the local gambling houses and luxury hotels, used for money laundering.

THE CUBAN REVOLUTION

After Batista's coup, a young lawyer, Fidel Alejandro Castro Ruz, an active student leader who associated with the Orthodox Party, denounced the illegitimacy of the new government to the magistracy, without effect. Since peaceful means did not work, on 26 July 1953 Castro made an unsuccessful attempt to capture the Moncada army barracks at Santiago (see p226). He was one of the few fortunate surviving rebels and was tried and sentenced to imprisonment in the Presidio Modelo, on Isla de la Juventud. Thanks to an amnesty, he was freed two years later and went into exile in Mexico, where he set about organizing the revolutionary forces, and was joined by a young Argentine doctor, Ernesto "Che" Guevara. This famous collaboration proved to be decisive for the success of the Revolution. In 1959, after years of armed struggle, the island was freed from dictatorships (see pp48–51).

Dancers at the Tropicana in the 1930s

12 August 1933 At night, Machado flees with a load of gold to the Bahamas

1940–4 Fulgencio Batista obtains presidential mandate thanks to a coalition of forces

1953–9 The Revolution liberates Cuba from dictatorship

1935 1940 1945 1950 1955

January 1934 Start of a period with a series of puppet presidents manoeuvred by the Cuban Army sergeant Fulgencio Batista

Sergeant Fulgencio Batista

10 March 1952 Coup d'état by Fulgencio Batista

The Cuban Revolution

IN EXILE IN MEXICO after the attack on the Moncada army barracks, on 2 December 1956 Fidel Castro left for Cuba on the yacht *Granma* with 82 other revolutionaries, including Che Guevara. Caught in a surprise attack by Batista's troops, only a few managed to escape to the Sierra Maestra, where they began to organize their guerrilla war. The miserable living conditions of the people, and the ever increasing corruption and repression, lent impetus to their struggle. The rebel army, which included farmers, students, women and regular army deserters, defeated Batista's troops after two years of fighting.

The attack against the Moncada barracks *took place on 26 July 1953 (the 100th anniversary of José Martí's birth). The rebels took advantage of the Carnival festivities to move unseen in the crowds, but the attack was a failure.*

Santa Clara was the scene of the battle that marked the triumph of the revolution. After the rebels' victory, Batista fled to Santo Domingo (31 December 1958).

Havana was occupied by Che Guevara's guerrillas, while Castro entered Santiago de Cuba (1 January 1959).

LEGENDA

-- Raúl Castro's march

-- Che Guevara's march

Havana • Matanzas

Pinar del Río •

Santa Clara

Cienfuegos •

Isla de la Juventud

The Sierra Escambray was reached by Che Guevara after an exhausting march; his men were without food or shoes and extremely weary but they were victorious (October 1958).

Radio Rebelde *was the guerrillas' radio station, set up in the Sierra Maestra by Che Guevara in February 1958. Its programmes were listened to avidly all over the island.*

THE PHASES OF THE WAR

The advance of two columns of guerrillas from the Sierra Maestra – one led by Che Guevara and Camilo Cienfuegos to the west (October 1958), the other by Raúl Castro bound for Guantánamo – marked the climax of the revolutionaries' struggle. After the battle of Santa Clara, conquered by Guevara's troops at the end of December, Batista escaped to Santo Domingo. On 1 January 1959 victory was declared by the revolution.

The Landing of the Granma *in Cuba took place in 1956. Because of a navigational error, the yacht landed on Las Coloradas beach instead of Niquero. Intercepted by a warship, the rebels tried to escape but were shot down by Batista's planes. Those captured were killed, while the survivors (including Castro) took refuge in the Sierra Maestra.*

Castro entered Havana *on 8 January 1959 and on 16 February was elected prime minister. At the time the president was Manuel Urrutia, elected after Batista's escape. The revolutionary government immediately abolished racial discrimination and reduced rents and the cost of electricity.*

Young women*, including Haidée Santamaría, Celia Sánchez and Vilma Espín, participated actively in the revolutionary war. After Havana was captured, they were entrusted with guarding strategic points.*

On the Sierra Maestra*, Cuba's largest mountain range, the rebels organized guerrilla warfare, recruiting soldiers from among the population (above, Castro recruiting farmers). The strategy was to ambush Batista's troops and take their supplies and weapons.*

• Camagüey

Holguín •

Playa Las Coloradas was where the *Granma* landed on 2 December 1956.

• Bayamo

Santiago de Cuba •
• Guantánamo

The attack at La Plata, a military barracks, was the rebels' first success (17 January 1957).

In the Sierra Maestra Fidel Castro, Che Guevara and the other survivors of the *Granma* worked out a strategy of guerrilla warfare with a growing number of *barbudos*, students, army deserters and reinforcements sent by the urban branch of the Movimiento 26 de Julio.

At Santiago de Cuba the rebels won an important victory on 17 January 1957.

TIMELINE

1953		1956		1958	1959
October 1953 Castro condemned to 15 years' imprisonment in Presidio Modelo	**30 November 1956** Bloody repression of revolt at Santiago	*Che Guevara*		**October** Che and Cienfuegos leave east to conquer central regions	**1 January** Che and Cienfuegos enter Havana; Castro, Santiago
26 July 1953 Attack on Moncada barracks	**15 May 1955** Castro freed, goes to Mexico in exile *Castro leaving prison*		**2 December 1956** Landing of *Granma* **1956–58** Guerrilla war in the Sierra Maestra	**24 February** Radio Rebelde set up **31 December** Santa Clara falls. Batista flees	**8 January** Castro enters Havana in triumph

The Heroes of the Revolution

THE SUCCESS OF THE REVOLUTION can be partly explained by the moral stature of the heroes who headed it, and partly by the unity of the movement – an entire population was determined to obtain freedom. After their triumphal entrance into Havana, the revolutionary leaders were entrusted with the task of realizing their objectives: the reorganization of the country's agriculture, afflicted with large landed estates and monoculture; the battle against illiteracy and unemployment; industrialization; the construction of homes, schools and hospitals. Fidel Castro became Prime Minister and Che Guevara was appointed Minister of Industry and president of the National Bank. The revolution continued, with its heroes and ideals.

Ernesto "Che" Guevara *was an Argentinian who met Castro in Mexico. Unpretentious, straightforward and ascetic, and an uncompromising idealist, he believed the Third World could be freed only through armed rebellion (see p172).*

The straw hats worn by the *barbudos* were those commonly used by farmers.

Camilo Cienfuegos, *a commander whose courage was legendary, was a direct, spontaneous person with a great sense of humour. He played a crucial role in the armed struggle, but took part in the government only for a brief period. He disappeared on 29 October 1959, while returning in his small plane from a tour of inspection in Camagüey, and was never seen again.*

Horses were the most common means of transport used by the revolutionaries.

Frank País *(seen here with his mother and fiancée), head of the Movimiento 26 de Julio, was entrusted with organizing a revolt in Santiago de Cuba that would coincide with the landing of the Granma. But because of the delay in the landing the revolt was repressed. País died in Santiago on 30 July 1957, in an ambush set up by the chief of police.*

Raúl Castro, *Fidel's brother, was one of the few survivors of the Moncada barracks attack and the landing of the Granma. He took part in the guerrilla war and became a member of the government, adopting a radical stance. As Minister of Defence he signed, with Khrushchev, the agreement for the installation of the nuclear missiles in Cuba that caused the 1962 crisis.*

The Cuban flag, used after the wars of independence, has the colours of the French Revolution. The three blue stripes represent the old provinces of the island.

Fidel Castro with Juan Almeida (left), *one of the strategists of revolutionary guerrilla warfare. Castro, a great orator and political strategist, the* Líder Máximo *and an uncompromising patriot, personified the Cuban state. As Alejo Carpentier wrote, "he accomplished what José Martí had promised". Born on 13 August 1926 in Mayarí in Eastern Cuba, the son of Spanish immigrants, he studied with the Jesuits and took a degree in law. He began to fight for the cause while at university.*

THE BARBUDOS

The rebels were referred to as *barbudos* (bearded men) because during their time in the mountains, they all grew long beards. A large number of farmers joined their famous marches. This photograph, taken by the Cuban photographer Raúl Corrales, expresses the epic and team spirit of the revolution.

Guillermo García Morales was one of the first Cuban farmers to join the revolutionary war of the Movimiento 26 de Julio. A guerrilla in the Sierra Maestra together with Castro, he was named Commander of the Revolution for his distinguished service.

Celia Sánchez Manduley espoused the revolutionary cause at an early age and fought in the Sierra Maestra. Considered Fidel Castro's right-hand "man" and companion, after 1959 she filled important political positions. Manduley died of cancer in 1980, while still young.

ERADICATING ILLITERACY, AGRICULTURAL REFORM

One of the first acts of the revolutionary government was a campaign against illiteracy, initiated in 1961: thousands of students travelled throughout the countryside, teaching the rural population to read and write. Che Guevara, who during the guerrilla warfare in the mountains had encouraged his men to devote some time to study, participated in the campaign. In a short time illiteracy was eradicated.

The next step was agrarian reform, which began with the abolition of ownership of large landed estates, especially those in foreign (in particular American) hands. US landholdings were drastically reduced. This marked the beginning of hostilities between the two countries. In October 1960 the US declared an economic boycott that blocked the export of petroleum to Cuba and the import of Cuban sugar. After nearly two years of growing tension, Cuba secured closer economic and political ties with the Soviet Union, Eastern Europe and China. In the meantime, the struggle against counter-revolutionary guerrillas in the Sierra del Escambray continued.

Marines arriving at the US naval base of Guantánamo during the missile crisis

against Cuba, which heralded a boycott by most other countries in the Americas (except Mexico and Canada). These countries also severed diplomatic relations with the island, as the US had done. The result was the establishment of even closer ties between Cuba and the communist world. A year later, when the US discovered the presence of nuclear missile sites in Cuba, President Kennedy ordered a naval blockade around the island and demanded that the missile installations be dismantled immediately. At the height of the crisis, with the world poised on the brink of nuclear war, the Soviet president Nikita Khrushchev ordered the missiles to be taken back to the Soviet Union.

Participants in the campaign against illiteracy in 1961

THE EMBARGO AND MISSILE CRISIS

On 17 April 1961 a group of Cuban exiles and mercenaries trained by the CIA landed at Playa Girón, in the Bay of Pigs, to invade the island. But the attack failed because, contrary to the expectations of the US, Cuban civilians did not rise up against Castro *(see p163)*. Eight days later President Kennedy declared a trade embargo

FROM THE *ZAFRA* CAMPAIGN TO THE EMIGRATION OF THE "*MARIELITOS*"

During the early stages, the government had aimed to create as much diversity in the economy as possible. However, in 1970, in order to inject life into the flagging economy, all efforts were concentrated on promoting the

TIMELINE

1961 April 17: landing at Bay of Pigs; US embargo begins on April 25

1962 Missile crisis

1965 Only legal political party is the Cuban Communist Party

1975 First congress of the Cuban Communist Party

1960 | 1970 | 1980

1961 January 3, diplomatic relations with US are broken

1967 Death of Che Guevara

1970 The *zafra* campaign

1980 125,000 Cubans emigrate from the small harbour at Mariel *zafra* (sugar cane harvest) campaign. A target was set of ten million tons, but in the end only 8,500,000 were harvested. In the same period some Latin American countries resumed diplomatic relations with Cuba. While the revolution had achieved a great deal in social terms, the country's economic problems had by no means been resolved. 1980 saw the emigration of 125,000 Cubans, the so-called *marielitos* – named after the small harbour of Mariel, near Havana, where they set off for Miami.

The Pope and Castro during his visit to Cuba

Many sectors of industry came to a standstill due to a lack of fuel, imports were reduced, interruptions in the supply of electricity and water became part of everyday life, transport virtually came to a halt, food rations were reduced, and wages were lowered. In 1991 the Soviet Union also withdrew its troops and technicians. The economic crisis continued to worsen until 1994.

THE *PERÍODO ESPECIAL*
The dismantling of the Berlin Wall in 1989 and the subsequent collapse of Communism in Eastern Europe deprived Cuba of economic partners; and Castro did not conceal his dislike of Gorbachev's *perestroika* policy. The suspension of Soviet aid was a crippling blow for the Cuban economy, and triggered a crisis that the government faced by imposing a programme of austerity. In 1990 the island went through one of the most difficult phases in its history, the Período Especial.

Empty shelves in a shop during the crisis period

THE ECONOMIC RECOVERY
At a time when more and more *balseros* (refugees who travelled on makeshift rafts, *balsas*) were fleeing to Miami, the first signs of change appeared. The government began to encourage foreign investment, private enterprise was granted a certain degree of freedom, relations were resumed with Eastern European nations, and the use of the US dollar in transactions was legalized. In the meantime Castro emerged from isolation and undertook official visits to a number of European countries. A sign of the change was Castro's visit to the Vatican to meet Pope John Paul II in 1996, and the Pope's visit to Cuba two years later. By the late 1990s, tourism had become the strongest sector of the economy. Today it is both a resource, and a cause for concern, in that the dual economy of the Cuban *peso* and American dollar (the currency used by foreign tourists) has created its own particular social problems. Cuba today faces all kinds of challenges, not least, how to change without losing its identity.

Rations coupon booklet

1990 Beginning of the Período Especial

1996 The Helms-Burton law tightens economic embargo

1998 Pope John Paul II's visit to Cuba (21–25 January), a significant turning point

1990

2000

1989 Berlin Wall comes down

1991 The Soviet Union withdraws troops and technicians

1996 In November, Castro visits Pope John Paul II in the Vatican

2000 1,774,000 tourists visit Cuba in one year

Seaside tourism

HAVANA
AREA BY AREA

Havana at a Glance

The crest of Havana

HAVANA IS A LIVELY, COLOURFUL capital city, full of bustle and entertainment, with some splendid architectural gems from the Colonial period and beyond, and numerous other sights. The city alone is worth the trip to Cuba. Many attractions are concentrated in three quarters: Habana Vieja (Old Havana), Centro Habana and Vedado. In the following pages Habana Vieja, the Colonial centre within the old city walls, is described first, followed by Centro Habana and the area known as the Prado. The western part of the city is covered in the chapter called Vedado and Plaza. For map references for major sights in Havana, refer to the Street Finder *(see pp118–23)*.

0 kilometres   1

0 miles   1

VEDADO AND PLAZA
(see pp96–105)

Necropolis Colón (see pp104–5) *is Havana's city cemetery as well as a national monument. Many famous people are buried here, often in striking tombs, and the site has become a place of pilgrimage for many.*

FURTHER AFIELD
(see pp106–17)

0 kilometres   20

0 miles   20

Castillo del Morro *(see p110), beyond the port canal, can be seen from many parts of the old city.*

Martí Memorial (see p103) *in Plaza de la Revolución is one of the symbols of Cuba. The white marble statue of the great patriot forms a focal point for national celebrations.*

◁ **Havana at sunset, with the dome of Capitolio rising up over the rooftops**

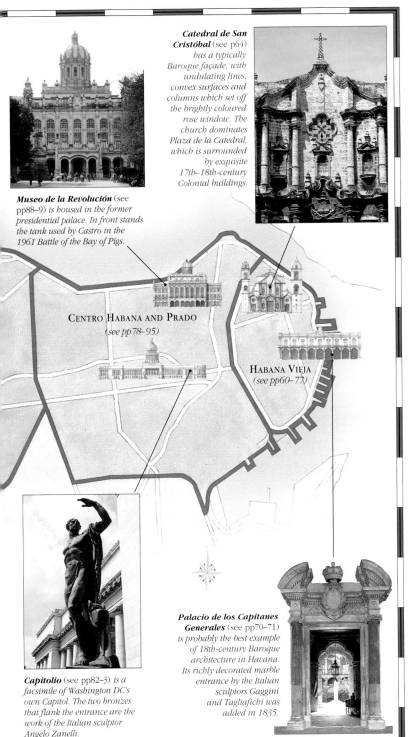

Catedral de San Cristóbal (see p64) has a typically Baroque façade, with undulating lines, convex surfaces and columns which set off the brightly coloured rose window. The church dominates Plaza de la Catedral, which is surrounded by exquisite 17th–18th-century Colonial buildings.

Museo de la Revolución (see pp88–9) is housed in the former presidential palace. In front stands the tank used by Castro in the 1961 Battle of the Bay of Pigs.

CENTRO HABANA AND PRADO
(see pp78–95)

HABANA VIEJA
(see pp60–77)

Capitolio (see pp82–3) is a facsimile of Washington DC's own Capitol. The two bronzes that flank the entrance are the work of the Italian sculptor Angelo Zanelli.

Palacio de los Capitanes Generales (see pp70–71) is probably the best example of 18th-century Baroque architecture in Havana. Its richly decorated marble entrance by the Italian sculptors Gaggini and Tagliafichi was added in 1835.

The Malecón

No OTHER PLACE REPRESENTS Havana better than the Malecón, and no other place thrills tourists and locals so much. This seafront promenade winds for 7 km (4 miles) alongside the city's historic quarters, from the Colonial centre to the skyscrapers of Vedado, charting the history of Havana from past to present. The busy seafront boulevard is lined with many attractive buildings, but it is the overall effect that is striking – and the Bay of Havana looks truly spectacular at sunset. In addition, the Malecón means tradition and religion to the people of the city: offerings to the gods *(see p21)* are thrown from the parapet into the sea.

LOCATOR MAP
See *Street Finder pp120–23.*

① ***The Caryatid Building*** *is one of the most important structures in the first stretch of the Malecón. Built in the early 20th century and recently restored, it was named after the Art Deco-style female figures that support the entablature of the loggia.*

② ***The area between Prado and Calle Belascoaín,*** *which has been scrupulously restored, is known for its pastel buildings. In the same part of the street, at No 51, is the "Ataúd" (the coffin), a 1950s skyscraper whose name derives from the shape of its windows.*

Varied decoration

Balconies with Neo-Moorish decorative patterns

ARCHITECTURE

The Malecón is lined with buildings whose pastel hues have faded in the sun and salty air, as well as early 20th-century structures, often with two or three storeys and a loggia on the upper floor, in a mix of different architectural styles.

Edificio Focsa

③ ***The Monument to the Victims of the Maine*** *was built in 1926 in memory of the sailors who died when the American warship* Maine *exploded in the Bay of Havana in 1898 (see p45). It stands in one of the wide stretches of the avenue on the edge of Vedado.*

Hotel Nacional

④ ***Between Calle 23 and Calle G*** *is the stretch of the Malecón that borders the Vedado quarter to the north. Dominated by Havana's tallest buildings, this is the seafront of a modern metropolis.*

On stormy days *the waves break against the rocks and crash over the sea wall onto the street. Children love it when this happens. Storms are also a source of inspiration for followers of* santería, *who view it as the wrath of Yemayá, the sea goddess (see p21).*

Fishing *on the Malecón is a popular pastime among the locals. Others are playing music, strolling, or simply sitting on the low wall and watching the horizon.*

ATMOSPHERE
The Havana seafront is especially magical at sunset, when the colours of the buildings are accentuated. The Malecón is at its busiest on Sundays, when the Havanans who cannot get to the Playas del Este flock here.

Young people love to gather along the Malecón, to meet friends, socialize, swim, sunbathe and drink rum.

The striking setting *of the Malecón, facing the sea and with the city behind it, makes it a popular place for romantic young couples. There is also the occasional single person on the lookout for female or male companionship.*

A WALK BY THE OCEAN: THE HISTORY OF THE MALECÓN

On 4 November 1901, the US authorities then occupying Cuba planned the Malecón as a tree-lined, pedestrian promenade to begin at the Castillo de la Punta. However the strong wind and rough sea obliged the engineers to change their original project and it was an American engineer named Mead, and Frenchman Jean Forestier, who came up with a more practical plan. In 1902 the open space in front of the Prado was completed

The Malecón in the early 1900s

with a municipal bandstand. Hotels and cafés were built near the old city, while bathing facilities were concentrated in Miramar. In 1919 the Malecón stretched as far as Calle Belascoaín, and in 1921 as far as Calle 23. It soon became a fast link between the old and modern cities – so much so that in the 1950s it was virtually abandoned by pedestrians. Today, despite the traffic, its original function has been partly revived.

HABANA VIEJA

Statue of Columbus, Palacio de los Capitanes Generales

THE HISTORIC HEART of Havana, which was declared part of the "cultural heritage of humanity" by UNESCO in 1982, is the largest Colonial centre in Latin America. After two centuries of neglect, restoration work under the direction of Eusebio Leal Spengler, the *historiador de la ciudad* (Superintendent of Cultural Heritage), is reviving the former splendour of this district. Habana Vieja is characterized by Hispanic-Andalusian architecture, vitalized by the tropical sun and lush vegetation. Time seems to stand still here but nonetheless the zone does not give the impression of being a museum. The restoration programme is not limited to monuments and major buildings, but also includes old shops and ordinary houses. The aim is to ensure the revival of both the beauty of Habana Vieja and its original vitality and everyday activities.

SIGHTS AT A GLANCE

Museums and Galleries
Fundación Destilería
   Havana Club **13**
Museo de Arte Colonial **2**
Museo José Martí **18**

Historic Buildings
Bodeguita del Medio **4**
Castillo de la Real Fuerza **5**
Palacio de los Capitanes
   Generales pp70–71 **8**
Seminario de San Carlos
   y San Ambrosio **3**
El Templete **6**

Historic Streets and Squares
Calle Obispo **9**
Calle Oficios **7**
Casa de Africa **11**
Casa de la Obra Pía **10**
Plaza de San Francisco **12**
Plaza Vieja **14**

Churches and Monasteries
Catedral de San Cristóbal **1**
Convento de Santa Clara **15**
Iglesia de Nuestra Señora
   de la Merced **17**
Iglesia del Espíritu Santo **16**

GETTING THERE
The easiest way to reach this quarter is by taxi, or by *cocotaxi (see p307)*, which is cheaper. Public transport services are infrequent and stops are not indicated. Habana Vieja can be easily explored either on foot or by hiring a rickshaw or carriage. These can be found behind the Castillo de la Real Fuerza, at the corner of Calle Mercaderes and Calle Empedrado.

KEY
Street-by-Street map *pp62–3*
Street-by-Street map *pp66–7*
i Tourist information
Ferry

0 metres 300
0 yards 300

◁ **Colonial buildings in Plaza Vieja** *(see p76)*

Street-by-Street: Plaza de la Catedral

DOMINATED BY THE ELEGANT PROFILE of its church, Plaza de la Catedral is one of the symbols of Habana Vieja. In 1592, the Zanja Real, the city's first aqueduct (and the first Spanish aqueduct in the New World), reached the square. Water was channelled from the Almendares river, 11 km (7 miles) away. The Zanja Real was built to provide water to ships docking in the harbour, as well as to local residents. A 16th-century plaque in the square marks the spot where the Zanja Real was located. In the 18th century the aristocratic buildings and present-day Cathedral were built here. Plaza de la Catedral is an unmissable attraction for anyone visiting the historic centre, with women in Colonial costume who stroll under the arcades and read fortunes, and a bar-restaurant where you can relax in the shade and listen to music.

A woman in Colonial costume on the Cathedral steps

Former entrance to the seminary

Centro Wifredo Lam, housed in an 18th-century palazzo, promotes contemporary art with exhibitions and lectures.

CALLE SAN IGNACIO

Seminario de San Carlos y San Ambrosio
The modern entrance of this 18th-century building echoes the Baroque decorative motifs of the Cathedral ❸

Palacio de los Marqueses de Aguas Claras was built in the second half of the 18th century. In the 1900s it housed the París Restaurant and then the offices of the Banco Industrial. It is now a bar-restaurant, El Patio, with tables in the inner courtyard as well as in the picturesque square.

CALLE EMPEDRADO

KEY

– – – Suggested route

STAR SIGHTS

★ Catedral de San Cristóbal

★ Museo de Arte Colonial

★ Bodeguita del Medio

Casa de la Condesa de la Reunión, a 19th-century building surrounding a splendid courtyard, is the headquarters of the Alejo Carpentier Foundation. This well-known 20th-century Cuban writer *(see p27)* set his novel *Siglo de las Luces* here.

LA BODEGUITA DEL MEDIO

★ **Bodeguita del Medio**
This restaurant is legendary thanks to the writer Ernest Hemingway, who came here to drink mojitos ❹

LOCATOR MAP
*See Street Finder, pp120–23,
map 4*

★ **Catedral de San Cristóbal**
*The Baroque façade of this church, declared
a national monument, is considered one of
the most beautiful in the Americas* ❶

Palacio del Conde Lombillo (1746)
is now home to the offices of the
Historiador De La Habana and hosts
temporary exhibitions of photographs
and lithographs.

**Palacio de los Marqueses
de Arcos**, built in the 1700s,
houses an art gallery where
handicrafts and prints are
on sale. The building was
once the main post office
and the original letter box is still
visible on the outside wall.

Plaza
de Armas
*(see
pp66–7)*

CALLE TACÓN

CALLE EMPEDRADO

CALLE MERCADERES

PLAZA DE LA
CATEDRAL

CALLEJÓN DEL CHORRO

CALLE SAN IGNACIO

| 0 metres | 40 |
| 0 yards | 40 |

**The Taller Experimental de
Gráfica** (1962) holds theoretical
and practical courses in graphic
art for Cubans and foreigners, and
houses a Gallery of Engravings.

★ **Museo de Arte Colonial**
*Dating from 1720, this is one of the
city's finest examples of early Colonial
domestic architecture. It houses an exhibition of Colonial furniture and objects* ❷

Catedral de San Cristóbal ❶

Calle Empedrado 156. **Map** 4 E2.
📞 (7) 8617 771. 🕐 10:30am–
3:30pm Mon–Fri, 10:30am–2pm Sat,
9am–12:30pm Sun. 🕀 8pm Mon,
Tue, Thu, Fri; 10:30am Sun. 📷

The austere nave of Catedral de San Cristóbal

CONSTRUCTION OF the Catedral de San Cristóbal (Cathedral of St Christopher) began in 1748 under the supervision of Jesuit priests, but after they were expelled from Cuba following conflict with the Spanish crown, the church was finished by Franciscans in 1777. It became a cathedral after the collapse of the old Parroquial Mayor (see p70), which was caused by the explosion of a ship in the nearby port.

In 1789, present-day San Cristóbal was consecrated as Catedral de la Virgen María de la Inmaculada Concepción, and the small square where it stands gained its current status. In 1796 it was renamed Catedral de San Cristóbal de La Habana, because, according to popular belief, from that year until 1898 it housed the relics of Christopher Columbus himself. A plaque to the left of the pulpit tells the same story, though there is no official historical record.

The architecture is in keeping with other Jesuit churches throughout the world: a Latin cross layout, chapels on the sides and to the rear, the nave higher than the side aisles. The Cuban

Baroque façade is grandiose, with two large, asymmetrical bell towers and an abundance of niches and columns, which Cuban author Alejo Carpentier described as "music turned into stone".

In comparison, the Neo-Classical interior is rather disappointing. Large piers separate the nave from the aisles, which have eight chapels. The largest one is the Sagrario chapel; the oldest (1755), designed by Lorenzo Camacho, is dedicated to the Madonna of Loreto and contains quaint, tiny houses used as ex votos.

The three frescoes behind the high altar are by Giuseppe Perovani, while the original wooden and plaster ceiling, demolished and then rebuilt in 1946–52, was the work of

Frenchman Jean Baptiste Vermay, who founded the Alejandro Fine Arts Academy (see p24). The high altar was created by Italian artist Giuseppe Bianchini in the 1800s. To the right is a huge wooden statue of St Christopher, carved by the Seville sculptor Martín de Andújar in 1636. The legs are out of proportion with the trunk, as they were cut in order to allow the statue to pass through the portal.

Statue of St Christopher

On 16 November, the saint's feast day, a solemn mass is held here, during which the faithful, who have to stay quiet during the service, file past the statue to silently ask for his blessing. This blessing is given as long as worshippers do not utter a word until they have left the church.

Pope John Paul II in front of the Cathedral

THE POPE'S VISIT

Pope John Paul II visited Cuba from 21–26 January 1998 (see p53). This carefully planned event was of great historical significance to Cuba and was greeted with enthusiasm not only by Catholics, but by virtually the entire population. The Cuban government had shown signs of favouring dialogue with the Church and greater religious tolerance in the 1990s. The Pope's visit and the outdoor masses were broadcast on television and the government also officially recognized Christmas Day as a holiday. On 25 January the "Celebration of the Word" was held in the Cathedral, during which the Pope met Cuban priests. Journalists from all over the world attended, and the Pope also held an audience with the faithful in Plaza de la Revolución.

Museo de Arte Colonial **②**

Calle San Ignacio 61. **Map** 4 E2.
📞 (7) 8626 440. ⏱ 9am–6:45pm daily. ● 25 Dec. 📷 📷 📷

THIS 18TH-CENTURY mansion, built by Don Luis Chacón, governor of Cuba, has been the home of a fascinating museum dedicated to Colonial art since 1963. The building is a fine example of a Colonial residence and is constructed around an elegant courtyard.

The 12 rooms on the ground floor and first floor contain furniture, chandeliers, porcelain and other decorative pieces from various 18th–19th-century middle-class and aristocratic houses in Havana, in which European, Creole and Colonial traditions are combined. Besides a remarkable collection of furniture made of tropical wood, the museum has an exceptional collection of stained glass windows (mediopunto), typical of Cuba's Creole craftsmen (see p23).

There is also a 13th room where exhibitions of contemporary art and crafts inspired by Colonial art are held. During the week the museum organizes tours for schoolchildren and leisure activities for the elderly in the area.

A small adjacent theatre, which has its own entrance on Calle San Ignacio, puts on a busy and wide-ranging programme of concerts and plays at weekends.

Seminario de San Carlos y San Ambrosio **③**

Calle San Ignacio 5. **Map** 4 E2. 📞 (7) 8626 989. ⏱ 8:30am–4pm Mon–Fri. ● 1 Jan, 26 Jul, 10 Oct, 25 Dec. 📷

THIS BUILDING WAS erected by the Jesuits in the mid-18th century to house a seminary first founded in 1689. Famous Cuban patriots

Colonial furniture in the Museo de Arte Colonial

and intellectuals studied here. One of them was Padre Félix Varela (1788–1853), who laid down the theoretical bases for the Cuban war of independence (see p26).

Besides the old portal on Calle San Ignacio, built in the Churrigueresque style which was common in Spain and her colonies in this period, there is also another entrance in 20th-century Neo-Baroque style on the Avenida del Puerto.

Museo de Arte Colonial: an arched mediopunto window

The large central courtyard is the only one of its kind in Cuba: it has galleries on three levels, the first with simple columns, the second with double columns, and the third with plain wooden piers. The

lavishly decorated inner stairway leading to the first floor has trapezoidal motifs instead of the more common arch, and fine black mahogany banisters. The seminary is still functioning, but is open to the public for visits.

Bodeguita del Medio **④**

Calle Empedrado 207. **Map** 4 E2. 📞 (7) 8671 374. ⏱ noon–12:30am daily. 📷

STANDING EXACTLY at the halfway point in a typical small street in old Havana, a few steps away from the Cathedral, the Bodeguita del Medio (literally, "little shop in the middle") has become a big attraction.

The place was founded in 1942 as a food shop. A bar serving alcoholic drinks was added, and the place became a haunt for intellectuals, artists and politicians. Today it is no longer a shop but a good restaurant offering typical Creole dishes, with a bustling bar serving shots of rum and Cuban cocktails. The walls are plastered with photographs, drawings, graffiti and visitors' autographs, including those of famous patrons such as the singer Nat King Cole, poets Pablo Neruda and Nicolás Guillén, and the writers Gabriel García Marquez, Alejo Carpentier (see p27), and Ernest Hemingway, who was a regular here.

The Bodeguita del Medio with its memento-covered walls

Street-by-Street: Around Plaza de Armas

THE ELEGANT, SPACIOUS PLAZA DE ARMAS is lined with Baroque buildings, giving it a delightful Colonial atmosphere. The space overflows with tropical vegetation and is enlivened by the stalls of the second-hand book market (see p69). The plaza was built in the 1600s to replace the old Plaza Mayor, the core of Havana's religious, administrative and military life, and up to the mid-1700s it was used for military exercises. After its transformation in 1771–1838, it became a favourite with rich Havana citizens and popular as an area for carriage rides. Careful restoration work has been carried out over recent years, and the square now attracts throngs of visitors and locals, many of whom simply gather here to sit and relax.

Palacio del Segundo Cabo
(1776), the former residence of the Spanish lieutenant governor, is now the home of the Cuban Book Institute.

★ **Palacio de los Capitanes Generales**
This fine Baroque palace, now the Museo de la Ciudad, was built for Cuba's old Colonial rulers. A statue of Columbus stands in the courtyard, beneath towering royal palms ❽

Plaza de la Catedral (*see pp62–3*)

CALLE TACÓN

CALLE O'REILLY

CALLE MERCADERES

CALLE OBISPO

STAR SIGHTS

★ Castillo de la Real Fuerza

★ El Templete

★ Palacio de los Capitanes Generales

★ Calle Obispo

Hotel Ambos Mundos

Former Ministerio de Educación

Farmacia Taquechel

★ **Calle Obispo**
Like an open-air museum of Colonial architecture, this street is lined with buildings of interest dating from the 16th–19th centuries, including old groceries and historic shops ❾

CALLE OBRAPÍA

Casa de la Obra Pía
This large 17th-century mansion is well-known for its elaborate Baroque doorway, which was reputedly sculpted in Spain ❿

★ Castillo de la Real Fuerza

This 16th-century castle, with its broad moat and characteristic angular ramparts, is the oldest military construction in Havana. A copy of the Giraldilla, the symbol of the city, stands on one of its towers ❺

LOCATOR MAP
See Street Finder, pp120–23, map 4

Calle Enna is Havana's narrowest and shortest street. It was named after a general active in the Colonial period.

★ El Templete

This Neo-Classical building, shaded by a majestic ceiba tree, evokes memories of the city's foundation ❻

Hotel Santa Isabel is in the former home of the Conde de Santovenia, built between the 18th and 19th centuries and recently opened after lengthy restoration *(see p248).*

La Casa de los Arabes housed the city's first school in the 17th century.

Calle Oficios

This perfectly restored Colonial street houses a number of shops and museums, including a vintage car museum ❼

0 metres		60
0 yards		60

KEY

‐ ‐ ‐ Suggested route

Stairway leading to the battle-ments, Castillo de la Real Fuerza

Castillo de la Real Fuerza ❺

Calle Tacón e/ Calle Obispo y O'Reilly.
Map 4 F2. (7) 8616 130.
9am–6:30pm daily. 1 Jan,
1 May, 26 Jul, 10 Oct, 25 Dec.

T HIS FORTRESS *(castillo)* was built in 1558–77 to protect the city from pirate attacks, following a raid by the French buccaneer Jacques de Sores in 1555, in which the original fort was destroyed and Havana devastated *(see p40)*. But despite the moat surrounding it and its thick walls, the castle soon proved to be quite inadequate as a defensive bulwark because of its poor strategic position, too far inside the bay. The castle then became the residence of governors, military commanders and

Painted pottery, Ceramics Museum

leading figures, as well as a safe place to store treasures brought from America and en route to Spain. In 1634, a weathervane known as La Giraldilla was placed on the lookout tower, which soon became the symbol of Havana. The original is now on display in the Museo de la Ciudad *(see pp70–71)* and a copy has been placed on the tower.
Today, the Castillo houses the **Museo Nacional de la Cerámica Cubana**, which houses a collection of ceramics, sculpture, mosaics and painted panels by modern and contemporary Cuban artists.

LA GIRALDILLA

There are various theories as to the meaning of the bronze weathervane sculpted by Gerónimo Martín Pinzón in 1630–34 and modelled on the one crowning La Giralda in Seville. Some people say it is the symbol of victory, others think it is the personification of Seville, the final destination of ships going to Europe. But others say the statue represents Inés de Bobadilla, wife of the Spanish governor Hernando de Soto. According to legend, she spent hours gazing at the horizon, waiting for her husband to return from his exploration of Florida and other parts of the US (in vain, since he died on the banks of the Mississippi). This is said to be the reason why the statue was placed on the highest point of the fortress dominating the port entrance.

The tower with its copy of the 17th-century weathervane

El Templete ❻

Plaza de Armas, Calle Baratillo y
O'Reilly. **Map** 4 F2.
(7) 8612 876.
9:30am–6:30pm daily.
1 Jan, 1 May.

S MALL AND AUSTERE, this Neo-Classical building, resembling a temple, stands on the spot where, according to legend, the city of San Cristóbal de La Habana was founded in 1599. Here, under a leafy ceiba – a tropical tree considered sacred by all the natives of Central America – the first meeting of the local government (the *cabildo*) and the first mass reputedly took place. A majestic ceiba tree

View of the Castillo de la Real Fuerza: the drawbridge and entrance, the moat, and the Giraldilla tower (left)

still stands in front of El Templete, although it is not the original. Next to it is the Columna de Cacigal, a column named after the governor who ordered its construction in 1754.

El Templete, completed in 1828, was modelled after a monument in the Basque town of Guernica. Inside are three enormous canvases by Jean-Baptiste Vermay *(see p24)*, depicting scenes from the history of Havana: the local authorities inaugurating the building, the first *cabildo*, and the first mass, which was celebrated by Bishop Juan José Díaz Espada y Land, who blessed the city as part of the ceremony.

The First Mass, one of Vermay's paintings in the Templete

Calle Oficios ❼

Map 4 F2.

THIS STREET was originally a link between the military centre of Plaza de Armas and the commercial and harbour activities centred around Plaza San Francisco. Together with Calle Obispo, this is one of the most atmospheric streets in Old Havana and should be toured slowly (don't miss the many interesting façades).

Approaching from Plaza de Armas, there are three buildings well worth visiting. The first, at No. 8, is the home of the **Museo Numismático**, built in the late 1700s and for a long time the premises of the Monte de Piedad bank. According to legend it was inhabited by the ghost of a Colonial lady dressed in white. It has a rich collection of coins, banknotes, old lottery tickets, medals, and Cuban and foreign bank documents.

At No. 16 is the 18th-century **Casa de los Arabes**, with displays of 18th- and 19th-century Hispanic-Arab bronzes, fabrics, rugs and furniture: the largest ethnographic display of Arab objects in Cuba, evidence of the presence of an old Lebanese, Syrian and Palestinian colony on the island. The building also houses the only mosque in Cuba and an Andalusian restaurant.

The third interesting and curious museum on the street is the **Museo del Auto Antiguo**, featuring vintage Cadillacs, Rolls-Royces, Packards and Fords dating from the 1930s, as well as the Bel-Air Chevrolet that once belonged to Che Guevara.

🏛 **Museo Numismático**
🚪 (7) 8615 811. ⏰ 9am–5pm Tue–Sat; 9am–1pm Sun. ⬤ 1 Jan, 26 Jul, 10 Oct, 25 Dec. 📷

The Casa de los Arabes patio, with narrow balconies and a Moorish-style fountain

🏛 **Casa de los Arabes**
🚪 (7) 8615 868.
⏰ 9:15am–4:45pm Tue–Sat.
⬤ 1 Jan, 26 Jul, 10 Oct, 25 Dec.
📷

🏛 **Museo del Auto Antiguo**
🚪 (7) 8615 811.
⏰ 9am–6:30pm daily. ⬤ 1 Jan, 26 Jul, 10 Oct, 25 Dec. 📷

THE MARKET IN PLAZA DE ARMAS

Since the early 1990s, when small businesses were officially authorized, this plaza *(see p67)* has been filled with colourful stalls. In the middle section, under the monument to Céspedes, is a market with second-hand books and periodicals of every kind, magazines published in the 1940s and 1950s, newspapers from the time of the revolution and Cuban classics now out of print. Next to the San Carlo y Ambrosio Seminary and behind the Castillo is the tourist handicrafts market, where skilfully made objects created from papier mâché and glass take their place alongside the more traditional and familiar ceramics and carved wood.

Second-hand books at the daily market in the Plaza de Armas

Palacio de los Capitanes Generales

Early 19th-century marble bathtub in the bathroom

Construction of this palace, a splendid example of Cuban Baroque *(see p22)*, took from 1776 to 1792. It was commissioned by the governor Felipe Fondesviela and designed by engineer Antonio Fernández de Trebejos y Zaldívar. The Palacio originally housed the Chapter House and the governor's residence as well as a house of detention, which until 1834 occupied the west wing. The seat of the Cuban Republic in 1902, the building became the Museo de la Ciudad (City Museum) in 1967, but the original structure of the sumptuous residence and political centre has not been altered. The complex as a whole offers an overview of the history of Havana, from the remains of the old Espada cemetery and Parroquial Mayor church to mementoes from the wars of independence.

Hall of Heroic Cuba
This hall contains objects from the independence wars, including the flag of Céspedes (see p42).

The Cabildo Maces
Considered the first major example of Cuban goldsmithery, these maces, by Juan Díaz (1631), are on display in the Sala del Cabildo, the room where local town council meetings were held in the governor's palace.

★ Cenotaph from the Parroquial Mayor Church
In 1557 the oldest Colonial monument in Cuba was placed in the old Parroquial Mayor (parish church), which then stood on this site. It commemorates the death of a young woman who was killed by accident while she was praying.

STAR SIGHTS
★ Cenotaph from the Parroquial Mayor Church
★ La Giraldilla
★ Salón de los Espejos

★ La Giraldilla
At the foot of the steps leading to the mezzanine is the oldest bronze statue in Cuba. It was commissioned by the governor, Juan Bitrián de Viamonte, for the lookout tower of the Castillo de la Real Fuerza (see p68).

Gallery
The monumental gallery, which overlooks a large, leafy courtyard, features a collection of busts of illustrious figures, the work of the Italian sculptor Luigi Pietrasanta in the early 1900s.

The White Room
has on display the escutcheons of Bourbon Spain and the city of Havana, and is decorated with 18th- and 19th-century Meissen porcelain.

Throne Room
Modelled on the large salon in the Palacio de Oriente in Madrid, this room was originally built for a Spanish monarch, but never used. It was restored in 1893 for the visit of Princess Eulalia of Bourbon.

The stained-glass windows brighten the grey of the *piedra marina*, a limestone encrusted with coral fossils.

The Espada Cemetery Room
has relics from the first city cemetery, founded by Bishop Juan José Díaz de Espada in 1806. They include the tomb of the French artist Vermay *(see p24)*.

★ Salón de los Espejos
The end of Spanish rule was proclaimed in 1899 in this light-filled salon with its 19th-century Venetian mirrors, and in 1902 the first president of the Republic of Cuba took office here.

The portico pavement, made of *china pelona*, a hard, shiny stone, dates from the 18th century.

Casa del Agua la Tinaja, vendor of purified well water

Calle Obispo �ⓐ

Map 4 E2.

Old filter, Taquechel pharmacy

THE LIVELIEST and most characteristic street in Old Havana is like a long, narrow bridge linking the two architectural souls of the historic centre, the Colonial and the Art Nouveau-eclectic. At one end is the Plaza de Armas, the Baroque heart of the old city, while at the other is Avenida de Bélgica and the famous El Floridita restaurant, which mark the start of the more modern district. The street is called Calle Obispo because in the past the city bishop (obispo) resided in the building situated on the corner of Calle Oficios.

Thanks to the recent restoration work promoted by the Oficina del Historiador de la Ciudad, headed by the charismatic Eusebio Leal Spengler, aimed at salvaging the best buildings in the old area, Calle Obispo has retained the elegance, vivacity and colours of the Colonial period. Newly installed street lighting makes for enjoyable evening strolling.

A plaque on the left-hand side of the Palacio de los Capitanes Generales bears quotations made by the great Cuban patriot José Martí concerning Garibaldi's stop at Havana. Opposite is the small

shop window of the **Casa del Agua la Tinaja**, which for centuries has been selling well water purified by very old but still quite efficient ceramic filters. Next door, **La Mina** restaurant serves food and cocktails outdoors and brightens up the whole block with live traditional music (see p268).

Among the most fascinating shops in this part of the street is the old pharmacy called **Taquechel**, which sells cosmetics and natural and homeopathic products, all created and produced in Cuba. Quaint shelves boast a pretty collection of 17th- and 18th-century glass and Italian majolica jars, as well as alembics and antique pharmaceutical and medical objects. No. 117–19 is the oldest house in Havana (see p22).

One of the major sights in the street is the restored **Hotel Ambos Mundos** (see p248). This charming, eclectically decorated hotel is rich in literary memories. The writer Ernest Hemingway stayed here for long periods from 1932 to 1939 (see p114), and began writing his famous novel For Whom the Bell Tolls in room 511.

Towards the end of the street, near the small Obispo y

Wooden *"azul avana"* blue doors of the Colonial house at No. 117

Bernaza square, there are more modern shops offering everything from embroidered shirts to books.

Next is **El Floridita** restaurant (see p268), known as "the cradle of the daiquiri". It was here, in the 1930s, that barman Constante (his real name was Constantino Ribalaigua) perfected the original cocktail mixed by Pagluchi (see p267). The new-style daiquiri, a blend of white rum, lemon, sugar and a few drops of maraschino and ice, was devised with the help of Ernest Hemingway, who was a regular. Today, in El Floridita's luxurious interior, besides Constante's classic cocktails you can feast on lobster and shellfish in the company of a bust of the great novelist. It was sculpted by Fernando Boada while Hemingway was still alive.

An old letter box at No. 115

Typical majolica jars on the shelves of the former Sala Museo

The upper gallery of the Casa de la Obra Pía, with its frescoed walls and polished wood balustrade

Casa de la Obra Pía ⑩

Calle Obrapía 158 esq. Mercaderes. **Map** 4 E2. ☎ (7) 8613 097. ☐ 9:30am–4:30pm Tue–Sat, 9:30am–12:30pm Sun. ● 1 Jan, 1 May, 26 Jul, 10 Oct. ☒ ☑ ☑

CALLE OBRAPÍA (literally, Charity Street) was named after this mansion, whose own name commemorates the pious actions of Martín Calvo de la Puerta y Arrieta, a wealthy Spanish nobleman who took up residence here in 1669. Every year he gave a generous dowry to five orphan girls for them to use to get married or enter a convent. A century later the residence became the home of Don Agustín de Cárdenas, who was given the title of marquis for taking Spain's side in 1762 during the British occupation of Havana (see p40). In 1793 new decoration, and the elaborate arch leading to the loggia on the first floor, were added to the building.

La Casa de la Obra Pía is regarded as one of the jewels of Cuban Baroque architecture, and its luxurious salons were used for young noblewomen to make their debut in society.

Majolica tile street sign for Calle de la Obrapía

Many colourful legends survive concerning the building's past. It was said that incredible treasures were hidden in its walls and that wailing and weeping could be heard from one of the rooms on the upper floor.

At the corner of Calle Obrapía and Calle Mercaderes is the **Casa de México**, a cultural centre that shows the close links between Mexico and Cuba. It has a library with more than 5,000 books and a museum displaying handmade glass, silver, fabric, terracotta and wooden objects. Lastly, on the other side of the street is the **Casa de Guayasamín**, named after the Ecuadorean painter whose works are on display.

Palo Monte objects (see p21), Casa de Africa

Casa de Africa ⑪

Calle Obrapía 157 e/ San Ignacio y Mercaderes. **Map** 4 E2. ☎ (7) 8615 798. ☐ 9:30am–4:30pm Tue–Sat, 9:30am–12:30pm Sun. ● 1 Jan, 26 Jul, 10 Oct, 25 Dec. ☑ ☑

OPPOSITE the Casa de la Obra Pía is a 17th-century building that was rebuilt in 1887 to accommodate a family of plantation owners on the upper floor and a tobacco factory, worked by slaves, on the ground floor. It is appropriate that the building is now a museum containing more than 2,000 objects linked to the history of sub-Saharan Africa and the various ethnic groups that were taken to Cuba on slave ships. Many of these items belonged to the ethnographer Fernando Ortíz, a specialist in the African roots of Cuban culture. Together with the section on religion, which includes objects from the various Afro-Cuban cults (see pp20–21), there are instruments of torture used on the slaves, batá drums, and paintings of plantation life. The museum also has a well-stocked library.

Plaza de San Francisco **⓬**

Map 4 F2. **Basílica Menor de San Francisco de Asís** ☎ (7) 8629 683, 8669 281. ⬤ 9:30am–6:30pm daily. ⬤ 1 Jan, 1 May, 26 Jul, 10 Oct, 25 Dec. 🖼 🚻 📷

BORDERING THE PORT, this picturesque square has an Andalusian character and evokes images of a distant age when galleons loaded with gold and other cargo set sail for Spain. In the middle of the square is the **Fuente de los Leones**, modelled on the famous fountain in the Alhambra in Granada. This work by the Italian sculptor Giuseppe Gaggini was donated in 1836 by the fiscal superintendent, Don Claudio Martínez de Pinillos, the Count of Villanueva, and for many years it supplied the ships docked here with drinking water.

The original commercial nature of the area can be seen in two buildings: the Aduana General de la República (the old customs house), built in 1914, and the **Lonja del Comercio** (the former stock exchange, 1908), with a dome crowned by a statue of Mercury, god of commerce. Restored in 1995, this building houses the offices of some of the top foreign firms now operating in Cuba.

The most important building in the square, however, is the **Basílica Menor de San Francisco de Asís**, built in

The Fuente de los Leones, Plaza de San Francisco

1580–91 as the home of the Franciscan community and partly rebuilt in the 1700s. The three-aisle interior has a Latin cross layout and contains some paintings by unknown 18th-century Cuban artists and a wooden statue of St Francis dating from the same period, again by an unknown artist. The basilica also has the remains of major Havana citizens, from the Marquis González, who died during the British siege of 1762, to José Martín Félix de Arrate, an illustrious historian of the Colonial period. Because of its exceptional acoustics, this church was recently converted into a concert hall for choral and chamber music *(see p280)*.

Attached to the church is a large, 42-m (138-ft) high bell tower that affords a lovely view of the city. Originally a statue of St Francis of Assisi stood on the top, but it was badly damaged by a cyclone in 1846.

In the cloister and rooms of the adjacent monastery, which dates back to 1739, is a museum of holy art with 18th–19th-century missals, a collection of votive objects made of precious metals, and 16th–18th-century majolica and ceramics.

Fundación Destilería Havana Club **⓭**

Calle San Pedro 262. **Map** 4 F3. ☎ (7) 8624 108. ⬤ 9am–5pm Mon–Thu, 9am–4pm Fri–Sat. ⬤ 1 Jan, 1 May, 26 Jul, 10 Oct, 25 Dec. 🖼 🚻 📷 🍴 💻

Logo of the Havana Club Foundation

THE DISTILLERIES of Havana Club, the most famous brand of Cuban rum, are open to the public, allowing visitors to see the production process of the spirit described as the "cheerful child of sugar cane" by Cuban writer and journalist Fernando Campoamor, a friend of Ernest Hemingway.

The organized tours begin in the Colonial courtyard of the Havana Club Foundation. After watching a brief video-tape on the history of sugar cane and its cultivation, visitors are taken to see the fermentation, distillation (in a room with old alembics), filtering and ageing processes. In the central hall, heavy with the intense smell of fermented molasses, is a model of an *ingenio (see pp42–3)*, or sugar plantation, which also includes a miniature steam train. Tours end in a bar where visitors can relax and sample the three year-old rum. The bar, which also serves excellent cocktails, is open from 9am to midnight.

Interior of the basilica of San Francisco, now used for chamber music concerts

Cuban Rum

THE HISTORY OF RUM dates back to the early 1500s, when an impure distillate was first obtained from sugar cane. With the arrival of Facundo Bacardí (see p224), a new technique of distillation was introduced, and Cuban rum (ron) went on to enjoy international success. Rum is part of everyday life in Cuba: a constant companion at parties and festivities, the main ingredient in cocktails, and an offering that is frequently given to the gods of santería. Rum-making begins with the main by-product of sugar, the sticky amber paste called molasses, which is diluted with water and fermented using special yeasts. The "must" thus obtained is then distilled and filtered to produce an eau de vie. Purified water and pure alcohol are then added 18 months later to produce Silver Dry, a young, clear rum.

Seal of guarantee of Cuban rum

Distillation, which used to be effected by means of alembics (left), is now carried out by using a series of connected tubes in which the molasses vapour is channelled until it condenses and is transformed into a colourless liquid that is then aged in special barrels.

The mezcla process is carried out under the expert guidance of a master taster and consists of mixing the new rum with other rums. Once blended, the rum rests for a few weeks in special vats until the right balance of taste and aroma is obtained.

Special oak barrels are used for the ageing process which takes at least three years. With time the rum becomes richer in colour and more full-bodied, like the seven-year añejo. The temperature, humidity level and ventilation in the ageing cellars are carefully regulated.

THE TYPES OF RUM

Besides Silver Dry, which is normally used in cocktails, the market offers rum aged for three years (carta blanca), five years (carta oro), and seven years (añejo), or even longer. Old rum, which is the most highly prized, should be drunk neat and at room temperature, while carta blanca, which is the most commonly seen, can be used in many ways and is often drunk with ice. There are assorted brands of Cuban rum, not all of which are internationally known like Havana Club.

Silver Dry · Carta Blanca · Carta Oro · Añejo

The cloister of the convent of Santa Clara, filled with tropical plants

Plaza Vieja ⓮

Map 4 E3.

THIS SQUARE was laid out in 1559 and was originally called Plaza Nueva (New Square). In the 19th century, after the widening of Plaza de Armas and the creation of other urban areas, it lost its role as the city's main public square and was renamed Plaza Vieja. From the 1950s to the 90s it was a car park, but it has now been restored to its original appearance.

The plaza is surrounded by arcades and a number of historic buildings from four different centuries. The most important of these is the **Casa del Conde Jaruco**, built in 1733–37. This was the home of the Countess de Merlin, a Cuban romantic novelist who

became a French citizen and also wrote a travel book about Cuba. The house is now used for art exhibitions. The spacious salon on the first floor, with its fine large stained-glass windows or *mediopuntos* (*see p23*), is well worth a visit.

Next door are two 17th-century buildings, and at the corner of Calle Muralla and Calle Inquisidor is the eye-catching Art Nouveau Hotel-Palacio Cueto. It was first built as a hotel in 1908, then later turned into apartments and is now being restored as a five-star hotel.

A fountain designed in 1796 stands in the middle of the square. It bears the crest of the city and of the Count of Santa Clara, then the city's governor. Nearby are two cultural institutions: a centre for visual arts and a photo gallery.

Convento de Santa Clara ⓯

Calle Cuba 602 e/ Sol y Luz.
Map 4 E3. *(7) 8613 335.*
8:30am–5:30pm Mon–Fri. 1 Jan, 26 Jul, 10 Oct, 25 Dec.

THE CONVENT OF SANTA CLARA is one of the oldest and most typical Colonial religious buildings in the New World. The convent occupies a considerable area of Habana Vieja and was founded in 1644 by Sister Catalina de Mendoza from Cartagena de Indias, to offer refuge for the poorer girls of the city.

The plain exterior, with its simple windows, makes a striking contrast to the interior, which has a colonnaded courtyard with elaborate inlaid wooden ceilings. Two of the three original cloisters have stood the test of time. In one of them, overflowing with luxuriant tropical vegetation and with an 18th-century fountain known as "The Samaritan", is the Centro Nacional de Conservación, Restauración y Museología, a body which coordinates the preservation and restoration of Cuba's historic architecture.

The second cloister is now part of a charming hotel decorated in Colonial style. Parts of the building are open to the public but it cannot be seen in its entirety.

Façade of Casa del Conde Jaruco, with typical *mediopunto* stained-glass windows on the first floor

The nave of the Iglesia de la Merced, illuminated by small light bulbs

Iglesia del Espíritu Santo ⓰

Calle Acosta 161. **Map** 4 E3.
[C] (7) 8624 310. ⬛ 8am–noon,
3–8pm daily. 📷 ✝ 6pm daily.

THE CHURCH of the Holy Ghost (Espíritu Santo) is of historical importance as one of the oldest Catholic churches in Havana. It was built in 1632 by some freed African slaves. Thanks to a papal bull and a royal decree from Carlos III, in 1772 it acquired the exclusive right to grant asylum to all those persecuted by the authorities.

From an architectural standpoint, the building's most striking feature is the tower, which is almost as tall as the one on the Basilica of San Francisco *(see p74)*. The church was radically rebuilt in the 19th century, retaining its Hispanic-Arab look only in the characteristic double pitch roof. The main chapel, with its stone vaulting and a crypt, was built by Bishop Jerónimo Valdés in 1706–29.

The area around the church plays host to one of the most picturesque religious markets in the city, in which the *yerberos*, or herbalist-healers, sell votive objects and various herbs that are used mostly in the local Afro-Cuban religious rites *(see pp20–21)*.

Iglesia de Nuestra Señora de la Merced ⓱

Calle Cuba 806. **Map** 4 E3.
[C] (7) 8638 873. ⬛ 8am–noon,
3–8pm daily. 📷 ✝ 9am daily.

CONSTRUCTION of this church began in 1637 but ended only in the following century, while the lavish decoration in the interior dates from the 19th century. The church is popular among those who follow *santería*, or local Afro-Cuban religion *(see pp20–21)*. According to the beliefs of this cult, Our Lady of the Merced corresponds to a Yoruba divinity known as Obbatalá, principal figure among the gods and the protector of mankind, who imparts wisdom and harmony. On the Catholic saint's feast day, 24 September, *santería* followers come dressed all in white – the colour associated with Obbatalá.

Museo José Martí ⓲

Calle Leonor Perez 314, esq. Egido.
Map 4 E4. [C] (7) 8613 778, 8615 095. ⬛ 9am–5pm Tue–Sat, 9am–1pm Sun. ⬤ 1 Jan, 1 May, 26 Jul, 10 Oct, 25 Dec. 📷 📷 📷 [W]
www.cult.cu/patrim/cnpc/museos/marti

THIS MODEST 19th-century building in the Paula quarter, near the port, became a national monument thanks to the special historic importance attached to José Martí *(see p45)*, who is the object of great patriotic veneration. The author and national hero, who died in combat on 19 May 1895 during the wars of independence against the Spanish, was born here in 1853. After his death, his mother Leonor Pérez lived in the building, and when she died it was given back to the religious congregation that had owned it. In 1925 it was purchased by the municipality after city-wide fund raising, and was turned into a museum, but government funding only became sufficient with the advent of Castro.

The house has been beautifully restored, and visitors can view furniture, paintings, and first editions of the writer's works. There are also objects of great historic value such as the inkpot and ivory pen used by Generalissimo Máximo Gómez to sign the *Manifesto de Montecristi*, which officially marked the beginning of the war against Spain. There are everyday objects on display, such as the penknife Martí had in his pocket when he died, and the album with photographs of his wedding to Carmen Zayas-Bazán.

Portrait of José Martí by Herman Norman in the museum

CENTRO HABANA AND PRADO

ENTRO HABANA has the air of an impoverished aristocrat – a noble creature whose threadbare clothes belie a splendid past full of treasures. This varied quarter developed beyond the city walls (which ran parallel to present-day Avenida Bélgica and Avenida de las Misiones) during the 1800s and was initially built to provide houses and greenery for the citizens. Most construction took place after 1863, when the walls began to be demolished to make more land available. The work was finally completed in the 1920s and 30s, when French architect Forestier landscaped the area of the Paseo del Prado, the Parque Central, the Capitolio gardens and Parque de la Fraternidad.

Remains of the old walls

SIGHTS AT A GLANCE

Historic Buildings
Capitolio pp82–3 ❸
Castillo de San Salvador de la Punta ❽
Hotel Inglaterra ❶
Palacio de Aldama ❻
Real Fábrica de Tabacos La Corona ⓬
Real Fábrica de Tabacos Partagás ❺

Historic Streets and Plazas
Avenida Carlos III ⓰
Callejón de Hammel ⓱
Parque de la Fraternidad ❹
Paseo del Prado pp86–7 ❼

Quarters
Barrio Chino ⓮

Theatres
Gran Teatro de La Habana ❷

Churches
Iglesia del Ángel Custodio ❿
Iglesia del Sagrado Corazón ⓯

Museums
Museo Nacional de la Música ❾
Museo de la Revolución pp88–9 ⓫
Museo Nacional de Bellas Artes pp92–5 ⓭

KEY

■ Street-by-Street map *pp80–81*
🚉 Railway station

GETTING THERE
The easiest way to get to this quarter is by taxi; and the best way to explore it is on foot. When map reading, bear in mind that the commonly used names of the streets differ from the official ones *(see p118)*.

Estación Central

0 metres 800
0 yards 800

◁ The bustling arcade alongside the Museo de la Música *(see p85)*

Street-by-Street: Around the Parque Central

L YING ON THE border of the old city and
Centro Habana, between the Capitolio
and the Prado promenade, the Parque
Central was designed in 1877 after the old
city walls were demolished. A statue of
Isabella II was put in the middle of the
square but was later replaced by one of
José Martí. The park is surrounded by
19th- and 20th-century monumental
buildings and adorned with large trees,
and is the heart of the city centre, a
popular meeting place. Towards evening,
when the air is cooler, people gather here
to talk until the small hours of the night
about baseball, music and politics.

**★ Gran Teatro
de La Habana**
*Renamed Teatro
García Lorca in
honour of the
great Spanish
poet, who stayed
in Havana for a
few months in
1930, the theatre
is a mixture of
influences with
slender, angular
towers* ②

**Real Fábrica de
Tabacos Partagás**
*This elegant red and cream-
coloured building is home
to a prestigious cigar
factory* ⑤

**Parque de la
Fraternidad**
*The park was
laid out in 1892
to celebrate
the 400th
anniversary of
the discovery
of America* ④

CALLE SAN MARTÍN (SAN JOSÉ)

CALLE INDUSTRIA

PASEO DE MARTÍ (PRADO)

CALLE DRAGONES

CALLE BRASIL

**The Cinema
Payret,** Cuba's first
motion picture theatre,
opened in 1897, a year after
the Lumière brothers presented
their invention in Paris.

STAR SIGHTS

★ Capitolio

★ Gran Teatro
de La Habana

★ Hotel Inglaterra

★ Paseo del Prado

★ Capitolio
*The dome of one of the
most imposing buildings
in Latin America towers
over the urban landscape
of Havana* ③

★ Hotel Inglaterra
This historic hotel has retained its 19th-century atmosphere. Despite the British name, the architectural elements and decoration are clearly Spanish-inspired ❶

LOCATOR MAP
See Street Finder, pp120–23, map 4

Calle San Rafael, known as *Boulevard*, is a narrow street for pedestrians only. Up to the 1950s it was famous for its luxury shops and boutiques.

The Hotel Parque Central was built recently. Its style and decor blend in well with the surroundings *(see p249).*

★ Paseo del Prado
This avenue, the locals' favourite for strolling, is lined with lovely buildings with recently restored arcades ❼

The statue of José Martí, Cuba's national hero, was sculpted in Carrara marble in Rome by José Vilalta y Saavedra and inaugurated on 24 February 1905 by Generalissimo Máximo Gómez.

0 metres 100
0 yards 100

KEY
– – – Suggested route

The Manzana de Gómez, a 19th-century building, was once a major commercial centre, and gradually shops are returning here.

Palacio del Centro Asturiano, with the characteristic towers on its corners, was designed by Spanish architect Manuel del Busto and opened in 1928. It is home to the Museo de Bellas Artes' international art collection *(see pp92–5).*

The Hotel Plaza, built in the 19th century as a private residence, became a hotel in 1909. It was frequented by great artists of the time, from Isadora Duncan to Enrico Caruso and Anna Pavlova *(see p269).*

Hotel Inglaterra ❶

Paseo de Martí (Prado) 416, esq. a San Rafael. **Map** 4 D2. *See p248.*

Aᴌᴛʜᴏᴜɢʜ ᴛʜɪꜱ ʜᴏᴛᴇʟ is built in the style of late 19th-century Havana Neo-Classical architecture, its soul is *mudéjar* (Moorish): the fine ochre, green and gold majolica tiles in the interior were imported from Seville, the foyer is decorated with Andalusian mosaics, and the wooden ceilings are reminiscent of Moorish inlay. Plus, one of the columns in the *salón-café* bears a classical Arabic inscription: "Only Allah is the victor". The Hotel Inglaterra dates from 1875,

when a small hotel merged with the lively Le Louvre night spot and its adjacent ballroom. The pavement outside the hotel, known as the "Louvre sidewalk", was an animated meeting point for Havana liberals. It was here that the young José Martí *(see p45)* advocated total separation from Spain, as opposed to more moderate liberal demands for autonomy. General Antonio Maceo, a hero of the wars of Cuban independence, prepared plans for insurrection in this hotel.

Among many illustrious guests were the great French actress Sarah Bernhardt and the Russian ballet dancer Anna Pavlova.

Gran Teatro de La Habana ❷

Paseo de Martí (Prado) y San Rafael, Central Havana. **Map** 4 D2.
📞 (7) 8613 078. ⬤ 9am–6pm daily. ⬤ 1 Jan, 1 May, 26 Jul, 10 Oct, 25 Dec. 🎫 📷

Oɴᴇ ᴏꜰ ᴛʜᴇ ᴡᴏʀʟᴅ'ꜱ largest opera houses is part of the monumental Palacio del Centro Gallego (1915), designed by Belgian architect Paul Belau to host the social activities of Havana's large and affluent Spanish community.

The magnificent façade is decorated with four sculpture

The staircase of honour, originally reserved for MPs

Capitolio ❸

Aꜱʏᴍʙᴏʟ ᴏꜰ ᴛʜᴇ ᴄɪᴛʏ, the Capitol (Capitolio) combines the elegance of Neo-Classicism with Art Deco elements. Inaugurated in 1929 by the dictator Gerardo Machado, it is a loose imitation of the Washington DC Capitol, but is even taller. It stands in an area once occupied by a botanical garden and later by the capital's first railway station. The home of government until 1959, the Capitol has seen major historic events: in 1933 the police fired on a crowd gathered here during an anti-Machado demonstration. Today the building houses the Ministry of Science, Technology and the Environment, but is open for tours, which include the former government chambers and the magnificent library.

National Library of Science and Technology

Chamber of Deputies
The Chamber still has its original furnishings and is decorated with bas-reliefs by the Italian artist Gianni Remuzzi.

Sᴛᴀʀ Sɪɢʜᴛꜱ

★ **Salón de los Pasos Perdidos**

★ **Dome**

Façade of the former Centro Gallego building, now home to the Gran Teatro

groups by the Italian sculptor Giuseppe Moretti, depicting Charity, Education, Music and Theatre. The building lies over the foundations of the Teatro Nuevo or Tacón. From 1837 to the early 20th century this was the venue for performances by world-famous artists, including the Austrian ballet dancer Fanny Essler, who made her debut here on 23 January 1841. In the mid-19th century Antonio Meucci, the inventor of the "talking telephone", worked here as a stagehand, and his invention was patented in the US, thanks to the support of the Gran Teatro's impresario.

The theatre was inaugurated on 22 April 1915 with a performance of Verdi's *Aida*, and became a stage for great dramatic occasions. Sarah Bernhardt performed here in 1918, and the pianist Arthur Rubinstein the following year. Cuban composer Ernesto Lecuona and the great Spanish guitarist Andrés Segovia have also appeared.

In 1959 the Gran Teatro, though continuing in its role as a concert hall and theatre, became the "home" of Alicia Alonso, the great Cuban ballet dancer. She founded the Ballet Nacional, which is the dance company and school known for organizing a famous annual ballet festival *(see p282)*.

★ Dome
Almost 92 m (300 ft) high, the dome was the highest point in the city until the 1950s.

Parliament

★ Salón de los Pasos Perdidos
This sumptuous hall, with fine marble floors and gilded lamps, takes its name ("Hall of Lost Steps") from its unusual acoustics.

A copy of a 25-carat diamond
is embedded in the floor beneath the dome. The original belonged to the last Tsar of Russia and was sold to the Cuban state by a Turkish jeweller. It was stolen and, mysteriously, later delivered to the President.

Statue of the Republic
This work, cast in Rome and covered with 22-carat gold leaf, stands 17 m (56 ft) high and weighs 49 tons.

Parque de la Fraternidad ❹

Map 4 D3.

THE SPACIOUS AREA of greenery behind the Capitol was called Campo di Marte (Parade Ground) in the 19th century, because it was near the Paseo Militar, used frequently for army drill. As the Parque de la Fraternidad (since 1928), it commemorates Cuba's common roots with the other people of the Americas, with monuments to major figures such as the Argentine José de San Martín, the Venezuelan Simón Bolívar, and US president Abraham Lincoln.

In the middle of the park is a gate with a plaque bearing an exhortation by José Martí: "It is time to gather and march together united, we must go forward as compact as the silver in the depths of the Andes. Peoples unite only through bonds of friendship, fraternity and love." Beyond the gate is a monument to American friendship and solidarity: a large ceiba – a tree sacred to both the Amerindians and the African slaves taken to the New World – planted here around 1920.

In front of the square is a white marble fountain, sculpted in 1831 by Giuseppe Gaggini. The fountain is known as the "Fuente de la India" or "La Noble Habana" – an allegorical representation of the city.

Nowadays the Parque de la Fraternidad is usually full of old American cars, most of which operate as private taxis.

The Fuente de la India symbolizing Havana

Façade of the Partagás cigar factory with its prominent pediments

Real Fábrica de Tabacos Partagás ❺

Calle Industria 524. **Map** 4 D3.
📞 (7) 8624 604. 🕐 9:30–11am, 12:30–3pm Mon–Sat. 🔴 1 Jan, 1 May, 26 Jul, 10 Oct, 25 Dec. 🎫 📷

CUBA'S LARGEST cigar factory, with its Neo-Classical façade, is a good example of 19th-century industrial architecture. It was founded in 1845 by the ambitious Catalan businessman Jaime Partagás Ravelo. However, he never revealed the sources of his tobacco leaves or how they were processed. The only information that survives is that he was the first person to use wooden barrels to ferment the leaves in order to heighten the aroma.

With the profits made from his high-quality cigars, Partagás bought a plantation in the province of Pinar del Río. He wanted to oversee all aspects of the cigar-making process personally, from growing the plants to the placing of a wrapper leaf around the filler and binder leaves rolled by the *torcedor (see p31)*. However, Partagás was assassinated in mysterious circumstances

Neon sign at the Partagás cigar factory

and the project failed. His factory was then purchased by another shrewd businessman, Ramón Cifuentes Llano.

Dozens of people work in the aroma-filled interior. Nowadays, there is no longer someone reading aloud to alleviate the monotony of the work by entertaining and educating the workers, as was the case in the 19th century (Partagás himself introduced this custom to Cuba).

However there is a loudspeaker that alternates reading passages with music and news on the radio. Connected to the factory is La Casa del Habano, an excellent shop with a back room that is used for sampling cigars.

Palacio de Aldama ❻

Avenída Simón Bolívar (Reina) y Máximo Gómez (Monte). **Map** 4 D3. 🔴 to the public.

THIS MANSION *(see p23)* was designed by Manuel José Carrera and built in the middle of the 19th century, having been commissioned by the rich Basque industrialist Domingo de Aldama y Arrechaga. He had to depend on his influential friends in order to obtain permission to build his residence in front of the Campo di Marte, or Parade Ground, which was reserved for military and administrative buildings. The monumental grandeur of this Neo-Classical building, considered the finest example of 19th-century architecture in Cuba, is still striking. The mansion is now the seat of the Instituto de Historia de Cuba. Sadly, it is not yet officially open to the public, but upon request the porter allows visitors to go into the courtyard to admire the impressive marble staircases, Baroque arches, splendid wrought iron with Imperial motifs and the two inner gardens with fountains made of Carrara marble.

The monument to General Máximo Gómez

Paseo del Prado **7**

See pp86–7.

Castillo de San Salvador de la Punta **8**

Malecón y Paseo de Martí (Prado). **Map** 4 D1. (7) 8603 196. ☐ 10am–5:30pm Wed–Sun. ☐ 1 Jan, 1 May, 26 Jul, 10 Oct, 25 Dec.

A MODEST FORTIFIED block on the west bank of the port entrance, this fortress *(castillo)* makes an ideal setting for political speeches and concerts because of its elevated position near the road. In the past it played a crucial role in the defence system of the capital but today it is a naval museum. Designed by Giovanni Battista Antonelli, Juan de Tejeda and Cristóbal de Roda and built in 1589–1610, it was part of the city's first line of defence together with the much larger Castillo de los Tres Reyes del Morro on the other side of the bay.

A large floating chain of wooden and bronze rings, an ingenious device added by the Italian engineer Antonelli in the late 16th century, connected the two fortresses. It was stretched tightly as soon as an enemy ship was sighted, to block access to the port.

In the open space in front of the Castillo are the three cannons to which the chain was tied.

The large forecourt has several monuments that are more important historically than artistically. In the middle is the equestrian statue of Generalissimo Máximo Gómez, the hero of the wars of independence, by Italian sculptor Aldo Gamba (1935). Behind this, a dilapidated chapel is used daily for stamp exhibitions and history lectures. It originally belonged to the Real Cárcel prison, where José Martí was kept for 16 years for subversive activities against the Spanish crown. Some cells still stand, as does a section of the wall against which some medical students were executed on 27 November 1871 as punishment for rebelling against Spanish rule. A cenotaph in their honour stands in the Columbus cemetery *(see p104).*

The Museo de la Música, an example of eclectic architecture

Museo Nacional de la Música **9**

Calle Capdevila 1, e/ Habana y Aguiar. **Map** 4 E1. (7) 8619 846, 8630 052. ☐ 10am–5:45pm Mon–Sat. ☐ 1 Jan, 1 May, 26 Jul, 10 Oct, 25 Dec.

T HE BUILDING (1905) that houses the National Music Museum is a mixture of different styles, a perfect example of 20th-century eclectic architecture. It was the residence of a family of opera lovers, whose guests included such illustrious figures as the great Italian tenor Enrico Caruso and the Spanish poet Federico García Lorca.

The museum was founded in 1971, and contains the largest collection of traditional musical instruments in Cuba, gathered by the ethnologist Fernando Ortiz, a pioneer in the study of Cuba's African roots. Besides the most complete collection of African drums in the world, there is the piano of singer and composer Bola de Nieve *(see p28)* and 40 guitars used by legendary figures of 20th-century Cuban music, such as the Trío Matamoros and Sindo Garay. Also on show are gramophones and phonographs, photos and famous composers' original manuscripts. In the foyer is a music stand with the score of the Bayamo, the Cuban national anthem. Visitors can consult specialist Cuban and foreign periodicals, as well as the archive of rare musical documents.

The Castillo de la Punta ramparts and the Morro fortress behind

Paseo del Prado **❼**

T HE MOST PICTURESQUE boulevard in Havana is popular in the daytime for a gentle stroll and gossip in the shade of the trees, and at sunset is one of the locals' main haunts. The Marquis de la Torre had the Paseo laid out in 1772 outside the city walls, and it rapidly became the favourite spot for city aristocrats to take their carriage rides. Bands were positioned in five spots along the boulevard to play for their enjoyment. The Paseo was used for military and carnival parades in the 19th century, when the paving was redone. In 1927 the French architect Forestier designed the Prado as we see it today: it was widened and lined with bronze lions and marble benches.

Lions
Eight lions, symbolizing Havana, were added in 1927, together with the marble benches.

Casa del Científico, residence of José Miguel Gómez, second President of the Republic of Cuba, is now a small hotel.

Neo-Moorish Building
The building at the corner of Calle Virtudes, richly decorated and with mudéjar *arches, shows many architectural influences and is typical of Havana.*

Hotel Sevilla
This historic hotel opened in 1908 and a ten-storey tower was added in 1918. It is a homage to Moorish architecture: the façade and hall decoration are mudéjar *(see p22) in style.*

Palacio de los Matrimonios
Named after the civil weddings celebrated on the first floor, this Neo-Baroque building was inaugurated in 1914 as the Casino Español.

Children playing in the shade during school break

Home of Dr Carlos Finlay, who discovered that mosquitoes spread yellow fever.

0 metres   60
0 yards   60

The Teatro Fausto was built in 1938 over the foundations of an old theatre of the same name.

Restored Buildings
These porticoed buildings were built along the avenue in the late 19th to early 20th century as private homes. They have been carefully restored, and the original bright pastel colours have been brought back to life.

Street Lamps
Elegant wrought-iron street lamps were added in 1834, together with the multi-coloured marble pavement.

Iglesia del Ángel Custodio ⑩

Calle Compostela 2, esq. Cuarteles.
Map 4 D2. ☎ *(7) 8610 469, 338 460.* ◻ *9am–noon, 3–6pm Tue–Sun.* ✝ *6pm Tue–Sat, 9am & 6pm Sun.*

B UILT IN 1689 on the Peña Pobre or "Loma del Ángel" hill as a hermitage and then transformed into a church in 1788, today the Neo-Gothic Ángel Custodio looks rather too white and unreal as a result of vigorous "restoration".

Standing in a key position between the former presidential palace (now the Museo de la Revolución) and the old town, it exudes literary references. The 19th-century Cuban novelist Cirilo Villaverde *(see p26)* used the Loma del Ángel hill as the setting for his story *Cecilia Valdés* about the tragic love affair between a Creole woman named Cecilia and a rich white man.

Félix Varela *(see p26)* and José Martí *(see p45)* were both baptised in this church.

The bell tower and spires of the church of Ángel Custodio

GRAHAM GREENE IN HAVANA

The classic espionage thriller *Our Man in Havana* (1958), by the English author Graham Greene, is an excellent description of Havana at the eve of the Revolution. In the book Greene narrates the adventures of a vacuum cleaner salesman who becomes a secret agent against his will. The novel is imbued with a dry sense of humour, and is set against an intriguing environment filled with casinos and roulette wheels, New York skyscrapers and decadent Art Nouveau villas, cabarets and prostitution. The Hotel Sevilla is a constant presence in the background.

Graham Greene (1904–91)

Museo de la Revolución ⓫

T HE IDEA OF PUTTING the Museum of the Revolution in
the former presidential palace of the dictator
Fulgencio Batista was clearly symbolic. Designed by the
Cuban architect Carlos Maruri and the Belgian architect
Paul Belau, the building was inaugurated in 1920 by
Mario García Menocal, and it remained the residence for
21 other presidents until 1959. The building has Neo-
Classical elements, and was decorated by Tiffany of New
York. It contains works by the leading Cuban decorators
of the early 1900s and by sculptors such as Juan José
Sicre, Esteban Betancourt and Fernando Boada. The
museum features documents, photographs and
memorabilia presenting an overview of the Cubans'
struggle for independence, from the Colonial
period on, but focusing in particular on
the Revolution, from the guerrilla
war to government reforms.

**Statues of Che Guevara
and Camilo Cienfuegos**
*These life-size wax statues
depict the two heroes
in combat.*

**The third
floor**
contains
the oldest
photos and
memorabilia.

**The side
wing** of the
palace, from
which Batista fled,
is not open to the
public at present.

GRANMA MEMORIAL

The large glass and cement pavilion in the tree-lined plaza
behind the museum contains the yacht *Granma* (named
after its first owner's grandmother). In 1956 this boat
brought Fidel Castro and some of his comrades from
Mexico to Cuba to begin the armed struggle against Batista
(see p48). There are also objects and vehicles relating to the
invasion of the Bay of Pigs (1961), an American spy plane
shot down in 1962 during the missile crisis, and
relics of Cuban activity in Ethiopia and Angola.

The American spy plane on display

STAR FEATURES

★ **Salón
de los Espejos**

★ **Main Staircase**

The Dome
The inside of the dome, visible from the staircase, consists of multicoloured ceramics. It includes four panels, decorated by Esteban Valderrama and Mariano Miguel Gonzáles, against a gold leaf background.

VISITORS' CHECKLIST

Calle Refugio 1, e/ Avenida de las Misiones y Zulueta.
Map 4 D2. (7) 8624 091.
10am–5pm daily.
(with charge)

The second floor gives an overview of Cuban uprisings from the Colonial period to the Revolution.

★ **Salón de los Espejos**
Lined with vast mirrors (espejos), the reception hall of the former presidential palace has ceiling frescoes by Cuban painters Armado Menocal and Antonio Rodríguez Morey.

The tall windows are similar to those in the Gran Teatro de La Habana, and were designed by the same architect, Paul Belau.

The terrace opposite the Salón de los Espejos has a fine view of the Bay of Havana.

Entrance

★ **Main Staircase**
The monumental staircase, which leads to the first floor, still bears marks of the bullets shot here on 13 March 1957, during an attack by some revolutionary university students on a mission to kill Batista. The dictator managed to save his life by escaping through a secret door in his office.

Real Fábrica de Tabacos La Corona ⑫

Calle Zulueta 106, e/ Paseo de Martí (Prado) y Colón. **Map** 4 D2. ☎ (7) 8626 173. ◷ 9am–3pm Mon–Fri. ● 1 Jan, 1 May, 26 Jul, 25 Dec. ✦ reduced fees for groups. ✦ ◎ ✦
Humidor and bar ◷ 9am–5pm Mon–Sat; 9am–3pm Sun.

THE ORIGINAL Miguel Fernández Roig cigar factory, known as "La Corona", was founded in 1842. After radical changes in the town plan caused by the demolition of the city walls, the factory moved to the Palacio Aldama (see p84); then in 1902 it moved again, this time to its definitive

The old sign of the prestigious La Corona cigar factory

home, a building also known as the "La Dama de Hierro" (Iron Lady), because it was the first to be built with a metal structure, in the late 1800s–early 1900s.

Visitors can take a tour of the factory and observe the work of the expert tobacco leaf rollers, known as torcedores. Various cigar-smoking-related items can be purchased here as well as high-quality, freshly made cigars. Smokers can also enjoy a cigar in the bar, where there are fine humidors – rooms in which the air is humidified in order to ensure proper storage and preservation of the cigars.

Museo Nacional de Bellas Artes ⑬

See pp92–5.

The austere interior of Iglesia de la Caridad

Barrio Chino ⑭

Map 3 C3.

THE CHINESE QUARTER of Havana, the Barrio Chino, which now occupies a small area defined by San Nicolás, Dragones, Zanja and Rayo streets, developed in the 19th century. In its heyday, in the early 1900s, there was a cultural association performing plays and operas, and a casino. The colourful streets were full of vendors of fritters and other Asian specialities, and people came to buy the best fruit and freshest fish in the city.

Today, all the Chinese shops are concentrated in the so-called Cuchillo de Zanja area (the intersection of Zanja and Rayo), a mixture of the oriental and the tropical; the architecture, however, is not particularly characteristic, except for the quarter gate, which has a pagoda roof. Another, much more impressive Ming and Ching-style portico was erected in 1998 at the corner of Calle Dragones and Calle Amistad. It is almost 19 m (62 ft) wide and was donated to Cuba by the Chinese government.

The Barrio Chino is also home to the **Iglesia de la Caridad**, dedicated to Cuba's patron saint (see p217). The church also has a popular statue, a Virgin with Asian features, brought here in the mid-1950s.

THE CHINESE COMMUNITY IN HAVANA

The first Chinese arrived in Cuba in the mid-1800s to work in the sugar industry, and they were treated like slaves. The first to gain their freedom began to cultivate small plots of land in Havana. In one of these, near the present-day Calle Salud, they grew Cuba's first mangoes, which were an immediate, spectacular success. Chinese restaurants began to appear in the area after the second wave of Chinese immigrants arrived from California (1869–75), armed with their American savings. Without losing any of their cultural traditions, the Chinese community has become assimilated into Cuban society, accepting and sharing the island's lot. A black granite column at the corner of Calle Linea and Calle L remembers the Chinese who fought for Cuban independence.

Entrance gate to Barrio Chino, the Chinese quarter in Havana

Callejón de Hammel, famous for its exotic and colourful murals

Iglesia del Sagrado Corazón ⓯

Avenida Simón Bolívar (Reina) 463.
Map 3 B3. 📞 (7) 8624 979.
🕐 7:30am–noon, 3–6pm daily.
✝ 8am, 4:30pm Mon–Sat, 8am, 9:30am, 4:30pm Sun. 📷 🎥 📷

WITH ITS IMPRESSIVE bell tower, 77 m (253 ft) high, the Church of the Sacred Heart can be seen from various parts of the city. It was designed in the early 1900s by the Jesuit priest Luis Gorgoza and consecrated in 1923, and is a rare example of the Neo-Gothic style in Cuba.

Dominating the façade is a figure of Christ resting on three columns decorated with a capital depicting the parable of the prodigal son. The interior

Entrance to the Iglesia del Sagrado Corazón, with its statue of Christ

has elaborate stained-glass windows narrating the life of Christ and a wealth of stucco-work and pointed arches. A Byzantine-style Sacred Heart with sculptures of saints and prophets is on the high altar.

Avenida Carlos III ⓰

(Avenida Salvador Allende) **Map** 3 B3.

LAID OUT IN 1850 during redevelopment under the supervision of Captain Miguel de Tacón, this boulevard (official name Avenida Salvador Allende) was designed to allow troops and military vehicles to go from the Castillo del Príncipe – built on the Aróstegui hill in the late 1700s – to their parade ground in the present-day Parque de la Fraternidad.

The middle section of the boulevard was reserved for carriages, while the two side avenues with their benches, trees and fountains were for pedestrians. First named Alameda de Tacón or Paseo Militar, it was renamed Avenida Carlos III in honour of the Spanish king who encouraged Cuban commerce and culture in the 18th century.

One of the most curious buildings on the street is the Grand National Masonic Temple, with a world map on the roof, built in the mid-1900s.

Representation of Ochún, the goddess of love

Callejón de Hammel ⓱

Map 3 A2.

THIS STREET IN the working-class Cayo Hueso quarter is a curious open-air Afro-Cuban sanctuary. Its name derives from a legendary French-German resident called Fernando Hammel, a wealthy arms dealer-turned-merchant, who took the entire quarter under his wing. The colourful, 200-m (656-ft) mural here, for which the street is now famous, is the work of naive painter Salvador González. He wanted to pay homage to his varied cultural roots by representing all the religious cults and movements of African origin that are still active in Cuba, hence the many symbols, writings, and images of African gods and Abakuá devils (see p21). He began this enormous project in 1990.

This alley has everything: from small shops selling hand-crafted religious objects to a Nganga, the large cauldron-like pot which forms the basis of Palo Monte, the religion of former Bantu slaves from the African Congo. On Saturdays Callejón Hammel becomes the venue for rumba shows, popular with the locals and tourists alike.

Museo Nacional de Bellas Artes ⓭

THE NATIONAL FINE ARTS MUSEUM was founded on 23
February 1913 thanks to the efforts of the architect
Emilio Heredia, its first director. After frequent moves,
the collections eventually found a definitive home in
the block once occupied by the old Colón market. The
original design was changed when the arcades of the
building were demolished and in 1954 the new Palacio
de Bellas Artes was inaugurated, a Rationalist building
with purely geometric lines designed by the architect
Rodríguez Pichardo. The museum is now divided
between two buildings: the original palacio recently
reconstructed by the architect José Linares, and the
Palacio del Centro Asturiano, by the Parque Central.

LOCATOR MAP
See Street Finder, map 4, p123

Virgin and Child
*This triptych by Hans Memling
(1433–94) exemplifies the vivid
style and masterful spatial
construction that made this
artist one of the great
masters of Flemish
painting.*

Sagrada Familia
*The Holy Family by the
Spanish artist
Bartolomé Esteban
Murillo (1618–82),
who enjoyed great
fame during his
lifetime, is a calm,
meditative scene.*

**PALACIO
DEL CENTRO
ASTURIANO**
*European painting
and sculpture, together
with the collection of
ancient art, are on display
in the Centro Asturiano,
designed in 1927 by the
architect Manuel Bustos
and recently restored.*

STAR FEATURES

★ **La Silla
by Wifredo Lam**

★ **La Habana en Rojo
by René
Portocarrero**

★ **Panathenaean
Amphora**

★ **Panathenaean Amphora**
*This terracotta amphora in the black
figure style is one of the most important
pieces in the museum's collection of
ancient Greek vases, which once
belonged to the Count de Lagunillas.*

★ La Habana en Rojo (1962)
Havana in Red *is part of a long series that René Portocarrero dedicated to the capital. This painting in particular expresses the passionate Baroque spirit that characterizes all of Portocarrero's work.*

The permanent collection is displayed in chronological order on the first and second floors.

Entrance

PALACIO DE BELLAS ARTES
The Palace of Fine Arts is entirely given over to Cuban art. Sculptures line the perimeter of the central courtyard, and the mezzanine houses service rooms and rooms for cultural education, the auditorium and the library. The two upper floors feature galleries divided into three sections: Colonial, academic and 20th-century art (divided into decades from the 1930s to the 1990s).

Form, Space and Light (1953)
This marble sculpture by Rita Longa, in the museum entrance, is characterized by a fluid concept of volume. Two male figures create a harmonious counterpoint.

★ La Silla (1943)
One of several fine works in which Wifredo Lam combines Cubism and Surrealism and adds a distinctively Cuban stamp: a Cubist chair with a vase on it is set in the magical context of the jungle.

Exploring the Museo Nacional de Bellas Artes

Duuring the reassessment of many of Cuba's cultural institutions after 1959, a large number of works were added to the original museum collection – the result of the confiscation of property that had been misappropriated. The collection was divided into three sections: Cuban, European and ancient art. The first consists of 4,336 paintings, 12,837 prints and drawings, and 285 sculptures; the second has 1,649 paintings and 126 sculptures, as well as drawings; the last has almost 600 works dating from the Egyptian to the Roman age.

Clotilde en los Jardines de la Granja by Joaquín Sorolla

PALACIO DEL CENTRO ASTURIANO (WORLD ART)

The building designed as the home of the collection of world art has maintained its original architectural elements, with furnishings, iron grilles, stained-glass windows and chandeliers. Besides the gallery, the place also has communal areas for the public, study rooms, a book shop, bar, a video room and an auditorium.

The collection comprises 548 paintings and 27 sculptures, displayed in sections: the Middle Ages, Italy, Germany, Flanders, the Netherlands, Great Britain, France and Spain. There are also works from various European schools, the US, Latin America, Japan and China, and a collection of icons.

Head of the god Amon, ancient Egyptian sculpture

Among the finest works are the Flemish paintings and the 19th-century Spanish pictures, including one by Joaquín Sorolla: *Entre Naranjos* (1903). In this the artist depicts a banquet in the countryside, using the play of the figures, light and shadow to create an Impressionist-like atmosphere. The same can be said of the movement of the water and the garden in the background in *Clotilde en los Jardines de la Granja*, which is a portrait of the artist's wife. Other Spanish artists represented are Murillo and Zurbarán. Then there are works by Constable, Bouguereau and Van Mieris. The Italian collection includes a group of landscape paintings, including one by Canaletto: *Chelsea College, Rotunda, Ranelagh House and the Thames* (1751), in which the painter brilliantly renders the atmosphere of London. There is also a scene of Venice by Francesco Guardi, *The Lagoon in front of the Fondamenta Nuove*, a youthful work with the delicate rendering that characterized his later production. Other Italian works are *St Christopher* by Jacopo Bassano (ca. 1515–92), *Alpine Landscape with Figures* by Alessandro Magnasco (1667–1748), and *The Spinstress* by Giovanni Battista Piazzetta. *The Reception of a Legation* by Vittore Carpaccio (1490) has a rigorously symmetrical composition. The 8,047 prints and drawings are exhibited on a rotating basis.

The ancient art section is also fascinating: 270 Greek, 195 Roman and 131 Egyptian works, as well as Mesopotamian, Phoenician and Etruscan finds. The 5th-century BC Greek amphora and the Fayoum portraits are especially interesting.

PALACIO DE BELLAS ARTES (CUBAN ART)

The permanent exhibition of 17th–21st-century Cuban art offers a complete overview of works by individuals and schools, and highlights the leading trends in each period. The temporary exhibition of prints and drawings, as well as of paintings, adds variety and

One of the many views that Canaletto painted of London

richness to the permanent collection, which has works by the great masters of contemporary Cuban art.

Two of the major figures are painter Wifredo Lam (*La Silla*, 1943) and sculptor Agustín Cárdenas, who were both influenced by the European avant-garde and African art. The free play of volumes in the wooden sculpture *Figure*, less than 1 m (3 ft) high, expresses to the full the African-derived sensuality that informs Cárdenas's style.

Cuban art in the 19th century, characterized by its technical skill, is represented by the portraits of Guillermo Collazo, an academic and painter, and landscapes by the Chartrand brothers. Other artists with an academic background are the Menocal brothers and Leopoldo Romañach, a painter and lecturer at the Academy.

The pioneers of modern Cuban art are particularly interesting. One of these is Víctor Manuel García, an exceptional landscape painter who conveys peaceful atmospheres with silently flowing rivers and figures with sinuous movements. García is the creator of the "mestizo" archetype: *Gitana Tropical* (Tropical Gypsy, 1929) includes a figure of a woman

El Malecón by Manuel Mendive, an extraordinary Naive painting

against the background of a barren landscape, which has become a symbol of Cuban painting *(see p24)*. There are several works by Amelia Peláez, who revived the still-life genre by merging Cubism and specifically Cuban motifs; among these are *Naturaleza Muerta sobre Ocre*, executed in 1930 in Paris, and *Flores Amarillas*, a mature work that marks a return to more simple compositions after a "Baroque" period.

Figure (1953) by Augustín Cárdenas

El Rapto de las Mulatas (1938), by Carlos Enríquez, is a dream-like "tangle" of human figures, horses and landscape that echoes the classical theme of the rape of the Sabine women. It is considered emblematic of Cuban painting and of this artist's oeuvre. The sensuality of the human bodies and the tropical atmosphere in this work provide a key to the interpretation of the motifs of traditional art.

The chronological display of works illustrates the development of Cuban art. In the 1950s there was a move away from figurative art, as seen in the work of Guido Llinás and Hugo Consuegra.

After the victory of the revolution in 1959, Cuban art embraced extremely varied styles. Servando Cabrera took guerrillas as his subject and then made an erotic series. Antonia Eiriz was a particularly powerful Neo-Expressionist, and Raúl Martínez began with abstract art and then absorbed elements of Pop Art.

Another renowned contemporary artist is Manuel Mendive who, in embracing Cuba's African heritage, searches for the hidden depths of existence. *El Malecón* (1975), one of his most significant works, depicts the city's famous promenade as if it were an almost sacred site where people mingle with African gods. The style here is at once naive and sophisticated.

Of the leading artists of the 1970s there are works by Ever Fonseca, Nelson Domínguez, and the unique illustrator Roberto Fabelo. Among the younger artists (all graduates of the historic San Alejandro Academy), Tomás Sánchez, with his archetypal landscapes, and José Bedia, with his bold installations, stand out. The artists who continue to emerge on the Cuban art scene – thanks to the Biennial Show – exhibit their works in the many temporary shows.

Of the considerable number of works in its possession, the museum now exhibits 639 paintings, 184 drawings and prints and 69 sculptures. The rest are on display on a rotating basis.

Flores Amarillas (1964), a still life dating from Amelia Peláez's mature phase

VEDADO AND PLAZA

THE UNUSUAL GRID PLAN of Vedado was the design of the engineer Luis Yboleón Bosque in 1859. It called for pavements 2 m (6 ft) wide, houses with a garden, and broad straight avenues. The name Vedado ("prohibited") arose because in the 1500s, in order to have full view of any pirates approaching, it was forbidden to build houses and streets here. In the late 19th and early 20th century the quarter was enlarged, becoming a prestigious residential

Sculpture at the corner of 23 and 12 Street

area for many of the city's leading families. Vedado has two different roles. It is Havana's modern political and cultural centre, with the city's main hotels, restaurants, shops, theatres, cinemas, offices and ministries; and it is also a historic quarter with a wealth of gardens and old houses with grand Colonial entrances. Plaza de la Revolución, the venue for major celebrations, is the political centre of Havana and the whole of Cuba, as well as a highly symbolic place.

SIGHTS AT A GLANCE

Museums and Galleries
Museo de Artes Decorativas ❸
Museo Napoleónico ❺

Historic Buildings
Casa de las Américas ❷
Quinta de los Molinos ❻
Universidad de La Habana ❹

Monuments
Memorial José Martí p103 ❽

Streets and Squares
Plaza de la Revolución ❼

Cemeteries
Necrópolis Colón pp104–5 ❾

Walks
A Walk through Vedado pp98–9 ❶

KEY

▢ Walk *pp98–9*
🛈 Tourist information
🚌 Coach station

GETTING THERE
This area is huge, but getting around on foot can be a rewarding experience if you have time. Otherwise, the best alternative is to go by taxi. In order to orientate yourself you will need to know how the street names work *(see p118).*

0 metres　　　1000
0 yards　　　1000

◁ **The end of the Malecón in Vedado with the mouth of the Río Almendares**

A Walk through Vedado ❶

THIS WALK TAKES IN the broad avenues which are typical of Vedado, providing a taste of the district's odd architectural mix of ugly 1950s high-rises and crumbling Neo-Classical mansions. There is only one museum on this route (Vedado has few conventional attractions), leaving you free to simply stroll and look around. Calle 23, modern Havana's most well-known street, is the main reference point for the walk. The most famous section is the first few blocks, known as La Rampa.

The Hotel Habana Libre, with the mosaic *La Fruta Cubana* (1957)

The Hotel Nacional viewed from the Focsa tower

KEY

···· Walking route

| 0 metres | 300 |
| 0 yards | 300 |

Malecón

The stretch of the Malecón where this walk begins is dominated by the headland occupied by the Hotel Nacional ①. This gem of Art Deco architecture opened in 1930 (*see p250*). Many famous guests have stayed here including Winston Churchill, Fred Astaire, Buster Keaton and Walt Disney. The hotel park offers lovely views across the bay.

La Rampa

Nearby is La Rampa (the first rising stretch of Calle 23 between the seafront and Calle N). Modern and lively, lined with offices, restaurants and bars with old-fashioned neon signs, La Rampa would pass for a typical 1950s street were it not for the façade of the Ministry of Sugar (or Minaz) with its revolutionary mural and the

"futuristic" Pabellón Cuba, which hosts exhibitions. This part of the walk is accompanied by the unmistakable profile of the Edificio Focsa ②, a skyscraper built in the 1950s.

This route also takes you past a small open-air crafts market and the Centro Internacional de la Prensa, which caters to foreign journalists.

Calle 23

In the middle of the park at the corner of Calle 23 and L is the Coppelia ice-cream parlour ③, a large glass and metal building (1966). This classic location in Havana was made famous by Tomás Gutiérrez Alea's

film *Strawberry and Chocolate* (*see p27*). Coppelia is the most popular ice-cream parlour in the city (hence the queues).

On the other side of Calle 23 is the impressive Hotel Habana Libre (*see p250*), with a tiled mural by renowned Cuban artist Amelia Peláez. The hotel first opened in 1958, and a year later was requisitioned from the Americans and became Fidel Castro's headquarters.

Inside are two mosaics by Portocarrero and Sosabravo (*see p24–5*).

At the intersection with Calle J is the Parque del Quijote ④, a tree-filled area with a modern statue of a nude Don Quixote on horseback by Sergio Martínez. Further along Calle 23 the buildings lessen in height and building styles are more varied.

The statue of Don Quixote by Sergio Martínez (1980)

ITINERARY

Hotel Nacional ①
Edificio Focsa ②
Coppelia ③
Parque del Quijote ④
Museo de la Danza ⑤
Casa de la Amistad ⑥
ICAIC ⑦

The constant queue for the
Coppelia ice-cream parlour

VISITORS' CHECKLIST

Departure: Hotel Nacional.
Arrival: corner of 23 y 12.
Length: 3.5 km (2 miles).
Where to eat: Coppelia ice-cream parlour, Casa de la Amistad, one of the bars at the corner of 23 y 12. It is advisable to plan stops and museum visits for the (hot) middle of the day.
Museo de la Danza ☎ (7) 8312 198. ☐ 11am–6:30pm Tue–Sat. ● 1 Jan, 1 May, 26 Jul, 25 Dec.

CALLE 13
AVENIDA DE LOS PRESIDENTES (G)
CALLE 17
CALLE L
CALLE N
②
①
MALECÓN
K
③
(RAMPA)
CALLE 23
④
CALLE 21
CALLE 23

Avenida de los Presidentes

The tour continues by turning right at Calle G (Avenida de los Presidentes), a wide, tree-lined avenue with luxurious 19th- and 20th-century French-style buildings. In the middle of the street are benches and neat flower beds. Behind the statue of Simón Bolívar is the junction with Calle Línea.

Calle Línea

The first street to be laid out in the Vedado quarter owes its name to the fact that it had a tramline *(línea)* connecting the original heart of the quarter and the historic centre. Calle Línea also has many French-style buildings as well as Colonial houses with stained-glass windows and wrought-iron grilles.

The recently restored building at the corner of Calle G is the Museo de la Danza ⑤, run by the legendary ballet dancer Alicia Alonso, founder of the Ballet Nacional *(see p83)*. It is the only dance museum in Latin

Alicia Alonso's shoes, Museo de la Danza

America, with mementoes of famous ballet dancers who have been to Cuba, drawings and sketches of stage sets, historic photos, period publications and works by contemporary artists.

Paseo

Once outside the museum, go along Calle Línea to the junction with one of the loveliest streets in Havana: Calle Paseo, which is like a long, thin park running all the way down to the Plaza de la Revolución *(see p102)*. It is lined with elegant buildings with splendid gardens: mostly ministries and public administration offices, very few of which can be visited. The Casa de la Amistad ⑥, at No. 406 between Calle 17 and 19, is a cultural centre with a bar and restaurant, and part of a lavish Art Deco building given by the wealthy Pedro Baró to his mistress Caterina Lasa, grande dame of Havana high society. They were forced to flee to Europe by the scandal caused by their affair, but returned in 1917, when Lasa managed to get a divorce from her first husband.

23 y 12

Continue on Calle Paseo for 200 m (220 yds) back to Calle 23, six blocks away from the busy central intersection where this walk ends. A plaque declares that on 16 April 1961, on the eve of the American invasion at the Bay of Pigs *(see p163)*, Fidel Castro announced that the Cuban Revolution was Socialist.

At Calle 23 y 12 there are restaurants and bars, shops, and cinemas like the Chaplin Cinematheque and the Cuban Institute of Cinematographic Arts and Industry (ICAIC) ⑦ *(see p27)*, with an art gallery featuring contemporary artists. Calle 12 leads south to Necrópolis Colón *(see pp104–105)*.

The permanent poster exhibition in the ICAIC building

The Art Deco building that is the home of the Casa de las Américas

Casa de las Américas ❷

Calle 3ra, esq. G. **Map** 1 C1. 📞 *(7) 552 706, 552 707.* 🕐 *10am–5pm Mon–Fri, 10am–3pm Sat.* ⬤ *1 Jan, 1 May, 26 Jul, 10 Oct, 25 Dec.* 📷

ON THE MALECÓN, beyond the Monument to the Victims of the *Maine (see p58)*, there is a kind of secular temple, with a bell tower but no cross. This is the Casa de las Américas, a cultural institution, which was built in just four months after the triumph of the Cuban Revolution. Haydée Santa-maría, one of the heroines of the stuggle, founded the Casa with the aim of promoting exchanges among artists and writers on the American continent.

The centre features Arte Nuestra América, the most comprehensive collection known of Latin American painting and graphic art from the 1960s to the present.

Museo de Artes Decorativas ❸

Calle 17, 502. **Map** 2 D2. 📞 *(7) 8309 848.* 🕐 *11am–6:30pm Tue–Sat, 9am–1pm Sun.* ⬤ *1 Jan, 1 May, 26 Jul, 10 Oct, 25 Dec.* 📷 🅆 *www.cult.cu/patrim/cnpc/museos*

THE WONDERFUL Museum of Decorative Arts is housed in the former residence of one of the wealthiest Cuban women of the 20th century: the Countess de Revilla de Camargo, sister of José Gómez Mena, the owner of

the Manzana de Gómez *(see p81)*. The mansion was built in 1927, and is well worth a visit for its French Rococo-Louis XV furnishings, as well as for the inner gardens.

The collection reveals the sophisticated and exotic tastes of the ruling classes and wealthy collectors of the Colonial period. Major works of art here include two paintings by Hubert Robert, *The Swing* and *The Large Waterfall at Tivoli*, and two 17th-century bronze sculptures in the foyer.

The main hall on the Louis XV-style ground floor has 18th-century Chinese vases, Meissen porcelain, a large Aubusson carpet dating from 1722 and paintings by French artists.

A bedroom on the second floor holds a collection of Chinese screens, while the Countess's room features a secretaire that once belonged to Marie Antoinette.

Last but not least is the pink marble Art Deco bathroom, which should not be missed.

Chinese porcelain, Museo de Artes Decorativas

Universidad de La Habana ❹

Calle 27 de Noviembre (Jovellar) y Ronda. **Map** 2F2. **Museo Antropológico Montané**, Felipe Poey Bldg, Plaza Ignacio Agramonte. 📞 *(7) 8793 488.* 🕐 *9am–noon, 1–4pm Mon–Fri.* ⬤ *1 Jan, 1 May, 26 Jul, 10 Oct, 25 Dec.* 📷 📷 📷

THE UNIVERSITY of Havana was founded under the auspices of a papal bull in 1721 and was initially housed in the Dominican monastery of St John Lateran, in the heart of Habana Vieja. In 1902, a few days after the proclamation of the Cuban Republic, it was transferred to the Vedado area to a site which had been utilized as an explosives store in the Colonial period.

The new univer-sity, housed in various buildings, was built between 1906 and 1940. In front of the main entrance, now the venue for political demonstrations and concerts, is the Alma Mater, the symbol of Havana

The Neo-Classical foyer of the Museo de Artes Decorativas

The austere façade of the University of Havana, with the statue of the Alma Mater at the top of the staircase

University. This statue, of a woman with her arms outstretched in a gesture of welcome, was cast in 1919 in New York by the Czech sculptor Mario Korbel. It was installed at the top of the broad granite stairway that forms the entrance to the complex in 1927. The student entrance to the university is in Calle San Lázaro, which broadens out into an open space where the ashes of Julio Antonio Mella *(see p46)* are kept, before sloping upwards.

In the Science Faculty, the Felipe Poey Museum of Natural History is open to visitors. Of much greater interest, however, is the **Museo Antropológico Montané**, in the Mathematics Department. Founded in 1903, this museum has exceptional pre-Columbian archaeological finds from Cuba, such as the Idolo del Tabaco found on the eastern tip of the island, the Idolo de Bayamo, one of the largest stone sculptures in the entire Caribbean area, and the Dujo de Santa Fe, a wooden ceremonial seat.

The oldest building on the hill is the Great Hall, with an austere façade behind which are allegorical paintings by Armando Menocal. The hall itself contains the old University of San Gerónimo bell, used to convene the professors, and the remains of Félix Varela *(see p26)*, brought to Cuba in 1911 from Florida, where the Cuban intellectual had died.

Idolo de Tabaco, Museo Montané

Museo Napoleónico ❺

Calle San Miguel 1159, esq. a Ronda. **Map** 2 F3. 🎫 *(7) 8791 412, 8791 460.* ⬜ *10am–5pm Mon–Sat.* ⬛ *1 Jan, 1 May, 26 Jul, 10 Oct, 25 Dec.* 📷 ✔ 📷 🆆 www.cult.cu/patrim/cnpc/museos

THE SURPRISING PRESENCE of a Napoleonic museum in Cuba is due to the passion of a sugar magnate, Julio Lobo. For years he sent his agents all over the world in search of Napoleonic mementoes. In 1959, when Lobo left Cuba, the Cuban government bought his collection.

Every room in this curious museum contains fine examples of imperial-style furniture as well as all sorts of surprising Napoleonic memorabilia, including one of the emperor's teeth and a tuft of his hair. There are two portraits, one by Andrea Appioni, painted in Milan during Napoleon's second Italian campaign, and another by Antoine Gros. There is also his death mask, cast two days before Napoleon's death by Francesco Antommarchi, the Italian physician who had accompanied him to the island of St Helena and who later settled in Cuba.

The mansion itself was built in the 1920s by Oreste Ferrara, counsellor to the dictator Gerardo Machado, who furnished it in a Neo-Florentine Gothic style.

Quinta de los Molinos ❻

Avenida Carlos III (Salvador Allende) y Luaces. **Map** 2 F3. 🎫 *(7) 8798 850.* ⬛ *for restoration.* **Grounds** ⬜ *7am–7pm Tue–Sun.*

A TYPICAL 19TH-CENTURY villa in the Vedado quarter, the Quinta de los Molinos was built as the summer residence of the captains-general in 1837. The villa stands in a leafy area with two tobacco mills *(molinos)*.

The rambling grounds around the villa were filled with tropical vegetation from the Botanical Garden, which was then in the Capitol area but was dismantled after the Parque Central was enlarged. The park is popular among local musicians, who come here to practise.

In 1899, General Máximo Gómez, Commander in Chief of the liberation army, stayed here, which is why it is now a museum dedicated to this hero of the wars of independence *(see p44)*.

A stained-glass window in the Quinta de los Molinos

A parade in front of the Ministerio del Interior, Plaza de la Revolución

Plaza de la Revolución ❼

Map 2 E5.

PLAZA DE LA REVOLUCIÓN has been Cuba's political, administrative and cultural centre since 1959. The square was designed in 1952 under the Batista regime, and most of the buildings visible today also date from the 1950s. What had been known as the Plaza Cívica was renamed Plaza de la Revolución following Fidel Castro's victory in 1959.

Though it does not distinguish itself by its architecture or design, the square is nonetheless an important place to visit because of its historic and symbolic importance. It was the venue for the first mass rallies following the triumph of the revolution and of the festivities for the campaign against illiteracy in 1961.

Since 1959, military parades and official celebrations have often attracted crowds of over a million people. During these events the area fills with people, and the speakers, including president Fidel Castro, take their place on the podium next to the statue of José Martí, at the foot of the obelisk.

On 25 January 1998 Pope John Paul II celebrated mass from this podium together with thousands of worshippers (see p53).

🏛 Ministerio del Interior
Calle Aranguren.

The façade of the Ministry of the Interior, which stands directly opposite the statue of Martí, is almost completely covered by a huge bronze wire sculpture of Che Guevara, which was completed in 1995. (The guerrilla fighter had his office in this building in the early 1960s.) This striking and symbolic image was inspired by the world-famous photograph taken by the press photographer Alberto Korda (see p172). Under the bust are the words: "Hasta la victoria siempre" (keep striving for victory). The façade is illuminated at night.

🏛 Museo Postal Cubano
Ave Rancho Boyeros,
19 de Mayo y 20 de Mayo.
📞 (7) 8815 551. ⏰ 9am–4:30pm Mon–Fri. 🌑 1 Jan, 1 May, 26 Jul, 10 Oct, 25 Dec. 🎫 📷

This fascinating postal museum has occupied a small corner of the Ministry of Communications since 1965. Through the medium of stamps, it illustrates the last two centuries of Cuban history, from the end of the Colonial period to the years following the fall of the Berlin Wall, including the wars of independence, and figures like Machado, Batista and Che Guevara.

The most curious item on display is a fragment of a "postal missile". In 1939, a group of Cubans decided to use a missile for "express airmail deliveries" from Havana to Matanzas, but the crude device exploded a few minutes after "take-off".

The Teatro Naciónal seen from Martí's memorial

🏛 Palacio de la Revolución
Calle Martí.

The former Ministry of Justice (1958) behind the Martí Memorial now houses the offices of the Council of State, the Council of Ministers and the Central Committee of the Communist Party. It was here that Fidel Castro received Pope John Paul II on 22 January 1998.

The elegant wooden card-index files in the Biblioteca Nacional

🏛 Biblioteca Nacional José Martí
Plaza de la Revolución.
📞 (7) 555 442. ⏰ 8:30am–6:30pm Mon–Sat. 🚻

The José Martí National Library has over two million books and is particularly strong in the humanities. The United States embargo, plus the Special Period crisis, have slowed the development of a library computerization programme, but all services are being modernized.

🎭 Teatro Nacional
Paseo y 39.
📞 (7) 8796 011, 8793 558.

Built with a striking convex façade, the National Theatre is Cuba's most important cultural complex. It was inaugurated in June 1959. There are two auditoriums: the Avellaneda, with a seating capacity of 2,500, and the Covarrubia, which seats 800 and has a mural by Cuban artist René Porto-carrero (see p24). Theatre pro-grammes include lectures, courses, theatre festivals, guitar and jazz concerts, and ballet. There is also a café chan-tant and a piano bar with live shows (see p280).

Memorial José Martí ❽

WORK ON THIS MONUMENT in the middle of the Plaza de la Revolución began in 1953, on the 100th anniversary of the birth of Cuba's national hero. The memorial was finished in 1959. It consists of a 109-m (358-ft) tower representing a five-pointed star and is built of grey marble from the Isla de la Juventud. At the foot stands a huge statue of José Martí in a meditative pose. The actual Martí Memorial is in the interior of the base, which also houses the Sala de Actos, an auditorium used for concerts, lectures and poetry readings.

★ Panorama
On clear days, the mirador on top of the tower, the highest point in Havana, affords a view of the entire city. The panorama shown here stretches from the Ministerio del Interior to the sea.

A lift goes to the top of the tower, which reaches a height of 139 m (458 ft) – the monument stands on a hill 30 m (100 ft) above sea level.

★ The Memorial
Two rooms contain manuscripts, portraits and mementoes of Martí; the third room describes the history of the monument and the square, while a fourth puts on contemporary art exhibitions. The mural in the lobby features the patriot's thoughts.

VISITORS' CHECKLIST

Plaza de la Revolución.
Map 2 E5.
📞 (7) 8820 906. 🕐 9:30am–5pm Tue–Sat, 10am–2pm Sun.
⬤ 1 Jan, 1 May, 26 Jul, 10 Oct, 25 Dec. 🈲 🗲 📷 ▢ 🛗
W www3.cuba.cu/memorial/

STAR FEATURES

★ Panorama

★ The Memorial

Statue of José Martí
The 18-m (59-ft) high, white marble statue, carved on site by Juan José Sicre, is surrounded by six half columns.

Necrópolis Colón

Havana's monumental Columbus cemetery is one of the largest in the world, occupying an area of 55 ha (135 acres) and with about two million graves, equal to the city's current population. It was designed in the 1860s by the Spanish architect Calixto de Loira, who based the layout on the rigorously symmetrical plan of Roman military camps. It was built between 1871 and 1886. Because of its many sculptures and monuments in different styles – from eclectic to the boldest expressions of contemporary art – the Necrópolis has been proclaimed a national monument. However, although it is full of fascinating funerary art, it is still the cemetery for and of Havana's citizens. People come here to visit their loved ones or simply to stroll around.

The Osario General, the ossuary built in 1886, is one of the cemetery's oldest constructions.

Martires del Asalto al Palacio Presidencial
This avant-garde memorial (1982) honours the students killed during their attack on Batista's Presidential Palace in 1957.

La Milagrosa

The Pantheon of Catalina Lasa *(see p99)*
was commissioned by her second husband, Juan Pedro Baró, who had her embalmed and brought from Paris to Havana.

★ **La Piedad de Rita Longa**
This delicate marble bas-relief pietà adorns the black marble tomb of the Aguilera family, which was built in the 1950s.

Chapel of the Six Medical Students

★ **Main Entrance**
The statue in Carrara marble of the three theological virtues, Faith, Hope and Charity, was sculpted in 1904 by the Cuban artist José Villalta de Saavedra in "Neo-Romantic" style.

JANUA SUM PACIS

Tomb of the author Alejo Carpentier (1904–80)

Entrance

Fuerzas Armadas Revolucionarias Monument (1955)
This pantheon houses the heroes of the Revolutionary Armed Forces.

VISITORS' CHECKLIST

Calle Zapata esq a Calle 12.
Map 1 C5.
(7) 8334 196.
8am–5pm daily.

Panteón de los Prelados

Capilla Central
Built in the late 1800s in the middle of Avenida Colón, the cemetery's main avenue, this chapel contains some impressive works of art, including frescoes by the Cuban artist Miguel Melero.

The Falla Bonet Pantheon
is a truncated grey granite pyramid with a statue of Christ by the Spanish sculptor Benlliure.

★ Las Víctimas de la Caridad
A monumental pantheon with the tombs of the victims of an accident that occurred in 1890 in the Isasí hardware store. The monument was designed by the Spanish architects Agustín Querol and Julio Zapata.

Tomb of Generalissimo Máximo Gómez *(see p44)*

STAR SIGHTS

★ **Main Entrance**

★ **La Piedad de Rita Longa**

★ **Las Víctimas de la Caridad**

LA MILAGROSA

"The Miraculous One" is the tomb of Amelia Goyri de la Hoz, who died in childbirth in 1901, along with her daughter. She was only 24. In keeping with the custom of the time, she and the child were buried together. According to popular legend, a few years later the tomb was opened and she was found intact, holding her baby in her arms. This "miracle", and the fact that the bereaved husband went to her tomb every day and never turned his back to it, made Amelia

A mother placing flowers on the statue of La Milagrosa

a symbol of motherly love. She became the protector of pregnant women and newborn children, and her tomb is a pilgrimage site for future mothers, who ask for her blessing and leave without turning their back to the tomb. The statue placed at the tomb in 1909 is by José Villalta de Saavedra.

FURTHER AFIELD

BEYOND THE CITY OF HAVANA, sights of interest are rather more scattered. The Miramar quarter lies to the west of the city, and the Castillo del Morro and Fortaleza de La Cabaña defence fortresses, evidence of Havana's strategic importance, are physically separated from the city but linked to it historically. Cubans are enthusiastic beachgoers and the long golden beaches at Playas del Este, east of Havana, are especially popular destinations at the weekend. Among the sightseeing highlights are the favourite haunts of Ernest Hemingway, including Finca La Vigía, the villa where he wrote some of his best novels, and the fishing village of Cojímar.

SIGHTS AT A GLANCE

Museums
Finca La Vigía ⑩

Monuments and Churches
Castillo del Morro ③
San Carlos de La Cabaña ④
Santuario di San Lázaro ⑬

Parks and Gardens
Jardín Botánico Nacional ⑫
Parque Lenin ⑪

Beaches
Playas del Este ⑨

Towns and Suburbs
Casablanca ⑤
Cojímar ⑧
Guanabacoa ⑦
Regla ⑥

Historic Places
Tropicana ②

Walks
A Walk through Miramar
  (pp108–9) ①

KEY

▢	Historic centre
▢	Built-up area
✈	Airport
⛴	Ferry
═	Motorway
━	Major road
─	Minor road

GREATER HAVANA

◁ **The lighthouse at Castillo del Morro, which can be seen from many parts of the old city**

A Walk through Miramar ❶

M IRAMAR is the most elegant part of Havana – as it was before the Revolution, when the city's richest inhabitants lived here. Life in this quarter revolves around the busy Avenida 5, a broad, tree-lined avenue flanked by splendid early 20th-century villas and now boasting a number of luxury hotels. Administratively, Miramar belongs to the municipality of Playa, as does the adjacent Cubanacán quarter, where many foreign embassies are located.

Looking down Avenida 5, the main avenue in Miramar

The compact Fuerte de la Chorrera

Arriving from Vedado

This walk begins at the Fuerte de Santa Dorotea de la Luna en la Chorrera fort ①, a national monument. The fort, designed by Giovanni Battista Antonelli and built in 1645, was crucial to the city's defence system (see p110) for over two centuries. Opposite the fort is the 1830 ②, a restaurant (see p268) in a house that once belonged to Carlos Miguel de Céspedes, Minister of Public Works under President Machado. Walk down to Calle 11 and over the iron bridge to reach the Miramar area. Turn right and go up to Avenida 5 ("Quinta Avenida").

Along Avenida 5

This broad, tranquil avenue with shrubs and benches in the middle begins at the exit of the northernmost tunnel under the Almendares river.

On both sides of the boulevard are large, imposing mansions built in the early decades of the 20th century and many Art Deco and eclectic-style houses, most of which were abandoned by their owners after Fidel Castro took power. The Cuban government has turned many of these buildings into ministries, embassies and even orphanages (an example is the residence of the former President of the Republic Grau San Martín at the corner of Calle 14). Further down the Avenida, at the corner of

KEY

•••• Walking route

0 metres   400
0 yards   400

ITINERARY

Fuerte de Santa Dorotea de la Luna en la Chorrera ①
Restaurante 1830 ②
Iglesia de Santa Rita ③
Maqueta de la Habana ④
Acuario Nacional ⑤

Dolphins performing at the Miramar aquarium

VISITORS' CHECKLIST

Point of departure: Fuerte de la Chorrera, Malecón.
Length: 5 km (3 miles).
Stops: Mesón La Chorrera, Calle Calzada 1252, before the tunnel; Cafetería Rumbos, Playita 16; Bar Media Noche, Calle 4 e/ Ave 3 y 5; Bar Dos Gardenias, Ave 7 y Calle 28.

Calle 26, is the modern Iglesia de Santa Rita ③, with three distinctive tall arches on its façade. Pop in to see the statue of St Rita by Cuban sculptress Rita Longa, to the left of the entrance. Walk up Calle 28 to Avenida 3 ("tercera"). In the block above is the fascinating Maqueta de La Habana museum ④, a detailed model of Havana measuring about 10 sq m (108 sq ft), with different areas colour-coded according to construction date, showing how the city developed from Colonial times onwards. Continue the walk along Avenida 3, taking in the stylish architecture, and then turn right to walk one block up to Avenida 1.

Statue by Rita Longa, Church of Santa Rita

The Seafront

Avenida 1 ("primera") lacks the liveliness and fascination of the Malecón, but the water is clear and there are peaceful spots for sunbathing, such as Playita 16 (at the end of Calle 16). At the corner of Calle 60 is the unmistakable pale blue building housing the Acuario Nacional ⑤, the city aquarium. Here, large saltwater tanks reproduce an assortment of Caribbean and ocean habitats. About 3,500 specimens represent 350 different species of sea fauna. The most spectacular section is the tank of *Tursiops truncatus* dolphins, more commonly known as bottle-nosed dolphins, which are typical of the Cuban seas. Dolphin shows are also performed here at regular intervals. The aquarium complex is open from 10am to 6pm every day except Monday.

The model of Havana: in the foreground, Castillo del Morro, behind, the Malecón

RÍO ALMENDARES

The Almendares river is no longer crystal-clear, but it must have been cleaner in the past, because in the 17th century a Spanish bishop called Almendáriz came to Havana in bad health and fully recovered after a stay along its banks. The river's name was changed from Casiguaguas to Almendares in the bishop's honour. Along its west bank, by the Calle 23 bridge from Vedado, is the Parque Almendares, an area filled with tropical plants and vegetation.

Thick vegetation in the Parque Almendares, Havana's "forest"

The early 20th-century Fountain of the Muses at the Tropicana

Tropicana ❷

Calle 72 e/ 41 y 45. Marianao.
C (7) 2671 717, 2670 110.

THE MOST FAMOUS nightclub in Cuba, America and perhaps the world is located in the outskirts of Havana, in the Marianao district. Many legendary figures of the 20th century have performed here, including Josephine Baker, Bola de Nieve, Rita Montaner and Nat King Cole.

The Tropicana was originally a farm estate belonging to Mina Pérez Chaumont, the widow of a wealthy man named Regino Truffin. In the 1930s she transformed her property into a vast nightspot with a restaurant and casino featuring extravagant floor shows with lavish costumes. The nightclub opened on 31 December 1939.

Perhaps surprisingly, given the change of regime, the Tropicana is still alive and kicking. Fortunately, the trees in the original estate were left intact, so that today the Tropicana stands in the middle of an extraordinary tropical forest. At night, floodlights illuminate the palm trees, partly hidden by clouds of artificial smoke. A reminder of the Tropicana's golden age is the enormous "Bajo las Estrellas" ballroom. With its capacity of 1,000 it is one of the largest of its kind.

At the main entrance is the Fountain of the Muses (1952). The garden's statue of a ballet dancer, by Rita Longa (1952), is now the symbol of the club.

Aerial view of the Castillo del Morro, situated on a rocky headland at the entrance to the bay of Havana

Castillo del Morro ❸

Carretera de la Cabaña, Habana del Este. **Parque Histórico Militar Morro Cabaña** ☎ (7) 8620 617-19, 8627 623. ⬤ 10am–10pm daily. ⬤ 1 Jan, 1 May, 26 Jul, 25 Dec.

CONSTRUCTION of this fortress, which was designed by the Italian military architect Giovanni Battista Antonelli, began in 1589 at the request of the governor, Juan de Texeda. The function of the Castillo de los Tres Reyes del Morro (its full title) was to detect the approach of any enemy (pirates especially). Various treasures of the New World were periodically concentrated in the port when

The old lamp in the Morro lighthouse

ships docked in Cuba on their way to Spain, and it was necessary to protect them.

The original lighthouse on the "Morrillo", the highest point of the hill, was rebuilt several times, until General Leopoldo O'Donnel ordered a new one to be built in 1845. This still stands today. It is made entirely of stone, and has its original lamp, the rays of which shine for a radius of 30 km (20 miles). Today the Castillo del Morro is open to visitors as the Parque Histórico-Militar. Many tourists and locals come simply to admire the outlook, as the fortress affords a magnificent view of the city and port of Havana.

Access to the castles is through an impressive gallery,

where plaques indicate the spot where the British opened a breach in 1762, allowing them to take the Morro and all of Havana after a 40-day siege.

On the northern side of the complex is the Plataforma de la Reina, with defence walls and a flight of steps leading to the upper terrace. From here visitors can gain an overall view of the fortress.

San Carlos de La Cabaña ❹

Carretera de la Cabaña, Habana del Este. ⬤ See Castillo del Morro. ⬛

AFTER THE BRITISH conquest of Cuba in 1762, it was 11 months before the Spaniards regained Havana. The bitter experience of foreign occupation convinced them of the need to fortify the hill

HAVANA'S DEFENCES

Havana was the most important port in the New World in the 1700s. It was a highly prized target for enemies and pirates because of its extremely favourable strategic position in the Caribbean, and it was also the most fortified city in any Spanish colony. Beyond the maritime canal affording access to the Bay of Havana were the two large fortresses of Morro and Cabaña. These two, together with the castles of Real Fuerza, Punta, Atarés and Príncipe and the city walls, constituted for centuries the city's impressive defence and attack system. From the outlying forts of Cojímar and La Chorrera, to the east and west respectively, any enemy approach could be sighted.

dominating the port in a more effective manner, so, on 4 November 1763, construction work began on the new Cabaña fortress. No fewer than 4,000 men laboured on the project, including Mexican and Indian prisoners transported from the Yucatán peninsula in conditions of semi-slavery.

The new fortification cost 14 million pesos, a sum so large that, according to an old legend, when King Carlos III of Spain was informed of the expense, he asked for a spyglass and reputedly commented: "Such an expensive construction should be visible from Madrid."

La Cabaña, which extends for more than 700 m (2,300 ft) along the entrance canal of the bay, is a huge 10-ha (25-acre) polygon designed in keeping with the principles of French military schools, but with detailing by the Spanish engineer Silvestre Abarca. With its crown-shaped plan, it is considered a fine example of a bastion-type defence fortification.

A visit to the fortress offers a variety of experiences. The fortress's central thoroughfare leads up to the Baluardo di San Ambrosio bastion and the

Entrance to the de La Cabaña parish church, which stands in the fortress parade ground

Teraza de San Agustín, where the poet Juan Clemente Zenea was executed for his separatist ideas in 1871. In the same area some Soviet nuclear missiles, left over from the 1962 Cuban Missile Crisis *(see p52)*, are on display.

The **Museo Monográfico** illustrates the history of the fortress through documents and photographs. The **Museo de Armas y Fortificaciones** is a military museum.

However, the one museum not to miss is the **Comandancia del Che**: on 3 January 1959 the *barbudos* (as Castro and his bearded revolutionaries were known) occupied La Cabaña and set up their headquarters in the 19th-century building that was once the residence of the Spanish military governor. Today it is a museum containing various items that belonged to Che Guevara, including his weapons, glasses and camera. The revolutionary's original office, which has been left intact, is also open to visitors.

Casablanca ❺

Regla (Havana). 🚢 *from Muelle de la Luz, La Habana Vieja, every 30 mins.* ☎ *(7) 977 473.* 🚉

THIS FISHING VILLAGE was built in the 1700s on the other side of the Bay of Havana from the city. Casablanca is best known for the huge Cristo de la Habana, an 18-m (60-ft) tall white marble statue of Christ, which looms over the village. The work of the Cuban sculptress Jilma Madera (1958), it was commissioned by President Batista's wife, Marta. She had made a vow that she would finance a large statue of Christ if her husband survived the attack by students on the presidential palace in 1957, during which he risked his life. The statue was completed a week prior to the Revolution. It can be seen from many parts of the city and is familiar to all Cubans.

The colossal Cristo de La Habana

THE CAÑONAZO

Every evening, at 9pm exactly, the picturesque "Cañonazo" ceremony is held in the La Cabaña fortress. On the hour, a volley of cannon shots is fired by a group of young soldiers of the Revolutionary Armed Forces, dressed in 18th-century uniforms. This theatrical ceremony is interesting from the historical point of view: in the Colonial period, a volley of cannon shots was fired at the end of each day to tell citizens that the city gates were closed and access to the bay had been blocked by a chain *(see p85)*.

The Cañonazo ceremony, a commemoration in historic costume

Regla ❻

Havana. 🏙 100,000. ⛴ from Muelle de la Luz, Habana Vieja, every 30 mins; (7) 977 473.
ℹ Infotur, Calle Albuquerque esq. Calixto Garcia, (7) 970 297.

Regla LIES on the east coast of the Bay of Havana, a few minutes by ferry from Muelle de la Luz. The town was founded in 1687 and over the years grew in economic importance as a fishing port and centre for huge sugar warehouses. In the 19th century freed slaves settled in Regla, and there is still a strong Afro-Cuban culture here today.

The church of **Nuestra Señora de la Virgen de Regla** was built here in the early 19th century, and the Liceo Artístico y Literario was

Interior of the Regla church with its ornate high altar

opened by José Martí in the late 19th century with a famous speech on Cuban independence.

Guanabacoa ❼

Havana. 🏙 100,000. 🚌

After its foundation in 1607, this town became an obligatory port of call for the slave traffic, which explains its fame as a city associated with Afro-Cuban culture. Its name, of Indian origin, means "land of many waters": there are several springs in this area which at one time encouraged wealthy Habaneros to build homes here. Today, Guanabacoa is proud of its Colonial houses and of having been the birthplace of three leading 20th-century Cuban musicians: pianist and composer Ernesto Lecuona, singer Rita Montaner, and *chansonnier* Ignacio Villa, better known as Bola de Nieve.

Guanabacoa has several interesting churches. Of these, the **Ermita de Potosí** in particular is well worth a visit.

The *Mano Poderosa* in the Guanabacoa Municipal Museum

Built in 1675, it is one of the oldest and most original Colonial period churches.

The interesting **Museo Municipal de Guanabacoa**, located in a well-restored Colonial house, illustrates the history of the town. The dominant figure is that of Pepe Antonio, the local hero in the struggle against the British in the 18th century.

The museum places particular emphasis on the *santería* and Palo Monte religions and on the rituals of the Abakuá cult *(see p21)*. An impressive piece in this section is the *Mano poderosa*, a multicoloured wooden sculpture about 1 m (3 ft) high. According to legend, it belonged to a woman who was able to make contact with the dead. Traditional Afro-Cuban events are held in the courtyard.

The museum is being restored, but two rooms linked to a nearby folk art shop are open to the public.

🏛 **Museo Municipal de Guanabacoa**
Calle Martí 108, esq. Versalles.
📞 (7) 979 117. 🕐 10am–6pm Tue–Sat, 9am–1pm Sun.
Annexe Rooms
Calle Martí y Lama. 📞 (7) 979 510.
🕐 9am–5pm Mon–Sat.

Cojímar ❽

Havana. 🏙 20,100.
🚌 ℹ Villa Panamericana, (7) 951 000.

A charming village with one-storey wooden houses – often with a garden, small porch and courtyard at the back – Cojímar was once inhabited only by fishermen. Now there are also many elderly people, including writers and artists, who have chosen to leave the capital for a more peaceful life.

In the 1950s however, there was only one author to be seen on the streets of Cojímar: Ernest Hemingway. Many of

LA VIRGEN DE REGLA

The Virgin of Regla has been the patron saint of fishermen and Havana since 1714. The Neo-Classical sanctuary dedicated to her contains an icon of a dark-skinned Virgin holding a white child that the faithful call "La Negra". The icon's origins are not known but one legend suggests it acquired its colour while being taken across the Black Sea. The statue was brought from Spain by a hermit in 1696, and in the 1900s was watched over by a certain Panchita Cárdenas, whose modest home next to the church is now open to worshippers.

La Virgen de Regla, the protector of fishermen

For followers of *santería* the Virgen de Regla is also Yemayá, the patroness of the sea and mother of all men, to whom food, flowers, candles and sweets are offered. On her feast day (Sep 8) the icon is borne through the town.

The 17th-century fort at Cojímar

the local fishermen were his friends and he liked to play dominoes and drink rum while listening to their stories. He made this village the setting for his famous novel *The Old Man and the Sea*.

In the small square named after Hemingway there is a monument featuring a bust of the author – a faithful copy of the one in El Floridita *(see p72)*. It is here thanks to the author's fishermen friends, who donated anchors, hooks and tools to pay for the casting.

Nearby, on the seafront, is a small fort, which was built as the easternmost defence point of Havana in 1645. It was designed by Giovan Battista Antonelli, architect of the Castillo del Morro *(see p110)*.

Cojímar is also the home of Hemingway's favourite restaurant, La Terraza *(see p269)*. It is still as elegant and well-run as it was during Hemingway's time. The cocktail lounge has a splendid wooden bar and is an ideal spot to enjoy a drink.

Playas del Este ❾

Havana.

HAVANA is one of the few cities in the world to have sizeable beaches only a 20-minute drive from the city centre. The Playas del Este consist of a stretch of about 50 km (31 miles) of fine sand and crystal-clear water, easy to reach via a good, fast road, with hotels, villages and tourist facilities of every kind. The beaches can offer a good compromise for people who want to spend some of their holiday at the seaside during

their visit to Havana. Bear in mind, however, that this area is also a popular haunt of *jineteros (see p292)*, though in places security guards have been drafted in to deter them.

Arriving from central Havana, the first beach is **Bacuranao**, a peaceful spot and a favourite with families. However, the loveliest places on the riviera are **Santa María del Mar** and **Guanabo**. Santa María del Mar is the most popular with tourists. It has the best beach, lined with pine and coconut trees, as well as a good choice of hotels and sports. Guanabo is more traditional, with small houses, restaurants and shops; at weekends this is the liveliest place along the coast when Habaneros arrive by the hundred. The Bajo de las Lavanderas, close to the shore, is a delight for scuba and skin divers, and deep-sea fishing trips can be arranged at the **Marina Veneciana**.

A small island, **Mi Cayito**, lies at the mouth of the Itabo river. There are fine views from Mirador Bellomonte.

One of the Playas del Este beaches popular with Havana residents

PLAYAS DEL ESTE

0 kilometres   1.5
0 miles   1.5

KEY

Major road

Playa El Mégano
Playa Santa María del Mar
Mi Cayito
Playa Boca Ciega
Playa Guanabo
Mirador Bellomonte
Marina Veneciana
HAVANA
VIA BLANCA
Itabo
462
VIA BLANCA
BARRERAS
MINAS
CAMPO FLORIDO

Ernest Hemingway in Cuba

Period print of the Ambos Mundos hotel

THE GREAT AMERICAN AUTHOR fell in love with Cuba on his first visit in 1932, attracted initially by the marlin fishing. It was not until 1939, however, that Hemingway decided to move to the island, initially settling down in the Ambos Mundos hotel in Old Havana *(see p248)*. Having decided to stay on, he found a quiet villa outside the town in which to write, Finca La Vigía, where he lived at first with journalist Martha Gellhorn (whom he married in 1940). His bond with Cuba lasted 20 years, through the Batista period and the beginning of the Revolution, and longer, in fact, than his relationship with Martha Gellhorn. Hemingway's last wife, Mary Welsh (married in 1946), joined the writer in Cuba and lived with him at Finca La Vigía. The villa is now a museum *(p115)*. He eventually returned to the US in 1960, a year before his suicide.

***A lover of cocktails**, Hemingway was a regular at Bodeguita del Medio (see p65) and El Floridita (see p72). Both bars were a stone's throw from his room on the fifth floor of the Ambos Mundos Hotel. The writer helped to invent the daiquiri.*

***Hemingway wrote** his most famous novels in Cuba. He was at Finca La Vigía in 1954 when he found out that he had received the Nobel Prize. "This prize belongs to Cuba, since my works were created and conceived in Cuba, with the inhabitants of Cojímar, of which I am a citizen." With these words, Hemingway placed the prize at the foot of the Madonna del Cobre (see p217).*

A marlin fishing tournament is held every year at the Hemingway Marina.

Gregorio Fuentes

Ernest Hemingway

Martha Gellhorn

THE SEA AND FISHING

Hemingway loved the sea and was passionate about swordfish and marlin fishing. He practised the sport with great commitment and courage – not on a luxury yacht, but on a small fishing boat, the famous *Pilar* – together with a fisherman, Gregorio Fuentes, who also became a good friend. The boat was moored at the picturesque village of Cojímar.

Finca La Vigía ⑩

Calle Vigía y Stheinhard, San Francisco de Paula, Havana. 🚉 *San Francisco de Paula.* 📞 *(7) 910 809.* 🕐 *9am–4pm Wed–Mon; 9am–12:30pm Sun.* 🔴 *1 Jan, 26 Jul, 10 Oct, 25 Dec.* 🗓️🎫📷♿🖥️

A T SAN FRANCISCO DE PAULA, on the outskirts of Havana, is the only residence Ernest Hemingway ever had outside the US. He lived here, in the periods between his various foreign trips, for almost 20 years.

The villa, built in 1887 to a design by Catalan architect Miguel Pascual de Balaguer, was bought by Hemingway in 1939. It was made a public museum in 1962, as soon as news of the writer's suicide in the US reached Cuba.

Everything in the villa is in the same meticulous order it was in when Hemingway lived here. There is his library with its 8,000 books; various hunting trophies from African safaris hanging in the living room; the author's personal possessions, such as his pipes and typewriter, and valuable artworks, including a ceramic medal by Picasso. The fact that all these objects have been left just as they were creates the atmosphere of a lived-in house rather than a museum.

Two curious features in the garden are the cat cemetery (Hemingway had 60 cats during his lifetime), and the *Pilar*, the author's fishing boat, which was transferred from

The façade of Finca La Vigía, surrounded by tropical vegetation

Cojímar to the museum and placed in a specially built pavilion in the garden. The *Pilar* was a comfortable and fast boat made of black American oak, and the author loved ploughing through the waves on fishing expeditions with his friend Gregorio Fuentes. During World War II he used it to patrol the sea north of Cuba, on the lookout for Nazi submarines that were in the area to sink ships laden with sugar intended for the Allied troops.

ENVIRONS: near Hemingway's villa is the village of **Santa María del Rosario**, founded in 1732 by Count Don José Bayona y Chacón on the estate of his large sugar factory. A real gem here is the church of the same name (it is also known as Catedral de los Campos de Cuba), notable for its splendid *mudéjar* ceilings.

The church was designed in 1760–66 by architect José Perera. The austere façade is reminiscent of the Spanish missions in the western US, while the interior contains some unusually lavish elements, such as the extravagantly gilded high altar, and paintings attributed to Nicolás de la Escalera, one of Cuba's early artists.

The living room of Hemingway's villa, with hunting trophies on the walls

Parque Lenin

Calle 100 y Carretera de la Presa, Arroyo Naranjo, Havana. *(7) 443 026-28.* 9am–5pm daily.
ExpoCuba
(7) 549 212. Wed–Sun.
Parque Zoológico Nacional
(7) 447 613. Wed–Sun.

Lᴇɴɪɴ ᴘᴀʀᴋ, 20 km (12 miles) south of Central Havana, occupies an area of 745 ha (1,840 acres). It was created in the 1970s as an amusement park for children and an area of greenery for a city in continuous expansion.

The impressive monument to Lenin designed by Lev Korbel

In the same period, thanks to an initiative by Celia Sánchez, Castro's personal assistant during the Revolution, the Russian architect Lev Korbel designed the vast monument honouring the Soviet leader. The statue of Lenin, which weighs 1,200 tons and is 9 m (30 ft) high, was completed in 1982 under the supervision of Antonio Quintana Simonetti, who also designed the park.

The most enjoyable way of getting around Parque Lenin is to take the narrow-gauge train which follows a route of 9.5 km (6 miles) in 45 minutes, making several stops. The train's old steam engines were used until a few years ago by Cuba's sugar factories to transport sugar cane. New open carriages allow passengers to admire the scenery. The park is popular with Habaneros, who love to walk among the palm, cedar, pine and araucaria trees. There is also a freshwater aquarium, stables, outdoor cinema, art gallery, swimming pools, café and the Las Ruínas restaurant. The latter occupies a 1960s building that incorporates the crumbling walls of an old plantation house.

Environs: near the park, among gardens and tree-lined paths, is the largest exhibition centre in Cuba, **ExpoCuba**, which stages various exhibitions and shows all year round. In autumn the pavilions are occupied by the famous Feria Internacional de La Habana, which offers an overview of Cuba's economic and socio-political life.

From Parque Lenin it is also easy to reach the 340-ha (840-acre) **Parque Zoológico Nacional**, where animals live freely in various natural habitats, often without cages. The savannah area is populated with zebras, hippopotamuses, giraffes and antelope. Another area is the habitat of lions.

Jardín Botánico Nacional ⑫

Carretera del Rocío km 3, Calabazar, Arroyo Naranjo (Havana). *(7) 547 278.* 9am–4:30pm daily.
1 Jan, 26 Jul, 25 Dec.

Tʜɪs ᴇɴᴏʀᴍᴏᴜs 600-ha (1,500-acre) botanical garden, set in an area of woods and cultivated fields, contains plants from all over

The tranquil Japanese Garden, part of the Jardín Botánico Nacional

the world. These are on display to the public and are also studied by specialists. The huge gardens are divided into geographical zones – Cuba, America, Africa, Asia and Oceania. The Caribbean section, which takes up one-fifth of the garden, has 7,000 flowering plants, half of which are unique to Cuba. There are also curiosities such as the Archaic Woods and the Palmetum. The former has plants descended from species that thrived in ancient geological eras, such as the *Palma corcho*, a fossil species that can still be found in the Pinar del Río region. The Palmetum has a large collection of palm trees from all tropical latitudes.

A must is the cactus area near the entrance. However, the most interesting part of this rather sparse park is the Jardín Japonés, a Japanese garden with artificial water-falls and a pond with a gazebo. It was donated to Cuba by the local Asian community in 1989.

Another fascinating sight here is the orchid garden, with numerous varieties.

The Sanctuary of San Lázaro at El Rincón

Santuario de San Lázaro ⓭

Calzada de San Antonio km. 23, El Rincón, Santiago de las Vegas (Havana). ☎ (683) 2396. ☐ 7am–6pm daily. ☩ 9am Wed–Fri, Sun. ☒ Feast Day of St Lazarus, Dec 16 and 17.

THIS SANCTUARY, dedicated to St Lazarus, the patron saint of the sick, lies in the small village of El Rincón, outside Santiago de las Vegas, next to an old lepers' hospital (now a dermatological hospital).

In Afro-Cuban religions Lazarus corresponds to Babalú Ayé. Both saints are represented in folk iconography as old men in tatters and covered with sores. In the case of the African saint, the skin disease was supposedly punishment from Olofi, the father of all the gods *(see p20)*, for the saint's adulterous and libertine past.

On 17 December, the simple white sanctuary welcomes thousands of worshippers, who flock here to make vows or ask the saint to intercede for them. Before the high altar, or in front of the image of St Lazarus (who is called *milagroso*, or "the miraculous one"), at a side altar, pilgrims light candles, leave flowers and make offerings.

The water from the fountain to the right of the sanctuary, considered miraculous by believers, is used to cure diseases and ease pain.

ITALO CALVINO AND CUBA

Santiago de las Vegas, most famous for its San Lázaro sanctuary, was also the birthplace of the great Italian novelist Italo Calvino (1923–1985). His father Mario was an esteemed agronomist who went to Cuba in 1918, following his appointment as director of the Estación Experimental de Santiago de las Vegas. This experimental field station covered 50 ha (123 acres) of land and employed 100 university graduates and 63 office workers. While in Cuba, Mario Calvino found ways of making genetic improvements to sugar cane and introduced new plants, including pumpkin and lettuce. He also worked on tobacco, corn and sorghum, while his wife Eva wrote articles exhorting Cuban women to emancipate themselves and acquire new dignity through education and training. When the Calvino family returned to San Remo in Italy, they took not only a son who would become a great writer, but also mango, avocado, flamboyant, cherimoya and even sugar cane seeds, which they cultivated at the San Remo Experimental Agriculture Station. In 1964 Italo Calvino was named a member of the jury for the Casa de las Américas prize *(see p100)* and visited Cuba, where he returned to his birthplace and also met Che Guevara.

Author Italo Calvino, born at Santiago de las Vegas

The altar of St Lazarus with flowers left by worshippers

HAVANA STREET FINDER

THE PAGE GRID shown on the *Area by Area* map below shows the parts of Havana covered by maps in this section. All map references in this guide refer to the maps in the *Street Finder* section. Addresses are indicated in keeping with the system used in Cuba so that people will understand your requests

Street sign, corner of Calle 13 and Ave de los Presidentes

for information. The street name (and sometimes house number) is followed by either "e/" (*entre*, or "between") and the names of the two streets between which the address you want is located, or "*esq.*" (*esquina*, or "corner") followed by the name of the street on the crossroad where the address is located.

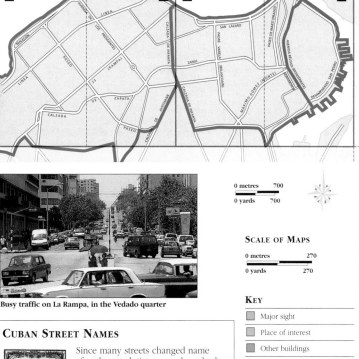

0 metres   700
0 yards   700

SCALE OF MAPS

0 metres   270
0 yards   270

Busy traffic on La Rampa, in the Vedado quarter

CUBAN STREET NAMES

CALLE
HABANA

Tile street sign in Habana Vieja

Since many streets changed name after the revolution, some have both an official name and an unofficial, more commonly used one. Where this occurs in this guide, the latter is followed by the former in brackets. In Vedado the streets are divided into neat 100-m (109-yd) long blocks or *cuadras*. The grid layout of the streets in this district is easy to follow. The streets parallel to the seafront are named with odd numbers, while the cross streets are indicated either with letters (from A to P) or even numbers. Street signs in the form of small stone blocks (see above) give coordinates at every corner.

KEY

- Major sight
- Place of interest
- Other buildings
- **P** Parking
- **H** Tourist information
- Hospital
- Police station
- Church
- Post office
- Coach station
- Train station
- Ferry

Street Finder Index

1

A　　　B　　　C

1

MALECÓN

Casa de las
Américas

VEDADO

2

MALECÓN

PASEO

CVD
Camilo Cienfuegos

LÍNEA

PASEO

Istituto de Cardiología
y Cirugía Cardiovascular

3

LÍNEA

Hospital Peadiátrico
Marfan

Hospital
Gineco-Obstétrico
Ramón González Coro

PASEO

Hospital
Gineco-Obstétrico
Clodomira Acosta

MONTERO
SÁNCHEZ

CRECHERIE

4

PLAZA DE LA REVOLUCIÓN

CALZADA DE ZAPATA

Necrópolis
Colón

5

AVENIDA 26

NUEVO

A　　　B　　　C

D **E** **F** **4**

LA HABANA
DEL ESTE

Castillo de San Salvador
de la Punta

Canal de Entrada

Fortaleza
de San Carlos
de La Cabaña

1

REGLA

CARRETERA DE LOS COCOS

AVENIDA CARLOS M. CÉSPEDES (AVENIDA DEL PUERTO)

MALECÓN
LÁZARO
CAPDEVILA
CÁRCEL

Museo Nacional
de la Música
PEÑA POBRE

REFUGIO
GENIOS
MORRO

COLÓN
Museo de la
Revolución
La Corona

CONSULADO
CHACÓN

TROCADERO
Iglesia
Ángel Custodio
TEJADILLO

ÁNIMAS
Museo Nacional
de Bellas Artes

CUARTELES
TACÓN

CUBA

Catedral +
Seminario
Castillo de la
Real Fuerza
Templete
BARN. LÓPEZ

PLAZA
DE LA
CATEDRAL
PLAZA
DE ARMAS

Bodeguita
del Medio
Museo
de Arte
Colonial
Palacio de los
Capitanes
Generales
JUSTIZ

2

PASEO DE MARTÍ (PRADO)
ZULUETA
AVENIDA DE LAS MISIONES

EMPEDRADO
PROGRESO
Iglesia y Convento
de Santa Teresa
O'REILLY
OBISPO

VIRTUDES

NEPTUNO
Hotel
Inglaterra
Palacio del
Centro
Asturiano
Edificio
Bacardí
VILLEGAS
COMPOSTELA
HABANA
AGUIAR
OBRAPÍA
CUBA
SAN IGNACIO

LA
Casa de la
Obrapía
Casa de
África
MERCEDES
OFICIOS
BARATILLO
CARPINETTI

PLAZA DE
SAN FRANCISCO

Gran Teatro
de La Habana
AGRAMONTE
AVENIDA BÉLGICA (MONSERRATE)
BERNAZA
AGUACATE
LAMPARILLA
AMARGURA

HABANA
Iglesia y Convento
de San Francisco

INDUSTRIA
Capitolio
Iglesia Del Cristo
CRISTO
BRASIL (TENIENTE REY)
PLAZA
VIEJA
CHURRUCA

rtagás
MURALLA

DRAGONES
VIEJA
Fundación
Havana Club

PARQUE DE LA
FRATERNIDAD
VILLEGAS
MURALLA
SOL
SANTA
CLARA
OFICIOS

AGUACATE
PORVENIR
Convento de
Santa Clara
LUZ
INQUISIDOR
SAN PEDRO

GÓMEZ (MONTE)
ECONOMÍA
AGRAMONTE
EGIDO
CURAZAO
LUZ
Iglesia y
Convento
de Belén
COMPOSTELA
ACOSTA
JESUS
SAN IGNACIO
Iglesia del
Espíritu Santo

3

CORRALES
FACTORIA
APONTE
CIENFUEGOS
CÁRDENAS
GLORIA
MISIÓN
PICOTA
MERCED
HABANA
DAMAS
CUBA
Iglesia de
la Merced

RALES
REVILLAGIGEDO
SUÁREZ
APODACA
(SOMERUELOS)
CONDE
BAYONA
LEONOR PEREZ (PAULA)
Iglesia
S. Francisco
de Paula

AGUILA
GLORIA
MISIÓN
ARSENAL
Museo
José Martí
SAN ISIDRO

Bahía de
La Habana

4

FLORIDA
ESPERANZA
SUÁREZ
AVE. DE ESPAÑA (VIVES)
FACTORIA
Estación Central
de Ferrocarriles
DESAMPARADO

RIQUE
PUERTA CERRADA
DIARIA
AGUILA
TALLA PIEDRA

AVENIDA DEL PUERTO

Ensenada de Atarés

ATARÉS

5

D **E** **F**

CUBA REGION BY REGION

Cuba at a Glance

THE LOVELY PALM-FRINGED BEACHES OF CUBA, such as those at Varadero and on Cayo Largo, are famous throughout the world, and justly so. But the interior of the island also offers a variety of unexpected experiences, from mountainous scenery to marshland and freshwater lagoons. The towns are full of interest, often with well-preserved architecture. Cuba really has two capitals. Havana is monumental and maritime, modern and Colonial, and represents the most European spirit of the country. The second, Santiago, embodies the Caribbean soul of Cuba. For the purposes of this guide, the island is divided into five regions – Havana, Western Cuba, Central Cuba – West, Central Cuba – East and Eastern Cuba. Each area is colour coded as shown here.

Varadero (see pp158–9), *known for its clear sea, is a popular holiday resort with sports centres and parks such as the Parque Josone.*

HAVANA

CENTRAL CUBA – WEST
(pp150–173)

WESTERN CUBA
(pp128–149)

The Valle de Viñales (see pp138–9) *has spectacular natural scenery with unique outcrops called* mogotes *and many cave formations. The most significant cave is the Cueva del Indio.*

Cayo Largo del Sur (see pp148–9), *a small island with splendid beaches on the shores of the Caribbean Sea, is a holiday paradise.*

Trinidad (see pp178–86) *is backed by the mountains of the Sierra del Escambray, which can be seen here beyond the Iglesia de San Francisco bell tower.*

◁ **The church and monastery of San Juan de Dios in Camagüey**

Cayo Coco is a natural reserve for flamingos in the Jardines del Rey archipelago (see pp194–5). The coasts, mostly marshland, are dotted with mangrove swamps.

Baracoa (see pp238–9), the isolated, easternmost city in Cuba, is the only one with traces of the island's first inhabitants. Near the town are remnants of the tropical forest that covered the entire island when Columbus first landed here.

CENTRAL CUBA – EAST
(pp174–203)

Camagüey (see pp196–9), in Central-Eastern Cuba, is full of well-preserved Colonial buildings and courtyards, with fine streets and squares such as Plaza San Juan de Dios, seen here.

0 km   90

0 miles   90

EASTERN CUBA
(pp204–241)

Santiago de Cuba (see pp218–27) is a fascinating town built around a bay, with its heart around the Catedral de la Asunción. Every summer Santiago plays host to the liveliest carnival in Cuba, in which the entire local population takes part.

WESTERN CUBA

PINAR DEL RÍO · ISLA DE LA JUVENTUD · CAYO LARGO DEL SUR

T HE WESTERN REGION OF MAINLAND CUBA *is characterized by swathes of cultivated fields and at times extraordinarily beautiful scenery. The main attraction here is the Viñales valley, where unusual limestone outcrops (called* mogotes*) loom over lush fields of tobacco. Off the coast, scattered islands with stunning white beaches offer a peaceful refuge from the bustle of Havana.*

According to the inhabitants of Santiago, Pinar del Río province is the least "revolutionary" part of Cuba. This, the island's most rural region, is populated by white farmers, who have never been known for their warlike passion, although western Cuba was the scene of several battles against the Spanish in the late 1800s, and in 1958 there was a revolutionary front here.

Pinar del Río was colonized in the 16th and 17th centuries by Europeans mainly from the Canary Islands. Historically Pinar has preferred to concentrate its efforts on producing what they claim is the best tobacco in the world. Tobacco fields are scattered among the Sierra del Rosario and Sierra de Organos ranges, which are barely 600 m (1,970 ft) above sea level – not high enough to be considered mountains yet high enough to create a breathtaking landscape. Palm trees mingle with pine trees, and delicate wild orchids thrive where the conditions are right. These low mountains provide excellent walking territory. The Sierra del Rosario is now a UNESCO world biosphere reserve, as is the Guanahacabibes peninsula in the far west. In both areas, the emphasis is placed on conservation-conscious ecotourism.

Ecotourism is less of a priority on Cayo Largo, a long-established island resort with lovely sea and sand, and numerous hotels. This island forms part of the Archipiélago de los Canarreos, in the Caribbean Sea, which is made up of 350 *cayos* or keys. All of these are uninhabited apart from Cayo Largo and Isla de la Juventud (Isle of Youth), a large island with a rich history and the best diving in Cuba.

Miles of white beaches and beautifully clear water at Playa Tortuga, Cayo Largo

◁ **Bike riding in the peaceful Viñales valley; in the background is a typical *mogote***

Exploring Western Cuba

THE EXTRAORDINARY TRANQUILLITY and agreeable climate of Western Cuba make it a lovely area for a relaxing break. However, there is also plenty to do. Besides walking and horse riding, there is the provincial capital of Pinar del Río to explore, while tempting coral beaches are easily accessible off the north coast. More effort is required to reach remote María La Gorda, in the far west, but keen divers are attracted to this up-and-coming diving centre. Isla de la Juventud attracts divers and visitors interested in curious attractions, from painted caves to the one-time prison of Fidel Castro. The Valle de Viñales hotels make the best base for a stay in Western Cuba.

View of a street in Pinar del Río, "the city of capitals"

Farmers with typical ox-drawn carts at the foot of a *mogote*

CAYO LEVISA ●

● CAYO JUTÍAS

VALLE DE VIÑALES ❾

❽ VIÑALES
PARQUE
LA GÜIRA

PINAR DEL RÍO ❼

SAN JUAN Y MARTÍNEZ ●   ❻ VUELTA ABAJO

GUANAHACABIBES RESERVE ⓫

● LA BAJADA

MARÍA ❿ LA GORDA

Schools of tropical fish, easily spotted on the sea bed along the Los Canarreos archipelago

GETTING AROUND

The motorway *(autopista)* connects Havana and Pinar del Río (about a two-hour drive), and another slower, but more picturesque, road follows the northern coastline. From Pinar a road runs southwest to Guanahacabibes. There are one-day tours that start off from Havana and include Soroa, Pinar and Viñales, but not the beaches: information is available at tourist offices. The best way to get to Isla de la Juventud and Cayo Largo is by air from Havana (40 mins). There is also a hydrofoil service to the former from Batabanó; the trip takes two hours. Excursions can also be booked to the two islands; departures are from Havana or larger towns.

SIGHTS AT A GLANCE

HAVANA

ARCHIPIÉLAGO DE LOS CANARREOS

ISLA DE LA
JUVENTUD

● MARIEL

● SAN ANTONIO
DE LOS BAÑOS

● BAHÍA
HONDA

② SIERRA
DEL ROSARIO

① SOROA

● BATABANÓ

● SAN CRISTÓBAL

MASPOTÓN
⑤

ARCHIPIÉLAGO DE LOS CANARREOS

● CAYO ROSARIO

● CAYO RICO

⑬

● CAYO CÁNTILES

*CAYO LARGO
DEL SUR*

SEE ALSO

• *Where to Stay* pp252–3

• *Where to Eat* pp270–71

● NUEVA GERONA

● LA FÉ

● EL
COLONY

PUNTA DEL ESTE ●

⑫

ISLA DE LA JUVENTUD

KEY

▬▬	Motorway
▬▬	Major road
▬▬	Minor road
～～	River
🌿	Viewpoint

0 kilometres   20

0 miles   20

Soroa ❶

Candelaria (Pinar del Río). **Road Map**
A2. 🚉 *Candelaria.* 🛈 *Rumbos, Pinar
del Río, (82) 771 402.*

THE VALLEY ROAD from
Havana to Soroa crosses a
peaceful area of cultivated
fields and rural villages. Soroa
itself lies 250 m (820 ft) above
sea level in the middle of
tropical forest. It was named
after two Basque brothers,
Lorenzo and Antonio Soroa
Muñagorri, who, in around
1856, bought various coffee
plantations in the area and
soon became the proprietors
of the entire territory. One of
the estates in the valley,
Finca Angerona, was
in the 19th century
the setting for a
legendary love story
involving the French-
German Cornelius
Sausse, who built
the farm in 1813,
and a Haitian girl,
Ursule Lambert.
   Soroa, today, is a
small town and a holiday
village (Villa Soroa), with a
number of tourist attractions.
The most photographed is the
Saltón, a spectacular waterfall

**A flower in the Soroa
orchid garden**

on the Manantiales river, a ten-
minute walk from the Villa
Soroa. But the major sight
here is the **Orquideario**, an
orchid garden which has been
declared a national monu-
ment. It has one of the largest
orchid collections in the
world, with more than 700
species, 250 of which are
endemic, in an area of 35,000
ha (86,500 acres). The park,
often visited by Hemingway,
was founded in 1943 by a
lawyer from the Canaries,
Tomás Felipe Camacho. He
had orchids sent here from all
over the world in memory of
his daughter, who had died at
the age of 20 in childbirth.
   Outside the town is the
Castillo de las Nubes,
a medieval-like
construction built in
1940 for Antonio
Arturo Sánchez
Bustamante, the land-
owner of this area.
The Castillo is
now a restaurant
with marvellous
views over the
Sierra del Rosario.

🌸 **Orquideario de Soroa**
Carretera de Soroa km 8. 📞 *(85)
2558.* ⬜ *daily.* 🈺 📷

**Bathing under the falls (*saltón*) of
the Manantiales river at Soroa**

Sierra del Rosario ❷

Pinar del Río. **Road Map** A2.
🛈 *Las Terrazas, Bureau of Ecological
Research; for information, ask the
telephone operator for number 16.*

THIS AREA OF 25,000 ha
(61,750 acres) of unspoilt
Cuba has been declared a
biosphere reserve by UNESCO.
Woods consisting of tropical
and deciduous trees and
plants cover the Sierra del

Beaches of the North Coast

AN ALTERNATIVE ROUTE to the Pinar region from
Havana is the road that skirts the coastline at the
foot of the Guaniguanico mountain range. The drive
from the capital to Viñales, with fine panoramic views
and scenery, takes about five hours. From the
northern coast there is access to the splendid beaches
on some of the small islands in the Los Colorados
Archipelago. For the most part, the locals make their
living by fishing, but the islands have already
attracted some tourism. The sea can be rough and a
general lack of facilities makes this area more suitable
for visitors who love water sports rather than a place
for a relaxing beach holiday.

***Cayo Jutías** is still unspoilt and
frequented more by Cubans than
by tourists. The island is an oasis
of peace and white sand,
populated by many species of
local and migratory birds.*

KEY

🟰 Motorway

➖ Major road

┈┈ Minor road

🚢 Ferry

Cayo Inés de Soto   Cayo Levisa

Cayo Jutías   Puerto
                      Esperanza

Santa Lucía

Minas de
Matahambre   **Around 3 km** (2 miles) from Santa Lucía, which
                has hotel facilities and connections, is a dam
                connecting the mainland with Cayo Jutías.

Rosario range, which is crossed by the San Juan river with its small falls. The area is home to abundant, varied fauna: 90 species of bird as well as many different reptiles and amphibians. The walks here are lovely (permission is needed from the Bureau of Ecological Research), on paths lined with flowers, including wild orchids.

Most of the farmers in the Sierra live in communities founded by a government programme in 1968. The best-known is **Las Terrazas**, whose name derives from the terraces laid out for the pine trees that are now a charac-teristic feature of the area.

The 900 inhabitants

make a living by maintaining the woods and from eco-tourism, which has increased since the building of the environmentally friendly Moka Hotel *(see p252)*. The hotel makes a good starting point for walks in the reserve, all of which are fairly easy and take no more than two hours to cover. Also open is the old, recently restored Buena Vista coffee plantation, which has a restaurant.

For birdwatching, hike along the San Juan river as far as the Cañada del Infierno, a shady pool frequented by local birds such as the *zunzún* hummingbird, the *tocororo* and the *cartacuba (see pp18–19)*.

The well-managed pine forest at Las Terrazas

Cayo Levisa ❸

Pinar del Río. **Road Map** A2. 🚌
from Palma Rubia (1 hr), departure 11:30am, return trip 5pm.
Excursions from Pinar del Río
ℹ️ *Rumbos, Calle Maceo 119 e/ Galeano y San Juan, (82) 778 053.*

THIS SMALL ISLAND, with its white sand beaches, an offshore coral reef and mangroves, is the most geared up for tourists in the Los Colo-rados archipelago, and the only one with diving facilities. Despite this, it is still unspoilt and is home to several species of bird and the surrounding waters have an abundance of fish, especially marlin.

The artificial pool at the heart of the Las Terrazas rural community

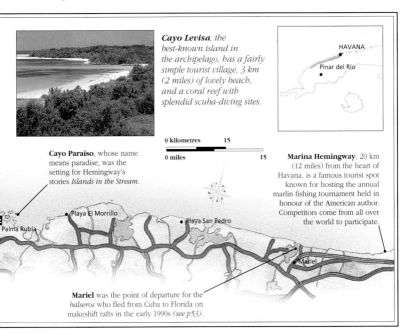

Cayo Levisa, the best-known island in the archipelago, has a fairly simple tourist village, 3 km (2 miles) of lovely beach, and a coral reef with splendid scuba-diving sites.

HAVANA

Pinar del Río

Cayo Paraíso, whose name means paradise, was the setting for Hemingway's stories *Islands in the Stream*.

0 kilometres   15

0 miles   15

Marina Hemingway, 20 km (12 miles) from the heart of Havana, is a famous tourist spot known for hosting the annual marlin fishing tournament held in honour of the American author. Competitors come from all over the world to participate.

Palma Rubia · Playa El Morrillo · Playa San Pedro · Mariel

Mariel was the point of departure for the *balseros* who fled from Cuba to Florida on makeshift rafts in the early 1990s *(see p53)*.

Parque La Güira 4

San Diego de Los Baños (Pinar del Río). **Road Map** A2. 🎿 *3,000.* 🍴 *La Güira Restaurant, (8) 826 11.* ⭕ *daily.* 📷

THE FORMER ESTATE of the landowner Don Manuel Cortina, who was forced to leave Cuba in 1959, this was one of the first properties to be nationalized after Castro's revolution. The large park includes the ruins of a medieval-style residence and an English garden with a small Chinese temple and statues of mythological figures including sphinxes and satyrs. Some of the trees have small treehouses hidden among the foliage which can be rented by anyone keen to live totally surrounded by nature.

About 5 km (3 miles) east of the Güira park is **San Diego de los Baños**, a peaceful village on the slopes of the Sierra de los Quemados, which has retained its original Colonial atmosphere. The village has always been a major tourist and therapeutic centre. The springs in the area produce sulphurous water that helps to cure rheumatism and skin diseases; it is available from the spa facility situated on a hill just outside town.

Don Manuel Cortina also owned a nearby cave, the **Cueva de los Portales**, discovered in the 19th century. This old hiding place was

The entrance to the Cueva de los Portales

The lovely gardens in Parque La Güira

used by the natives as a refuge from the massacres waged by the Spanish in the early 16th century. In more recent times, during the missile crisis, the cave became the headquarters of Che Guevara, some of whose personal belongings and mementoes are on display.

Maspotón 5

Los Palacios (Pinar del Rio). **Road Map** A3. 🍴 *Tourist Centre.* ⬤ *for renovation.*

THE BEST-KNOWN of the many hunting reserves in Cuba, Maspotón includes three lagoons and 61 covers. Besides the endemic birds, migratory birds also come here to escape the cold in North America. Game includes ducks, snipe, pheasants and wild guinea fowl.

Hunting and fishing at Maspotón are regulated. Open season is from October to March, and hunters may not kill more than 40 birds per day. Maspotón's location close to the sea means that fishermen can choose to catch either freshwater or saltwater fish. The hunting lodge hires out all necessary equipment, including everything needed for hunting on horseback, and will also provide hunters with expert guides. Maspotón is a 25-km (15-mile) drive from

A Hoyo de Monterrey cigar band

Pinar del Río by dirt road. The reserve is currently closed to the public because the visitor centre is being renovated. Organized excursions in the nearby area are also available.

Vuelta Abajo 6

Pinar del Río. **Road Map** A3.

THE SMALL AREA between Pinar del Río, San Juan y Martínez and San Luís produces very high quality tobacco. Good growing conditions are the result of a series of factors: for example, the Sierra del Rosario protects the plants from heavy rainfall, and the sandy red soil in which the tobacco plants grow is well drained and rich in nitrogen. This is a unique environment; in fact, the former landowners who left Cuba in 1959 have tried in vain to reproduce the miracle in Nicaragua, Honduras, Santo Domingo and the US.

On the road from the provincial capital to San Juan y Martínez, the prestigious Hoyo de Monterrey plantations can be visited. Here plants are protected from the sun by cotton cloth in order to maintain the softness of the tobacco leaves. There are also the *ranchos*, windowless storehouses where the leaves are left to dry on long poles.

Cuban Tobacco

THE TOBACCO PLANT (*Nicotiana tabacum*) grows from small, round, golden seeds. Cuban tobacco seeds are in demand throughout the world, because their quality is considered to be so good. The plant reaches its full height in the three or four months from November to February. Like cigar-making *(see pp30–31)*, tobacco growing is the result of age-old expertise handed down from generation to generation. Tobacco plants are quite delicate, and need skilful handling. There are two types: *Corojo*, grown in greenhouses, which has the prettiest leaves, selected for use as wrapper leaves for the cigars, and *Criollo*, which grows outdoors and provides the other leaves.

Criollo leaves *are separated into three grades: ligero, seco and volado. The first, which is the best, has the most aromatic leaves, which absorb most sun and are harvested only when completely mature.*

Floating cultivation *is a technique of experimental hydroculture in which the seeds germinate ten days earlier than those grown with traditional methods.*

Poles for transport and drying

Traditional cultivation in rows

TOBACCO HARVEST
Harvesting tobacco is a delicate and laborious operation. The leaves are tied in bunches, hung on horizontal poles and then transported to drying rooms. In the case of the *Corojo* plant, the harvest is carried out in various stages, at intervals of several days.

Drying *takes from 45 to 60 days. The leaves, hung on small poles in storehouses known as* casas del tabaco, *gradually turn from bright green to brown.*

Humidification *is a hydrating process carried out after the drying so that the leaves do not dry out and become brittle. Once sprayed, the bunches of leaves are suspended in order to eliminate excess water.*

By establishing a tobacco monopoly *in 1717, the Colonial authorities obliged farmers to sell all their tobacco to Spain. Now, although the Cuban government allows private tobacco growers to have 7-ha (17-acre) plots, the state is still the sole manufacturer and distributor of cigars.*

Pinar del Río **7**

Road Map A3. 👥 *200,000.*
ℹ️ *Rumbos Cuba, Calle Marti 109,
esq Rafael Ferro, (82) 771 401.* 🚉
🚌 *from Havana.*

In 1778, when the Cuban provinces were founded, the town of Nueva Filipina was renamed Pinar because of a pine grove in the vicinity, on the banks of the Guamá river. Nearby, General Antonio Maceo fought a number of battles in 1896–7 that were crucial to the Cubans' victory in the third war of Cuban independence.

Today, the pines no longer grow here, but the clean air and Colonial atmosphere of Pinar del Río are unchanged. The town has long been a centre for the cultivation and industrial processing of tobacco. The most striking aspect about the historic centre of this small, orderly and peaceful town is the abundance of columns: Corinthian or Ionic, simple or decorated. Not for nothing is Pinar del Río known as the "city of capitals".

The most important buildings lie on the arcaded main street, Calle Martí (or Real). In the **Cultural Heritage Fund** shop, at the corner of Calle Rosario, visitors can buy local crafts as well as art reproductions. In the evening, the **Casa de la Cultura** (at No. 125) hosts shows and concerts of traditional music such as

A capital with bas-relief decoration

punto guajiro (from *guajiro*, the Cuban word for farmer), which is of Spanish derivation, and is generally characterized by improvisation.

At Nos. 172, 174 and 176 in Calle Colón, there are three unusual buildings designed by Rogelio Pérez Cubillas, the city's leading architect in the 1930s and 1940s.

🏛️ **Palacio de Guasch**
Calle Martí, esq.
Comandante Pinares.
Museum 📞 *(82) 3087.*
⏰ *Tue–Sat, Sun am.*
⏺️ *1 Jan, 1 May, 26 Jul, 10 Oct, 25 Dec.* 🈲 🅿️ 📷
This somewhat extravagant building is a mixture of Moorish arches, Gothic spires and Baroque elements. It was built in 1909 for a wealthy physician who had travelled widely and who wanted to reproduce in his new residence the architectural styles that had impressed him the most. After 1959 the mansion was transformed into a Museo de Ciencias Naturales (natural history museum) named after Tranquilino Sandalio de Nodas, a well-known land surveyor in this region. The museum illustrates the natural and geological

One of the three eclectic-style buildings on Calle Colón

THE CENTRE OF PINAR DEL RÍO

Catedral de
    San Rosendro ⑤
Casa Garay ④
Fabrica de Tabacos
    F Donatién ⑥
Museo Provincial
    de História ②
Palacio de Guasch ①
Teatro Milanés ③

0 metres   400
0 yards   400

KEY

🚉 Railway station

🚌 Coach station

ℹ️ Tourist information

The unusual façade of the Palacio de Guasch, Pinar del Río

history of Pinar and has on display stuffed birds and animals, including the tiny Cuban *zunzún* hummingbird, and a crocodile more than 4 m (12 ft long), as well as rare plants and butterflies. In the inner courtyard are sculptures of prehistoric animals.

🏛 Museo Provincial de Historia
Calle Martí 58 e/ Colón y Isabel Rubio.
☎ (82) 754 300. ◯ Tue–Sat, Sun am. ● 1 Jan, 1 May, 26 Jul, 10 Oct, 25 Dec. 🗹 🗹 🗹

This museum illustrates the history of the province from the Pre-Columbian period to the present. On display is a major collection of 19th-century arms, Colonial furniture, works by local painters, including a huge landscape by Domingo Ramos (1955), and mementoes of the musician Enrique Jorrín, the father of the cha-cha-cha.

🎭 Teatro Milanés
Calle Martí y Colón.
☎ (82) 753 871.
● for restoration (phone to check).
A Neo-Classical gem and the city's pride and joy, this theatre is named after the local romantic poet José Jacinto Milanés, who was a senator during the Cuban Republic. It started out as the Lope de Vega theatre, which first opened in 1838 and was then bought in 1880 by one Félix del Pino Díaz. He totally renovated it, modelling it on the Teatro Sauto in Matanzas *(see p154)*.

This simple but functional structure has a rectangular plan, a linear façade and a portico with tall columns. Its opulent, three-level, U-shaped wooden auditorium has a seating capacity of 500.

🎭 Casa Garay
Calle Isabel Rubio 189 e/ Ceferino Fernández y Frank País.
☎ (82) 752 966. ◯ Mon–Fri; Sat every other week. ● 1 Jan, 1 May, 26 Jul, 10 Oct, 25 Dec. 🗹 🗹

Since 1892 the Casa Garay has produced Guayabita del Pinar, a famous liqueur based on an ancient recipe. It is made by distilling brandy from the sugar of the *guayaba* (guava), which is grown in this area.

Guided tours of the small factory finish up at the tasting area, where visitors can try the sweet and dry versions of this popular drink.

🎭 Fabrica de Tabacos Francisco Donatién
Calle Maceo 157 Oeste.
☎ (82) 3424. ◯ Mon–Fri, Sat am. ● 1 Jan, 1 May, 26 Jul, 10 Oct, 25 Dec. 🗹 🗹 🗹

This tiny cigar factory, housed in a former 19th-century hospital, is open to the public. Visitors can watch the 40 or so workers making *veguero* cigars, which are not exported. These and other cigars are sold in the small shop. The factory is also a training school for *torcedores (see p31)*.

Viñales ❽

Pinar del Río. **Road Map** A3.
🚶 4,000. 🚌

VIÑALES, whose name derives from a vineyard planted here by a settler from the Canary Islands, was founded in 1607.

This small town, the economy of which has always been based on agriculture, is now the subject of government protection as an example of a perfectly preserved Colonial settlement. The main street, named after a 19th-century nationalist, Salvador Cisneros Betancourt, is lined with many Colonial houses with characteristic arcades, which make useful shelters from the hot sun and any sudden violent tropical rainstorms.

The town's most important architecture is in the main square, the **Parque Martí**, on which stand the Iglesia del Sagrado Corazón de Jesús (1888), and the former Colonia Española (diplomatic headquarters of the Spanish gentry). This is now the home of the Casa de la Cultura, which offers an interesting programme of cultural activities.

Viñales also boasts a minor architectural gem, the **Casa de Don Tomás**, built in 1887–8 for Gerardo Miel y Sainz, a rich merchant and agent for a shipping line. The building, designed by the Spanish architect Roger Reville, was restored in 1991 and turned into a good fish restaurant *(see p270)*.

The main street in Viñales, with its one-storey porticoed houses

Valle de Viñales ➒

A UNIQUE LANDSCAPE awaits visitors to the Viñales Valley. The *mogotes*, the characteristic, gigantic karst formations that resemble sugar loaves, are like stone sentinels keeping watch over the corn and tobacco fields, the red earth with majestic royal palm trees and the farmhouses with roofs of palm leaves. According to legend, centuries ago some Spanish sailors who were approaching the coast thought the profile of the *mogotes* they glimpsed in the fog looked like a church organ. Hence the name, Sierra de los Organos, given to the network of hills in this area.

A storehouse for drying tobacco near a *mogote*

Sierrita de San Vicente
is famous for its hot springs. A farm near the village breeds gamecocks – cockfighting is still quite popular in Cuba.

Mural de la Prehistoria
On the face of a mogote the Cuban painter Leovigildo González, a pupil of the famous Mexican artist Diego Rivera, painted the history of evolution (1959–62), from ammonites to Homo sapiens. The mural, restored in 1980, makes use of the cracks in the rock to create special effects of light and colour.

KEY

▲ Peak

--- Paved road

=== Path

~~~ River

-·- Underground river

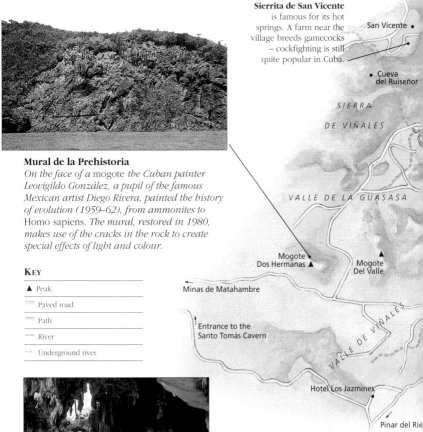

San Vicente •

• Cueva del Ruiseñor

SIERRA DE VIÑALES

VALLE DE LA GUASASA

Mogote Dos Hermanas ▲   ▲ Mogote Del Valle

Minas de Matahambre

Entrance to the Santo Tomás Cavern

VALLE DE VIÑALES

Hotel Los Jazmines

Pinar del Río

Gran Caverna de Santo Tomás
This is the largest network of caves in Cuba and the whole of Latin America. With its 18 km (11 miles) of galleries and up to five levels of communicating grottoes, the Gran Caverna is a speleologist's paradise. In the 19th century, the Cueva del Salón was used by local farmers for festivals.

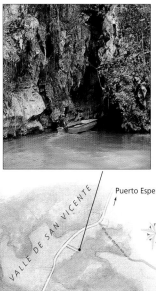

Cueva del Indio
This cave, discovered in 1920, lies in the San Vicente Valley. The first part of the tour here is on foot through tunnels with artificial lighting. Then a small motorboat takes visitors up the underground San Vicente river for about a quarter of a mile.

Puerto Esperanza

VALLE DE SAN VICENTE

La Palma

eva De San Miguel

▲ Mogote La Esmeralda

▲ Mogote De Robustiano

Río Palmarito

▲ Mogote Rustico

• Viñales

• Hotel La Ermita

0 kilometres 1

0 miles 1

Viñales still has a Colonial feel *(see p137)*. It is a tranquil, pleasant little town, ideal for a short stay.

Palenque de los Cimarrones
In the depths of Cueva de San Miguel, past the bar at its mouth, is a spectacular cave that was once a refuge for runaway African slaves (cimarrones). It now houses a small museum and a pleasant restaurant.

THE STRUCTURE OF A MOGOTE

The *mogotes* are among the most ancient rocks in Cuba, and all that remains of what was once a limestone plateau. Over a period lasting millions of years, underground aquifers eroded the softer limestone, giving rise to large caverns whose ceilings later collapsed. Only the hard limestone pillars, or present-day *mogotes*, were left standing. *Mogotes* generally have only a thin covering of soil, but those in the Sierra de los Organos are covered with thick vegetation. Some endemic plant species have adapted to life on their craggy crevices; these include the mountain palm tree *(Bombacopsis cubensis)*, and the corch palm *(Microcycas calocoma)*.

Limestone wall of the ancient cave

Thick vegetation on the sides

Friable terrain

The jetty at María La Gorda, the departure point for boats taking people to dive sites

María La Gorda ⑩

Pinar del Río. ℹ *María La Gorda Diving Centre, La Bajada, (82) 778 131, 778 077.*

THE BEST-KNOWN BATHING SPOT on the southwestern coast owes its name to a sad legend. A few centuries ago, a plump *(gorda)* girl named María was abducted by pirates on the Venezuelan coast and then abandoned here. In order to survive, she was forced to sell herself to the buccaneers who passed by. The place still bears her name today.

The extraordinary beauty of the coral reefs – populated by sea turtles, reef sharks and other rare species of tropical fish – makes these 8 km (5 miles) of coastline with fine

white sand and a warm, translucent sea a real tropical aquarium. The reefs are also easy to reach, lying just a short distance from the shore (the coral and fish can even be seen without swimming under water).

From the jetty opposite the diving area, a boat with a doctor on board takes divers twice a day to the various dive sites. Areas of particular interest include the so-called Black Coral Valley, a wall of coral over 100 m (328 ft) long, and the Salón de María, a sea cave at a depth of 18 m (60 ft), which is the habitat of rare species of fish.

Guanahacabibes Reserve ⑪

Pinar del Río. **Excursions** *from Pinar del Río.* ℹ *Rumbos, Calle Maceo 119, Pinar del Río, (82) 778 053.* ☑

A *cotorra,* **a species of parrot seen in the reserve**

THE PENINSULA of Guanahacabibes, named after a Pre-Columbian ethnic group, is a strip of land 100 km (62 miles) long and 6–34 km (4–21 miles) wide. In 1985 it was declared a world biosphere reserve by UNESCO, to protect the flora and fauna.

Access to the inner zone, in the vicinity of La Bajada, is therefore limited. Permission to visit is granted by the Pinar del Río forest rangers at the tourist offices in local hotels, and visits to the park are made in jeeps with a local guide.

The mixed forest of deciduous and evergreen trees contains about 600 species of plants and many animals, including deer, boar, reptiles and *jutías,* rodents similar to opossums that live in trees. Among the bird species are woodpeckers, parrots, hummingbirds, *cartacuba* and *tocororo (see p18).*

Cabo San Antonio, the western tip of Cuba, is identifiable by the Roncalli lighthouse, built in 1849 by the Spanish governor, after whom it was named.

Cabo Corrientes at the southern end of the Guanahacabibes reserve

◁ **The Valle de Viñales with** *bohíos,* **farmers' houses characteristic of rural Cuba**

Diving in the Caribbean Sea

THE CARIBBEAN sea beds off the island of Cuba offer some of the most exciting coral reef scenery imaginable. The coral formations lie at a maximum depth of 150 m (495 ft), at an average temperature of about 23° C (73 °F), and never less than 18° C (64 °F). The most fascinating areas for

A scuba diver surrounded by a school of grunts

divers are situated at María la Gorda, the Archipelago de los Canarreos, Playa Santa Lucía and Jardines de la Reina. Qualified scuba-diving centres *(buceo)* take visitors on trips out to the reefs. In some areas it is possible to see tropical fish and coral simply by snorkelling *(see p285)*.

Sea plume is a type of gorgonia that looks much like a feather.

"Soft coral" results from an evolutionary process during which the hard skeleton turns into a flexible structrure.

The grouper, *with its unmistakable colouring, is one of the most common fish in the Caribbean, together with the queen triggerfish and the* Pomacanthus paru *angelfish. Other widespread species are the tarpon, with its silvery colouring, and the barracuda, with its powerful teeth. Sharks are less common.*

Sponge

The blue surgeon fish is born with bright yellow colouring that later turns blue.

Coral

THE SEA FLOOR

The coral reef is a rich and complex ecosystem. The Caribbean sea beds are home to numerous varieties of coral and a great many sea sponges and gorgonias, as well as tropical fish, sea turtles and various crustaceans.

Brain coral *is one of many types of coral common to the Cuban seas, along with black coral, iron wire coral with its rod-like structure, and elkhorn coral with its flat branches.*

Tubular sponges *vary in size, the largest ones being 2 m (6 ft) high. If they are squeezed or stepped on they emit a purple dye that will stain your skin for several days. There are also barrel- and vase-shaped sponges.*

Gorgonian sea fans (Gorgonia ventalina) *are quite widespread on Caribbean sea beds. It is possible to see splendid examples of huge proportions.*

Isla de la Juventud

Billboard welcoming visitors to Nueva Gerona

THE NATURALIST Alexander von Humboldt *(see p181)* described this island as an abandoned place, Robert Louis Stevenson called it *Treasure Island*, the dictator Batista wanted to turn it into a paradise for rich Americans, and Fidel Castro repopulated it with young people, and changed its name to the Isla de la Juventud (youth). With a surface area of 2,200 sq km (850 sq miles) and 86,000 inhabitants, this is the largest island in the Archipiélago de los Canarreos. Comparatively few tourists venture to the island, but there are a few interesting sights and the diving is excellent.

Nuestra Señora de los Dolores, in Nueva Gerona

Nueva Gerona

The capital of the island is a small and peaceful town. Surrounded by hills that yield multicoloured marble, Nueva Gerona was founded in 1828 on the banks of the Las Casas river by Spanish settlers who, together with their slaves, had left countries on the American continent that had won their independence.

The town is built on a characteristic grid plan (intersecting and parallel streets, with a main avenue and a central square) and the modern outskirts are in continuous expansion.

A good starting point for a visit to Nueva Gerona is **Calle 39**, the graceful main street flanked by coloured arcades. Here can be found the local cinema, theatre, pharmacy (which is always open), post office, hospital, bank, Casa de la Cultura, tourist office and bars and restaurants.

This street ends at the Parque Central, Nueva Gerona's main square, where the **Iglesia de Nuestra Señora de los Dolores** stands. First built in Neo-Classical style in 1853, this church was totally destroyed by a cyclone in 1926 and rebuilt three years later in Colonial style.

South of the Parque Central, the former City Hall building is now the home of the **Museo Municipal**, or town museum. This has on display many objects and documents concerning pirates and buccaneers – the main protagonists in the island's history – as well as the inevitable photographs and mementoes of the revolution. There is another museum in town that is dedicated solely to the struggle against Fulgencio Batista's dictator-ship: the **Museo de la Lucha Clandestina**.

Lastly, another must for visitors is the **Museo de Ciencias Naturales**, the natural history museum. The geological and natural history of the island is illustrated and there is also a fine Planetarium, the only one in the world in which the North Star can be seen together with the Southern Cross.

The harbour at Nueva Gerona, where fishermen moor their boats

KEY

▬▬	Motorway
▬▬	Major road
▬▬	Minor road
▭▭	Unpaved road
✕	Domestic airport
🚢	Ferry
🏖️	Recommended beach
⋔	Pre-Columbian site
𐬾	Viewpoint

The monumental façade of the Presidio Modelo prison

🏛 Museo Municipal de Nueva Gerona

Calle 30 e/ 37 y Martí.
📞 *(46) 323 791.*
🕑 *Tue–Sat, Sun am.*
🛇 ✦ ◎

🏛 Museo de Ciencias Naturales

Calle 41, esq. 54.
📞 *(46) 323 143.*
🕑 *Tue–Sat, Sun am.*
● *1 Jan, 1 May, 26 Jul, 10 Oct, 25 Dec.* 🛇 ✦ ◎

Strolling along the arcades on Nueva Gerona's Calle 39

♟ Presidio Modelo

4 km southeast of Nueva Gerona, Reparto Delio Chacon. 📞 *(46) 325 112.* 🕑 *Tue–Sat, Sun am.* ● *1 Jan, 1 May.* 🛇 ✦ ◎

On the road that connects the capital with Playa Bibijagua, a popular beach of black sand frequented by the inhabitants of Nueva Gerona, is Cuba's most famous penitentiary. Originally built by Machado, it was modelled on the famous one in Joliet, Illinois (US) and converted into a museum in 1967. The prison consists of tiny cells in the interior of four enormous multi-storeyed round cement blocks. In the middle of each stood a sentry-box from which guards could keep a close watch on all the prisoners. Guards and prisoners never came into contact with one another. Guards circulated in underground galleries, keeping constant watch over the prisoners above.

It was in the Presidio that the organizers of the attack on the Moncada army barracks in Santiago, led by Fidel Castro, were imprisoned in October 1953. They were liberated two years later, in May 1955.

At the entrance to the first pavilion is cell 3859, where Castro, despite his isolation, managed to reorganize the revolutionary movement, starting with the defence plea he made in court, *History Will Absolve Me* (see p47).

Exploring Isla de la Juventud

U NLIKE OTHER ISLANDS in the Archipelago de los
Canarreos, there are no grand luxury hotels on the
Isla de la Juventud. As a result it seems to have a more
genuine Cuban atmosphere, and the tourist industry
works alongside other island activities without pressure.
The island is not new to habitation, unlike other *cayos*
which have only recently seen housing development,
and retains vestiges of five centuries of Cuban history.
The town of Nueva Gerona and its surroundings make a
good starting point for a visit, followed by the southern
coast. The main hotels are in the southwestern part of
the island, while the eastern tip has some fascinating
ancient cave paintings by Siboney Indians.

**Coral formations on the island's
sea floor**

🏛 Finca El Abra

Carretera Siguanea km 1.5 (5 km
southwest of Nueva Gerona).
◻ Mon–Sat, Sun am. ● 1 Jan,
1 May, 26 Jul, 10 Oct, 25 Dec.
🔲 🔲 🔲

On the edge of the Sierra de
las Casas is an elegant villa
where, in 1870, the 17-year-
old José Martí was held for
nine weeks before being
deported to Spain for his
separatist views. Part of the
building is now a museum
with a display of photographs
and documents relating to the
national hero's presence on
the island. The rest of the
villa is occupied by the
descendants of the original
owner, a rich Catalan.

Nearby is the vast Parque
Natural Juan Antonio Mella,
which has a botanical garden,
a zoo, an amusement park, an
artificial lake, and a viewpoint
overlooking the entire island.
To the south the Ciénaga de
Lanier is visible, a marshy
area in the middle of which is
the village of Cayo Piedra.

Hotel Colony

📞 (46) 398 181. 🚌 to the Centro
de Buceo, daily at 9am, return trip
at 4:30–5pm.

This low-rise hotel *(see p253)*
– a landmark for all scuba
divers on the island – blends
in well with the natural environment. The nearby sea is
green and translucent, with a
sandy floor that is often
covered with swathes of the
submerged marine aquatic
plant *Thalassia
testudinum*.

The hotel overlooks
Playa Roja, the large,
palm-shaded beach
where an important
diving centre, the
**Centro Inter-
nacional de Buceo**,
is also located.

In the mornings a van takes
guests from the Hotel Colony
to the diving centre, where all
kinds of diving equipment can
be rented (although it is
advisable to take a 3 mm
wetsuit and an oxygen tank
or bottle with you), and which

A hotel sign

provides boats to take visitors
to the dive sites. At noon,
lunch is served at the Ranchón,
a restaurant on a platform on
piles connected via a pontoon
to a beach at Cabo Francés.

The 52 dive sites, between
Cabo Francés and Punta
Pardenales, lie at the end of a
shelf which gently slopes
down from the coast
to a depth of 20–25 m
(65–82 ft), and then
abruptly drops for
hundreds of metres.
This vertical wall is a
favourite with passing
fish, which literally rub
shoulders with divers.

While dives on the
platform can be made
by beginners, those
along the shelf are
more difficult and suited to
divers with more experience.

Among the most fascinating
dives are: the one at La Pared
de Coral Negro, which has an
abundance of black coral as
well as sponges as much as
35 m (115 ft) in diameter; El
Reino del Sahara, one of the
most beautiful shallow dives;
El Mirador, a wall dive among
sponges and large madre-
pores; and El Arco de los
Sábalos, which is the domain
of tarpons. At Cayo Los Indios
shipwrecks can be seen on
the sea bed at a depth of
10–12 m (33–40 ft).

There are also two
wonderful boat trips that
can be made from the Hotel
Colony. One goes to the
Península Francés, which is
better known as **Costa de
los Piratas**. This is a paradise
for divers because of its
wonderfully colourful and

The Hotel Colony, surrounded by tropical vegetation

View of Punta del Este beach with its white sand and crystal-clear sea

varied underwater flora and fauna. A variety of other activities can also be enjoyed here, including water skiing, surfing, sailing, deep sea fishing and even horse riding.

The second excursion goes to **Cocodrilo**, formerly called Jacksonville. This traditional fishing village was founded in the early 20th century by a small community of emigrants from the British colony of the Cayman Islands. In fact, there are still a few inhabitants who speak English as their first language.

The settlers at Cocodrilo introduced a typical Jamaican dance known as the Round Dance, which blended with a variation of traditional Cuban *son* music (the *Son Montuno*), has resulted in the creation of a new and interesting dance which is highly popular among the locals, who call it the Sucu-Sucu.

Pre-Columbian drawings which may represent a calendar, in the Cuevas del Este

☖ Cuevas de Punta del Este
59 km (37 miles) southeast of Nueva Gerona. **☖** *Rentamicar, Nueva Gerona, (46) 324 432.*
Punta del Este, on the southeastern tip of the island, has a stunning white sand beach. It is however, most famous for its seven caves, which were discovered in 1910 by a French castaway who took refuge here. On the walls of the caves are 235 drawings made by Siboney Indians in an age long before the arrival of Christopher Columbus.

The drawings in the largest cave – a series of red and black concentric circles crossed by arrows pointing eastward – probably represent a solar calendar. The complexity of these drawings led the Cuban ethnologist Fernando Ortíz, who studied them in 1925, to call them "the Sistine Chapel of the Caribbean". Protect yourself against mosquitoes – the caves are full of them.

HISTORY OF THE ISLAND

The corsair Sir Francis Drake

The Taíno and Siboney peoples knew of the Isla de la Juventud *(see p38)* long before Columbus "discovered" it in 1494 on his second journey. The Spanish crown licensed the island to cattle breeders, but in practice handed it over to pirates. Because of the shallow waters, heavy Spanish galleons were unable to approach the island, while the buccaneers' light vessels could land there. This meant that such mythical figures as Francis Drake, Henry Morgan, Oliver Esquemeling and Jacques de Sores were able to exploit it as a hiding place for booty captured from Spanish ships.

After Nueva Gerona was founded (1828), the island was used as a place of detention for Cuban nationalists, including José Martí. Its use as a prison island continued for 50 years in the 20th century; construction of the Presidio Modelo began in 1926. In 1953 Batista turned the island into a free zone where money could be laundered. The dictator also wanted to turn it into a holiday paradise for rich Americans, but his plans failed. On New Year's night in 1958, as Castro's *barbudos* were entering Havana, a group of soldiers in the rebels' army took over the island during the opening ceremony of the Hotel Colony, and arrested the mafiosi in the hotel.

In 1966, after a devastating cyclone, the Cuban government decided to plant new citrus groves on the island which would be worked by students from Cuba and around the world. The idea was such a success that in ten years the island's population grew from 10,000 to 80,000.

An old map of Isla de la Juventud from the Museo Municipal of Nueva Gerona

Cayo Largo del Sur ⑬

The Cayo Largo logo

Tʜɪs ɪsʟᴀɴᴅ ɪs a wonderful holiday destination for those who love sun, sea and sand. It is 25 km (15 miles) long and has a surface area of 37.5 sq km (15 sq miles). There are no extremes of climate here. It rains very little, the temperature is 24° C (75° F) in winter and less than 30° C (86° F) in summer, the coast is flat, the sand as white and fine as talcum powder, and the sea is clear and calm. It is safe for scuba diving, and the island offers other sporting activities such as horse riding, sailing, tennis and surfing. And if you prefer not to swim, you can walk for miles in the shallow water. There are no villages except those built for tourists, with recently built, comfortable hotels, as well as restaurants, bars, discos and swimming pools.

View of Playa Tortuga

Marina Cayo Largo
is the point of departure for boat trips to several scuba diving sites. In shallow water there are coral gardens populated by multicoloured fish, and a black coral reef 30 km (19 miles) long. Fishing equipment can be hired in the water sports centre.

★ Playa Sirena
This 2.3-km (1.5-mile) beach is very tranquil: sheltered from the wind, the sea is calm all year round.

Combinado is a marine biology centre which is open to the public.

Playa Paraíso is very secluded, making nude sunbathing possible.

Isla del Sol   Las Piedras

Playa Lindamar is a shell-shaped beach, 5 km (3 miles) long, sheltered by white rocks, with many hotels, holiday villages and bathing facilities.

STAR SIGHTS

★ Playa Sirena

★ Playa Los Cocos

★ Playa Tortuga

Holiday Villages
Exclusive holiday resorts, with family bungalows and cottages, are concentrated on the southwestern coast. Right, the Villa Iguana (see p252).

VISITORS' CHECKLIST

Archipiélago de los Canarreos (Isla de la Juventud). **Road Map** B3. 🏯 *500.* ✈ *Vilo Acuña, (45) 248 205.* ⓘ *Abatur, (45) 248 241; Cubatur, Hotel Isla del Sur (45) 482 18; Havanatur (45) 482 15; Rumbos, (45) 483 27.* **Excursions** *from Marina Cayo Largo: departure in the morning, return at sunset.*

★ **Playa Tortuga**
This beach in the eastern part of the island is popular with nature lovers: it is a nesting area for marine turtles and has become a natural reserve for Chaelonidae (species of marine turtle), which are also raised at Combinado.

KEY

▬	Major road
▬	Minor road
═	Unpaved road
🛧	International airport
🏖	Beach
⛴	Ferry

Playa Los Pinos

CAYO LARGO

0 km 1

0 miles 1

Playa Blanca, surrounded by white rocks, is the longest beach on the island (7.5 km/5 miles). It also offers some of the best tourist facilities.

★ **Playa Los Cocos**
The coconut palms along the shore provide some shade here and the shallow water makes it ideal for children. The nearby coral reefs and shipwrecks attract scuba divers.

An iguana in Cayo Iguana

VISITING THE NEARBY ISLANDS

The small *cayos* nearby offer many natural attractions. Cayo Rico, an island surrounded by brilliant green water and fringed with beaches of sand as fine as sugar, is only a few minutes away by boat. The sea beds, which are especially rich in lobsters and molluscs, are fascinating and can be admired from glass-bottomed boats. While various species of fish abound at Cayo Rosario, which is a scuba diver's dream, the only inhabitants of Cayo Iguana, just off the western tip of Cayo Largo, are the harmless iguanas, which can be as much as 1 m (3 ft) long. Cayo Pájaro is the craggy habitat of ocean birds, while Cayo Cantiles, rich in flowers, birds and fish, is also home to several species of monkey.

CENTRAL CUBA – WEST

THE CENTRAL-WESTERN *provinces are the rural heart of Cuba, with cultivated fields and a gentle landscape, even where the plain gives way to the Sierra del Escambray. Apart from Varadero, the famous holiday resort, the main attractions in this region are two lively towns – Santa Clara and Cienfuegos – and the natural scenery of the Zapata peninsula and the Escambray mountains.*

In 1509, while circling Cuba, the Spanish navigator Sebastián Ocampo caught sight of a bay on the northern, Atlantic coast inhabited by Siboney Indians. Their land was requisitioned almost immediately and assigned to settlers from the Canary Islands. The Indians opposed this injustice so fiercely that the city of Matanzas, which was built in that bay in the 1600s, probably owes its name to the memory of a massacre *(matanza)* of Spaniards by the natives.

Another bay, on the south coast, was sighted by Columbus in 1494. The Jagua Indians living there were later wiped out, but it wasn't until 1819 that Cienfuegos was founded by Catholic settlers from the former French colonies of Haiti and Louisiana, who were granted this territory to counterbalance the massive presence of African slaves. From the mid-1500s to the mid-1700s, both coasts in this region had to face the serious threat of pirate raids, against which the many redoubts, citadels and castles that are still visible along the coastline had very little effect. As a result, in 1689, 20 families from the village of Remedios, not far from the sea, decided to move to the interior, to be at a safe distance from the buccaneers' ships and cannons. In this way the city of Santa Clara was founded.

Santa Clara, capital of Villa Clara province, holds a special place in Cuban hearts since it was the setting for heroic acts by Che Guevara and his *barbudos*. On 28 December 1958, they captured the area after what was to be the last battle of the revolution (see p48) before Batista fled.

A typical wooden house along the Punta Gorda peninsula, Cienfuegos

◁ **Varadero, extremely popular with international holidaymakers**

Exploring Central Cuba – West

THIS PART OF CUBA boasts some exceptional attractions: the beaches of Varadero – perhaps the best and certainly the most well-equipped in Cuba – and the swamp *(ciénaga)* of Zapata, a nature reserve which is particularly good for birdwatching. Cienfuegos, Matanzas and Santa Clara are all appealing towns, this last a must for those interested in Che Guevara's life. A good route for a tour could begin with Matanzas and Varadero, before turning south to Cienfuegos, perhaps via the Península de Zapata. From there it is an easy ride to Santa Clara and beyond to Remedios.

Aerial view of Cayo Libertad, off the coast of Varadero

One of the bronze statues by Rita Longa in the reconstruction of the Indian village at Guamá

GETTING AROUND

The provinces of Central Cuba – West are traversed by the Carretera Central; although the motorway (Autopista Nacional) which links Havana and Santa Clara is a much faster (though less scenic) road. The railway line connecting Havana to Santiago passes through Matanzas and Santa Clara, while another links Havana and Trinidad via Cienfuegos. There are also daily return flights from Havana to Cienfuegos, Varadero and Santa Clara. For visitors with limited time, it may be best to go on an organized tour. These typically cover a province or a few cities, and include visits to parks.

SIGHTS AT A GLANCE

The arcades of the Prado with Corinthian columns in Cienfuegos

Iglesia de San Juan Bautista, the cathedral of Remedios

0 kilometres   30

0 miles   30

SAGUA LA GRANDE ●

CARRETERA CENTRAL

CAYOS DE LA HERRADURA

⑪ REMEDIOS

SANTA CLARA ⑨

CIENFUEGOS ⑦

⑧ JARDÍN BOTÁNICO SOLEDAD

⑩ SIERRA DEL ESCAMBRAY

Sancti Spíritus

● LAGO HANABANILLA

Trinidad

SEE ALSO

• *Where to Stay* pp253–7

• *Where to Eat* pp271–2

KEY

▦	Motorway
▬	Major road
▭	Minor road
～	River
✳	Viewpoint

Villa Clara

Historia viva   Decisión   Victoria

Signpost at the entrance to the province of Villa Clara

Matanzas ❶

Stained-glass window, Triolet pharmacy

S ITUATED ON THE SHORES of a large bay, Matanzas is the capital of the province of the same name. It is a major industrial town, with the fourth most important port in the world for sugar exports. Because of the many bridges over the Yumurí and San Juan rivers, linking the historic centre to the various quarters of Matanzas and its two suburban districts (Versalles and Pueblo Nuevo), the city has been called the "Creole Venice", a match for the no less ambitious "Athens of Cuba". These two names date back to the 19th century, when the artistic and cultural life of the city, the hub of a flourishing agricultural region, outshone that of Havana.

Teatro Sauto in Matanzas with its beautiful wood-panelling

The Centre of Matanzas

The streets in Matanzas are officially indicated by a number, but in practice their Colonial names are still commonly used.

The historic centre can be seen in a few hours. A good place to start is **Plaza de la Vigía**, connected to the outskirts by the Concordia and Calixto García bridges. In the square is the statue of an unknown soldier of the wars of independence, and around it stand several of the city's key sights: the Neo-Classical fire station (1898), the Palace of Justice (1826), the Museo Provincial, the Sauto Theatre and Ediciones Vigía.

🏛 Museo Provincial

Calle Milanés, e/ Magdalena y Ayllon.
📞 (45) 243 464. 🕐 Tue, Fri, Sat;
Sun am. ⬤ 1 Jan, 1 May, 26 Jul,
10 Oct, 25 Dec. 🖼 🎫 📷
This museum occupies the Palacio del Junco, a bright blue porticoed building constructed in 1835–40.

The collection includes documents and objects concerning the history of the province from the Pre-Columbian period to 1959. The section devoted to the Colonial period, with documents on slavery and sugar cane farm tools, is of particular interest. Copies of *Aurora*, the most interesting Cuban periodical of the 19th century, are also on display.

🎭 Teatro Sauto

Calle Magdalena y Milanés.
📞 (45) 242 721. 🕐 Tue–Sun.
⬤ Dec 20–Jan 5. 🖼 🎫 📷
The pride and joy of the city, this theatre was designed by the Italian architect Daniele Dell'Aglio, who was also responsible for the church of San Pedro in the Versalles district. On 6 April 1863 the auditorium was opened to the public as the Esteban Theatre, in honour of the provincial governor who had financed the construction. It was later renamed the Sauto Theatre because of the Matanzeros' affection for the local pharmacist, Ambrosio de la Concepción Sauto, a passionate theatre-goer. He was famous for having cured Queen Isabella II of Spain of a skin disease, using a lotion he had himself prepared.

A solidly built Neo-Classical structure with several Greek-inspired statues made of Carrara marble, the theatre has various frescoes of Renaissance inspiration, executed by the architect Dell'Aglio himself. The U-shaped interior is almost entirely covered with wood-panelling.

Because of its exceptional acoustics, the versatile theatre has been the chosen venue for all kinds of shows and great 19th- and 20th-century Cuban artists have appeared here. World-famous performers have included actress Sarah Bernhardt (in *Camille* in 1887), ballet dancer Anna Pavlova and the guitarist Andrés Segovia.

THE DANZÓN

In the 19th century two composers, José White and Miguel Failde, were born in Matanzas, which was at that time a major cultural centre. In 1879 the latter composed *Las Alturas de Simpson*, which introduced a new musical genre to Cuba, the Danzón. This Caribbean and Creole adaptation of European country dancing became the most popular dance on the island for about fifty years. It is still danced

Period print of people dancing the Danzón

in Matanzas, in the Casa del Danzón, the house where Failde was born, which is now a music museum.

Bookbinding at the Ediciones Vigía publishing house

Ediciones Vigía
Calle Magdalena 1, Plaza de la Vigía.
(45) 244 845. ☐ Mon–Sat. ● 1 Jan, 1 May, 26 Jul, 10 Oct, 25 Dec.
This publishing house's products are entirely hand-crafted – duplicated, painted and bound – on special untreated or recycled paper. Visitors can watch the various stages of production and buy books (on poetry, theatre and history) by Cuban and foreign authors, as well as periodicals.

Parque Libertad
Calle Milanés, an important commercial street, leads to the city's other large square, Parque Libertad (formerly the parade ground), where military parades were held in the 1800s. The square was built on the site of the Indian village of Yacayo. In the

middle of the plaza is an impressive statue of José Martí, surrounded by some attractive buildings: the Liceo Artístico y Literario (1860); the Casino Español, built in the early 1900s; the Palacio del Gobierno; the **Catedral de San Carlos**, dating from the 17th century but mostly rebuilt in the 19th century; and, next to Hotel El Louvre, the Museo Farmacéutico Ernesto Triolet.

Museo Farmacéutico Ernesto Triolet
Calle Milanés 4951, e/ Santa Teresa y Ayuntamiento. (45) 243 179.
☐ daily.
This fine example of a 19th-century pharmacy, overlooking Parque Libertad, was founded on 1 January 1882 by Ernesto Triolet and Juan Fermín de Figueroa and turned into a museum in 1964.

On the wooden shelves stand the original French porcelain vases decorated by hand, others imported from the US, and an incredible quantity of small bottles with herbs, syrups and elixirs. The museum also has a collection of three million old labels, mortars and stills, and advertising posters boasting

about the miraculous curative powers of Dr Triolet's remedies. The façade of the pharmacy faces the square.

The shop also serves as a bureau of scientific information, with more than a million original formulae and extremely rare books on botany, medicine, chemistry and pharmaceuticals, in several foreign languages.

The wooden shelves at the Museo Farmacéutico Ernesto Triolet

MATANZAS TOWN CENTRE

Catedral de San Carlos ⑤
Ediciones Vigía ④
Museo Farmacéutico Ernesto Triolet ⑥
Museo Provincial ②
Parque Libertad ⑦
Plaza de la Vigía ①
Puente Concordia ⑧
Teatro Sauto ③

KEY
Hershey station (p156)
Church
Tourist information

The Bacunayagua bridge, 110 m (360 ft) high, spanning the Yumurí river

Valle de Yumurí ❷

Matanzas. **Road Map** B2.

THE BACUNAYAGUA BRIDGE, 7 km (4 miles) west of Matanzas, is a fine work of Cuban engineering. At 110 m (360 ft), it is the highest bridge in Cuba. Built over the Yumurí river in the early 1960s, it offers lovely views of the peaceful, wooded valley below, which can be reached via a road running parallel to the river.

This attractive area of undulating land dotted with royal palm trees is well known for its many centres and clinics specializing in treatments for stress, asthma and high blood pressure. From the Monserrat hill,

where the Nuestra Señora de Monserrat Sanctuary is located, there is a fabulous view of the bay of Matanzas.

Legends vary concerning the origins of the word "Yumurí". The most fantastic associates it with the lamentation of the Indians massacred by the

A huge limestone formation in the Cuevas de Bellamar

Spanish. Another version came in a letter written by the Swedish writer Fredrika Bremer, who visited Cuba in the late 19th century. According to her, in order to escape from slavery, Siboney Indians used to commit suicide by throwing themselves into the river while screaming "*Yo morí*" (I am dying).

Cuevas de Bellamar ❸

Carretera de las Cuevas de Bellamar, Matanzas. **Road Map** B2.
◯ *daily.*

DISCOVERED BY CHANCE in 1861 by a slave who was surveying the terrain in search of water, the fascinating Bellamar caves lie just 5 km (3 miles) southeast of Matanzas.

Only the first 3 km (2 miles) of these extensive caves have been explored to date, and expert speleologists say there are still many surprises in store. Access to the public, with a specialist guide, is limited to the first 1,500 m (5,000 ft) of the caves. This stretch includes caves and galleries covered with crystal formations in intriguing shapes. The temperature is a constant 26° C (79° F), thanks to the continuous seepage of the cave walls. This impressive tour (available

THE HERSHEY TRAIN

The small Hershey electric train

The first stretch of the Hershey rail line, inaugurated in 1916, connected the Hershey sugar factory and the village of Canasí, both near the coast west of Matanzas. The electrical system was one of the first in Cuba. In 1924 there were 38 pairs of trains, though only four covered the full distance between Havana and Matanzas. Today, the Hershey train links Casablanca (*see p111*) and Matanzas (*pp154–5*) via beautiful scenery, covering 89 km (55 miles) in 3 hours 20 minutes, with frequent stops.

daily) goes 26 m (85 ft) below sea level, and visitors can see marine fossils dating from 26 million years ago. Trained speleologists are allowed to enter a cave that is 50 m (164 ft) below sea level.

At Varadero guided tours of the Bellamar caves can be booked at the larger hotels.

Varadero ❹

See pp158–9.

Cárdenas ❺

Matanzas. **Road Map** B–C 2.
🏛 100,000. 🚌 *Rumbos, Calle Zaes e/ Minerva y Mercedes, (45) 524 717.*

The linear façade of the historic Dominica building at Cárdenas

O N ARRIVING IN Cárdenas, 50 km (31 miles) east of Matanzas and 18 km (11 miles) south of Varadero, visitors may feel they are entering another age. This is mostly due to the presence of gigs and one-horse carriages which, having regained popularity during the Periodo Especial *(see p53)*, circulate in their dozens through the streets.

The town, considered one of the most symmetrical on the island, was founded in 1828 as San Juan de Dios de Cárdenas. In the 19th century the town thrived thanks to the flourishing sugar industry. Today, however, except for a rum factory near the port,

Cárdenas offers only two possible areas of employment: work on a farm or a job of some kind in Varadero's important tourist industry.

A closer look at the squares and monuments allows visitors to appreciate the little hidden gems in this town. Parque Colón, one of the two main squares in Cárdenas, is dominated by the first statue of Christopher Columbus erected in Cuba, inaugurated in 1862 by Gertrudis Gómez de Avellaneda, the 19th-century Hispanic-Cuban author *(see p26)*.

Next to the Iglesia de la Inmaculada Concepción (1846) is a very important monument: the **Dominica** building. In 1850, when it was the headquarters of the Spanish government in Cuba,

Cuban nationalist troops led by Narciso López hoisted the Cuban flag here for the first time.

In the second major square, Parque Echevarría, is a fine Neo-Classical building, erected in 1862, which was once the city's district prison. It was turned into the **Museo Municipal Oscar María de Rojas** in 1900, making it the oldest town museum in Cuba. It houses a collection of coins, arms, shells and minerals.

Cárdenas is also famous for being the birthplace of José Antonio Echevarría (1932–57), the revolutionary who was president of the University Students' Federation in Havana. He waged an anti-Batista campaign and was assassinated by the police. The house he was born in is now a museum with an interesting historical survey of revolutionary Cuba; it also has on display items that once belonged to Echevarría and José Martí.

🏛 **Museo Municipal Oscar María de Rojas**
Calzada 4, e/ José Antonio Echevarría y José Martí. ☎ *(45) 522 417.* ⏰ *Tue–Sat; Sun am.* ● *1 Jan, 1 May, 26 Jul, 25 Dec.* 🎫 ✔ 📷

🏛 **Museo Casa Natal de José Antonio Echevarría**
Plaza José A Echevarría.
☎ *(45) 524 145.* ⏰ *Tue–Sat.* ● *1 Jan, 1 May, 26 Jul, 25 Dec.* 🎫 ✔ 📷

Cárdenas, the city of horse-drawn carriages

Varadero ❹

Monument to the Indians

CUBA'S TOP RESORT, which occupies the 19-km (12-mile) long Península de Hicacos, is connected to the mainland by a drawbridge, a sign of Varadero's exclusivity. When, in the late 19th century, some families from Cárdenas bought part of the land on the peninsula and built themselves summer residences on the north coast, Varadero became a fashionable beach for the wealthy. After Castro took power in 1959, the area was opened up to all kinds of people. Now, however, Cubans are rarely to be seen on holiday at Varadero, since services and facilities have to be paid for in dollars.

The attractive home of Varadero's municipal museum

Exploring Varadero

The peninsula – which can be toured by hiring a bicycle, scooter or one-horse carriage – is a succession of hotels, restaurants, holiday villages, bars, discos, shops, cinemas, camping sites and sports centres, all set among lush greenery that includes bougainvillea, royal poinciana, coconut palms and seagrapes.

The main road along the northern side of the peninsula is Avenida Primera (1ra), the eastern part of which is named Avenida Las Américas. It is here that the main luxury hotels, the major yacht clubs and a golf course are located. The Autopista Sur (motorway) runs along the southern coast.

The Historic Centre

The old centre of Varadero, which has no significant historical monuments, lies around the Iglesia de Santa Elvira and the **Parque Central**, in Avenida 1ra between Calle 44 and 46. The oldest hotel of note is Hotel Internacional (at the western end of Avenida Las Américas), which was built in the 1950s, complete with a casino and extravagant swimming pool.

♣ Parque Retiro Josone

Avenida Primera y Calle 56.
📞 (45) 667 228.
🕐 daily.

This is a beautiful park, with elegant trees, tropical flowers and plants, three restaurants and a small lake where birds gather and tourists row boats. It was established in 1942 by José Uturrió, the owner of the Arrechabala *ronera*, the rum factory just outside Cárdenas. He named it Josone, a combination of the first syllable of his Christian name and that of his wife, Onelia.

⌂ Museo Municipal

Calle 57 y Playa. 📞 (45) 613 189.
🕐 daily. 📷 🎟 📷

The Municipal Museum recounts the history of Varadero both as an urban and tourist centre and also has a collection of Indian handicrafts on display. It is interesting primarily because of the building which it occupies.

The white and blue wooden chalet with terracotta roof tiles is characteristic of the architectural style imported from the US and in fashion in Varadero and the Caribbean area in the early 1900s. These prefabricated buildings, easy to assemble and easily adapted as holiday houses, were made in Louisiana.

The architect Leopoldo Abreu, the original owner of this villa, landscaped splendid gardens which visitors to the museum can still enjoy. One side of the museum faces the sea, and the balcony on the first floor offers a fine view over the splendid beach and the coastline.

VARADERO

Straits of Florida

Airport

PENÍNSULA DE HICACOS

Cárdenas

Bahía de Cárdenas

0 km   1
0 miles   1

KEY

═══ Autopista Sur motorway

━━━ Major road

━━━ Minor road

∩ Pre-Columbian site

ℹ Tourist information

A stretch of the magnificent beach at Varadero

VISITORS' CHECKLIST

Matanzas. **Road Map** B2.
🏠 10,000. ✈ 6 km (4 miles) W,
(5) 613 016. 🚗 Cárdenas,
18 km (11 miles) SW.
🚌 Autopista Sur y 36, (45) 612
626. ℹ Rumbos, Ave. 1, esq. 23.

Upon request, golf players can book accommodation in the few luxury bedrooms in the villa.

🍽 Restaurante Las Américas (Villa Xanadú)
Avenida Las Américas,
Reparto Las Torres. 📞 (45) 667 750.
🕐 lunch and dinner.

During the years from 1920 to 1950 an American millionaire, chemical engineer Alfred Irénée Dupont de Nemours, gambled a great deal of money by purchasing most of the beautiful Hicacos peninsula from the heirs of the Spanish landowners. At that time there were only a few villas and one hotel here. Dupont then parcelled the land out to Cubans and Americans who, within a few years, had transformed Varadero into a centre for gambling and prostitution.

At the height of his property dealings, Dupont asked the two Cuban architects Govantes and Cabarrocas, who had designed the Capitolio in Havana (see pp82–3), to design a villa for the rocky promontory of San Bernardino, the highest point in Varadero. This sumptuous four-storey building, completed in 1929 and named Villa Xanadú, was dressed with Italian marble and precious wood. The roof was covered with green ceramic tiles with thermal insulation. The house was surrounded by a huge garden with rare plants and features which included an iguana farm and a golf course. This extravagant construction cost $338,000, an enormous sum at the time.

In 1959, after the Revolution, Dupont escaped from Cuba, leaving the villa to the Cuban government, which, in 1963, turned it into "Las Américas", the most elegant restaurant in Varadero. It specializes in French cuisine, but can be visited without any obligation to eat there. The dining room still has its original furniture, and in the library there are books and photographs of the Dupont family on display. The large terrace overlooking the Varadero Golf Club course is part of the bar area.

∩ Punta Hicacos
For those interested in wildlife, the most fascinating part of Varadero is the area near Punta Hicacos, which has become a nature reserve. Here you can visit several caves, including the Cueva de Ambrosio, with Pre-Columbian rock paintings, a lagoon area (Laguna de Mangón), and some quiet, secluded beaches.

The peninsula is also an attraction for scuba divers, who have 23 dive sites to choose from.

The former Villa Xanadú, now a bar-restaurant, with its distinctive green roof

Straits of Florida

Golf course

Bahía de Cárdenas

VARADERO

Península de Zapata 6

Pineapple plants, common here

THIS PENINSULA is named after the landowner who was granted the land by the Spanish crown in 1636. It is one of the least populated areas of the island, and mostly consists of a huge swamp, partly covered by forest. In the past the inhabitants made their living by extracting peat and making charcoal. Zapata is one of the most complete wildlife reserves in the Caribbean, rich in birds and animals, and one part, the area around the Laguna del Tesoro, has been designated a national park, the Gran Parque Natural de Montemar. The Caribbean coast, with its sandy beaches, attracts scuba divers and fans of other water sports.

A mangrove swamp, characteristic of some tropical coastal areas

STAR SIGHTS

- ★ Guamá
- ★ Playa Larga
- ★ Playa Girón

Corral de Santo Tomás is a refuge and observation point for migratory birds. It can only be visited with an official guide (ask at the reception desk of the Villa Playa Larga Hotel).

Santo Tomás
Quemado Grande
Maneadero

ZAPATA

The Laguna de las Salinas is the winter home of many species of migratory bird from November to May.

THE FAUNA OF THE ZAPATA SWAMP

This habitat supports about 150 species of bird, including the *zunzuncito (see p19)*, the Cuban Pygmy owl, the Zapata rail, a rare type of baldicoot, waterhen, various species of parrot, and heron. Along the coast manatees can be seen (the Caribbean species is over 4 m/13 ft long and weighs about 600 kg/1,320 lbs). The beaches and roads are invaded each spring by crabs leaving the water to mate.

The local crocodile (Cocodrilo rhombifer) *has been protected since the 1960s.*

The Cuban Pygmy owl (Glaucidium siju) *is a small nocturnal raptor.*

The grey heron *lives in the mangrove swamps and feeds on small fish and amphibia.*

The zunzuncito (Mellisuga helenae) *is multi-coloured (male) or black-green (female).*

KEY

▬	Major road
▬	Minor road
✈	Aerotaxi
ℹ	Tourist information
🏖	Recommended beach
⚹	Nature reserve
✚	Medical centre

Central Australia
The headquarters of the Cuban Armed Forces in 1961, during the Bay of Pigs conflict, this sugar refinery now houses the Museo de la Comandancia.

VISITORS' CHECKLIST

Matanzas. **Road Map** B2.
🏠 10,000.
🚤 from Boca de Guamá to Guamá.
ℹ️ Rumbos, Villa Playa Larga, (459) 7228.

★ Guamá
Home to a holiday resort, built on ten islands in the Laguna del Tesoro, Guamá also features the Aldea Taína, a reconstruction of a typical pre-Columbian village.

★ Playa Larga
With its decent beach and hotel, Playa Larga is a good base for exploring the swamp.

Caleta Buena, a splendid cove 8 km (5 miles) from Playa Girón, is perfect for scuba diving.

La Cueva de los Peces is a natural pool *(cenote)*, 70 m (230 ft) deep, lying along a fault line. It is an ideal spot for scuba diving and snorkelling.

★ Playa Girón
This beach is best known as the site of the final battle between Fidel Castro's armed forces and the counter-revolutionary army, which took place on 17–19 April 1961.

Exploring the Península de Zapata

A welcome sign at the Península de Zapata

THE PENÍNSULA DE ZAPATA is synonymous with unspoiled nature and luxuriant tropical vegetation. It is a place where visitors can walk among lianas, mangroves and swamp plants, lie in a hammock in the shade of palm trees, observe birds with multicoloured plumage, go fishing, or row a boat on the Laguna del Tesoro. The tranquil Gran Parque Natural de Montemar attracts lovers of wildlife and untouched habitats, rather than adventure seekers. In any case, there is nothing to be feared from the wildlife – there are no ferocious beasts or poisonous snakes on the island.

Statue of Manguanay by the Cuban sculptress Rita Longa, Guamá

Boca de Guamá

Arriving from the north, after passing through Jagüey Grande, which has the largest citrus groves in Cuba, and Central Australia (*see p161*), you reach Boca de Guamá. Here a picturesque *ranchón*, a kind of rustic hut, converted into a restaurant, indicates that you are near the **Criadero de Cocodrilos**, or crocodile farm. Visitors can watch and photograph the crocodiles from an observation point overlooking the farm in the Zapata swamp.

Founded in 1962 to safeguard 16 endangered species of reptile, this is the largest crocodile farm in Cuba and includes about 100,000 animals kept in separate pools according to size, age and species.

✕ Criadero de Cocodrilos
🔲 *daily.* 🖾

Guamá

This unusual holiday village (*see p253*) in the Laguna del Tesoro (Treasure Lake), measuring 90 sq km (35 sq miles), is named after Guamá, a Taíno warrior who resisted the Spanish conquistadors until he was killed in 1533.

The village consists of 49 huts standing on several small islands in the lagoon. Built of royal palm wood and thatched with palm leaves, the huts provide simple accommodation. However, they are equipped with modern amenities, including air-conditioning. Make sure you take adequate supplies of mosquito repellent if you plan to stay here.

The huts are supported on stilts and are connected to one another by hanging bridges or by canoe. In fact, the only way to reach this tourist village is by boat, which takes an hour to travel along the luxuriantly fringed canal to the lagoon from Boca de Guamá.

This unusual resort also includes a restaurant, a disco, and a small museum, Muestras Aborígenes, which has on display some finds dating back to the Taíno civilization, discovered in the Laguna del Tesoro area.

Also of interest is the reconstructed Taíno village of Aldea Taína, which occupies another of the islands in the lagoon. It comprises four earth *bohíos* (typical Indian huts), a *caney* (a larger round building), and 25 life-size statues of natives by the well-known Cuban sculptress Rita Longa. The figures form the Batey Aborigen, or native Indian square, and represent the few people who lived in the village: a young girl named Dayamí; a crocodile hunter, Abey; Cajimo, hunter of *jutías* (a type of rodent, *see p142*); Manguanay, the mother who is preparing *casabe* (cassava) for her family; Yaima, a little girl who is playing; and the key figure, Guamá, the heroic Taíno warrior.

One of the 49 thatched huts in the Laguna del Tesoro

Playa Larga

At the end of the Bay of Pigs is one of the better beaches along this part of Caribbean coastline, where thick vegetation usually grows down as far as the shore. The coral reef offshore offers magnificent dive sites. Playa Larga's resort area is a popular destination with Cubans and there are also enough facilities to attract international tourists.

Near the car park, a monument commemorates the landing of the anti-Castro troops in 1961, while along the road to Playa Girón there are numerous monuments honouring the Cuban defenders who died in the famous three-day battle.

Northeast of Playa Larga is an ornithological reserve, and the Centro Internacional de Aves (International Bird Centre) of Cuba.

Cueva de los Peces *(see p161)*, near Playa Larga, ideal for diving

Playa Girón

This beach was named in the 1600s after a French pirate, Gilbert Giron, who found refuge here. It became famous three centuries later, when it was the site of the ill-fated, American-backed landing in 1961. A large sign at the entrance to the beach reads: "Here North American imperialism suffered its first major defeat".

Situated on the eastern side of the Bay of Pigs, this is the last sandy beach in the area, ideal for fishing and diving and also equipped with good tourist facilities.

A must is a visit to the small **Museo Girón**, which covers the anti-Castro invasion using photos, documents, weapons, a tank and the wreckage of aeroplanes that took part in the last battle, as well as films taken during the invasion.

🏛 **Museo Girón**
Playa Girón, Península de Zapata.
📞 *(459) 4122.* ⭕ *daily.*
📷 ✔ 📷

Playa Girón, the easternmost sandy beach in the Bay of Pigs

THE BAY OF PIGS INVASION

The long, narrow Bay of Pigs *(Bahía de Cochinos)* became known throughout the world in 1961. On April 14 of that year, at the height of the Cold War, a group of 1,400 Cuban exiles, trained by the CIA with the approval of the president of the United States, John F Kennedy, left Nicaragua for Cuba on six ships. The next day, six US B-26 aeroplanes attacked the island's three military air bases, their bombs killing 7 people and wounding 53.

On April 16 the group of counter-revolutionaries landed on the main beaches along the bay, Playa Larga and Playa Girón. However, they were confronted by the Cuban armed forces, headed by Fidel Castro himself, who were well prepared for the battle and had the support of the local population. The fighting lasted just three days and ended in the rapid defeat of the invaders. In order to avoid an international crisis, which could have escalated into an extremely serious situation, given the Soviet Union's support of Cuba, the US suddenly withdrew its aerial support, leaving the invading forces at the mercy of Cuban troops.

The abandoned invaders, many of whom were mercenaries, were taken prisoner and immediately tried. After 20 months in prison, they were allowed to return to the US in exchange for supplies of medicine, foodstuffs and equipment for Cuban hospitals.

The hostages released by Cuba on their return to the US

Cienfuegos ❼

The triumphal arch (1902)

THE CAPITAL of the province of the same name, Cienfuegos is a maritime town with a well-preserved historic centre and one of the most captivating bays in the Caribbean Sea, which helped earn the city the name "Pearl of the South" in the Colonial era. When Columbus discovered the gulf in 1494, it was occupied by Jagua Indians. In order to defend the bay from pirates, the Spanish built a fortress here in 1745. The first town was founded in 1819, and was named after the Cuban Governor General of the time, José Cienfuegos. The town was planned according to a geometric layout typical of Neo-Classicism.

The "zero kilometre" in the Parque Martí

Parque Martí

The "zero kilometre", the central point of Cienfuegos, is in the middle of Parque Martí, the former Plaza de Armas (parade ground). The vast square, a 200 x 100 m (655 x 330 ft) rectangle, has been declared a national monument because of the surrounding buildings and its historic importance. It was here that the foundation of Cienfuegos was celebrated with a solemn ceremony in the shade of a hibiscus tree, chosen as a marker for laying out the city's first 25 blocks.

Lions on a marble pedestal flank a monument to José Martí, erected in 1906. On Calle Bouyón stands the only triumphal arch in Cuba, commissioned by the local workers' corporation in 1902 to celebrate the inauguration of the Republic of Cuba. One side of the square is entirely

occupied by the **Palacio del Ayuntamiento**, now the home of the provincial government assembly, supposedly modelled on the Capitolio in Havana (*see pp82–3*).

🎭 Teatro Tomás Terry
Ave. 56 No. 2703 y Calle 27.
📞 (432) 513 361. ◯ daily.
This theatre was built in 1886–89 to fulfil the last will and testament of Tomás Terry Adams, an unscrupulous sugar factory owner who had become wealthy through the slave trade and then became mayor. World-famous figures such as Enrico Caruso and Sarah Bernhardt performed here in the early 1900s.

The theatre was designed by Lino Sánchez Mármol as an Italian-style theatre, with a splendid U-shaped, two-tiered auditorium and a huge fresco by Camilo Salaya, a Philippine-Spanish painter who moved to Cuba in the

late 1800s. The austere, well-proportioned façade on the Parque Central has five arches corresponding to the number of entrances. The ceramic masks on the pediment, made by the Salvatti workshops in Venice, represent the Three Graces.

To the left of the theatre is the Neo-Classical Colegio de San Lorenzo, built thanks to a generous donation by the academic Nicolás Jacinto Acea to ensure that needy children in the town would be educated.

🏛 Catedral de la Purísima Concepción
Ave. 56 No. 2902 y Calle 29.
📞 (432) 525 297. ◯ Mon–Sat; Sun am. 🚻
The cathedral of Cienfuegos, which was constructed in 1833–69, is one of the major buildings on the central square. Its distinguishing features are the Neo-Classical façade with two bell towers of different heights, and stained-glass windows made in France depicting the Twelve Apostles.

🏛 Museo Provincial
Ave 54 No. 2702 esq. Calle 27.
📞 (432) 519 722.
◯ Tue–Sat; Sun am.
⬤ 1 Jan, 1 May, 26 Jul, 25 Dec.
The Provincial Museum is in the former Casino Español, an eclectic-style building first opened on 5 May 1896. The furniture, bronze, marble and alabaster objects, crystal and porcelain collections, bear witness to the refined taste and wealth of 19th-century families in Cienfuegos.

The austere façade of the Teatro Tomás Terry

**Palacio Ferrer, with its
unmistakable blue cupola**

🏛 Palacio Ferrer

Ave. 54 esq. Calle 25. 📞 *(432)
516 584.* ⬤ *for cultural events.*
🎟 *access to viewpoint.*

The palacio that houses the
Casa Provincial de la Cultura
was built in the early 1900s by
the sugar magnate José Ferrer
Sirés. Enrico Caruso is said
to have stayed here when
he performed at the Teatro
Tomás Terry.

This building stands on the
western end of the plaza and is
the most bizarre and eclectic
in the square. It is distinguished by its cupola with blue
mosaic decoration. It is worth
climbing up the wrought-iron
spiral staircase to enjoy the
fine views over the city.

🏛 Museo Histórico Naval Nacional

Ave. 60 y Calle 21, Cayo Loco.
📞 *(432) 519 143.* ⬤ *Tue–Fri; Sat,
Sun am.* ⬤ *1 Jan, 1 May, 26 Jul, 25
Dec.* 🎟 📷

A short walk northwest of
Parque José Martí, on the
Cayo Loco peninsula, is the
most important naval museum
in Cuba, featuring a series of
documents concerning the
anti-Batista insurrection of
5 September 1957, and an
interesting display recording
the history of the Cuban Navy.

VISITORS' CHECKLIST

Cienfuegos. **Road Map** C3.
🚶 *150,000.* ✈ *5 km (3 miles)
northeast, (432) 552 267.*
🚉 *Ave. 58 y Calle 4.*
🚌 *Calle 49, e/ Ave. 56 y 58.*
ℹ️ *Rumbos, Ave. 20, e/ 37 y
39, (432) 551 121.*

Paseo del Prado

The liveliest street in town is
known for its elegant, well-
preserved buildings and the
monuments honouring
leading local figures. It crosses
the historic centre and goes
south as far as Punta Gorda.
It was laid out in 1922.

Paseo del Prado, the main street in the historic centre of Cienfuegos

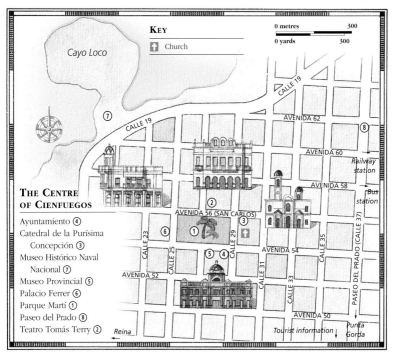

KEY

🏛 Church

0 metres 300
0 yards 300

Cayo Loco

CALLE 19

AVENIDA 62

AVENIDA 60

Railway
station

AVENIDA 58

Bus
station

THE CENTRE OF CIENFUEGOS

Ayuntamiento ④
Catedral de la Purísima
Concepción ③
Museo Histórico Naval
Nacional ⑦
Museo Provincial ⑤
Palacio Ferrer ⑥
Parque Martí ①
Paseo del Prado ⑧
Teatro Tomás Terry ②

AVENIDA 56 (SAN CARLOS)

AVENIDA 54

AVENIDA 52

AVENIDA 50

CALLE 23
CALLE 25
CALLE 29
CALLE 31
CALLE 33
CALLE 35
CALLE 37
PASEO DEL PRADO (CALLE 37)

Reina

Tourist information

Punta
Gorda

Exploring Cienfuegos

THE PRESENCE OF THE SEA at Cienfuegos makes itself felt more and more the further you go from the historic centre towards the Reina and Punta Gorda districts, two narrow strips of land almost entirely surrounded by water. However, for a fuller taste of the sea, go to the mouth of the bay, which is dominated by the Castillo de Jagua fortress with the picturesque Perché fishing harbour. Southeast of Cienfuegos is one of Latin America's most spectacular botanic gardens.

The interior of Palacio de Valle, with its Neo-Moorish decoration

The characteristic wooden houses of Punta Gorda

Punta Gorda

At the southern tip of the bay of Cienfuegos lies Punta Gorda – the aristocratic quarter of the city in the early 1900s – which affords a lovely panoramic view of the bay. A short walk along the seafront takes you past many Art Nouveau villas. Various brightly coloured wooden houses can be seen towards the tip of the peninsula. They were modelled on the American prefabricated "balloon frame" homes that were so much in vogue in the early 20th century.

🏛 Palacio de Valle

Calle 37 e/ Ave. 0 y 2, Punta Gorda.
📞 (432) 551 226.
🕐 daily. 📷
🌐 www.pvalle.islagrande.cu

The most original building in the area, Palacio de Valle was designed by local and foreign architects engaged by the sugar merchant Acisclo del Valle Blanco, one of the wealthiest men in Cuba. It was built in 1913–17. This two-storey building, which is now a restaurant, is lavishly decorated with Gothic, Venetian and Neo-Moorish motifs, much in the Arab-Spanish style of the Alcázars in Granada and Seville. The façade has three towers of different design symbolizing power, religion and love. The terrace is open to the public.

🏛 Cementerio Monumental Tomás de Acea

Ave. 5 de Septiembre. 📞 (432) 515 257. 🕐 daily. 📷 📷

This impressive monumental cemetery lies in the eastern suburb of Cienfuegos. Varied in stylistic influences, it was conceived as a large garden with paths and fruit trees. The entrance is a replica of the Parthenon in Athens.

Palacio de Valle, which Batista turned into a casino, now home to a restaurant

🜛 Cementerio General La Reina

Ave. 50 y Calle 7, Reina.

⭘ daily. 🜨

The municipal cemetery of La Reina is located at the western end of the city, and has been declared a national monument. Laid out in the 1830s, this Neo-Classical cemetery includes a famous funerary statue of La Bella Durmiente (Sleeping Beauty).

The statue of Sleeping Beauty in La Reina cemetery in Cienfuegos

♣ Castillo de Jagua

Poblado Castillo de Jagua. 🜨

📞 (43) 96402. ⭘ Tue–Sun.
🌑 1 Jan, 1 May, 26 Jul, 25 Dec.
🜨 🜨 🜨

Built by engineer José Tantete, following a design by Bruno Caballero, to protect the bay and the region from Jamaican pirates, the Castillo was the third most important fortress in Cuba in the 18th century and the only one in the central region of the island.

The original moat and drawbridge are still intact, while the interior is now a restaurant specializing in fresh fish dishes.

According to legend, the citadel was inhabited by a mysterious lady dressed in blue, who every night walked through the rooms and corridors, frightening the guards. It is said that one morning one of the guards was found in a state of shock while wringing a piece of blue cloth in anguish. The unfortunate man never got over this experience and ended up in an asylum.

At the foot of the Castillo is the fishing village of **Perché**, with picturesque wooden houses, in striking contrast to the majestic military structure above.

Most visitors arrive by ferry from Pasacaballos hotel (29 km/18 miles south of Cienfuegos), from the dock in Cienfuegos, or on a boat from Punta Gorda.

ENVIRONS: Cienfuegos province is interesting to eco-tourists. Besides the **Ciego Montero** spa north of the capital, other noteworthy sights are **El Nicho**, to the southeast, which is famous for its waterfalls, and the conservation area of Aguacate.

However the main sight is the **Valle de Yaguanabo**, in the southern region, which is traversed by the river of the same name, which forms small waterfalls and clear freshwater pools. On the slopes of one of the mountains in this valley, populated by mammals such as boar, deer and opossums, is the entrance to the **Cueva de Martín Infierno**. This cave has been a national monument since 1990, because it has one of the largest stalagmites in the world (67 m/220 ft high) and other rare mineralogical sites such as Moonmilk and Flores de Yeso.

About 20 km (12 miles) south of Cienfuegos is **Playa Rancho Luna**, with golden sand and a hotel (see p253). It is popular with tourists and local families alike.

BENNY MORÉ

A great source of pride to Cienfuegos is the figure of Maximiliano Bartolomé Moré, better known as Benny Moré, who was born at nearby Santa Isabel de las Lajas on 24 August 1919. Moré inspired many generations of Cubans and foreigners with his supple, unique voice, which enabled him to interpret a variety of musical genres. For this reason the artist was nicknamed el bárbaro del ritmo (the barbarian of rhythm). He was self-taught, and when still quite young performed with famous orchestras such as those led by the Matamoros brothers and Pérez Prado (see pp28–9). He died in the early 1960s. For some time Cienfuegos – a city with a great musical tradition and the birthplace of cha-cha-cha – has paid tribute to him with the Benny Moré International Festival. The Cabildo Congo di Lajas in his home town puts on performances of Afro-Cuban popular songs and dances.

The Cuban singer, Benny Moré

Jardín Botánico Soledad ❽

IN 1912 EDWIN ATKINS, owner of the Soledad sugar works 15 km (9 miles) from Cienfuegos, transformed 4 ha (10 acres) of his estate into a sugar cane research centre, and filled the garden with a great number of tropical plants. In 1919 the University of Harvard bought the property and founded a botanical institute for the study of sugar cane and Caribbean flora. The botanical garden has been run by the Cuban government since 1961, and is one of the largest in Latin America, with a surface area of 90 ha (222 acres) and more than 2,000 different species of plant, including 300 palms. Besides the endemic species there are also huge bamboo trees. Guided tours, made partly on foot and partly by car, reveal the exceptional diversification of the garden.

★ **Garden Drive**
Lined with royal palm trees, the drive borders one entire side from the entrance to the glasshouse.

Leguminous plants

Laboratory

Ticket office, library

Medicinal plants, which are grown throughout the country, can be viewed in this small plot.

Forest plants

STAR SIGHTS

★ **Banyan Tree**

★ **Garden Drive**

Protected woodland

★ **Banyan Tree**
Among over 80 varieties of fig in the botanical garden, perhaps the most striking is a huge Ficus benghalensis *or banyan tree, a species with aerial roots (with a circumference of over 20 m/65 ft). The roots, trunks and branches form an impenetrable barrier.*

Cacti
Over 200 species of cactus are housed in this glasshouse. They are young specimens, grown after the serious damage inflicted by hurricane Lilly (1996).

Water Lilies
The pool near the glasshouse is entirely covered with water lilies of different colours: bright pink, white, dark purple, violet, blue and yellow.

Santa Clara ⑨

See pp170–72.

Sierra del Escambray ⑩

Villa Clara, Sancti Spíritus, Cienfuegos. **Map** C3. 🛈 *Topes de Collantes Tourist Centre, (42) 401 80.*

THE SIERRA DEL ESCAMBRAY mountain range, with an average height of 700 m (2,300 ft) above sea level, covers a large part of southern Central Cuba, across three provinces: Villa Clara, Cienfuegos and Sancti Spíritus *(see p187)*. In the heart of the range is the **El Nicho** nature reserve, which is of great scientific and ecological value with its abundant mountain fauna and varied plantlife. **Pico San Juan** (1,156 m/ 3,790 ft), dotted with conifers and lichens as well as coffee plantations, is the highest mountain in the Sierra.

A long steep road leads from the northern side of the mountains up to stunning **Embalse Hanabanilla**, a large artificial lake overlooked by a hotel. The Río Negro path, which skirts the waterfall of the same name, leads to a belvedere viewing point from which one can see the entire lake.

In the village of Macagua is the **Comunidad Teatral del Escambray**, an international theatre school. The school was founded in 1968 by members of the Havana Theatre, who used to rehearse here before touring rural communities.

Mimosa
With its deeply divided leaves, the mimosa makes a very attractive ornamental plant.

PALM TREES

For many Cubans, palm trees represent the power of the gods. A great variety of species, many of them native to Cuba, grow throughout the island: the royal palm *(Roystonea regia)*, the national plant; the bottle palm *(Colpothrinax wrightii)*, called *barrigona* (pregnant one), because the trunk swells in the middle; the sabal, whose fan-like leaves are used for roofing; the local coccothrinax *(C. crinita)*, with its unmistakable foliage; and the corcho *(Microcycas calocoma, see p139)*.

Royal palm   **Bottle palm**   **Coccothrinax palm**

Santa Clara ❾

Bust of Leoncio Vidal

The Teatro de la Caridad, where Enrico Caruso performed

Founded on 15 July 1689 by a group of inhabitants from Remedios *(see p173)*, who had moved away from the coast to escape from pirate raids, Santa Clara was for centuries the capital of the province of Las Villas, which included the present-day provinces of Cienfuegos, Sancti Spíritus and Villa Clara. One important historical event has made Santa Clara famous: in 1958 it was here that the last battle of the guerrilla war led by Che Guevara took place, the battle which marked the end of Batista's dictatorship. Santa Clara is now known as "the city of the heroic guerrilla". Today, it is a lively city and has several interesting sights.

Santa Clara's well-tended main square, Parque Leoncio Vidal

Parque Leoncio Vidal

The heart of the city, this charming square with its pristine flower beds, wrought-iron benches and period street lamps has retained its original 1925 atmosphere.

An obelisk stands here. It was commissioned by the rich heiress Martha Abreu de Estévez in honour of two priests, Juan de Conyedo and Hurtado de Mendoza. The heiress also financed the construction of the Teatro de la Caridad, the town's first four public bathhouses, the astronomical observatory, the electricity station, a hospital and a fire station.

There is also a bust of Leoncio Vidal, a colonel in the national independence army who died in battle in 1896, here in this square. There is also a fountain, and a sculpture entitled *Niño de la Bota* (child in boots), purchased by mail order from the J L Mott Company, an art dealer in New York.

Until 1894 the square was partly off limits to blacks, who could only walk along certain areas of the pavement.

🎭 Teatro de la Caridad

Parque Vidal 3.
📞 *(42) 205 548.*
Built to a design by the engineer Herminio Leiva y Aguilera for the heiress Martha Abreu de Estévez, this theatre was inaugurated in 1885.

An antique vase in a hall in the Museo de Artes Decorativas

The theatre offered many additional services – a barber shop, ballroom and gambling room, café and restaurant – with the aim of collecting money to be given to the poor in the city (hence its name, Charity Theatre).

The building has a simple, linear façade, in contrast to the ornate interior, with its profusion of chandeliers and painted panels and a stage with all kinds of mechanical gadgets and draped curtains. The auditorium itself, which has three tiers of boxes with wrought-iron balusters, had folding seats in the stalls right from the start – something completely new in Cuba at the time.

Perhaps the best feature of the theatre is the frescoed ceiling, executed by the Spanish-Philippine painter Camilo Salaya, representing the allegorical figures of Genius, History and Fame.

🏛 Museo de Artes Decorativas

Calle Martha Abreu esq. Luis Estévez
📞 *(42) 205 368.*
⏰ Mon, Wed, Thu; Fri–Sun pm.
🔴 1 Jan, 1 May, 26 Jul, 25 Dec.

The excellent Decorative Arts Museum, housed in a building dating from 1810, contains 18th-, 19th- and 20th-century furniture, as well as furnishings and paintings that belonged to leading local families. Among the objects on display here, those donated by the Cuban poetess Dulce María Loynaz *(see p27)* are particularly elegant and delightful: five fans, eleven sculptures and two Sèvres porcelain jars, the largest of their kind in Cuba.

The Tren Blindado Monument, a work by José Delarra

VISITORS' CHECKLIST

Villa Clara. **Road Map** C3.
250.000. *Luis Estévez 323.*
Carretera Central km 2.5.
*Havanatur, Calle Maximo
Gomez, (42) 204 001; Izla Azul,
Calle Lorda 6 (42) 202 589.*

♨ Tren Blindado Monument

Carretera Camajuaní, junction with railway line.

On 28 December 1958, with the aid of only 300 men, Che Guevara succeeded in conquering the city, which was fiercely defended by 3,000 of Batista's soldiers. The following day Guevara handed the dictator another severe setback by derailing an armoured train that was supposed to transport 408 soldiers and weapons of all kinds to the eastern region of Cuba in order to halt the advance of the rebels.

Cuban sculptor José Delarra commemorated this event by creating a museum–monument on the spot where it took place, in the northeastern part of Santa Clara, on the line to Remedios. The sequence of events is re-created using original elements such as four wagons from the armoured train, military plans and maps, photographs and weapons.

Also on show is the D-6 Caterpillar bulldozer that was used by the guerrillas to remove rails and cause the derailment. The episode ended with the surrender of Batista's men.

Parque Tudury

This square, in front of the Neo-Classical Iglesia di Nuestra Señora del Carmen (1756), is also known as Parque El Carmen. Here stands a monument commemorating the foundation of the town of Santa Clara. It was erected in 1951 around a tamarind tree, on the spot where, on 15 July 1689, the first mass was celebrated in the new city. The monument consists of 18 columns on which are carved the names of the first families in Santa Clara, crowned by a cross.

THE CENTRE OF SANTA CLARA

Museo de Artes Decorativas ③
Parque Leoncio Vidal ①
Parque Tudury ⑤
Teatro de la Caridad ②
Tren Blindado Monument ④

Railway station

CALLE SAN VINCENTE
CALLE MÁXIMO GÓMEZ
CALLE LUIS ESTÉVEZ
CALLE MACEO
CALLE MARTÍ
CALLE MARTÍ
CALLE INDEPENDENCIA
CALLE MARTHA ABREU
CALLE MACEO
CALLE PEDRO ESTÉVEZ
CALLE RAFAEL TRISTA
CALLE COLÓN
CALLE EDUARDO MACHADO

0 metres   300
0 yards   300

Che Guevara Memorial, bus station

KEY

🏛 Church

🏛 Tourist information

The group of sculptures in Santa Clara, dedicated to Che Guevara

🏛 Memorial "Comandante Ernesto Che Guevara"

Plaza de la Revolución Ernesto Guevara, Santa Clara.
📞 (42) 205 878. ⏰ Tue–Sun.
🔴 1 Jan, 1 May, 26 Jul, 25 Dec.
🖼 📷 📷

The monument in Plaza de la Revolución was built to commemorate the 30th anniversary of the battle of Santa Clara. It was designed by the architect Jorge Cao Campos and the sculptor José Delarra, and was unveiled on 28 December 1988.

The complex comprises a museum and the mausoleum of Che Guevara. Dominating the monument is an impressive bronze statue of Che, with his arm in plaster (he had broken it during the battle). Beneath, a bas-relief depicts scenes from the battle, on which are carved the historic words that Che wrote in his farewell letter before leaving for Bolivia.

Under the monument (the entrance is at the back) is the museum, designed by the architect Blanca Hernández Guivernau, which has some of Che's personal belongings on display, together with a chronological reconstruction of his life, which clearly

SE ASIGNA AL COMANDANTE ERNESTO CUEVARA LA MI. SION DE CONDUCIR DESDE LA SIERRA MAESTRA HASTA LA PROVINCIA DE LAS VILLAS UNA COLUMNA REBELDE

Part of the bas-relief memorial to Che Guevara

reveals the evolution of his revolutionary ideas.

Che's personal effects include his pistol holster, his uniform, watch, pipe, the container from which he used to drink *mate* tea, his beret, jacket, and the telephone he used during the battle of Santa Clara, along with his binoculars, camera and radio.

The newest construction in the square is the mausoleum containing the bodies of Ernesto Che Guevara and six other comrades, found in Bolivia 30 years after their death and transferred to Cuba in July 1997. The tomb is in the shape of a cave and consists of numbers of niches with ossuaries as well as a central brazier where an eternal flame burns. Cubans flock here daily in order to pay their respects.

ERNESTO CHE GUEVARA

When Ernesto Guevara de la Serna was killed in Bolivia upon orders from the CIA, he was only 39 years old. In the summer of 1997 – while Cuba was celebrating the 30th anniversary of the death of the *guerrillero heroico* – the body of Che Guevara was returned to the island. He was one of only two foreigners in the history of Cuba (the other is the Dominican general Máximo Gómez) to be proclaimed a Cuban citizen "by birth". Watching his coffin being lowered from the aeroplane to the sound of the *Suite de las Américas* served to remind everyone, especially young Cubans, that Che had died and had therefore really existed; he was not merely a 20th-century legend, but a reality for millions of people who had shared his ideas. Further testimony is given by his children, his widow Aleida March, many of those who fought with him on the Sierra and in the Congo, and also Alberto Granado, with whom Che made his first trips to Latin America and who, after the Revolution, moved to Cuba on his friend's invitation. Though Che suffered from asthma, he had an iron will, loved books as well as sports, and had a great spirit of sacrifice; he could appreciate beauty and was a perfectionist but had a sense of humour. He was a man of action who also found time to meditate on reality and to write.

The photographer Korda with his famous portrait of Che Guevara

Interior of the Iglesia de San Juan Bautista, Remedios cathedral

Remedios ⑪

Villa Clara. **Map** C3. 🏛 50,000.
🚉 🚌 🛈 Hotel Mascotte, Calle
Máximo Gómez 114, (42) 395 144.
🎭 Parrandas (24 Dec).

F OUNDED AROUND 1514 by
Vasco Porcallo de Figueroa
and given the name of Santa
Cruz de la Sabana, this town
was renamed San Juan de
los Remedios del Cayo after
a fire in 1578.

This peaceful place has a
small, well-preserved Colonial
historic centre in the area
around Plaza Martí. Over-
looking this square is the
Iglesia de San Juan Bautista,
the city cathedral, which is
considered one of the most
important churches in Cuba.
What we see today is the
result of restoration carried
out in the 20th century thanks
to the rich landowner Eutimio
Falla Bonet, who revived its
original Baroque splendour
without touching the Neo-
Classical bell tower. Most
striking are the lavish Baroque
altar and the magnificent
decorative ceiling.

Behind the cathedral is the
**House of Alejandro García
Caturla**. Here, the musical
instruments, photographs and
some personal belongings of
this talented 20th-century
personality are on display.
García Caturla was a
composer, pianist, saxophone
player, percussionist, violinist
and singer, as well as a fine
tennis player and rower,
journalist and art critic. He
caused a scandal by marrying
a black woman, by whom he
had 11 children. He defended
the poor and was regarded as
a fair and honest judge. His
honesty was ultimately the
cause of his assassination on
12 November 1940, at the age
of 34, by a defendant who
had tried to bribe him.

Also in the square are three
other noteworthy buildings.
The Mascotte hotel was the
site of an important meeting
between Generalissimo
Máximo Gómez and a US
delegation in 1899. The
former Casino Español, now
Casa de la Cultura, and the
El Louvre café, founded in
1866, also stand here.

However, Remedios is
probably most famous for the
Parrandas, the local festival
documented in the fascinating
**Museo de las Parrandas
Remedianas**. Here, photographs, musical instruments,
costumes, sketches, carriages
and *trabajos de plaza* –
decorated wooden structures
– bring to life Parrandas
past and present.

🏛 **House of Alejandro
García Caturla**
Calle Camilo Cienfuegos 5.
⏰ Tue–Sat, Sun am. ⏺ 1 Jan,
1 May, 26 Jul, 25 Dec. 🈵 🎬 📷

🏛 **Museo de las Parrandas
Remedianas**
Calle Máximo Gómez 71, esq. Andrés
del Río. ⏰ Tue–Sat, Sun am.
⏺ 1 Jan, 1 May, 26 Jul, 25 Dec.
🈵 🎬 📷

THE PARRANDAS

**A 19th-century print showing
people gathering in the square**

In 1829 the parish priest of
Remedios, Francisco Virgil
de Quiñones, had the idea
of getting some boys to
bang on sheets of tin in
order to get the lazier
church members out of
their homes to participate
in the nighttime cele-
brations of the Advent
masses (Dec 16–24).

In time this strange
concert developed into a
fully fledged festival, with
music, dances, parades
with floats and huge
wooden contraptions
(trabajos de plaza). The
festivity is a sort of cross
between Mardi Gras and
the Italian Palio horse race,
based on the competition
between two quarters of
Remedios, San Salvador
and Carmen.

The Parrandas begin on
December 4 with concerts
performed with various
percussion instruments,
and end with a great
crescendo on Christmas
Eve. The two *trabajos de
plaza*, one per quarter,
which are made during the
year, are left in Plaza Martí
during the festivities. They
are illuminated at nine in
the evening and may have
a historical, patriotic,
political, scientific or architectural theme. Later on
there are fireworks to welcome the entrance of the
floats *(carrozas)*, which
never occurs before 3am.
These *tableaux vivants*
move among the crowd.

The most endearing
aspect of the Parrandas,
enlivened by songs, polkas
and rumbas, is that all the
inhabitants, of all ages,
take part.

Plaza Martí, the tranquil central square in Remedios

CENTRAL CUBA – EAST

SANCTI SPÍRITUS · CIEGO DE ÁVILA · CAMAGÜEY · LAS TUNAS

*T*HIS AREA IN THE HEART OF THE ISLAND *presents two different facets. One is Colonial, with Spanish traits which are visible in the architecture and local customs and is best expressed in beautiful Baroque Trinidad, and fascinating, labyrinthine Camagüey. The other aspect is unspoilt nature, the coastline dotted with cayos, which has attracted visitors from abroad only in recent years.*

Trinidad, Camagüey and Sancti Spíritus, the main cultural centres in this region, were three of seven cities founded in the 16th century by a small group of Spaniards led by Diego Velázquez. The 1600s and 1700s were marked by the threat posed to Cuba by England and by pirate raids such as that made by Henry Morgan at Camagüey (then Puerto Príncipe) in 1666. At that time Trinidad had political and military jurisdiction over the whole of central Cuba, where the economy was based solely on sugar cane cultivation and the sale of sugar. The great landowners resided in luxurious mansions in these three cities.

In the second half of the 19th century, a period of crisis began with the advent of new technology, for which there was no skilled labour. Slave revolts, the first of which broke out in Camagüey in 1616, became increasingly frequent and violent, while competition from Cienfuegos was becoming more intense. In the late 1800s the major landowners left the cities and as time went on they gradually ceded their sugar factories to American businessmen, who converted them into one large sugar-producing business. Camagüey concentrated on livestock raising, still an important resource in the province, while Trinidad had to engage in other activities such as handicrafts and cigar-making. It remained isolated from the rest of Cuba for a long time, since the railway was not extended to Trinidad until 1919 and the road to Cienfuegos and Sancti Spíritus was only laid out in the 1950s. One result of this isolation, however, is that the historic centres of Trinidad and Sancti Spíritus have preserved their Colonial atmosphere.

Aerial view of the causeway linking Cayo Coco to the mainland

◁ Calle Simón Bolívar in Trinidad, sloping down towards the plain

176   CUBA REGION BY REGION

Exploring Central Cuba – East

FROM A CULTURAL POINT OF VIEW, the most interesting place in the area is the delightful town of Trinidad. This small town also has a lovely beach nearby and makes a good base for tours to the Sierra del Escambray or for excursions to the Valle de los Ingenios. A transit town, Sancti Spíritus can seem disappointing after Trinidad, while Camagüey is appealing both for its fascinating Colonial architecture and as an authentic, vibrant Cuban city. The Atlantic coast in the province of Ciego de Ávila is good for swimming and diving, especially at Cayo Coco and Guillermo, where there are good tourist facilities.

Playa Prohibida at Cayo Coco, fringed by sand dunes

KEY

— Motorway
— Major road
— Minor road
— River
❀ Viewpoint

The Salto del Caburní, between rocks and red earth, near Topes de Collantes

SEE ALSO

• *Where to Stay* pp272–3
• *Where to Eat* pp257–9

One of the Colonial houses around the peaceful pedestrian square of San Juan de Dios, in Camagüey

8 **JARDINES DEL REY**

GETTING AROUND

There is at least one domestic airport in each of these provinces. The cities are linked by road and by trains bound for Oriente, while from Trinidad the Valle de los Ingenios can be toured on a delightful small steam train. Cayo Coco can be reached by car along the causeway, as well as by air. The most difficult area to travel around is the Sierra del Escambray *(see p169)*, although organized tours now include Topes de Collantes as one of their stopping points.

The Cockerel Festival at Morón, celebrating the city's symbol

11 *SIERRA DE CUBITAS*

13 *CAYO SABINAL*

NUEVITAS ●

12 *PLAYA SANTA LUCÍA*

10 *CAMAGÜEY*

● *PUERTO PADRE*

GUÁIMARO ●

14 *LAS TUNAS*

● *SANTA CRUZ DEL SUR*

| 0 km | 15 |
| 0 miles | 15 |

Trinidad ❶

A cannon used as a bollard

THIS CITY WAS FOUNDED by Diego Velázquez in 1514, and was declared a World Heritage Site by UNESCO in 1988. The original cobblestone streets and pastel-coloured houses give the impression that time has scarcely moved on since Colonial times. From the 1600s–1800s, the city was a major centre for trade in sugar and slaves, and the buildings around the Plaza Mayor, the heart of Trinidad, bear witness to the wealth of the land-owners of the time. A long period of isolation from the 1850s to the 1950s protected the city from any radical new building and the original town layout has been left largely unchanged. The historic centre has recently been skilfully restored, down to details like the street lights.

★ Palacio Brunet
This mansion is now the Museo Romántico, with a collection of furniture and items that belonged to the wealthiest local families (p181).

Casa de la Música

Nuestra Señora de la Popa (see p186)

SIMÓN BOLÍVAR

CALLE HERNÁNDEZ ECHERRI

CALLE PIRO GUINART

CALLE MARTÍNEZ VILLENA

★ Iglesia y Convento de San Francisco
The monastery is the home of the Museo de la Lucha contra Bandidos, while the church bell tower, the symbol of the city, offers fine views. The bell dates from 1853 (p185).

Canchánchara
This typical casa de infusiones, housed in an 18th-century building, is known for its namesake cocktail canchánchara, made from rum, lime, water and honey. Live music is played here.

In Plazuela del Jigüe, where an acacia tree *(jigüe)* stands, Father Bartolomé de Las Casas celebrated the first mass in Trinidad in 1514 *(p185)*.

The Museo de Arqueología Guamuhaya occupies an 18th-century building where the naturalist Humboldt once stayed *(see p181)*.

STAR SIGHTS

★ Palacio Brunet

★ Palacio Cantero

★ Iglesia y Convento de San Francisco

KEY

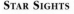
– – – Suggested route

Iglesia Parroquial de la Santísima Trinidad
The church of the Holy Trinity was built in the late 1800s on the site of a 17th-century church that had been destroyed by a cyclone. It has an impressive carved wooden altar decorated with elaborate inlaid wood (p180).

VISITORS' CHECKLIST

Sancti Spíritus. **Road Map** C3.
👥 50,000. 🚌 Calle Piro Guinart 224, e/ Maceo e Izquierdo, (419) 2404, 3737.
🚃 Ave. Simón Bolívar 422, (419) 3348. 🛈 Rumbos, Calle Maceo y Simon Bolívar, (419) 6495. 🔓 daily.

The Casa de los Conspiradores, with a wooden balcony on the corner, was the meeting place of the nationalist secret society, La Rosa de Cuba.

La Casa de la Trova, a venue for listening to live music *(see p279)*, stands on the Plazuela de Segarte, a small square surrounded by 18th-century houses.

Museo de Arquitectura Colonial
Housed in the beautifully restored Casa de los Sánchez Iznaga, this museum illustrates the main features of Trinidadian architecture (p180).

Casa de la Cultura (p185)

Casa de Aldemán Ortiz
Besides being a fine example of 19th-century architecture, this building has an interesting art gallery with works by local artists, as well as handicrafts (p180).

★ Palacio Cantero
This Neo-Classical gem was built in the early 19th century and is now the home of the Museo Histórico Municipal, which recounts the history of the region. The tower has a commanding view of the historic centre (p185).

PLAZUELA DE SEGARTE

PLAZA MAYOR

CALLE MARTINEZ VILLENA

CALLE JAVIER

CALLE SIMÓN BOLÍVAR

0 metres 100
0 yards 100

Trinidad: Exploring Plaza Mayor

Decorative element in Plaza Mayor

THE MUSEUMS AND BUILDINGS facing the main square in Trinidad lend historic weight and depth to the "suspended-in-time" feel of this city. It is worth stopping in the town centre for at least half a day to see the museums, relax on the benches in the shade of the palm trees, enjoy a cocktail at the bar by the cathedral steps, or stroll around the stalls in the crafts market.

A 19th-century shower in the Museo de Arquitectura Colonial

🔒 Iglesia Parroquial de la Santísima Trinidad

Plaza Mayor.
⭕ *variable.*

Completed in 1892, this austere church with a Neo-Classical façade stands at the top of the sloping Plaza Mayor.

The four-aisle interior has a fine Neo-Gothic altar dedicated to the Virgin of Mercy, with a painting by the Cuban painter Antonio Herr on the rear wall. But the real attraction of this church is an 18th-century wooden statue made in Spain, the *Señor de la Vera Cruz* (Lord of the True Cross), which is associated with a curious story. The sculpture, made for one of the churches in Vera Cruz, Mexico, left the port of Barcelona in 1731, but three times in succession the ship was driven by strong winds to the port of

Casilda, 6 km (4 miles) from the city of Trinidad. While preparing to make a fourth attempt to reach Mexico, the ship's captain decided to leave behind part of the cargo, which included the huge chest containing the statue of Christ. The locals regarded the arrival of the sacred image as a sign from Heaven, and from that time on the *Señor de la Vera Cruz* became an object of fervent worship.

The Maundy Thursday procession, which was suspended in 1959 and revived again in 1997, is dedicated to this statue.

🏛 Museo de Arquitectura Colonial

Calle Ripalda 83, e/ Hernández Echerri y Martínez Villena, Plaza Mayor. 📞 *(419) 3208.* ⭕ *Tue–Thu, Sat–Sun.* ⬛ *1 Jan, 1 May, 26 Jul, 10 Oct, 25 Dec.* 📷 💰 📷

The front of the 18th-century mansion of the Sánchez Iznaga family, now the home of the Museum of Colonial Architecture, features a lovely portico with slim columns, a wrought-iron balustrade and wooden beams. Originally, the building consisted of two separate houses, both of which belonged to sugar magnate Saturnino Sánchez Iznaga. The houses were joined during the 19th century.

The museum, the only one of its kind in Cuba, covers the different architectural

Bronze knocker, Museo de Arquitectura Colonial

elements seen in Trinidad and illustrates the building techniques used during the Colonial period. There is a collection of various locks, latches, doors, hinges, windows and grilles, as well as parts of walls and tiles.

In one of the bathrooms facing the inner courtyard is a fine example of a 19th-century shower, with a complicated network of pipes supplying hot and cold water.

🏛 Casa de Aldemán Ortiz (Galería de Arte)

Calle Martínez Villena y Bolívar, Plaza Mayor. 📞 *(419) 4432.* ⭕ *Sat–Thu.*

This beautiful mansion with a long wooden balcony, reminiscent of the Colonial buildings in Habana Vieja, is evocative of the city's golden age. It was built in 1809 for Ortiz de Zúñiga, a former slave trader who later became the mayor of Trinidad. The house now belongs to the Fondo de Bienes Culturales.

The first floor, home to an art school, has paintings on display (and for sale) by contemporary Cuban artists, including Antonio Herr, Juan Oliva, Benito Ortiz, Antonio Zerquera and David Gutiérrez. Of interest in the gallery itself are frescoes, the great staircase, and, in the upper hall, a ceiling decorated with figures. From the balcony there is a fine view of the entire square.

The statue of Señor de la Vera Cruz (1731), in one of the chapels inside Santísima Trinidad

Museo de Arqueología Guamuhaya, seen from the Casa Ortiz; behind is Palacio Brunet

🏛 Museo de Arqueología Guamuhaya
Calle Simón Bolívar 457, e/ Hernández Echerri y Martínez Villena, Plaza Mayor. ((419) 3420. ● currently closed for restoration.

Alexander von Humboldt

HUMBOLDT IN CUBA

The German naturalist Alexander von Humboldt (1769–1859), the father of modern geography, made two trips to Cuba (1800–1, 1804), which are recorded in a museum at Calle Oficios 252 in Havana. The book that followed, *Political Essay on the Island of Cuba*, in which he described Cuba as "the land of sugar and slaves", illustrated its geography, rivers, population, economy, government and slave system. Because of its abolitionist ideas the book was soon banned.

The building that is now the home of the Archaeological Museum was constructed in the 18th century and was purchased in the 1800s by the wealthy Don Antonio Padrón, who added a portico with brick columns and Ionic capitals.

The Guamuhaya (the native Indian name for the mountainous Escambray area) collection includes Pre-Columbian archaeological finds as well as objects associated with the Spanish conquest and slavery in Cuba, and stuffed animals, including the *manjuari*, an ancient species of fish that still lives in the Zapata swamp.

In the courtyard is a bronze bust commemorating the German geographer and naturalist Alexander von Humboldt, who stayed here as Padrón's guest in 1801, during his travels in the New World.

🏛 Palacio Brunet (Museo Romántico)
Calle Hernández Echerri 52, esq. Simón Bolívar, Plaza Mayor. ((419) 4363. ● 9am–5pm Tue–Sun.

Built in 1812 as the residence of the wealthy Borrell family, Palacio Brunet now contains the Museo Romántico. The decoration of the mansion blends in well with the objects on display, most of which once belonged to Mariano Borrell, the family

founder. They were inherited by Borrell's daughter, the wife of Count Nicolás de la Cruz y Brunet (hence the name Palacio Brunet).

The museum's 14 rooms all face the courtyard gallery with its elegant balustrade. The spacious living room has a Carrara marble floor, a coffered ceiling, Neo-Classical decoration, furniture made of precious wood, Sèvres vases and Bohemian crystalware. There are also English-made spittoons, which reveal that the 19th-century aristocratic landowners were partial to smoking cigars. In the dining room the fan windows are a particularly attractive feature.

Other rooms of interest are the countess's bedroom, with a bronze baldachin over the bed, and the kitchen, which is still decorated with its original painted earthenware tiles.

One of the elegant frescoes decorating Palacio Brunet

The Houses of Trinidad

THE HISTORIC CENTRE of Trinidad has an extraordinarily dense concentration of old Colonial houses, many still inhabited by the descendants of old local families. The oldest, single-storey buildings have two corridors and a porch parallel to the street, with a courtyard at the back. In the late 1700s another corridor was introduced to the layout.

A *mampara*, an interior door with two leaves

In the 19th century, the houses formed a square around an open central courtyard. In general, the houses of Trinidad, unlike those in Havana, have no vestibule or portico. The entrance consists of a large living room that gives way to a dining room, either through an archway or a *mampara*, an inner, double door.

Barrotes, small turned wooden columns, characterize the 18th-century windows.

Red tile roof

Wooden supports

Wooden beams support the two- or four-pitch sloping roof, which is covered with terracotta tiles. Inside, mudéjar-style coffered ceilings can often be found.

TRINIDAD FAÇADES

The façade of the typical Trinidad house has a large central door, with a smaller door (or doors) cut in it for easy access. The windows, set slightly above ground level, are almost the height of the door. They have strong wooden shutters instead of glass. This house is in Plaza Mayor, next to the Casa Ortiz.

Wrought-iron ornamental motifs

Wooden shutters

The arched windows so characteristic of Trinidad have radiating wooden slats instead of mediopunto windows. These allow the air to enter but keep out the sunlight.

The 19th-century iron grilles replaced the wooden barrotes and typically have simple decoration at the top and bottom.

The wooden front door is sometimes framed by plaster motifs: flattened pilasters, moulding, half-columns either with simple Tuscan capitals or with upturned bowls at the top.

◁ **The view from the San Francisco bell tower: in the foreground, Plaza Mayor, beyond, the coast**

Trinidad: Around Plaza Mayor

WALKING ALONG THE STREETS leading from Plaza Mayor is a fascinating experience even if you have no particular destination. A slow stroll allows time to observe the detail of a window, a small balcony, the irregular cobblestones, or the cannons used as bollards. The historic centre is more or less free of traffic. In the evening the houses glow in the warm hues of sunset, and music fills the streets: the Casa de la Trova *(see p179)* and Casa de la Música *(p178)* put on daily concerts by local bands.

The river cobblestones *(chinas pelonas)* used in Trinidad's streets

The frescoed entrance hall in Palacio Cantero and its Italian marble floor

�blank Casa de la Cultura Trinitaria
Calle Zerquera 406. **C** *(419) 4308.*
During the day, the spacious, well-lit vestibule is used as permanent exhibition space by local artists (some of whom also have their studios here), who sell their paintings. In the evening, performances of various kinds of entertainment are held in the rear courtyard: theatre, dance, concerts and shows for children.

�blank Palacio Cantero (Museo Histórico Municipal)
Calle Bolívar 423. **C** *(419) 4460.*
⭘ *Sun–Thu.* ● *1 Jan, 1 May, 26 Jul, 10 Oct, 25 Dec.*
This mansion, which originally belonged to Don Borrell y Padrón – one of the major figures in local sugar production – was purchased in 1851 by a landowner from the Valle de los Ingenios. He renamed it after himself, and transformed it into one of the most sumptuous Neo-Classical residences in the city. The building is now the Museo Histórico Municipal.

From the grand entrance hall, with frescoed arches, the route takes in the dining room, the kitchen, the courtyard and an area for domestic servants.

The history of Trinidad can be traced through exhibits, maps, and monuments related to different themes: the Cantero family, piracy, the plantations in the Valle de los Ingenios, the slave trade and the wars of independence. The *mirador* (viewing platform), on the top of the tower, is also open to the public.

Plazuela del Jigüe
This peaceful little square, where a spreading acacia tree offers shady respite from the sun, is rich in history *(see p178)*. El Jigüe restaurant is housed in a lovely porticoed building decorated with panels of painted tiles.

⏛ Iglesia y Convento de San Francisco
Calle Hernández Echerri, esq. Guinart.
Museo de la Lucha contra Bandidos **C** *(419) 4121.*
⭘ *Tue–Sun.* ● *1 Jan, 1 May, 26 Jul, 10 Oct, 25 Dec.*
This elegant church was built in 1813 by Franciscan monks, but it was taken from them in 1848 in order for it to be used as a parish church. In 1895 the authorities transformed the monastery into a garrison for the Spanish army. Then in 1920, because of the lamentable state of the place, the monastery and part of the church were demolished. Only the bell tower was salvaged, along with adjacent buildings, which were used as a school until 1983, when the complex became the home of the **Museo de la Lucha contra Bandidos**.

The museum illustrates with documents, photographs and exhibits the struggle against the "bandits", the counter-revolutionaries who fled to the Sierra del Escambray after 1959. Old tanks are displayed in the cloister of the former monastery.

The small Plazuela del Jigüe, with its handful of handicrafts stalls

Beyond Trinidad's Historic Centre

Away from the centre there are more interesting areas to explore. One spot to head for is Parque Céspedes, where locals, young and old, gather to listen and dance to live music in the evenings. Or, walking eastwards, lively Plaza Santa Ana draws people at all times of day. From the hill north of Plaza Mayor there are marvellous views over the valley, especially beautiful at sunset.

The Cabildo de San Antonio, with votive offerings and sacred drums

Façade of Nuestra Señora de la Candelaria de la Popa hermitage

🔒 Ermita de Nuestra Señora de la Candelaria de la Popa

This small 18th-century church on a hill north of the centre is connected to Plaza Mayor by a narrow, steep street. The striking three-arch bell tower loggia was added in 1812, when work was done to the church to repair the damage done by a violent cyclone. Despite deterioration, the church is still intact. Even though it is closed, it is worth a visit because the location is so beautiful.

Plaza Santa Ana

A short walk from Plaza Mayor, in the eastern part of the city, this square is dominated by the 18th-century Iglesia de Santa Ana. It was partly rebuilt in 1800, and the bell tower was added 12 years later. The now decaying church is flanked by a royal poinciana tree.

The square is a popular place to gather, thanks to the cultural centre in the former prison. Set around a lovely courtyard, the centre includes a restaurant, café and art gallery.

🏛 Cabildo de los Congos Reales de San Antonio

Calle Isidro Armenteros 168.

In the picturesque working-class quarter of El Calvario, in the northern part of Trinidad, is the Cabildo de los Congos Reales, a temple founded in 1859 for the worship of Afro-Cuban divinities. In the 1800s Cuba witnessed the rise of many *cabildos*, cultural centres differentiated by ethnic group which aimed to preserve the spiritual and musical heritage of the slaves. The Cabildo in Trinidad, dedicated to Oggún – a warrior god whose Catholic equivalent is St Anthony of Padua – is for the followers of the Palo Monte religion (*see p21*).

Environs: on a rise 1 km (half a mile) northeast of the centre, near Motel Las Cuevas (*see p259*) is the **Museo Espeleológico**, opened on 20 May 1999. Located inside a cave of 3,700 sq m (4,440 sq yds), it can be visited with an expert guide as far as the Salón de las Perlas, a smaller cave where water drops "fall like pearls". According to legend, an Indian girl called Cacubu took refuge (and died) here, escaping from the lecherous Spanish conquistador Porcallo de Figueroa. Karstic fossils from caves near Matanzas are also on show.

Iglesia de Santa Ana, on the square of the same name, in eastern Trinidad

Topes de Collantes ➋

THE UNSPOILT LANDSCAPE of the Sierra del Escambray *(see p169)*, where pine and eucalyptus grow alongside deciduous trees, ferns and tropical plants, offers extraordinarily beautiful scenery that can best be seen by hiking from Topes de Collantes, a steep 30-minute drive north of Trinidad. Here, two itineraries are suggested, indicated by a letter and colour. Itinerary A consists of a walk of average difficulty through the tropical forest as far as the Caburní falls. Itinerary B is longer but easier and less tiring, and includes a detour to the Batata thermal cave.

TIPS FOR HIKERS

Departure points: *Topes de Collantes.*
🛈 *Topes de Collantes Tourist Centre, (42) 402 28.* **Length:** *Itinerary A: 3.5 km (2 miles); Itinerary B: 4.5 km (3 miles).*
Stopping-off point: *Hacienda Codina.*

KEY

▬▬	Major road
═══	Path
▬▬	Itinerary A
▬▬	Itinerary B
🅿	Parking
✚	Hospital

0 kilometres 1
0 miles 1

La Batata ⑤
This cave is traversed by an underground river, with natural pools at a temperature which never rises above 20° C (68° F).

Hacienda Codina ④
The Codina farm has orchid and bamboo gardens, a pool with mud baths, and fine views. The route continues for 1 km (half a mile) among medicinal plants.

↗ Santa Clara Manicaragua

Trinidad ↙

Topes de Collantes ①
At 800 m (2,625 ft) above sea level and with good clean air, this spot was chosen as the location for a sanitarium for lung diseases, now used as an anti-stress centre.

Salto del Caburní ③
After a two-hour walk you will come to a cliff with a steep, plunging waterfall. Water gushes over rocks and collects further down, forming a pool where it is possible to bathe.

The Forest ②
The path leading to Salto del Caburní crosses untouched tropical forest with curious rock formations.

Secluded La Boca beach, shaded by royal poinciana trees

Península Ancón ❸

Road Map C3.

ABOUT 10 KM (6 miles) south of Trinidad is one of the first coastal areas in Cuba to be developed for tourism, the peninsula of Ancón, where foreign visitors have been coming since 1980. The fine white sand and turquoise water (not as clear here as along the north coast, though) make this promontory a miniature Varadero, with hotels, bars, restaurants and water sports clubs. However, unlike Varadero, this area is visited by visitors and locals alike. Cubans head mainly for **La Boca**, 6 km (4 miles) from Trinidad, near the neck of the peninsula, especially on warm Sundays and in summer.

At **Playa Ancón**, 5 km (3 miles) of white sand in the southern part of the peninsula, there are comfortable hotels, a splendid beach and a diving school. From the beach by Hotel Ancón, assorted boat excursions are available to take divers to snorkelling sites out on the coral reef.

For some fascinating dive sites, divers should take an excursion to **Cayo Blanco**, 8 km (5 miles) off the coast. At the western tip of this small coral island with white sand beaches, is the largest black coral reef in Cuba, where divers can choose from a number of different dive sites. On the rocky coasts near **María Aguilar**, on the other hand, there are pools where swimmers only need a mask to easily spot a great variety of tropical fish.

As with Varadero *(see pp158–9)*, bicycles can be hired and make a pleasant way of getting around the Ancón peninsula.

Opposite the peninsula, across the bay, is the old port of **Casilda**, 6 km (4 miles) from Trinidad, where in 1519 Hernán Cortés recruited the troops that went on to conquer Mexico.

Once a prosperous port thanks to the sugar trade, Casilda has long since declined, and is now above all a place that people pass through on their way to the local beaches.

Valle de los Ingenios ❹

Road Map C3. 🚗 🚌
Excursions *from Trinidad* ℹ *at railway station, (419) 3348; Rumbos, Calle Simón Bolívar 422, (419) 6495.*

LEAVING TRINIDAD and heading northeast, along the road to Sancti Spíritus, one can appreciate the beauty of the fertile plain, with the green hills of the Sierra del Escambray forming a backdrop. Only 12 km (7 miles) separate Trinidad from the Valle de los Ingenios, whose name derives from the sugar mills *(ingenios, see pp42–3)* built here in the early 19th century. Today,

The bell on the Iznaga bell tower

Valle de los Ingenios, from the Mirador de la Loma: green swathes of sugar cane at the foot of the Sierra

The Iznaga estate tower, with a commanding view of the valley

fields of sugar cane form a blanket of green, interrupted only by towering royal palms.

The valley is rich in history with ruins providing evidence of the time when the sugar industry was at its peak. These buildings also help visitors to understand the social structure that was the order of the sugar plantations. The whole zone, which has a surface area of 270 sq km (104 sq miles), includes more than 70 old *ingenios*. UNESCO has declared the valley a World Heritage Site.

A good way to visit the area is to take the steam train which departs from Trinidad and covers the entire valley. One of the places accessible only to those with a car is the **Mirador de La Loma del Puerto** (6 km, 4 miles east of Trinidad, on the road to Sancti Spíritus). This observation point (*mirador*), 192 m (630 ft) above sea level, offers a magnificent view of the whole valley. There is also an outdoor café where you can sample the drink *guarapo*, sugar cane juice.

However, the most impressive destination is the **Manaca Iznaga Estate**, where about 350 slaves lived in the 1840s. The landowner's house survives and has been

converted into a bar and restaurant. Also still standing are the *barracones* (slaves' huts), and a monumental seven-level tower 45 m (147 ft) high. Each level is different from the next in shape and decoration: the first three are square, the top four are octagonal. The symbolic meaning of this tower is apparent. It was built in 1830 as an assertion of authority over the valley by Alejo Iznaga, a rival to his brother Pedro, who was also a major landowner and sugar producer. The tower also functioned as a lookout for supervising the slaves.

The top of the tower, which is reached via a steep wooden stairway, today offers lovely, wide-ranging views of the surrounding countryside. At the foot of the tower is the bell that once tolled the work hours on the plantation.

There are other estate mansions to be seen in this area, including one at Guachinango, which was built in the late 18th century in a dominating position over the Río Ay.

The village of **San Pedro** is an example of the urban settlements that developed in association with the sugar plantations and works.

SUGAR PRODUCTION IN CUBA

For centuries, sugar cane (*Saccharum officinarum*), which was introduced to the island in 1512 by Spanish settlers, has been the mainstay of the Cuban economy. Sugar extraction takes place in various phases: after being washed, the cane stalks are pressed by special mills and the juice (*guarapo*) is extracted from the fibrous mass (*bagassa*), which is used as fuel and as livestock fodder. The juice is treated chemically, filtered and then evaporated so as to obtain a concentration of dark syrup that is then heated. This produces crystals of sucrose. The syrupy mass then goes into a centrifuge. Other by-products are obtained from sugar cane, including molasses, a residue of the syrup, which still contains 50 per cent sugar and is used as the basic ingredient in the production of rum (*see p75*).

Ripe cane *is from 2–5 m (6–16 ft) tall with a diameter of 2–6 cm (1–3 in). Once cut, the plant shoots again and becomes ripe again in a year. Newly planted cane, grown from cuttings 30–40 cm (12–16 in) long, ripens in 11–18 months.*

The zafra (harvest) *takes place between December and June. Before harvest begins, the cane field is burned to remove the outer leaves, which obstruct harvesting. In the plains cutting is done with machines, while in the hills the machete is still used.*

Transport *has to be rapid to minimize the deterioration of the sucrose in the heat. To this end, in the late 1800s a special railway network was built and steam trains travelled between the cane fields and the sugar works. Some are still running.*

Sancti Spíritus ❺

Statue of Christ beside the cathedral

THE CITY OF Sancti Spíritus, deep in the heart of fertile agricultural countryside, was founded by Diego Velázquez on the banks of the Tuinucú river in 1514. It was moved to its present site, near the Yayabo river, eight years later. In 1586 British pirates set fire to the town along with all the documents relating to its foundation. The political, economic and military centre of the area, Sancti Spíritus was embellished with elegant mansions throughout the 17th and 18th centuries. Today, its small, attractive Colonial centre receives few visitors, despite its "national monument" status.

🚇 Yayabo Bridge

Its medieval appearance and large terracotta arches make this bridge, built in 1825, unique in Cuba, and for this reason it has been declared a national monument. According to one bizarre legend, in order to make the bridge more robust, the workmen mixed cement with goat's milk.

The Yayabo bridge is an important part of the city's street network: it is the only route into town for those coming from Trinidad.

Exploring Sancti Spíritus

The central part of the city can be explored on foot in a few hours. It is pleasant to simply stroll along the recently restored streets (many of which are for pedestrians only), where brightly coloured Colonial houses with wrought-iron balconies are characteristic. The most famous approach to the town is the southern one, across the lovely old bridge over the Yayabo river. The narrow, quiet streets leading up from the bridge to the city centre are the oldest in Sancti Spíritus. They are paved with irregular cobblestones and lined with one-storey houses with shingle roofs.

Calle Máximo Gómez, which leads to the main square, Parque Serafín Sánchez, is lined with 18th- and 19th-century monuments, museums and mansions. These include the **Teatro**

The Yayabo Bridge, leading to the Colonial centre

Principal, a bright blue porticoed construction built in 1876 and restored in 1980; a large 19th-century mansion that is now the Pensamiento bar; the **Casa de la Trova**; a typical bar-restaurant, Mesón de la Plaza; and the Placita, a small square with a statue of Dr Rudesindo Antonio García Rijo, an illustrious citizen.

🏛 Museo de Arte Colonial

Calle Plácido 74. ☎ (41) 254 55.
◻ Tue–Sat, Sun am.
⬤ 1 Jan, 1 May, 26 Jul. 📷 📹 🔲

This fine 18th-century building once belonged to the Iznaga family (see p189). It is now a museum with crystal, porcelain, furniture, paintings (many of them Spanish), and a splendid courtyard.

Recently restored Colonial homes, with their original colours, in one of the streets near the river

The interior of the Parroquial Mayor during mass

🔒 Parroquial Mayor del Espíritu Santo

Calle Agramonte Oeste 58.
📞 *(41) 248 55.* ⏰ *Tue–Sat, Sun am.* ✝ *Tue–Sun.*

Using money donated by Don Ignacio de Valdivia, the local mayor, the Parroquial Mayor of Sancti Spíritus was built of stone in 1680, over the original 16th-century wooden church that had been destroyed by pirates. It is one of Cuba's oldest churches. The simple and solid building is reminiscent of the parish churches of Andalusia, and still has its original, exquisitely worked wooden ceilings. The

30-m (100-ft) bell tower, with three levels, was added in the 18th century, and the octagonal Cristo de la Humilidad y la Paciencia chapel, built next to the church in the 19th century, has a remarkable half-dome.

Parque Serafín Sánchez

The heart of the city consists of a tranquil square with trees and a charming *glorieta* (gazebo), surrounded by Neo-Classical buildings. A national monument, the Parque is dedicated to Serafín Sánchez, a local hero in the wars of independence, whose house is open to the public in the nearby Calle de Céspedes. In the evenings, the plaza is a popular gathering place.

The most notable buildings here are the Centro de Patrimonio, with broad stained-glass windows and Seville mosaics, the large **Biblioteca** (library), and the **Hotel Perla de Cuba**, one of the most exclusive hotels in Cuba in the early 1900s. The **Hotel Plaza**, whose bar is popular with the locals, forms part of a Colonial building.

ENVIRONS: around 8 km (5 miles) east of Sancti Spíritus, in the direction of Ciego de Ávila, nature lovers and fans of fishing can enjoy **Presa Zaza**, an artificial lake well stocked with trout and black bass. Tours of the lake depart from the Zaza hotel, while the shores are ideal spots for birdwatching. Presa Zaza is Cuba's largest man-made lake and is the venue for a major international fishing competition every September.

Chatting in the Parque Serafín Sánchez in the evening, a popular pastime

THE CENTRE OF SANCTI SPÍRITUS

0 metres   300
0 yards   300

KEY

🔲 Church

🚉 Railway station

Parque Martí in Ciego de Ávila, with a monument to José Martí

Ciego de Ávila ❻

Road Map D3. 🏛 *100,000.*
🚆 🚌 ✈ ℹ *Rumbos, Carretera Central (33) 201 952.*

WHEN CIEGO DE ÁVILA was founded in 1538 by the conquistador Jácome de Ávila, it was just a large farm in the middle of a wood, a *ciego*. It only became a bona fide city in 1840. Today, it is a rural town with two-storey houses fronted with Neo-Classical columns, and streets filled with one-horse carriages.

The few visitors who come here are mostly on their way to the *cayos* in the Jardines del Rey archipelago.

Anyone who does stop off should visit the **Teatro Principal** (1927) and the **Museo Histórico Provincial**. This last has four rooms of documents and photographs concerning the history of the province, in particular the story of La Trocha. This line of defence was constructed in the 19th century. It was devised by the Spanish to block the advance of the Cuban nationalists *(mambises)* by cutting the island in half, from Morón, north of Ciego de Ávila, to Júcaro, on the Caribbean coast. Some surviving La Trocha towers, built about 1 km (0.6 mile) from one another, lie a short distance outside town and are open to the public.

One of La Trocha's redoubts

The multi-ethnic character of the city means that visitors can enjoy both the rural festivals of Spanish origin *(parrandas)*, similar to those in Remedios *(see p173)*, and merengue and congo dance shows, especially in the quarter where Jamaican and Haitian immigrants live. Ciego de Ávila also has a cycling school which is attended by children from all over the island. At Epiphany the town is the starting point for the month-long Vuelta Internacional por la Paz, a cycle race much like the Tour de France.

(see p173)

THE COCKEREL OF MORÓN

"Be careful not to end up like the cockerel of Morón, which lost its feathers as well as its crest". This Spanish saying dates back to the 1500s, when the governor of the Andalusian village of Morón de la Frontera, who lorded it over the local farmers and was known as "cockerel" *(gallo)* for his arrogance and presumptuousness, was punished with a good thrashing and thrown out of town by the angry citizens. The event became well known and to commemorate it, a statue of a plucked rooster was set up in the main avenue. When a community of Andalusians emigrated to Cuba in the 18th century and founded a city they called Morón, to maintain their traditions they put a statue of the rooster at the entrance to the town. It was taken down in 1959, and replaced in 1981 by a new bronze sculpture placed next to a tower. At 6am and 6pm daily, a recording of a cock crowing is played here.

The bronze statue (1981) of the legendary cockerel of Morón

Morón ❼

Ciego de Ávila. **Road Map** D3.
🏛 *45,000.* 🚌 ℹ *Cubanacán, Calle Colón 49, (335) 2181.* 🐓 *Cockerel of Morón: end of June.*

MORÓN lies on the road that runs north from Ciego de Ávila (a town with a long-standing rivalry with Morón). The road is known for its occupation in 1896 by nationalist rebels *(mambises)* after they had managed to breach the Spanish defence.

Morón was founded in 1750 and retains a small, well-preserved Colonial centre. The **Museo Municipal** has more than 600 archaeological finds, brought to light in 1947

A street in Morón with pastel-coloured houses and arcades

Isla Turiguanó, the unusual "Dutch village" near Morón

a short distance from town, including a famous statuette, the Idolillo de Barro.

🏛 Museo Municipal
Calle Martí 374 e/ Antuña y Cervantes. **📞** *(33) 228 1280.* **◻** *Tue–Sun.* **●** *1 Jan, 1 May, 26 Jul, 25 Dec.* 🖼 📷 📷

ENVIRONS: north of Morón are two freshwater lagoons: the **Laguna Redonda**, which owes it name to its almost circular form and is known for its great abundance of trout, and the **Laguna de Leche**. This latter is called the "Lagoon of Milk" because of its colour, caused by the limestone deposits in the water. It is the largest stretch of brackish water in Cuba, with a surface area of 67 sq km (26 sq miles). It abounds in carp and pike and is a refuge for herons and flamingos.

Immediately north of the Laguna de Leche is the **Isla Turiguanó**, a peninsula with a village of Dutch-style houses surrounded by grazing land for cattle. The animals are also Dutch, having been imported by Celia Sánchez *(see p51)*.

Florencia, about 20 km (12 miles) west of Morón, is the starting point for hikes in the small **Sierra de Jatibonico**. This range can also be explored on horseback, along the route followed by Camilo Cienfuegos's column in 1958 *(see p48)*.

The Canal Viejo de Bahamas is used for platform fishing for large tropical fish. There are also hunting reserves: the Coto de Caza de Morón and Coto de Caza Aguachales de Fala.

Jardines del Rey ❽

Ciego de Ávila, Camagüey.
Road Map D3.

I N THE ATLANTIC OCEAN, north of the province of Ciego de Ávila, the Sabana and Camagüey archi-pelagoes, known collectively as "Jardines del Rey", include about 400 small islands, almost all of which are uninhabited.

The lighthouse at
Cayo Paredón Grande

They were discovered in 1522 by the conquistador Diego Velázquez, who was so struck by them that he dedicated them to the king *(rey)*, Carlos V. They later became a hiding place for pirates and, after the official abolition of slavery, a clandestine landing point for slaves.

A causeway 17 km (10 miles) long, built in 1988 as a link between the archipelago and mainland Cuba, makes it easy for visitors to get to the lovely beaches, the coral reef, and the holiday villages which are currently concentrated on **Cayo Coco** and **Cayo Guillermo** *(see pp194–5)*. However, Cuban nationals themselves have limited access to the archipelago.

Cayo Paredón Grande, 6 km (4 miles) long, is the third largest island in the Jardines. Although there are no hotels, it is worth visiting for the lovely beaches, and the coral has some fine dive sites, too. There are good views of the distinctive black and yellow Diego Velázquez Lighthouse, built by Chinese immigrants in 1859.

Although part of the province of Camagüey, **Cayo Romano** belongs naturally to this archi-pelago. Its marshy coastline is the habitat of manatees.

The pristine white sandy beach of Cayo Paredón Grande, Jardines del Rey

Cayo Coco ❾

A boat heading out to a coral reef

With 22 km (14 miles) of white sandy beaches and 370 sq km (143 sq miles) of partly marshy land abounding in mangroves and coconut palms, Cayo Coco is an important natural reserve for marine birds. Flamingos can be spotted easily in the lagoon areas near the coast. The name of the island derives from another rare species of bird that lives here: the white ibis, known to Cubans as the "coco". The island is peaceful, and tourist amenities have been built and organized with environmental concerns in mind. The beaches are lovely, with fine sand washed by clear turquoise water. The warm, shallow water makes Cayo Coco particularly suitable for families with children, but the island is also popular among diving and water sports enthusiasts, who can take advantage of the modern sports facilities here.

The *Coccothrinax litoralis* palm tree, common on Cayo Coco

CAYO GUILLERMO

Archipelago de Sab

The Duna de la Loma del Puerto is a natural viewing point which can be reached via a path that goes through tropical vegetation.

C A Y

Cayo Guillermo
Linked to Cayo Coco, this small island (13 sq km, 5 sq miles) is covered with mangroves and palms as well as mahogany, juniper and mastic trees. At Playa Pilar beach the dunes rise as high as 16 m (52 ft).

Playa Prohibida, surrounded by sand dunes reaching heights of 14 m (46 ft), is a particularly peaceful, secluded beach.

KEY

▬▬	Major road
▬▬	Minor road
🏖	Recommended beach
✕	Domestic airport

Bahía de Perros

The Pedraplen
A major work of civil engineering, this causeway links the islands with the mainland. It has caused some concern to ecologists, since it blocks the tide and may disturb the ecosystem of the bay.

La Loma

•San Rafae

★ Playa Flamencos
This beach, almost 3 km (2 miles) long, is regarded as one of the best on the island because of its lovely clear sea and fine sand. The shallow water is only knee-deep even 200 m (650 ft) from the shore.

VISITORS' CHECKLIST

Ciego de Ávila.
Road Map D3. ✈ *Carretera Cayo Guillermo, (33) 309 165.*
🛈 *Cubanacán, Sol Club Cayo Coco, (33) 301 280; Havanatur, Hotel Tryp Cayo Coco, (33) 301 300.* ⚓ *Marina Marlín, Cayo Coco; Marina Puertosol, Cayo Guillermo, (33) 301 637.*

Centro de Investigaciones de Ecosistemas Costeras
This centre for the environment studies the effects of tourism on local ecosystems. It is open to the public, and illustrates the bird species on the island, including the roseate spoonbill seen here.

Güira, a village founded in the early 1900s, still has its traditional houses. It is a starting point for horse riding excursions.

Camagüey

Villa de los Trabajadores

Bautista

OCO

0 km   5.5
0 miles   5.5

Cayo Paredón Grande *(see p193)*

CAYO ROMANO

Manatí

★ Parador La Silla
This is an ideal spot for viewing a spectacular array of pink flamingos, which flock here in great numbers during the wet season, from April to November, to breed.

STAR SIGHTS

★ **Playa Flamencos**

★ **Parador La Silla**

Camagüey ⑩

THIS CITY LIES IN THE MIDDLE of a vast area of pasture-land. It is nicknamed "the Legendary" for its traditions of heroism and patriotism as well as for its Neo-Classical architecture. There is a large, rich Colonial-style historic centre, the result of 19th-century planning, and the city has an active cultural life. Founded in the bay of Nuevitas on the northern coast as Nuestra Señora de Santa María del Puerto Príncipe, the city was moved to the interior to escape from revolts by the Indians, who staunchly resisted Spanish domination in the 1500s, and from pirate attacks. The irregular, intricate street network that distinguishes Camagüey from other Cuban cities resulted from the need to protect itself from raids.

An example of 19th-century Neo-Classical architecture in Camagüey

Parque Agramonte: the equestrian statue and the Cathedral

Parque Ignacio Agramonte

The former Plaza de Armas is dominated by an equestrian statue of Agramonte, a Cuban independence hero, sculpted by the Italian artist Salvatore Boemi and inaugurated by Amalia Simoni, Agramonte's wife, in 1912. At the four corners of the square stand royal palms, planted in memory of a group of nationalists executed here on 24 February 1851. As so often during the wars of independence, the palms were symbolic monuments to the rebels, as the Spanish would never have allowed real monuments to be built.

Buildings of interest on the square include the **Palacio Collado** (1942), **Bar El Cambio**, opened in 1909, a Colonial building housing **La Volanta** restaurant, the **Casa de la Trova Patricio Ballagas** in an 18th-century building with a courtyard, the **Biblioteca Julio Antonio Mella** and the cathedral.

✝ Catedral de Nuestra Señora de la Candelaria

Calle Independencia 64, Parque Agramonte. 📞 (322) 949 65. ⭕ daily. ✝ daily.

Camagüey's cathedral, dedicated to Our Lady of Candelaria, the patron saint of the city, was designed by Manuel Saldaña and built in the early 1700s. In 1777 a bell tower was added, but it collapsed only a month later.

Since that time, the church has been through several phases of reconstruction, taking on its present-day appearance in 1864.

It now has a monumental façade surmounted by a pediment, and a bell tower on six levels, crowned by a statue of Christ.

CALLE PADRE VALENCIA
CALLE MÁXIMO GÓMEZ
CALLE ASTILLEROS
CALLE RAM...
CALLE SAN RAMÓN
CALLE HERMANOS AGÜERO
CALLE LUGAREÑO
CALLE CISNEROS
CALLE INDEPENDENCIA
CALLE MARTÍ
CALLE CRISTO
CALLE RAÚL LAMAR

0 metres   200
0 yards   200

THE CENTRE OF CAMAGÜEY

CALLE IGNACIO AGRAMONTE

CALLE REPÚBLICA

CALLE BARTOLOMÉ

CALLE LUACES

CALLE SAN PABLO

Casino Campestre

Carretera Central, Bus station

...ADERO

KEY

† Church

ℹ Tourist information

The courtyard at Casa Agramonte, where concerts are performed

🏛 Casa Natal de Ignacio Agramonte

Calle Ignacio Agramonte 459, e/ Independencia y Cisneros. **【** (322) 971 16. ☐ Tue–Sun. ● 1 Jan, 1 May, 26 Jul, 25 Dec. 📷 📷 📷

Near Plaza de los Trabajadores, where a large ceiba tree marks the middle of the old town, is the former home of Ignacio Agramonte. This famous local patriot died in battle in 1873 at the age of 32. The two-storey house dates from 1750 and has a beautiful inner courtyard with old *tinajones*.

Plaque on Nicolás Guillén's birthplace

The museum has documents concerning the war of independence, the hero's personal belongings, such as his 36-calibre Colt pistol made in 1851, and family furniture, including the piano of Agramonte's wife, Amalia Simoni. She was reputed to be one of the richest, loveliest, most virtuous women in the city.

A short walk away is another famous home. The **Casa Natal Nicolás Guillén** *(see p26)*, birthplace of Cuba's poet laureate who died in 1989, is at Calle Hermanos Aguero 58.

VISITORS' CHECKLIST

Camagüey. **Road map** D3.
🏠 300,000. ✈ Ignacio Agramonte, (322) 610 10. �G Ave Avellaneda y Finlay, (322) 887 44. 🚌 Carretera Central km 3, (322) 734 63. ℹ Islazul, Calle Ignacio Agramonte 448, (322) 92 550. 🎭 Jornadas de la Cultura Camagüeyana (first half of Feb); Carnival (26 Jul).

🏛 Iglesia de la Merced

Plaza de los Trabajadores 4.
【 (322) 927 83.
☐ daily. 🕇 daily.

The Iglesia de la Merced was built in 1601 but was rebuilt from 1748 to 1756, and now has a Baroque façade with a central bell tower. Inside the church are striking, almost Art Nouveau-style murals. The choir and catacombs are also of interest. Most famous, however, is the Holy Sepulchre with an 18th-century statue of Christ by the Mexican sculptor Juan Benítez Alfonso. It was cast from 23,000 silver coins collected from the faithful by Manuel Agüero, a citizen who, after his wife's death in 1726, became a monk in the Mercedarios order and devoted himself to restoring the church.

🎭 Teatro Principal

Calle Pedro Valencia 64.
【 (322) 930 48.

First opened in 1850 and rebuilt in 1926 after a devastating fire, the local theatre is famous as the home of the Camagüey Ballet, one of the leading dance companies in Latin America *(see p282)*.

THE *TINAJONES*

These symbols of the city can be seen everywhere – in parks and gardens and especially in the courtyards of the local Colonial houses. *Tinajones* are large jars, which may be as much as 2 m (6 ft) tall, made of clay from the nearby Sierra de Cubitas. The jars were introduced by Catalonian immigrants in the early 1700s, and are used today to collect rainwater and to store food.

A *tinajón* in the central square

Exploring Camagüey

THE VAST HISTORIC CENTRE of Camagüey, a complex 16th-century labyrinth of winding alleyways, dead ends, forks and squares, is not easy to navigate. The centre consists mainly of two-storey houses without arcades, pierced by large windows protected by wooden grilles. Each house has an inner courtyard. There are numerous old churches, most of them well attended, whose bell towers jut above the red tile roofs of the Colonial houses. As with Trinidad, the well-preserved architecture is the result of the town's geographic isolation: the railway line only arrived in 1903, and the Carretera Central road in 1931.

The Cinco Esquinas (Five Corners), one of the town's more complicated junctions

Other City Centre Sights
Many interesting sights are just a short walk away from Parque Ignacio Agramonte.

Calle Martí runs west from the square up to Plazuela de la Bedoya, a delightful Colonial square in need of restoration. An old Ursuline convent stands here, as well as a church, the **Iglesia del Carmen**. Although not completed until 1825, it has a distinctly Baroque character.

Calle Cristo leads to Plazuela del Cristo, which is dominated by the Iglesia del Santo Cristo del Buen Viaje and the Cementerio General

Author Gertrudis Gómez de Avellaneda

(1814), the oldest cemetery in Cuba. Back near Parque Agramonte, there is a complex interchange, the **Cinco Esquinas** (five corners), near the top of Calle Raúl Lamar, which is a good example of the intricate layout of the city centre.

Another route to explore runs along or near Calle República, a narrow, straight street that crosses the entire city from north to south. At the northern end, beyond the railway line, is the Museo Provincial Ignacio Agramonte (see p199).

Further south, a right turn at the Hotel Colón leads eastwards across to Calle

Avellaneda. Here, at No. 22, is the birthplace of Gertrudis Gómez de Avellaneda, the 19th-century author of anti-slavery novels.

Further south stands the **Iglesia de Nuestra Señora de la Soledad**, built in 1776. It was here that local patriot Ignacio Agramonte was baptized and also got married. The façade features pilasters and moulding typical of early Cuban Baroque architecture, but the real attractions here are the decoratively painted arches and pillars and the wooden *alfarje* ceiling (see p222) inside.

By going south to the far end of this street you will reach Calle Martí, which will take you back to Parque Agramonte.

Plaza San Juan de Dios
This square is commonly called Plaza del Padre Olallo, in honour of a priest who is soon to be canonized because he dedicated his life to caring for the sick in the city hospital.

Today, the totally restored Plaza San Juan de Dios is a quiet, picturesque spot, but also a gem of Colonial architecture. Around it are 18th-century pastel buildings, two of which have been converted into restaurants. One whole side of the plaza is occupied by an important group of buildings that include a church and an old hospital, which is now the home of the Dirección

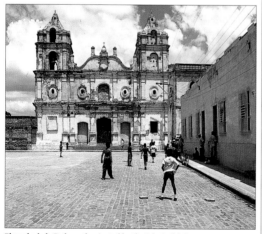

Plazuela de la Bedoya, dominated by the Iglesia del Carmen

Provincial de Patrimonio and the Oficina del Historiador de la Ciudad, a body that takes care of the province's cultural heritage. Construction of the building began in 1728.

Despite its small size, the **Iglesia de San Juan de Dios** is one of the most interesting churches in Camagüey. It still has its original floors, ceiling and wooden choir, and, most importantly, the high altar with the Holy Trinity and an anthropomorphic representation of the Holy Ghost, the only one in Cuba. The church façade is simple and rigorously symmetrical.

The old **Hospital** was used in the 20th century as a military infirmary, then a teacher training school, a refuge for flood victims, a centre for underprivileged children and, most recently, as the Instituto Tecnológico de la Salud (Technological Institute of Health). The square plan with two inner courtyards (clearly of *mudéjar* influence) was modelled on Baroque monasteries. The enclosure walls are thick and plain; in contrast the window grilles and wooden balustrades in the galleries are elegant and elaborate.

Iglesia y Hospital de San Juan de Dios

Plaza San Juan de Dios. ◯ *daily.*
● *1 Jan, 1 May, 26 Jul, 25 Dec.*

One of the cloisters in the old San Juan de Dios hospital

🏛 Museo Provincial Ignacio Agramonte

Avenida de los Mártires 2, esq. Ignacio Sánchez. 【 *(322) 82425.* ◯ *10am–6pm Tue, Wed, Thu, Sat; 2pm–10pm Fri; 9am–1pm Sun.*

The only military building in town was the headquarters of the Spanish army cavalry in the 19th century. Since 1948 it has housed a large museum given over to the history, natural history and art of the city and its province. The prestigious art collection is second only to that in the Museo de Bellas Artes in Havana, and has three works by the famous Cuban artist Fidelio Ponce.

The museum also has an exceptional collection of books, including some manuscripts by the Canaries writer Silvestre de Balboa, author of

The Holy Trinity high altar

Espejo de Paciencia, a poem (1608) regarded as the first literary work in Cuba *(see p26).*

🌸 Parque Casino Campestre

The largest natural park in any Cuban city, the Casino was for a long time used for agricultural fairs, and became a public park in the 19th century. The Hatibonico river flows through it. Besides the many statues of patriots and illustrious figures from Camagüey and Cuba, it has a monument to the Seville pilots Barberán and Collar, who on 10 June 1933 made a historic transatlantic flight from Seville to Camagüey in 19 hours 11 minutes.

ENVIRONS: the plains north of Camagüey are cattle country. **King Rancho**, a former cattle ranch, has a restaurant *(see p272)* and rooms and offers horse-riding trips and rodeos. King Ranch is most easily accessed from Santa Lucía, 26 miles (16 km) to the north.

Plaza San Juan de Dios, known for its well-preserved Colonial architecture

A country road north of Camagüey, leading to Sierra de Cubitas

Sierra de Cubitas ⑪

Camagüey. **Map** D3.

THE RANGE OF HILLS that lies 40 km (25 miles) north of Camagüey forms the largest local reserve of flora and fauna, with over 300 plant species. To date, however, this area has no tourist facilities on any scale.

The main attractions are caverns such as Hoyo de Bonet, the largest karst depression in Cuba, and the Pichardo and María Teresa grottoes, where cave drawings have been discovered. Expert speleologists, on the other hand, can visit the Cueva de Rolando, a cave 132 m (435 ft) long with a subterranean lake 50 m (165 ft) across, the bottom of which has not yet been explored.

In the neighbouring Valle del Río Máximo is the **Paso de los Paredones**, a long, deep ravine with holes caused by water erosion, some as much as 100 m (328 ft) deep and up to 1 km (0.6 mile) wide. The thick vegetation, through which sunlight penetrates for only a few hours, is home to a variety of native birds (*tocororo and cartacuba; see pp18–9*) and migratory birds, as well as harmless reptiles and rodents.

Playa Santa Lucía ⑫

Camagüey. **Map** D3.
 Rumbos, Tararaco, Playa Santa Lucía, (32) 336 106.

THE MOST FAMOUS beach resort in the province offers 21 km (13 miles) of fine white sand lapped by turquoise waves. The large coral reef only 3 km (2 miles) from the shore is a scuba diver's paradise (*see p285*). It shelters the coast from the currents of the Canal Viejo de Bahamas, thus safeguarding calm swimming conditions for adults and children alike, as well as creating a good area for practising all water sports. There are more than 30 dive sites along the reef, which can be reached with the help of the international diving centres, while Virgen de Altagracia and Shark's Point offer dives full of romance, exploring the wrecks of pirate and Spanish vessels. For the brave there is also the chance to observe a special type of shark, the *Carcharinus leucas*, which is fed and trained and so can be viewed at close range.

At the bay of Nuevitas, 6 km (4 miles) west of Santa Lucía, near the tiny seashore village of La Boca, is **Playa Los Cocos**. This lovely unspoilt beach has fine white sand and clear water, and is a must for visitors to Santa Lucía.

A beach at Cayo Sabinal, accessible by car or catamaran

Cayo Sabinal ⑬

Camagüey. **Map** D3.
 Rumbos, Bahia de Nuevitas, (32) 447 54.

TOGETHER WITH Cayo Romano and Cayo Guajaba, this small island forms part of a protected area. It is the home of deer and the largest colony

The pier at Playa Santa Lucía, departure point for boats going out to the coral reef

◁ **Playa Los Cocos, near Playa Santa Lucía**

of flamingos in Cuba, as well as a nesting area for four species of sea turtle. Cayo Sabinal can be reached either via a causeway or by catamaran from Playa Santa Lucía.

In the past it was home to permanent residents: first the natives, then pirates and Spanish coalmen. Today, the key is visited mostly for its three beautiful beaches, Playa Bonita, Playa Los Pinos and Playa Brava. The Colón Lighthouse dates from 1894.

South of Cayo Sabinal is the Bay of Nuevitas, where the city of Camagüey was first founded. The three small islands in the bay, known as **Los Ballenatos**, are popular destinations for boat trips.

Las Tunas ⑭

Las Tunas. **Map** E3.
🏘 100,000. ✈ 🚉 🚌
ℹ Hotel Las Tunas, Ave. 2 de diciembre, (31) 450 14. 🎭 Jornada Nacional Cucalambeana (end of Jun).

UNTIL 1975, Las Tunas was just one of the cities in the old Provincia de Oriente. Then administrative reform made it the capital of an autonomous province. The town was founded on the site of two native villages that were razed to the ground by the *conquistador* Alonso de Ojeda in the early 1500s. However, the town only really began to develop three centuries later, progressively

A scuba diver grasping a barracuda

taking on the character of a frontier town between central and eastern Cuba and an obligatory transit point for anyone going to Santiago. The historic centre has some Colonial buildings but no major monuments of note. However, the city does have many artists' studios.

The town hall of Las Tunas

The **Museo Histórico Provincial**, in the town hall, has archaeological finds and documents relating to the history of the province. The Memorial a los Mártires de Barbados commemorates a terrorist act against Cuba carried out in 1976: a bomb exploded on a Cubana aeroplane headed for Havana, killing 73 passengers and the entire crew.

Every year Las Tunas springs to life on the occasion of the Jornada Nacional Cucalambeana, dedicated to Juan Cristóbal Nápoles Fajardo, known as El Cucalambé, a farmer and poet born here in 1829. Local and other Cuban artists, as well as foreign scholars, take part in this festival of music and folk traditions.

ENVIRONS: near Las Tunas are many sites linked with the wars of independence. They include the **Fuerte de la**

Loma, now a national monument, built by the Spanish to halt the advance of the Mambí, and the city of **Puerto Padre**, the scene of major battles in the Ten Years' War (1868–78).

The best beach here is **Playa Covarrubias**, near Puerto Padre, on the Atlantic coast.

Jardines de la Reina ⑮

Ciego de Ávila, Camagüey. **Map** D4.
🚤 Júcaro, Embarcadero Avalón, (33) 981 04.

THIS ARCHIPELAGO in the Caribbean Sea was discovered by Christopher Columbus and called Jardines de la Reina in honour of the queen *(reina)*, Isabel of Castile. Currently, these islands can be reached by boat from the pleasant fishing village of Júcaro, but will soon be linked to the mainland by a causeway. Initially, a 20-km (12-mile) road will connect Providencia and Júcaro, and later the latter will be connected to Cayo Caoba.

The great number of unspoilt *cayos*, the secluded beaches, the rich fauna consisting of crocodiles, iguanas, turtles and tropical birds, and a 200-km (125-mile) coral reef make this archipelago a paradise for nature lovers.

At Cayo Caballones, only about 100 m (328 ft) from the coast, is a floating hotel reserved for fishermen, divers and photographers. Traditional tours usually take place in daytime, departing from Cayo Blanco, an hour from the coast. Navigating the entire archipelago takes five hours.

EASTERN CUBA

GRANMA · HOLGUÍN · SANTIAGO DE CUBA · GUANTÁNAMO

C UBANS REFER TO THE EASTERN PART OF CUBA *as the Oriente, giving it an exotic, magical appeal. The landscape, stretching out towards Haiti and other Caribbean islands, is varied, with majestic mountains, magnificent coastlines and an area of arid desert, unusual in Cuba. The eastern cities, often rich in history, include Santiago de Cuba, host to one of Latin America's most famous carnivals.*

From the 17th to the 19th centuries, thousands of black slaves were brought to Cuba from Africa, men and women who became the ancestors of the multi-ethnic mix visible in Eastern Cuba today, part African, but also part Spanish, part French and Chinese. In this cultural melting pot, African and European, Catholic and pagan traditions are blended, sometimes inextricably.

The area is full of apparent contradictions: there is the combative Oriente, rebellious and indomitable; and yet there is also the laid-back Oriente, an oasis of pleasure, and the sonorous Oriente, the cradle of great musicians. It is true that the people of Eastern Cuba have always fought with great fervour. One eloquent example is the Indian chief Hatuey, who was burned at the stake in the 16th century for organizing resistance against the Spanish. Then, in the 19th century, local nationalists led the wars of independence. The citizens of Bayamo even burned down their town rather than hand it over to the enemy. In the 20th century, there were the *rebeldes* (many of whom were from Eastern Cuba, including Fidel Castro himself), who launched the struggle against Batista's dictatorship by attacking the Moncada barracks in Santiago.

Yet the people of eastern Cuba also know how to have a good time, adore music, rhythm and dance of all kinds, and each year put on a colourful Carnival at Santiago de Cuba which rivals that of Rio de Janeiro, and is one of the most celebrated in Latin America.

Cacti growing along the Costa Sur, the only arid zone on the island, east of Guantánamo

◁ The steps on Calle Padre Pico, in the heart of Santiago de Cuba

Exploring Eastern Cuba

THE CLASSIC STARTING POINT for touring the eastern
provinces is Santiago de Cuba, a city rich in
history, with lovely Colonial architecture and sites
associated with the revolution. To the west rises the
majestic Sierra Maestra, also with its own associations
with the guerrilla war of the 1950s. The Sierra is most
easily reached, in fact, from the north, near Bayamo.
To the east, the Parque Baconao has all kinds of
attractions, ideal for families with children, while
more adventurous souls can head further east, to the
province of Guantánamo, famous for its US naval
base, and Baracoa, Cuba's oldest city. The province
of Holguín, further north, has some fine beaches,
and Cuba's most interesting archaeological site.

The small islands of Bahía de
Naranjo, now a holiday village

GIBARA ②
BAHÍA DE BARIAY ③

HOLGUÍN ①

SEE ALSO

• *Where to Stay* pp259–61

• *Where to Eat* p273

MANZANILLO ⑩
YARA
BAYAMO ⑨

AMEDIA LUNA ●
⑪
BARTOLOMÉ MASÓ
GRAN PARQUE NACIONAL ⑫
SIERRA MAESTRA
BASÍLICA DEL COBRE ⑬

CABO CRUZ ●
MAREA DEL
PORTILLO

```
0 kilometres    20
0 miles         20
```

KEY

═══ Motorway
─── Major road
⋯⋯ Minor road
━━━ Scenic route
≈≈≈ River

A group of musicians improvising a concert
in Parque Céspedes, Santiago de Cuba

SIGHTS AT A GLANCE

Bahía de Bariay ③
Banes ⑥
Baracoa pp238–9 ⑳
Basílica del Cobre ⑬
Bayamo ⑨
Boca de Yumurí ㉓
Castillo del Morro pp228–9 ⑮
Cayo Saetía ⑧
Chorro de Maita ⑤

Costa Sur ⑱
El Yunque ㉑
Gibara ②
Gran Parque Nacional Sierra Maestra ⑫
Guantánamo ⑰
Guardalavaca ④
Holguín pp208–9 ①
La Farola ⑲
Manzanillo ⑩

Mayarí ⑦
Parque Baconao pp230–33 ⑯
Río Toa ㉒
Santiago de Cuba pp218–27 ⑭

Tour
Towards Santiago via Cabo Cruz pp214–5 ⑪

④ GUARDALAVACA
⑤ CHORRO DE MAITA
⑥ BANES
CAYO SAETÍA ⑧
⑦ MAYARÍ
MOA
SAGUA DE TÁNAMO
RÍO TOA ㉒
EL YUNQUE ㉑ BARACOA ⑳
㉓ BOCA DE YUMURÍ
⑰ GUANTÁNAMO
LA FAROLA ⑲
⑱ COSTA SUR
⑭ SANTIAGO DE CUBA
⑮ CASTILLO DEL MORRO ⑯ PARQUE BACONAO

The *azulejos* decoration in the Colonia Española in Manzanillo

GETTING AROUND
Although sights on the outskirts of Santiago can be reached by bus or taxi, by far the best way to get around Eastern Cuba is to hire a car. Some journeys are among the most picturesque in Cuba, especially the drive to Baracoa via "La Farola" *(see p235)*. Another option would be to fly to the main eastern towns. Various organized tours are also available, starting off from Santiago or from the beach resorts of Holguín province, especially Guardalavaca. These tours can be booked through travel agencies.

A perfectly restored Neo-Classical building in the centre of Baracoa

Holguín ●

A peanut vendor in Parque García

CALLED THE CITY OF PARKS because of its many leafy squares, Holguín is a modern town built on a grid layout and situated between two hills, Cerro de Mayabe and Loma de la Cruz. The people of Holguín took an active part in the wars of independence under the leadership of Calixto García, the famous general who liberated the city from the Spanish in 1872. The house he was born in is now a museum; the square named after him marks the centre of the city and is dominated by a statue of the heroic general.

Exploring Holguín

Calle Maceo and Manduley – two parallel streets with shops, hotels, bars and clubs, including the Casa de la Trova – cross three squares: **Parque San José**, **Parque Calixto García** and **Parque Peralta**. Parque García, always buzzing with people, is the site of the town's chief monuments and museums including **Casa Natal de Calixto García**.

🚩 La Periquera (Museo Provincial de Historia)

Calle Frexes 198, e/ Manduley y Maceo. 🕻 (24) 463 395. ◯ Tue–Sun. ● 1 Jan, 1 May, 26 Jul, 10 Oct, 25 Dec. 🖾 🖅 🖾

This large Neo-Classical building with a courtyard overlooks Parque Calixto García. It was built in 1860 as a ballroom and casino for the local upper middle class. In 1868, at the beginning of the Ten Years' War *(see p44)*, the building was occupied by Cuban patriots and converted into a barracks, where a handful of Spanish soldiers were taken prisoner. Hence the building's nickname, *La Periquera*, which translates as "parrot cage", a reference to the brightly coloured uniforms of the Spanish army.

Today, the building is the home of the Museo Provincial de Historia, where five rooms illustrate the main stages in the history of Holguín. Also on display are archaeological relics of the Taíno Indians, who lived here from the 8th to the 15th centuries. The most famous item in the collection is the Hacha de Holguín, a stone axe head carved as a human figure. It was discovered in the hills around Holguín, and has become the symbol of the city.

Hacha de Holguín

🏛 Museo de Historia Natural Carlos de la Torre y Huerta

Calle Maceo 129, e/ Martí y Luz Caballero. 🕻 (24) 423 935. ◯ Tue–Sun. ● 1 Jan, 1 May, 26 Jul, 10 Oct, 25 Dec. 🖾 🖅 🖾

One of the most interesting natural history museums in Cuba has 11 rooms with 7,000 specimens of Cuban and Caribbean flora and fauna. There is an outstanding collection of birds and shells, including *Polymita* snails from the beaches of Baracoa *(see p241)*, and a 60 million year-old fossil fish, found in a quarry in the Sierra Maestra.

San Isidro Cathedral, in the spacious Parque Peralta

⛪ Catedral de San Isidro

Calle Manduley, e/ Luz Caballero y Aricoches, Parque Peralta. 🕻 (24) 422 107. ◯ daily. 🚩 daily.

Consecrated as a cathedral as recently as 1979, San Isidro was built in 1720 on the site of the first mass held to celebrate the foundation of the city: in Parque Peralta. It is also known as Parque de Flores because a flower market used to be held here.

The church contains a copy of the popular Madonna of Caridad, the original of which is in the Basílica del Cobre near Santiago de Cuba *(see p217)*. On 4 April there is a celebration in honour of the Virgin, during which worshippers put palm leaves on the altar beneath her image.

Loma de la Cruz

There are marvellous, far-reaching views from the top of the Loma de la Cruz (Hill of the Cross). The engineers who founded Holguín used this site to plan the layout of the town, but it was only much later (from 1927–50) that the 458-step stairway was built to the top. Every year on 3 May, the people of Holguín

Parque Calixto García, with La Periquera; behind, the Loma de la Cruz

A panoramic view of Holguín from the top of the Loma de la Cruz

climb up the hill for the Romerías de Mayo, a celebration of Spanish origin. The top of Loma, about 3 km (2 miles) northwest of Parque Calixto García, is marked by a Spanish lookout tower and by a cross placed there on 3 May 1790 by friar Antonio Alegría.

Plaza de la Revolución
Situated east of the city centre, behind Hotel Pernik, this vast square contains a monument to the heroes of Cuban independence, the mausoleum of Calixto García and a small monument to his mother. The square is the main venue for political rallies and popular festivities.

ENVIRONS: another, more distant viewing point over the city is the **Mirador de Mayabe** on the Cerro de Mayabe, which is about 10 km (6 miles) southeast of the city centre.

From the mirador there is a view of the valley with its fruit orchards and of Holguín in the distance. This spot is also home to an *aldea campesina* (country village), with simple lodgings and a restaurant, as well as an open-air museum. This illustrates the lives of Cuban farmers living in a small village, with various examples of a *bohío real*, a typical rural home with a palm-leaf roof

and earth floor, a hen-house and a courtyard containing jars for transporting water.

At No. 301 on the road leading to Gibara, a mile or so north of the centre, is the small **Fábrica de Órganos**, the only factory in Cuba that manufactures mechanical organs. The factory is open to the public.

A mechanical organ made in the Holguín factory

THE CENTRE OF HOLGUÍN

Casa de la Trova ③
Casa Natal de Calixto García ⑦
Catedral de San Isidro ⑥
La Periquera ②
Museo de Historia Natural Carlos de la Torre y Huerta ④
Parque Calixto García ①
Parque Peralta ⑤
Parque San José ⑧

0 metres   250
0 yards   250

KEY
🏛 Church
ℹ Tourist information

View of Gibara, an appealing seaside town with a Colonial centre

Gibara ❷

Holguín. **Road Map** E3.
🏚 *100,000.* 🚌 *from Holguín.*

SOUTH OF THE bay that
Columbus named Río de
Mares (the river of seas)
is the picturesque town of
Gibara. In the 19th century
this was the main port on the
northern coast of the province
of Oriente, and it has the most
important Colonial architecture
in the area. Gibara is sometimes known as "Villa Blanca"
(white town) because of its
white houses.

The shady Malecón
(seafront) has a statue of
Columbus shown gazing at
the horizon, a ruined garrison
and views of the small fishing
harbour. From here, narrow
streets lead to the main
square, overlooked by the
Iglesia de San Fulgencio
(1854), and an old theatre.

Façade of the Iglesia de San
Fulgencio at Gibara

The **Museo de Ciencias
Naturales** (Natural History
Museum) has one of the best
butterfly collections in Cuba,
and the **Museo de Artes
Decorativas** (Decorative Arts
Museum) is housed in a
magnificent 19th-century
mansion. This last contains
fine examples of *mediopuntos
(see p23)* and *mamparas (see
p184)* as well as furniture and
Art Nouveau objects.

🏛 **Museo de Ciencias
Naturales**
Calle Maceo 12, e/ Martí y Luz
Caballero. 📞 *(24) 423 935.* ⭕
Tue–Sat, Sun am. ● *1 Jan, 1 May,
26 Jul, 10 Oct, 25 Dec.* 📷 📷
🏛 **Museo de Artes
Decorativas**
Calle Independencia. ⭕ *Tue–Sat;
Sun am.* 📷

Bahía de Bariay ❸

Holguín. **Road Map** E3.

EAST OF GIBARA is a bay with
a spit of land in the middle
called Cayo de Bariay. Most
historians (but not Baracoans,
see p238) agree that Columbus
first landed here in 1492. With
its abundant flowers and trees
laden with fruit, it looked like
paradise to the explorer. In
1992, on the 500th anniversary
of Columbus' landing in Cuba,
a monument called *Encuentro*
("Encounter"), dedicated to the
Taíno Indians, was erected
here. The site is relatively
remote if travelling by car,
but boat trips can be arranged
from Guardalavaca *(see p211)*.
East of Cayo de Bariay is the
beautiful **Playa Don Lino**.

COLUMBUS IN CUBA

On 28 October 1492, when he first set
foot on Cuban land, Columbus wrote in
his travel journal: "I have never seen a
more beautiful place. Along the banks of
the river were trees I have never seen at
home, with flowers and fruit of the
most diverse kinds, among the
branches of which one heard the
delightful chirping of birds. There
were a great number of palms.
When I descended from the
launch, I approached two

**Christopher Columbus,
explorer of the New World**

fishermen's huts. Upon seeing me, the natives took fright
and fled. Back on the boat, I went up the river for a good
distance. I felt such joy upon seeing these flowery gardens
and green forests and hearing the birds sing that I could not
tear myself away, and thus continued my trip. This island is
truly the most beautiful land human eyes have ever beheld."

Guardalavaca ❹

Holguín. **Road Map** F3.

CONVERTED in the mid-1980s into a holiday resort, the beach of Guardalavaca is the most popular holiday destination in Cuba after Varadero *(see pp158–9)*. Although the resort is within easy reach of Holguín, 58 km (35 miles) to the southwest along a road through curious conical hills, the location still feels remote.

The 4-km (2-mile) crescent-shaped beach, enclosed at either end by rocks, is backed by abundant vegetation. The sea is crystal-clear, the sand is fine, and there is a coral reef quite close to the shore. Behind the beach is a modern tourist resort with the usual holiday facilities.

The name "Guardalavaca" (watch the cow) derives from the Spanish word for the cattle egret *(see p18)*, a bird which is common throughout Cuba, and especially prevalent here.

West of the beach is **Bahía de Naranjo**, a natural park that comprises 32 km (20 miles) of coastline and 1,000 ha (2,470 acres) of woods, with karst hills covered with thick vegetation. There are three small islands in the bay; on one, Cayo Naranjo, there is an aquarium featuring shows with sea lions and dolphins. Boat tours, diving and fishing trips are also organized here.

Skeletons found in the necropolis of Chorro de Maita

Chorro de Maita ❺

Cerro de Yaguajay, Banes (Holguín). **Road Map** F4.
🚪 *Tue–Sat.* ⏰ *1 Jan, 1 May, 26 Jul, 10 Oct, 25 Dec.* 🎟️ ⚡ 📷

NEAR THE COAST, just 5 km (3 miles) south of Guardalavaca, is Chorro de Maita, the largest native Indian necropolis in Cuba and the Antilles. At this unmissable site archaeologists have found 56 skeletons and a number of clay objects, bone amulets, funerary offerings and decorated shells.

All this material can be seen from a boardwalk inside the *aldea taína*, a reconstruction of a pre-Columbian rural village, built for entertainment, but historically accurate. Visitors can buy souvenirs and sample the food that the Amerindians themselves used to eat. In front of the huts are some life-size statues of natives.

Banes ❻

Holguín. **Road Map** F4.

THIS COUNTRY TOWN, 32 km (20 m) southwest of Holguín, is located in the middle of a vast and rich excavation zone (the province of Holguín has yielded one-third of the archaeological finds in Cuba). Banes is the home of the **Museo Indocubano Bani**, Cuba's most important archaeological museum outside Havana. The museum has over a thousand objects on display, including axes, terracotta vases, flint knives and, most notably, a 4-cm (2-in) high figure of a woman in gold, known as the Ídolo de Oro. It was found near Banes, and dates from the 13th century.

Ídolo de Oro, Museo Indocubano Bani

🏛 **Museo Indocubano Bani**
Calle General Barrero 305, e/ Martí y Céspedes. 📞 *(24) 824 87.* 🚪 *Tue–Sat, Sun am.* ⏰ *1 Jan, 1 May, 26 Jul, 10 Oct, 25 Dec.* 🎟️ ⚡ 📷

The lovely clear turquoise sea at Guardalavaca, Eastern Cuba's Varadero

The coves at Cayo Saetía, known for their fine white sand

Mayarí **7**

Holguín. **Road Map** F4.
👤 30,000.

MAYARÍ, 100 km (62 miles) southeast of Holguín, was founded in 1757 and, together with Gibara *(see p210)*, is the oldest city in the province. The small Colonial centre can be explored in a short time.

Nearby are the **Farallones de Seboruco**, caves where objects left by the Taíno people have been found. Nearby is an important eco-tourist site, the **Meseta de Pinares de Mayarí**, a large forest cloaking the hills up to an altitude of 1,000 m (3,280 ft).

Southwest of Mayarí is Birán, where Fidel Castro was born on 13 August 1926. His parents' house is still standing.

Cayo Saetía **8**

Holguín. **Road Map** F4.

LYING AT THE MOUTH of the Bay of Nipe, this small island covering 42 sq km (16 sq miles), with wonderfully fascinating coves, is connected to the mainland by a drawbridge. It was formerly a private hunting reserve, and in the woods and meadows, antelopes and zebra still live side by side with species native to Cuba. On safaris, led by expert guides, visitors travelling on horseback or in jeeps can observe and photograph the animals. The few tourist facilities on this island are for residents only and were designed with every care for the environment.

Bayamo **9**

Granma. **Road Map** E4.
👤 130,000. ✈ 🚂 Saco y Línea, (23) 424 955. 🚌 Carretera Central y Jesús Rabí (23) 424 036. ℹ Islazul, Calle Mármol 120, (23) 425 105.

THE SECOND OLDEST town in Cuba after Baracoa, Bayamo was founded in 1513 by Diego Velázquez. Until 1975 it was part of the large Oriente province, but after administrative reform it became the capital of a new province, Granma. It is a pasture and livestock breeding area, but has also been the home of nationalists and the cradle of political revolts and struggles.

In 1869, rather than surrender their town to Spain, the citizens burned Bayamo down. As a result, the centre is relatively modern. Daily life revolves around the **Plaza de la Revolución** (Parque Céspedes), the main square, dominated by a statue of local plantation owner and war of independence hero Carlos Manuel de Céspedes (1955). The square is home to almost all the important buildings in town: the Cultural Centre, the Royaltón Hotel, the offices of the Poder Popular, and the historic Pedrito café.

The statue of Carlos Manuel de Céspedes at Bayamo

Adjacent to the main square is **Plaza del Himno** (Square of the Hymn). It gained its name after *La Bayamesa*, the Cuban national anthem, was first played in the church here on 20 October 1868. Marking this event is a sculpture that includes a bronze plaque on which are engraved the words and music by Perucho Figueredo. His bust stands next to the nationalists' flag.

Plaza de la Revolución, also known as Parque Céspedes, in Bayamo

Bayamo "the Rebellious"

Bayamo has a long tradition of rebellion. In the early 1500s, the native Indians, led by their chief, Hatuey, fiercely resisted the Spanish *(see p215)*. A few years later an African slave killed the pirate Gilberto Giron, displaying his head as a trophy in the central plaza. This episode inspired the epic poem *Espejo de Paciencia* by Silvestre de Balboa, the first major work of Cuban literature *(see p26)*. But the most dramatic episode in the history of Bayamo concerns the struggles for independence, during which, on 10 October 1868, a group of local nationalists and intellectuals – Juan Clemente Zenea, Carlos Manuel de Céspedes *(see p43)*, Pedro Figueredo, José Fornaris and José Joaquín Palma – organized an anti-Spanish revolt. They entered the town on 20 October, and declared it the capital of the Republic in Arms. On 12 January, faced with the fact that Bayamo would be recaptured by Colonial troops, the citizens decided to set fire to their own town, an act which later led to the choice of *La Bayamesa* as the national anthem.

The monument dedicated to the national anthem, *La Bayamesa*

Interior of the Parroquial Mayor de San Salvador

In the smaller **Parque Maceo Osorio**, formerly Parque de San Francisco, north of Plaza de la Revolución, is the Casa de la Trova Olimpio La O, one of the town's few 18th-century buildings. The courtyard is used by local groups for concerts *(see p282)*.

Casa Natal de Carlos Manuel de Céspedes

Calle Maceo 57, e/ Marmol y Palma. (23) 423 864. Tue–Sat, Sun am. 1 Jan, 1 May, 26 Jul, 10 Oct, 25 Dec.

The house where the leading figure in the first war against Spain in the 19th century was born on 18 April 1819 is a handsome, two-storey Colonial building facing Plaza de la Revolución. Architecturally it is the most important building in the city.

The rooms on the ground floor, which open onto a courtyard with a fountain, contain the heart of the collection, with Céspedes's documents and personal items, including his steel and bronze sword.

Upstairs are several furnished rooms, one of which has a bronze bed with mother-of-pearl medallions, a fine example of Colonial furniture. A gallery leads to the old kitchen, which still has its original ceramic oven.

Façade of the birthplace of Carlos Manuel de Céspedes

Parroquial Mayor de San Salvador

Calle Saco 18. (23) 422 514. daily.

When the nationalists of Bayamo chose to burn down their own town rather than leave anything for the Spanish, they put the holy images kept in the Parroquial Mayor (the Cathedral) into safekeeping. That was the plan, at all events. Unfortunately, the only things spared by the fire were the font (which had been used for the baptism of Carlos Manuel de Céspedes) and the Capilla de los Dolores, a chapel built in 1740, which contained an image of the Virgin Mary and a Baroque altarpiece made of gilded wood. The altarpiece has a particularly fine frame decorated with tropical motifs and representations of local fruit and animals, an unusual and very Cuban element in the art of the 18th century.

In 1916, Bishop Guerra commissioned the re-construction of the old Parroquial Mayor, dedicated to Jesus the Saviour, the patron saint of Bayamo. The original building had been finished in 1613 and in the course of time had been transformed into a large three-aisle church with two choirs, nine altars and a finely wrought pulpit.

The new church was opened on 9 October 1919, with the old image of Jesus the Saviour salvaged from the fire, a new marble altar, a patriotic painting by the Dominican artist Luis Desangles, and plastered brick walls frescoed by Esteban Ferrer.

Manzanillo ⑩

Granma. **Road map** E4.
✈ *"Sierra Maestra", 8 km (5 miles)
south of town.* 🚌 🚏 *Bayamo,
Camagüey, Havana, Pilón, Yara.*

BUILT ALONG THE Caribbean
bay of Guacanayabo,
Manzanillo is a charming
seaside town. It was founded
as Puerto Real in 1784, and
reached its apogee in the
second half of the 19th
century, thanks to sugar and
the slave trade.
  Memories are still strong
of the feats of Castro's rebel
forces in the nearby Sierra
Maestra, especially those of
Castro's assistant Celia
Sánchez, who organized a
crucial rearguard here. She
is honoured by a striking
monument in the town.
  In Parque Céspedes, the

The Glorieta Morisca de Manzanillo, where the municipal band plays

central square, a brickwork
bandstand for concerts by
local bands was opened on
25 June 1924. The so-called
Glorieta Morisca gained its
name because of its Arab-
influenced decoration,
designed by José Martín del
Castillo, an architect from

Granada. Other monuments
in town, all near the Parque
Céspedes, include the Neo-
Classical Iglesia de la Purísima
Concepción, built in the
1920s; the atmospheric Café
1906, the 19th-century town
hall, now the Asamblea
Municipal del Poder Popular;

Towards Santiago via Cabo Cruz ⑪

THIS FASCINATING ROUTE BY ROAD TO SANTIAGO skirts
the high slopes of the Sierra Maestra which,
along the south coast, almost force the road into the
sea in places. The surrounding scenery is unspoiled
and at times wild, and conceals several places of
historical significance. The route can be covered in a
day, but for a more relaxing drive visitors could
consider staying in Marea del Portillo.

La Demajagua ①
Céspedes's estate still has
sugar-making equipment,
such as these *calderas* used
for making molasses.

Playa Las Coloradas ③
  It was here that 82 rebels
landed aboard the *Granma*
in December 1956 *(see p48)*.

Media Luna ②
This is the birthplace of
the revolutionary Celia
Sánchez *(see p51)*. The
house is now a museum.

El Guafe ④
This archaeological site has
pre-Columbian finds on
display in a small museum.

**Parque Nacional
Desembarco del *Granma*** ⑤
This park has few facilities but
is rich in local flora, including
some extraordinary orchids.
Interesting natural sights
include caves. There are also
various sites commemorating
the journey of the
revolutionaries following
their arrival on the *Granma*.

Niquero

Punto Nuevo

Bélic

③

④ Cabo Cruz

⑤

and the Colonia Española, a social club for Spanish immigrants that was completed in 1935. The club is located in a building with an Andalusian courtyard and a panel of painted tiles representing Columbus's landing in Cuba.

ENVIRONS: 10 km (6 miles) south of Manzanillo are the remains of La Demajagua, the estate belonging to Carlos Manuel de Céspedes (*see pp42 & 213*). On 10 October 1868, he freed all of his slaves, urging them to join him in fighting the Spanish.

Yara, 24 km (15 miles) east of Manzanillo, is where Céspedes proclaimed Cuban independence, and where the Indian hero Hatuey was burned at the stake. There is a small museum in the central square, Plaza Grito de Yara.

HATUEY'S SACRIFICE

Over the centuries, the sacrifice of Hatuey acquired great patriotic significance and gave rise to numerous legends, including *La Luz de Yara* (The Light of Yara), written by Luis Victoriano Betancourt in 1875. The author relates that from the stake on which the Indian hero was being burned, there arose a mysterious light that wandered throughout the island, protecting the sleep of the slaves who were awaiting their freedom. This light was the soul of Hatuey. Three centuries later, the wandering light returned to the site of the Indian's sacrifice, and in a flash all the palm trees in Cuba shook, the sky was lit up, the earth trembled, and the light turned into a fire that stirred Cubans' hearts: "It was the Light of Yara, which was about to take its revenge. It was the tomb of Hatuey, which became the cradle of independence. It was 10 October" – the beginning of the war of independence.

The Indian chief Hatuey being burned at the stake

VISITORS' CHECKLIST

Departure point: Manzanillo.
Length: 350 km (220 miles).
Stop-off points: Campismo Las Coloradas (huts and restaurant), 4 km (2 miles) southwest of Bélic. For lodging: Hotel Farallón del Caribe and Hotel Marea del Portillo, Pilón (see p261).

Southern Coast ⑧
The southern coastline of the province of Granma is fascinating, with scenic cliffs and bays. The coastal road connecting Marea del Portillo and Santiago de Cuba is flanked by mountains covered with vegetation on one side and sparkling sea on the other.

Pilón ⑥
This sugar-producing town has a thriving commercial port. It is also the home of the Museo Municipal Celia Sánchez Manduley.

0 km 15
0 miles 15

KEY
— Tour route
= Other roads
= Path
☼ Viewpoint

Marea del Portillo ⑦
In an inlet surrounded by rocks, this beach of black sand has a handful of hotels. It is a good starting point for hikes and horse rides, boat trips and diving excursions.

Gran Parque Nacional Sierra Maestra ⑫

Granma, Santiago de Cuba.
Road Map F4.
🛈 *Cubanacán, Santiago de Cuba, (22) 642 202, 641 752, 641 891; for excursions: Villa Turística Santo Domingo, Bartolomé Masó (23) 565 302; Cubanacán, Calle Maceo 63, Bayamo, (23) 427 202.*

View from the Pico Turquino, the highest mountain in Cuba

THIS NATIONAL PARK, which covers an area of 38,000 ha (95,000 acres), spans the provinces of Granma and Santiago de Cuba. This is where the major peaks of the island are found, including Pico Turquino (at 1,974 m/ 6,390 ft, the highest in Cuba), as well as sites made famous by the guerrilla war waged by Fidel Castro and the *barbudos*.

The main starting point for exploring the Sierra Maestra is **Villa Santo Domingo**, about 35 km (22 miles) south of the Bayamo– Manzanillo road (there is simple accommodation in Santo Domingo).

From Santo Domingo, you can make the challenging 5-km (3-mile) journey – on foot or in a good off-road vehicle – to the **Alto del Naranjo** viewpoint (950 m/3,120 ft). With a permit (obtainable from the forest

The *gavilán del monte*, common in the Sierra Maestra

rangers in Villa Santo Domingo), you can go on to **Comandancia de la Plata**, Castro's headquarters in the 1950s. Here there is a museum, a small camp hospital and the site from which Che Guevara made his radio broadcasts. Comandancia de la Plata is accessible only on foot – an hour's walk through lovely, though often foggy, forest. The area was made into a national park in 1980, and is not only important historically. The dense, humid forest conceals many species of orchid and various kinds of local fauna. The mountains of the Sierra Maestra are excellent hiking territory, and also attract mountain climbers. The scenery is spectacular but be prepared for spartan facilities.

A limited number of treks can be organized in Villa Santo Domingo, where guides can be hired. Overnight accommodation in the mountains is available either at campsites or in simple refuges. Note however that since much of this area is a military zone, it is not always open to the public.

At present, it is possible to do a three-day guided trek across the park, beginning at Alto del Naranjo and ending at Las Cuevas, a small town on the Caribbean Sea. Hikers do not need to be expert mountaineers in order to take part in this walking tour, because the path is equipped with ladders, handrails and rock-cut steps. However, it is still advisable to do a certain amount of training beforehand. The final descent from Pico Turquino onwards is fairly strenuous and walkers need to be reasonably fit.

It is important to take proper mountain gear with you: walking boots, thick socks, a hat to protect you from the sun, as well as a sweater, a windproof jacket, perhaps even a waterproof groundsheet and a good tent. The humidity in the Sierra, which is often enveloped in mist, is very high, and showers are common.

The coast at the southern edge of the Sierra Maestra, known as the **Riviera del Caribe**, is spectacular. The coastal road runs close above the waters of the Caribbean Sea and offers excellent views of coastal stacks and coves.

View of the splendid coastline south of Sierra Maestra

Basílica del Cobre ⓭

Santiago de Cuba.
Road Map F4.
📷 Carretera Central 21, (22) 361 31.
🕐 daily. ✝ 🎨 procession (8 Sep).

THE VILLAGE OF El Cobre, about 20 km (12 miles) west of Santiago de Cuba, was once famous for its copper *(cobre)* mines. A great number of slaves worked here up until 1807. Nowadays the village is best known for Cuba's most famous church, the Basílica de Nuestra Señora de la Caridad del Cobre. Here the main attraction is a statue of the Virgen del Cobre. This black Madonna is richly dressed in yellow, and wears a crown encrusted with diamonds, emeralds and rubies, with a golden halo above. She carries a cross of diamonds and amethysts. The statue is kept in an air-conditioned glass case behind the high altar.

It is taken out every year on 8 September when a procession takes place to commemorate the Virgin's saint's day. The Virgen del Cobre was proclaimed the protectress of Cuba in 1916 and was blessed and crowned by Pope John Paul II during his visit to Cuba in 1998 *(see p64)*.

The Basílica del Cobre, surrounded by tropical vegetation

This fine three-aisled church, built in 1926, stands on a hill, the Cerro de la Cantera, which is linked to the village by a flight of 254 steps. The elegant central bell tower

The austere interior of the Sanctuary of the Virgen del Cobre

and two side towers crowned by brick-red domes are a striking sight above the light-painted façade.

The basilica is the object of pilgrimages from all over the island. In the Los Milagros chapel, thousands of ex-votos left by pilgrims are on display. Some are rather curious, such as the Nobel Prize medal won by Ernest Hemingway, beards left by some of the rebels who survived the guerrilla war in the Sierra; an object belonging to Castro's mother; and earth collected by Cuban soldiers who fought in Angola.

THE VIRGEN DEL COBRE

According to legend, in 1606 three slaves who worked in the copper mines of El Cobre were saved in the Bay of Nipe, off the north coast of Cuba, by the statue of a black Virgin Mary holding the Holy Child in her arms. They had been caught in a storm while out in a boat and would have drowned

The statue of the Virgen del Cobre

had not the Virgin, whose image was floating among the waves, come to their aid. In reality, it seems that the statue arrived in Cuba by ship from Illescas, a town in Castile, upon the request of the governor Sánchez de Moya, who wanted a Spanish Madonna for the village of El Cobre. Whatever the truth, in 1611 the Virgen de la Caridad was given a small sanctuary and immediately became an object of veneration for the locals, who continued to attribute miraculous powers to her. The devotion for this Madonna has always been very strong, even among non-practising Catholics. Her

figure is associated with the Afro-Cuban cult of Ochún *(see p20)*, the goddess of rivers, gentleness, femininity and love, who is also always depicted as a beautiful black woman wearing yellow. Now that the *santería* religion is widespread in Cuba, the sacred image of the Virgin of El Cobre and the more profane, sensuous image of the beautiful African goddess are often combined in prayers and discussion, and set beside each other on rustic home altars, often without any apparent awareness of contradiction.

A group of ex-votos offered by the *barbudos*

Santiago de Cuba ⓮

Sign for the Rum Museum

Tʜɪs ɪs ᴘᴇʀʜᴀᴘs ᴛʜᴇ ᴍᴏsᴛ ᴀꜰʀɪᴄᴀɴ, the most musical and the most passionate city in Cuba. In 1930 the Spanish poet Federico García Lorca likened it to "a harp made of living branches, a caiman, a tobacco flower". Except for the cars and some modern buildings, Santiago has not altered much since those days. This is a city where the heat – and the hills – mean that people move to a slow rhythm. It is a lively, exciting place where festivities and dancing are celebrated with fervour, never more so than during Carnival. Santiago's citizens also take pride in the fact that Santiago is called the "Cradle of the Revolution". Sandwiched between the Sierra Maestra mountains and the sea, this is the second city in Cuba in population size.

A restored Neo-Classical building in the historic centre

Parque Céspedes

The city centre spreads out in chaotic fashion around Parque Céspedes in a maze of alleys and narrow streets. Any visit to the historic centre of Santiago must start in Parque Céspedes, the main square. From here visitors are inevitably drawn along **Calle Heredia**, the most famous, popular and festive street in the town. Every house bears signs of the city's great passions: music, dancing, carnivals and poetry. At certain times, including in the summer when the Festival del Caribe is held, this street becomes a stage for amateur artists. Traditional *son* music, on the other hand, can be heard in the courtyard of the Casa de la UNEAC *(see pp282–3)* at No. 266, while No. 208, the former "Cafetín

de Virgilio", became the Casa de la Trova in 1968, and local and foreign bands can be heard here day and night. Photographs of great Cuban musicians past and present such as El Guayabero and Compay Segundo cover the walls.

West of Parque Céspedes

The picturesque area west of Parque Céspedes called Tivoli and the bay can be seen from the **Balcón de Velázquez**, a viewpoint situated

at the corner of Calle Mariano Corona and Bartolomé Masó.

A small fort was built here in the 16th century to house artillery to be used in the event of an attack. Today, only fragments of the original walls remain. Inside the viewpoint area itself are some attractive bronze tondos (circular carvings in relief) with portraits of Diego Velázquez, Hernán Cortés, Bartolomé de Las Casas and the Indian Guamá.

Calle Heredia, the liveliest street in Santiago de Cuba

KEY

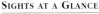

- 🔲 Street-by-Street, *pp220–21*
- 🚌 Coach station
- 🚉 Railway station
- ✝ Church

0 metres   200
0 yards   200

Plaza de la Revolución ↗

Cementerio de Santa Ifigenia

Tourist information

VISITORS' CHECKLIST

Santiago de Cuba. **Road Map** F4. 🧍 400,000. ✈ 7 km (4 miles) south of town. 🚉 Ave. Jesús Menéndez, esq. Hechevarria. 🚌 Ave. de los Libertadores, esq. Yarayó, (22) 628 484. 🛈 Havanatur, Hotel Santiago, Calle M y Ave de las Americas, (22) 643 445. 🎭 Festival del Caribe (first half of Jul), Carnival (second half of Jul).

Calle Padre Pico seen from the top of the steps

South of Parque Céspedes

Around 100m (330 ft) southwest of the square, the **Steps of Padre Pico** lead to Tivolí, the most authentic, picturesque mixed quarter in Santiago. Here, over the centuries, various peoples have arrived and stayed, including Puerto Ricans, Jamaicans, Arabs, Dominicans and Chinese. In the 1700s a colony of French people from Haiti also settled here, setting up shops, music schools, theatres and hotels.

East of Parque Cespedes

To the east of the square, at the corner of Calle Bartolomé Masó and Calle Hartmann (San Félix), is the **Museo del Ron** (Rum Museum), housed in a late 19th-century building. Displays illustrate how rum is distilled and matured *(see p75)*, alongside the history of the Bacardí factory, with an exhibition of labels from bottles of rum, new and old.

Another place to visit is Parque Dolores, a leafy square surrounded by buildings adorned with wrought-iron balconies. A small old café in the square, **La Isabelica**, serves excellent coffee.

Customers at La Isabelica, an atmospheric historic café

SIGHTS AT A GLANCE

Ayuntamiento ②
Balcón de Velázquez ⑪
Café La Isabelica ⑨
Casa de Diego Velázquez ①
Casa de la Trova ⑤
Casa Natal de Antonio Maceo ⑭
Casa Natal de José María Heredia ⑥
Catedral de la Asunción ④
Cuartel Moncada ⑮

Hotel Casa Granda ③
Museo de la Lucha Clandestina ⑬
Museo del Carnaval ⑧
Museo del Ron ⑩
Museo Provincial Bacardí Moreau ⑦
Parque Histórico Abel Santamaría ⑯
Plaza de Marte ⑰
Steps of Padre Pico ⑫

Street-by-Street: Parque Céspedes

THE FORMER PLAZA DE ARMAS in Santiago is the heart of the city, both geographically and spiritually. Renamed Parque Céspedes in honour of the nation's founding father (see p44), whose statue stands in the middle, this square is a place for socializing, relaxing, chatting and celebrating. At all hours of the day and night, the benches are filled with people, young, old, women, children and visitors. No one is alone here for long. Everyone sooner or later gets involved in a conversation or entertainment of some kind, because this square's other role is as an open-air venue where music – live, recorded, or improvised – takes the leading role. Restored in Neo-Classical style in 1943, the square consists of four areas, each with fountains and greenery, divided by lanes.

Casa de la Trova
Live music is performed here daily.

The house where the poet José Heredia was born is a fine 18th-century building around a leafy courtyard (*p223*).

★ **Museo Provincial Bacardí Moreau**
The oldest museum in Cuba, housed in an elegant Neo-Classical building, is also the most eclectic. Items on display range from an Egyptian mummy to mementoes of the wars of independence and works by living artists (p224).

CALLE GENERAL LACRE

CALLE HARTMANN

CALLE HEREDIA

CALLE AGUILERA

KEY

– – – Suggested route

STAR SIGHTS

★ **Casa de Diego Velázquez**

★ **Museo Provincial Bacardí Moreau**

★ **Catedral de la Asunción**

Seafront

Hotel Casa Granda
One of Cuba's historic hotels (see p261), the Casa Granda opened in 1920. Graham Greene (see p87) described it in Our Man in Havana *as a hotel frequented by spies. Its terrace overlooks the square.*

★ **Catedral de la Asunción**

The Cathedral façade is Neo-Classical, but the original church is four centuries old. It is believed that Diego Velázquez is buried somewhere beneath the building, but there is no proof of this (p223).

Paseo de Martí

CALLE BARTOLOMÉ MASÓ

CALLE FÉLIX PEÑA

CALLE HEREDIA

CALLE MARIANO CORONA

PARQUE CÉSPEDES

Balcón de Velázquez

This spacious viewing terrace, built over the site of a Spanish fortress, offers a magnificent view of the picturesque quarter of Tivolí, as well as the port and the bay of Santiago. There is an admission charge (p218).

★ **Casa de Diego Velázquez**

Built in 1516–30, the residence of the Spanish conquistador Diego Velázquez is considered by some to be the oldest building in Cuba. Restoration was carried out in 1965, and it is now the home of the Museo de Ambiente Histórico Cubano (p222).

0 metres	50
0 yards	50

The Casa de la Cultura Miguel Matamoros, an eclectic building (1919) housing the sumptuous Salón de los Espejos, is a venue for artistic and cultural events.

Ayuntamiento

The Ayuntamiento (town hall), a symbol of the city, was built in 1950 according to 18th-century designs found in the Indies Archive. It was from this building's central balcony that Fidel Castro made his first speech to the Cuban people, on 1 January 1959.

Exploring Parque Céspedes

Ceramic plate,
Casa de Velázquez

O NE OF THE LIVELIEST SQUARES in Cuba, Parque Céspedes is not only a place for socializing, but also has sites of cultural and architectural importance. Allow half a day to visit three of the most important monuments around the Parque: the house of Diego Velázquez, the impressive cathedral, and the residence of the great 19th-century poet José María Heredia.

The courtyard in the 19th-century wing of Diego Velázquez's house

A room with Colonial furniture in Diego Velázquez's house

🏛 Casa de Diego Velázquez (Museo de Ambiente Histórico Cubano)

Calle Félix Peña 61, e/ Heredia y Aguilera. ☎ (22) 652 652.
🕐 Mon–Sat, Sun am. 🔴 1 Jan, 1 May, 26 Jul, 25 Dec. 📷 ✦ ⬛

This building, constructed in 1516–30 as a residence for the governor Diego Velázquez, is the oldest private home in Cuba, according to architect Francisco Prat Puig, who restored the house in 1965. (Other scholars dispute this assertion, however, and not everyone has praised the restoration.) Whatever the truth, this splendid residence is still fascinating.

In the 1600s it was the so-called House of Transactions (the ground floor still has an old furnace in which gold ingots were made). It passed from one owner to another, and in the 19th century was joined to the building next door. The upstairs gallery facing the courtyard is closed off by a Moorish wooden blind, to screen residents from the eyes of strangers. Also upstairs, some of the original *alfarje* ceilings survive.

The building now houses the Museo de Ambiente Histórico Cubano, covering the history of furniture in Cuba. It contains superb examples from all Colonial periods. Among the mostly austere Creole furniture, dating from the 16th and 17th centuries, are a splendid priest's high-backed chair and a finely wrought coffer – two excellent examples of Moorish-style objects.

The basement has 18th-century "Luis Las Casas" furniture, a style peculiar to Cuba which combines English influences and French rococo motifs. These pieces of furniture are massive, lavish and intricately worked, often finished at the base with feet shaped like claws. The 19th-century section includes a dining room with stained-glass windows and French furniture, including rocking chairs, a console table and a Charles X mirror.

Another important item is a tapestry with the coat-of-arms of the Velázquez family, the only piece in the museum that is directly related to this Spanish *conquistador*.

THE 16TH-CENTURY MUDÉJAR-STYLE HOUSE

Considered the oldest private building in Cuba and declared a national monument because of its historic value, the 16th-century section of Velázquez's house is a fine example of the Cuban version of the *mudéjar* (Moorish) style – although much of what is there is the result of restoration.

The courtyard, in mudéjar style, is narrow and long and runs around a central well.

Wooden screens protect the gallery and balconies from the sun and public gaze.

Frescoes, known as cenefas, decorate the lower part of the walls, but they are not original.

Cedar ceilings with geometric patterns, called alfarjes, were common in the 16th century.

The lovely wooden inlaid choir in the Catedral de Nuestra Señora de la Asunción

🛕 Catedral de Nuestra Señora de la Asunción

Calle Heredia, e/ Lacret y Félix Peña.
📞 (22) 628 502. 🕐 daily.
🕐 daily.

The cathedral of Santiago has a basilica layout, with a central nave and four aisles, an apse and a narthex or vestibule at the back. The church has been rebuilt several times over the centuries. The original was built in 1555, but in the early 17th century a series of pirate raids caused so much damage that the church was rebuilt in 1666–70. In the 18th and 19th centuries it was further damaged, this time by earthquakes.

Interior of the cathedral's dome

Today the cathedral, which has been declared a national monument, displays a mixture of styles, the result of a series of changes made in 1922 by the architect Segrera, who added the bell towers, had the interior painted, and also reworked the façade. A marble angel was set over the main entrance and statues of Christopher Columbus and Bartolomé de las Casas were placed in side niches.

The cathedral also has a museum, the **Museo Eclesiástico**, which has on display interesting frescoes by the Dominican friar Luis Desangles, liturgical objects, statues and an important collection of ecclesiastical music scores.

🏛 Casa Natal de José María Heredia

Calle Heredia 260, e/ Hartmann (San Félix) y Pío Rosado (Carnicería).
🕐 Tue–Sat; Sun am.
⬤ 1 Jan, 1 May, 26 Jul, 10 Oct, 25 Dec.

This is the modest but elegant 18th-century house where the nationalist poet José María Heredia (1803–39) was born. Heredia, highly regarded for his odes to nature (see p26), should not be confused with his cousin, a French Parnassian poet, who was also born in Cuba but spent practically all his life in Europe.

The well-preserved house contains period furniture and objects, wooden ceilings and tiled floors, and is well worth a visit. From the large entrance hall, with a coffered ceiling and paintings of the poet's ancestors on the walls, a large arch leads into the central peristyled courtyard. Here there are wooden columns, a stone well and abundant vegetation.

Other rooms in the house include Heredia's bedroom, which has an impressive mahogany bed and elegant antique lamps.

Cultural events and poetry readings are often held in the museum's large porticoes. In addition, every year literary seminars and workshops are held here as part of the Festival del Caribe, or Fiesta del Fuego. This summer cultural event takes over the entire city of Santiago (see p35).

Entrance hall of Heredia's house, its arch leading to the courtyard

Around Calle Heredia

T HIS STREET IS ONE OF THE LIVELIEST in Cuba. It buzzes
with music and activity, and the sound of guitars,
maracas, percussion and voices can be heard at all
hours of the day, not just in the Casa de la Trova or the
Casa de la UNEAC, but also in the Museo del Carnaval,
where concerts are held in the courtyard. The nearby
Museo Bacardí is devoted to Cuban history.

**Techos de Santiago de Cuba by
Felipe González, Museo Bacardí**

🏛 Museo Provincial
Bacardí Moreau

Calle Pio Rosado (Carniceria), esq.
Aguilera. ☎ *(22) 628 402.* ○ *Tue–
Sat, Sun & Mon pm.* ● *1 Jan, 1 May,
26 Jul, 10 Oct, 25 Dec.* 🎟 ✔ 📷
This is the oldest museum in
Cuba. It was founded in 1828
and is a rich source of relics
dating from the Spanish
conquest to the wars of
independence. The
objects were collected
and organized in
the late 1800s and
early 1900s by
Emilio Bacardí,
founder of the
famous rum
distillery. Bacardí
was also a famous
patriot and the
first mayor of
Santiago when
Cuba became a
republic. His aim
was to display the origin and
development of the Cuban
nationalist movement from a
cultural point of view, and he
asked the architect Segrera
to design a building for the
objects and works of art he
had collected.

The museum is housed in
an eclectic building with a
broad staircase and an atrium
dominated by two large
statues of Minerva and
Liberty. On the ground floor
is a large collection of arms

**The statue
of Liberty
in the foyer**

used by nationalist generals
and heroes such as Antonio
Maceo, Máximo Gómez and
José Martí. There is also an
important collection of works
by 19th-century Cuban
painters, including Felipe
López González, Juan Emilio
Hernández Giro, José Joaquín
Tejada Revilla and Buena-
ventura Martínez. Twentieth-
century artists represented
here are Wifredo Lam and
René Portocarrero *(see
pp24–5).* The archaeology
section is in the basement
and includes the only
Egyptian mummy in Cuba.

🏛 Museo del Carnaval

Calle Heredia 303, esq. Pio Rosado
(Carniceria). ☎ *(22) 626 955.*
○ *Tue–Sun.* ● *1 Jan, 1 May,
26 Jul, 10 Oct, 25 Dec.* 🎟 ✔ 📷
This lovely late 18th-century
building was converted into
an elementary school in the
mid-1900s, then into an office
building, and eventually
became the offices of the
Carnival Commission. The

**Part of an elaborate float in the
Museo del Carnaval**

**Decorated *tumbadoras (see p29)*
in the Museo del Carnaval**

Museo del Carnaval was
opened here in 1983.
The three rooms contain
photographs with explanatory
captions, chronologies,
banners, musical instruments,
costumes and papier mâché
masks – a well-documented
survey of the Carnival
festivities held in Santiago.
Carnival here differs from the
traditional Spanish model and
combines many African and
Franco-Haitian elements.

The courtyard is used for
folk events and concerts,
as well as for rehearsals by
bands preparing to perform
during Carnival.

🏛 Museo de la
Lucha Clandestina

Calle Rabí 1, e/ San Carlo y Santa
Rita. ☎ *(22) 624 689.*
○ *Tue–Sun.* ● *1 Jan, 1 May, 26
Jul, 10 Oct, 25 Dec.* 🎟 ✔ 📷
The Museum of the
Clandestine Struggle
overlooks a pleasant
square in the district of
Tivolí, southwest of
Parque Céspedes. The
building was the head-
quarters of Batista's
police from 1951 to
1956. On 30 November
1956 it was burnt down
by revolutionaries, led
by Frank País *(see p50).*

The four rooms in
the restored building
commemorate the
activities of the Movi-
miento 26 de Julio, the
movement headed in
Santiago by Frank País
up to 30 July 1957,
when the young rebel
leader was arrested
and assassinated by
Batista's police.

Carnival in Santiago de Cuba

THE ROOTS of the Carnival in Santiago are religious: since the end of the 17th century there have been processions and festivities from 24 June to 26 July in honour of the city's patron saint, Santiago Apostolo. At the end of the parade, slaves who were members of the *cabildos* – societies that kept alive African languages, traditions and beliefs – were allowed to go out into the streets, where they sang to the

Playing the trompeta china

accompaniment of drums, rattles and other instruments. These were the forerunners of the *comparsas*, the soul of Carnival: groups of people wearing masks or costumes, dancing to the rhythm of the *conga* and carrying streamers, banners and *farolas* (brightly coloured paper street lamps). In the second half of July the whole town celebrates, every district taking part in the parades, each with at least one *comparsa*.

The young people in each quarter meet every evening except Monday in the *focos culturales*, places where they prepare for Carnival by rehearsing the dances and music they will perform in July.

The type of *tumbadora* used in the *conga*

Parades go through the streets of Santiago. Some of the comparsas, such as the Carabalí Izuama (see p282), date from the 19th century.

The musicians in each group are dressed alike. They are followed by a crowd swaying to the rhythm of the music.

THE CONGA
The chief dance for Carnival is the *conga* (also a genuine musical genre). People form a procession and dance through the streets, following a band playing various instruments, including different kinds of drums and the *trompeta china*, introduced to Cuba in the late 1800s.

The *bombo*, a drum with a deep sound

The Tropicana de Santiago joins the procession with the other comparsas, and also presents open-air performances in lavish costumes.

Papier mâché masks are an essential part of a Carnival float. Huge and brightly coloured, they often represent animals or caricatures of human faces.

Beyond Santiago's Historic Centre

CALLE SACO (also known as Enramada), Santiago's main commercial street, links the heart of the old city with the port. After passing through a working-class quarter, with early 20th-century wooden houses, the street ends at Paseo Marítimo. Laid out in the Colonial era as a seafront promenade for the city's high society, this broad street retains echoes of its former beauty and still has its original 1840 paving, stretching out along the port, where cruisers and yachts are moored. An alternative route to explore is to go in the opposite direction, east of the centre, where there are important historic sites, including the Moncada barracks.

🏛 Casa Natal de Antonio Maceo

Calle Los Maceos 207, e/ Corona y Rastro. 🅲 (22) 623 750.
🕐 Mon–Sat. ⬤ 1 Jan, 1 May, 26 Jul, 10 Oct, 25 Dec. 🈸 🗹 🖸
The house where this great general was born on 14 June 1845 (he died near Havana on 7 December 1896; see p44) is a modest place. Visitors can see some of the hero's personal belongings and family photographs, including one of his brother José, who was also a general, and one of his mother, Mariana Grajales.

🎴 Cementerio de Santa Ifigenia

Avenida Crombet.
🅲 (22) 632 723.
🕐 daily. 🈸 🖸
This monumental cemetery (1868) is the second most important in Cuba after the Colón cemetery in Havana (see pp104–5). It was originally laid out with a Latin cross plan and divided into courtyards, the most important of which were

The mausoleum of Martí in the Santa Ifigenia Cemetery

reserved for those of higher social status. A visit to the Santa Ifigenia cemetery evokes two centuries of Cuban history, past the tombs of such illustrious 19th-century figures as José Martí, Carlos Manuel de Céspedes, Emilio Bacardí and the mother of Antonio Maceo, as well as the 20th-century revolutionaries of the Movimiento 26 de Julio such as Frank País, who was killed in 1957 (see p50).

The funerary monuments themselves are fascinating. The Neo-Classical tombs nearest the entrance are the oldest, followed by the eclectic and then Modernist tombs. The Rationalist tombs built from the mid-20th century on include Martí's large octagonal mausoleum.

🏛 Museo Histórico 26 de Julio – Cuartel Moncada

Calle General Portuondo (Trinidad), e/ Moncada y Ave de los Libertadores.
🅲 (22) 620 157. 🕐 Tue–Sun.
⬤ 1 Jan, 1 May, 26 Jul, 10 Oct, 25 Dec. 🈸 🗹 🖸
On 26 July 1953, at the height of the Carnival festivities, Fidel Castro led about 100 rebels in an attack on the Moncada barracks (see p48). Capturing Moncada, the second largest garrison in Cuba, built in the 19th century, would have meant securing a large stock of weapons and thus triggering a general revolt. Abel Santamaría was to attack the Saturnino Lora hospital, a strategic site on a promontory overlooking the barracks, and Raúl Castro was to capture the law courts building. This bold attempt failed, but it did succeed in increasing public awareness of the activity of the young revolutionaries. Eight of them died during the attack, while 55 were taken prisoner, tortured and executed.

Since January 1959 the barracks, which still bear bullet holes, have housed the Ciudad Escolar 26 de Julio school. Part of the building houses the Museo Histórico 26 de Julio, which in fact

The impressive façade of the former Moncada army barracks, now a school and museum

The monument to General Maceo in Plaza de la Revolución

illustrates the history of Cuba from the time of Columbus, but devotes most space to the guerrilla war of the 1950s. There is a model reproducing the attack on Moncada. There are also possessions which belonged to Fidel Castro, his brother Raúl and Che Guevara when they were waging war in the Sierra Maestra.

🏛 Museo Abel Santamaría Cuadraro – Parque Histórico Abel Santamaría

Calle General Portuondo (Trinidad), esq. Ave de los Libertadores.
📞 (22) 624 119. ⏰ Mon–Sat.
● 1 Jan, 1 May, 26 Jul, 10 Oct, 25 Dec. 🎟 🚫 📷

The Moncada barracks, Saturnino Lora hospital and law court buildings form part of the Parque Histórico Abel Santamaría. In the 1953 raid, the former hospital was the target of a group of rebels led by Abel Santamaría, who was captured and killed by the police after the failed attempt.

The hospital now houses a museum with documents and photographs relating to the trial of Fidel Castro and the other rebels, which was held a few days after the attack on the barracks in one of the rooms here.

Besides the photographs illustrating the difficult social and economic conditions in Cuba during the 1950s, there is the manuscript of Castro's landmark self-defence in court, later entitled *History Will Absolve Me (see p145).*

Plaza de Marte

East of Plaza Dolores is the third largest square in Santiago, laid out in the 19th century. It is of great historic importance: for here capital punishment was meted out both in the Colonial period and under General Machado. At its centre is a 20-m (65-ft) column (1902) celebrating Cuban independence.

🏛 Bosque de los Héroes

East of the centre, behind the unmistakable Hotel Santiago, lies a small, unobtrusive hill. A white marble monument was erected here in 1973 to honour Che Guevara and the comrades-in-arms who died with him in Bolivia. Their names are engraved here.

The column in Plaza de Marte

Plaza de la Revolución

In the northeastern part of Santiago, beyond the Moncada barracks, is Plaza de la Revolución, a large, rather soulless square at a crossroads of three major avenues. The square is dominated by a vast monument executed in the early 1990s by the Santiago sculptor, Alberto Lezcay, representing General Maceo *(see p44)* on horseback, surrounded by 23 stylized machetes. Plaza de la Revolución marks the start of the modern, residential area of the city, where the architecture shows a marked Soviet influence.

Vista Alegre

The Vista Alegre quarter has fine eclectic-style buildings constructed in the 1920s and 1930s. The quarter also has two important institutions: the **Centro Africano Fernando Ortíz**, with African masks, statues and musical instruments on display, and the **Casa del Caribe**, which houses a historical archive, library, and centre for conferences, workshops and events *(see p283).* During the Festival del Caribe, the Casa del Caribe presents examples of Yoruba, Congo and voodoo rites.

Bosque de los Héroes, honouring Che Guevara and comrades

Castillo del Morro ⑮

A T THE ENTRANCE TO THE BAY OF SANTIAGO, 10 km (6 miles) southwest of the city centre, stands an imposing castle, declared a World Heritage site by UNESCO in 1997. The Castillo del Morro combines medieval elements with a modern sense of space, adhering nonetheless to classical Renaissance principles of geometric forms and symmetry. The fortress was designed in 1637 by engineer Giovan Battista Antonelli for the governor Pedro de la Roca, who wanted to defend the city against pirate raids. Construction of the citadel, large enough to house 400 soldiers, took from 1638 to 1700. The Castillo was converted into a prison in 1775, becoming a fortress once again in 1898 during the wars of independence, when the US fleet attacked the city.

A cannon, part of the old battery used to defend the bay

In the casemates a display of prints illustrates the history of Santiago's forts.

Artillery area

★ View of the Bay
The parapets and lookouts on the upper parts of the fortress were used by the sentries to keep watch. Visitors today can appreciate the setting and enjoy a marvellous view over the bay.

Underground passageways link the various parts of the castle. This one leads to the artillery area.

The stone stairway on the side of the castle facing the sea is part of an open-air network of steps leading to the upper levels.

STAR FEATURES

★ **View of the Bay**

★ **Central Square**

Plataforma de la Punta (*morrillo*, or bluff)

Triangular Lunette
*Built in 1590–1610 as the main
protection for the fortress
gate, this structure
originally stood separately
from the castle. It was
later incorporated into
the main structure.*

Drawbridge
*This bridge passes over
a dry moat that runs
alongside the fortification
on the inland side. It is
well preserved, and still
has the original winch
which was used to raise
and lower the bridge.*

Dry moat

★ Central Square
*This square, the nerve
centre of the castle, was
used as an area for
organizing daily activities.
The square provides access
to the chapel, barracks,
garrison and
underground rooms.*

THE BAY OF SANTIAGO

About 8 km (5 miles) southwest of the centre of Santiago, at
the end of the Carretera Turística (which, despite its name, is
a rather poorly maintained, traffic-filled road), is Marina Punta
Gorda. From here ferries cross
over to a small island in the
middle of the bay. This is Cayo
Granma, home to a picturesque
fishing village made up of
multicoloured huts and small
houses built on piles. This
island is a peaceful place off
the beaten track, with only
one restaurant (*see p273*) and
abundant greenery – a good
place to relax in and round off
a visit to Santiago de Cuba.

**View of Cayo Granma from
the Carretera Turística**

**Three separate main
structures,** built on five
different levels, form the
skeleton of the castle.
This unusual construction
is a result of the uneven
terrain of the headland.

Parque Baconao ⑯

L YING BETWEEN THE CARIBBEAN SEA and
the eastern fringes of the Sierra
Maestra, and straddling the provinces
of Santiago and Guantánamo, Parque
Baconao has been declared a biosphere
reserve by UNESCO. The largest and
most original amusement park in Cuba
(80,000 ha/197,600 acres) combines
mountains and beaches with old coffee
plantations and an unusual range of
attractions. The park was developed in
the 1980s thanks to the voluntary work
of students and labourers, and has been
updated periodically. Today, visitors can
appreciate a wide range of cultural and
outdoor activities and attractions, and
there is plenty of hotel accommodation.

Gran Piedra
*This is an enormous monolith, from the
top of which, at an altitude of 1,234m
(4,048 ft), you can even see Jamaica
and Haiti on clear days (see p232).*

**The Cafetal La
Isabelica**, the
oldest coffee
plantation in the
province, has
been converted
into a museum
(see p232).

**Jardín
Botánico
(Botanic
Garden)**

Siberia

La Isabélica

Perseverancia

Tres Arroyos

Prado de las Esculturas
*This sculpture garden,
with 20 works by Cuban
and foreign artists, was
laid out in the late 1980s.
The display extends for
1 km (0.6 mile) and can
also be viewed by car.*

Abel Santamaría

Las Guásimas

Damaiayabo

El Palenque

El Oasis

Juraguá

Siboney

Granjita Siboney
(see p232)

At the Oasis, a centre
managed by artists,
visitors can go horse
riding and watch
rodeo shows.

**Museos y
Exposiciones
de la Punta,
*(see p233)***

Playa Siboney is the favourite
beach of the citizens of
Santiago. Only 19 km (12 miles)
from town, it can be reached by
regular bus service.

KEY

▬	Major road
=	Path
—	River
⚓	Recommended beach
☀	Viewpoint
⋔	Ruins of old *cafetales*

Valle de la Prehistoria
*This children's park features huge sculptures of
dinosaurs and there is also a Natural History Museum.*

Laguna Baconao
At this lagoon boats can be hired for trips around the lagoon or up the Baconao river. There is a crocodile farm near the Casa de Rolando restaurant at the lakeside.

VISITORS' CHECKLIST

Santiago de Cuba.
Road Map F4.
Tours in the park 🛈 *Rumbos, Hotel Las Américas, Avenida Las Américas y General Cebreco, Santiago de Cuba, (22) 641 554.*

SIERRA MAESTRA

SIERRA LARGA

Indio

⚲ Kentucky

⚲ San Jimy

⚲ Gran Sofia

Baconao

SIERRA DE LA GRAN PIEDRA

0 kilometres   3

0 miles   3

• María del Pilar

BACONAO

Sigua

Sigua

Exposición Mesoamericana
(see p233)

Jardín de Cactus
(Cactus Garden)

The sea bed in the area between Playa del Indio and Playa Larga is dotted with shipwrecks.

Acuario Baconao
This aquarium has a good display of sharks, sea lions and other fish. Above is the tunnel from which the fish can be seen at close range. There is a pool where dolphins perform a show three times a day.

Playa Daiquirí
This small, quiet beach – behind the Daiquirí Hotel – is where American troops landed in 1898, during the US occupation (see p44).

Exploring the Parque Baconao

The 1960 Maya Cuba car, a museum piece

IT IS POSSIBLE TO EXPLORE THE PARK by car or taxi in a day, although accommodation is available. Heading east from Santiago, along Avenida Raúl Pujol, you will pass the zoo (Parque Zoológico), and, nearby, the Arbol de la Paz (Tree of Peace), a ceiba tree beneath which the Spanish signed the surrender agreement in 1898. The entrance to Parque Baconao is not far beyond the confines of the city. Most of the attractions are suitable for families and can be reached by car, but the peak of the Gran Piedra and the easternmost beaches are only accessible on foot.

The spectacular view from the Gran Piedra

A strelitzia in flower at the Gran Piedra Jardín Botánico

species of orchid and multicoloured strelitzias (flowers more commonly known as bird of paradise), a flight of 459 steps leads up to the top of the Gran Piedra (1,234 m/4,048 ft asl). This gigantic, 25-m (82-ft) monolith rests on the crater of an extinct volcano.

It is best to make the climb in the morning, because the afternoon can bring foggy weather and you may not see far into the distance. However, on clear days the view is simply superb: it stretches from the mountains to the coast, and even as far as Haiti.

🏛 Cafetal La Isabelica

Carretera de la Gran Piedra km 14.
⏰ daily. ● 1 Jan, 1 May, 26 Jul, 10 Oct, 25 Dec. 🎫 📷 🚹

There are numerous old coffee plantations around the Gran Piedra, all of which were recently added to the World Heritage List by UNESCO. Almost all of the plantations are in ruins, but one exception is the Cafetal La Isabelica, which can be reached easily via a

🐴 Granjita Siboney

Carretera Siboney km 13,5.
📞 (22) 391 68. ⏰ daily.
● 1 Jan, 1 May, 26 Jul, 10 Oct, 25 Dec. 🎫 📷 🚹

By the roadside 16 km (10 miles) east of Santiago, this is the farm rented by Abel Santamaría in 1953 as a base of operations in the run-up to the assault on the Moncada barracks. It was from here, on 26 July, that the young rebels drove into Santiago to launch the attack. Their attempt failed and Granjita Siboney itself was later attacked by Batista's men. The (reconstructed) bullet holes can be seen around the door.

Granjita Siboney is now a museum with the uniforms and some of the weapons that the revolutionaries wore and carried that day. Next door is the Generación del Centenario gallery, with paintings honouring the rebels who died during the attack on the barracks, as well as photographs, documents and the car Castro used in the attack.

🌿 Gran Piedra

Jardín Botánico ⏰ daily.
🎫 📷

Heading west from Granjita Siboney, you come to a turn-off to Gran Piedra: this 12-km (7-mile) road with hairpin bends provides one of the best panoramas in Cuba and views of the intense green of the tropical and mountain forests. Beyond the Jardín Botánico, with its many

Granjita Siboney farm, showing the signs of the July 1953 attack

path from the foot of the
Gran Piedra.

This plantation belonged to
Victor Constantin, a French
landowner who, together with
many others, fled from Haiti
in the late 1700s following
a slave uprising there. He
brought with him numerous
slaves and his mistress, Isabel
María, after whom he named
his plantation.

The largest structure is the
manor house. The ground
floor was partly for the
labourers and partly used
to store tools and implements.
The first floor consists of a
bedroom, living room,
dining room and studio, all
with 18th-century furniture
and furnishings.

The house overlooks a
terrace where coffee beans
were left to dry – actually the

Reproductions of pre-Columbian objects, Exposición Mesoamericana

roof of a large storehouse.
Nearby are the kitchens,
behind which is the water
tank; the whole area is
surrounded by coffee plants.
Visitors to the *cafetal* museum
are offered a demonstration
of how coffee is grown and
processed for consumption.

The provincial authorities
have approved a project to
restore the Cafetal La
Isabelica, which will then
become the home of an
ethnographic museum.

🏛 **Conjunto de Museos
y Exposiciones de la Punta**
Carretera de Baconao.
🔲 *daily.* 📷 ⭕
A cross between a museum
and a trade fair, this collection
of buildings contains displays
of all kinds of things from
stamps and dolls to ceramics

and archaeological finds. Of
particular interest is the Salon
de Historia del Transporte
Terrestre por Carretera, which
houses a fascinating collection
of 2,000-plus miniature cars
and an array of old vintage
cars, including a local Maya
Cuba – a tiny, one-cylinder
car. The oldest is a 1912
Model T Ford. There are
also vehicles of historical
significance, including cars
that once belonged to Fidel
Castro and Benny Moré.

🏛 **Exposición
Mesoamericana**
Carretera de Baconao.
🔲 *daily.* 📷 ⭕
This series of sea caves
along the road are showcases
for reproductions of Central
American pre-Columbian
works of art.

**Interior of the Cafetal La Isabelica
owner's manor house**

THE ORIGINS OF COFFEE GROWING IN CUBA

Coffee was introduced to Cuba at the end of
the 18th century, by which time it had been a
fashionable drink among the European
aristocracy and bourgeoisie for some time. The
French coffee growers who had fled to Eastern
Cuba from Haiti in 1791 were well aware of
this: they were the ones who brought the "new"
plant to the island. The hills around Santiago
and the valleys
between Baracoa and
Guantánamo were
ideal for coffee grow-
ing, because they
offered both water
and shade. Coffee
was an immediate
success, and demand
increased so much that
it was planted along
the coast too. In 1803
there were 100,000
coffee trees; by 1807

this figure had increased to four million,
cultivated on 191 plantations. The French
growers became very wealthy, building palatial
manor houses on their plantations. As the
cultivation of coffee required plenty of manual
labour, and there weren't enough workers from
Haiti, there was a "boom" in the slave trade in
the early 19th century. Cuban archives mention
7,654 "dead souls" at the
beginning of the cen-
tury, and 42,000 in 1820.
While this immigration
contributed to the eco-
nomic fortune of the
island, it proved to be
the end of the land-
owners. It was not long
before the slaves,
increasingly numerous
and organized, began to
rebel against their
condition *(see p42)*.

Coffee growing beneath the trees in the mountains

Guantánamo

Guantánamo. **Road Map** F4.
👥 *200,000.* ✈ 🚌 🚉

I F IT WERE NOT FOR the US
naval base and the famous
song *Guantanamera* (girl
from Guantánamo), this town
would probably only be
known to Cubans and music
experts. Its name, in fact, is
linked with the *changuí*, a
variation of *son* music that
developed in the coffee
plantations in the mountains,
music made famous by the
musician Helio Revé.

Guantanamera was
composed by Joseíto Fernández in the 1940s almost for
fun, drawing inspiration from
a proud local girl who had
not reacted to a compliment
he paid her. Later, some
"literary" verses from the
Versos Sencillos by José Martí
were adapted to the music.

The town of Guantánamo
was founded in 1796 to take
in the French fleeing from
Haiti and developed during
the 19th century. The capital
of a varied province where
desert areas studded with
cactus alternate with green
mountains, Guantánamo has
few sights of note. A tour of
the small historic centre is
little more than a walk around
Parque Martí, dominated by
the **Parroquial de Santa
Catalina de Riccis** (1868).

Opposite the church is a
statue of General Pedro A
Pérez, sculpted in 1928.

An interesting Colonial
building facing the square
is the old Spanish prison,
now the home of the modest
Museo Provincial, which

**Joseíto Fernández, composer of
the song *Guantanamera***

contains a collection of
documents, photographs and
objects related to the history
of the province.

🏛 Museo Provincial
de Guantánamo
Plaza Martí, esq. Prado. 📞 *(21) 325
872.* ⏰ *daily.* ⚫ *1 Jan, 1 May, 26
Jul, 10 Oct, 25 Dec.* 💳 ✔ 📷

**A stone gorilla in the Museo
Zoológico de Piedra**

ENVIRONS: Around 20 km (12
miles) east of Guantánamo, on
the road to Lomas de Yateras,
a coffee-growing area, is an
unusual open-air museum, the
Museo Zoológico de Piedra.
It was founded by Angel Iñigo,
a farmer and self-taught
sculptor. Since 1978 he has
produced sculptures of about
40 animals in stone, including
lions, boa constrictors, tapirs,
buffaloes, rhinoceroses and
gorillas. All are on display.

At the mouth of Guan-
tánamo bay, some 20 km (12
miles) south of the city are two
Cuban ports, **Caimanera** and
Boquerón, both close to the
US naval base. The former is
within a Cuban military zone
and is off-limits to everyone
except those who live there

and those with a special pass.
There is a hotel in Caimanera
(see p260) but you need a
permit to stay.

The US naval base is not
open to the public. However,
it can be "spied" on from an
unusual viewing point *(mirador)*, purpose built above an
existing military command
post by the Cuban authorities,
who now make the most of
their view over the base.

To visit the **Mirador Los
Malones**, situated on a hill
off the Baracoa road, about
15 miles (24 km) east of Guantánamo, make arrangements
either in Santiago, with the
Gaviota tourist agency, or in
Guantánamo, in the epony-
mous hotel.

After going past the main
gate of the Cuban military
zone, visitors proceed for
about 10 km (6 miles) through
forests of cacti before reaching
the mirador. Firstly, the tour
goes into an underground
museum, where a Cuban
military attaché explains the
reasons why Cuba wants the
US to give back this territory.
A detailed model of the base
is also on view here.

Stairs or a lift then take
visitors to the viewing point at
the top of the hill (where there
is also a small restaurant). A
telescope enables visitors to
have a good look at the base
and – unusually within a
military zone – it is permitted
to film and take photographs.

Museo Zoológico de Piedra
Boquerón de Yateras. ⏰ *Mon–Sat.*
⚫ *1 Jan, 1 May, 26 Jul, 10 Oct,
25 Dec.* 💳 📷

The Parroquial de Santa Catalina de Riccis in the Parque Martí

Costa Sur ⑱

Guantánamo. **Road Map** F4.

TRAVELLING EASTWARDS from Guantánamo, visitors will pass through the most barren part of Cuba, where the climate is desert-like because of the hot winds blowing here. This is a unique area on the island where cacti and succulents are the main vegetation. The coast road, tucked in between the mountains and the blue sea, is spectacular. The rocky coast has tiny coves with pebble beaches, home to an assortment of seashells and *Polymita picta* snails *(see p241)*.

La Farola ⑲

Guantánamo. **Road Map** F4.

CAJOBABO – a southern coastal town where José Martí and Máximo Gómez landed to begin the 1895 war against Spain – marks the beginning of La Farola, a spectacular 49-km (30-mile) road that wends its way upwards over the mountains to Baracoa, through vegetation that becomes more and more luxuriant as the coast is left behind.

Until 1959 Cajobabo could only be reached by ship. In order to connect it to the rest of the island, in the 1960s engineers excavated sections of mountainside in the Sierra

THE AMERICAN NAVAL BASE

In 1903 the US – the victors, together with the Cubans, in the war against Spain – obliged the Cuban Republic to accept the Platt Amendment *(see p45)*, whereby the latter had to grant the US Navy the right to install a naval base in the bay of Guantánamo. This territory should be given back to Cuba in 2002, when the 99-year lease granted to the US expires. For this occupancy, the American government pays $2,000 per year, though it is said that the Cuban government has regularly returned this sum to the US since 1959. In the past the situation has taken on the dramatic overtones of the Cold War and highlighted a difficult state of co-existence. Inside the base, the menial jobs are done by Puerto Ricans, the wives of the servicemen do their shopping in supermarkets stocked with food flown in from the US, and there are two English-language radio stations and one TV station. The base, US territory in Cuba, covers 110 sq km (43 sq miles), and has two runways for military planes. The whole area is surrounded by 27 km (17 miles) of fence.

Mirador Los Malones: a telescope looking over the American base

del Purial in order to create a kind of "flying highway". The road acquired its name *(farola* means beacon) because in some stretches it looks like a beam, suspended in air. It is regarded as one of the great engineering feats of recent Cuban history.

This highway and the periodic viewing points offer incredible views of the peaks of the Sierra Maestra, lush valleys, tropical forests, pine groves, banana plantations, rivers, waterfalls and royal palm trees. The luxuriant vegetation seems to swallow up the road in places. Along the road, people sell local produce such as coffee, red bananas and tangerines.

View from one of the observation points along La Farola road

Baracoa ⑳

Cocoa fruit, a
local crop

THE OLDEST CITY IN CUBA lies at the far eastern tip of the island. Its name in the Arauaca language, spoken by the former inhabitants of the area, means "the presence of the sea". Nuestra Señora de la Asunción de Baracoa church was founded on 15 August 1511, on a curved bay that had been discovered some 20 years earlier by Columbus, and immediately became the political and ecclesiastical capital of Cuba. However, this status was short-lived. In 1515, the city founder Diego Velázquez transferred his residence to Santiago, marking the beginning of a long period of social and economic isolation for Baracoa.

A street in Baracoa, dominated by lush vegetation

Exploring Baracoa
"Baracoa means nature", the Cubans say, and it is certainly true: enclosed by tropical forest and the sea, for four centuries this town has managed to live by fishing, cultivating cocoa, coconuts and bananas, and by gathering wood. While the isolation has created inconveniences, it has also allowed the locals to maintain their traditions and preserve the ecosystem.

The historic centre of Baracoa is not Colonial, but a mixture of styles, with some Neo-Classical and French influences. Thick vegetation towers over the buildings and has even invaded some houses, many of which are built of wood.

The best view of the town is seen from the terrace of an 18th-century fortress on a hill above the town: the **Castillo de Seboruco**, now El Castillo hotel (see p259). From here you can see the roofs and the bay of Baracoa, dominated to the west by the rock of El Yunque (see p240).

Parque Central
In the main square, overlooked by the cathedral, is a famous bust of the Indian leader Hatuey (see p215). Nearby are the **Casa de la Trova**, the **Fondo de Bienes Culturales**, which exhibits works by local painters, sculptors and craftsmen, and the **Casa de la Cultura**, an eclectic building with Colonial elements that hosts evening performances and events.

At No. 123 Calle Maceo is the **Casa del Chocolate**, which serves excellent hot chocolate. Baracoa cocoa is famous throughout Cuba.

The Cruz de la Parra, perhaps brought to Cuba by Columbus

⌂ Catedral de Nuestra Señora de la Asunción
Calle Maceo 152.
☎ (21) 433 52. ◷ variable.
✝ Tue–Sun.

This modest church, built in 1512 and restored in 1833, is most famous as the home of the Cruz de la Parra, a wooden cross that is said to be the oldest symbol of Christianity in the New World.

According to legend, the cross was brought to Cuba by Columbus on his first voyage to America, and on 1 December 1492 it was placed on the spot where Baracoa was later founded. It is said that the cross disappeared mysteriously one day and was then miraculously found under the climbing vine (parra) in a settler's garden, hence its name. The four tips of the cross are now covered with metal sheets, because in the past worshippers used to pull off splinters and keep them as relics.

The cathedral is not always open, but if you want to see the Cruz de la Parra and want information about it, or about the city in general, just ask for the sacristan and he will try to help you.

A typical single-storey wooden house in Baracoa

◁ The bay of Baracoa viewed from the Castillo de Seboruco

🏛 Fuerte Matachín (Museo Municipal)

Calle Martí y Malecón. 📞 *(21) 421 22.* 🕐 *daily.* 🎫 📷

This small museum, which provides an interesting overview of local history, is housed in a military fortress built during the Colonial period to defend the city from pirates. (Piracy was particularly active in the 18th and 19th centuries.)

The displays start with archaeological finds of the pre-Columbian era, and are followed by documents, maps, paintings and prints related to Spanish domination, pirates, slaves and the plantations.

There is an interesting natural history section with specimens of *Polymita* snails *(see p241)* and *almiquí* (a rat-sized mammal, *see p240*). The museum is also a historical and geographical research centre and fosters initiatives to preserve and develop local culture.

Along the fort walls is a battery of cannons facing seawards, and a small garden.

Statue of Columbus, Museo Municipal garden

El Malecón

This is the seafront that connects the two 19th-century forts in Baracoa: Fuerte Matachín, to the east, and **Fuerte de la Punta**, to the west, now a restaurant. The Malecón is ideal for a quiet stroll during the week. On Saturdays a bustling food market is held here in the morning, and in the evening the road is prepared for the *noche baracoesa*, a lively folk festival during which people eat, drink and dance along the seafront.

Hotel La Rusa

Halfway along the Malecón is Hotel La Rusa, a historic hotel that once belonged to the Russian princess Magdalena Rowenskaya, who fled her country with her husband in 1917 after the October Revolution. She eventually settled in Baracoa, where she ended up opening a restaurant and giving singing lessons. Much later,

VISITORS' CHECKLIST

Guantánamo.
Road Map F4. 🏠 *50,000.*
✈ *4 km (2 miles) west of town, (21) 422 16.* 🚍 *Ave. Los Mártires, esq. Martí, (21) 422 39.* ℹ *Calle Antonio Maceo y Paralejo, (21) 452 24.* 🛍 *Sat.*

she became active in the 26 July Movement and entertained Castro, Che and other revolutionaries.

The hotel foyer has photographs and relics belonging to this eccentric figure, who was later immortalized by the novelist Alejo Carpentier *(see p27)* in his work *The Consecration of Spring.*

The rundown exterior of the Hotel La Rusa

THE CENTRE OF BARACOA

Casa de la Cultura ③
Casa de la Trova ④
Castillo de Seboruco ①
Catedral de Nuestra Señora de la Asunción ②
Fuerte Matachín (Museo Municipal) ⑦
Fuerte de la Punta ⑤
Hotel La Rusa ⑥

KEY

ℹ Tourist information
🚌 Coach station
✚ Church

The mountain of El Yunque, dominating the bay of Baracoa

El Yunque ㉑

Guantánamo. **Road Map** F4.
🄷 Buró de Turismo, Hotel El Castillo, Baracoa, (21) 421 03.

A LIMESTONE FORMATION, 575 m (1,885 ft) high, covered with thick vegetation, El Yunque was a sacred site for the Taíno Indians for many centuries. Later it became a natural landmark for navigators about to land at the port of Baracoa. The Spanish called it "El Yunque" (the anvil) because of its unmistakable outline. The outcrop's shape has led to local misapprehension that this was the rock that Columbus described as "a square mountain that looks like an island" in 1492. In fact, he was referring to a similarly shaped rock at Bariay near Gibara (see p210).

The slopes of the mountain, which has been declared a biosphere reserve by UNESCO, are home to botanical rarities, including two carnivorous plants and *Podocarpus*, one of the oldest plant species in the world, as well as an endemic palm tree, *Coccothrinax yunquensis*.

El Yunque is also the habitat for some endangered species of bird such as the *carpintero real (Campeophilus principalis)* and the *caguarero* hawk *(Chondrohierax wilsonii)*, as well as for the smallest amphibian in the world, the *Sminthillus limbatus*, less than 1 cm (0.4 inch) long, and another very ancient species, the *almiquí (Solenodon cubanus)*, a mammal similar to a rat.

Río Toa ㉒

Road Map F4.

T HE VALLEY FED by the Río Toa, Cuba's biggest river, was recently made a nature reserve, the **Parque Natural Río Toa**. Still lacking in roads and facilities, this park is part of a wide-ranging project to create refuges and camping sites that will not interfere with the local ecosystems.

Local farmers still use an old-fashioned craft to travel upstream – the *cayuca*, a flat canoe of Indian origin. From the river, visitors can admire the majestic Pico Galán (974 m/3,200 ft) and the great waterfalls that cascade into the river from steep cliffs. Enquire in Baracoa if you are interested in exploring the area.

Going up the Río Toa in a rowing boat

ENVIRONS: northwest of Baracoa, 21 km (12 miles) past the mouth of the Río

Playa Maguaná, one of the unspoilt beaches near Baracoa

Río Miel, flowing through virtually virgin tropical forest between Baracoa and Boca de Yumurí

Toa, is **Playa Maguaná**, the most beautiful beach in the province, with dazzling white sand. The beach's Indian name refers to the presence of a nearby archaeological site. A 2-km (1-mile) coral reef lies only 500 m (1,640 ft) from the shore. Be warned though that the sea can often be rather choppy in this area.

There is a modern holiday village hidden among the coconut palms, where villas can be rented, but this place is still delightfully unspoilt.

Boca de Yumurí ㉓

Road Map F4.

AROUND 30 KM (18 MILES) east of Baracoa, this village of *bohíos* (traditional dwellings with palm-leaf roofs) takes its name from the Yumurí river, which flows into the sea here. Its inhabitants live by fishing, but earn a little extra by taking tourists on boat rides on the river (and by selling *Polymita* shells).

A short boat ride across the Yumurí river will take you to an enchanting beach. Another interesting trip is to go upstream, where the river course reaches an impressive canyon with walls as much as 180 m (590 ft) high.

The Río Yumurí flows through an area interesting for its ecology. Colourful tropical birdlife abounds, including the *zunzún*, the *tocororo* and the *cartacuba* (*see pp18–9*).

ENVIRONS: East of Boca de Yumurí, also accessible from Cajobabo, is the tiny, isolated village of **Maisí** and beyond is the easternmost tip of Cuba, Punta Maisí. On clear days it is possible to see as far as Haiti from the headland. This area has been turned into the Parque Natural Terrazas de Maisí and the building of further roads and facilities is planned.

POLYMITA SNAILS

A genus endemic to the Baracoa area, the *Polymita* is a snail with a brilliantly coloured shell. According to the colour, six species of *Polymita* can be identified: *P. picta*, *P. muscarum*, *P. sulphurosa*, *P. versicolor*, *P. venusta* and *P. brocheri*. All these species live on trees and plants, and feed on mushrooms and lichens, contributing to the health of the plants, especially coffee trees. *Polymita* snails can be easily recognized, because the shell with coloured stripes looks as though it has been painted, and stands out clearly against the bright green vegetation. Legend has it that the snail acquired its colours from a young Indian who had no pearls or jewels to give to his beloved. He painted a snail shell with the yellow of the sun, the green of the woods, the red of the flowers, and the white from the foam of the waves. But when he decided to take the blue from the sky, it was too late in the day, and he had to be content with the black of night. Today this snail, highly prized for its shell, is an endangered species. Although selling or gathering *Polymita* is not illegal, both locals and visitors are urged to leave them alone.

Patterned Polymita shells

Viewing Haiti from Punta Maisí, at the eastern-most tip of Cuba

TRAVELLERS'
NEEDS

WHERE TO STAY

SINCE 1980, when Cuba decided to open its frontiers to foreign visitors, the growth in tourism has obliged the government to invest heavily in the hotel industry. Some of the old historic hotels have been restored and equipped with international standards of comfort, and new infrastructure has been created, often through joint ventures involving the Cuban Ministry of Tourism and foreign companies. Today, visitors can choose from a variety

Carro de la Revolución, ceramic piece by Sosabravo (*see p25*) Habana Libre hotel, Havana

of accommodation, with choices ranging from modern luxury hotels with swimming pools and good sports facilities to Colonial, city centre hotels and all-inclusive holiday villages on small uninhabited islands. The cheapest hotels are still decidedly spartan and rarely meet international standards. Since 1996, Cubans have been allowed to let out rooms in their own homes or even entire apartments, an increasingly popular arrangement with tourists.

Hostal Conde de Villanueva (*see p248*)

HOTEL CHAINS

MOST VISITORS to Cuba come on package holidays and a number of hotel chains cater for this type of tourism. All hotels are state-owned, although some are managed by joint venture agencies.

One upmarket chain is the Cuban **Gran Caribe**, whose hotels include the historic Hotel Nacional in Havana (*see p98*), an architectural gem built in 1930, the Hotel Plaza and the Hotel Inglaterra (*see pp81–2*) in Havana's Parque Central, and the elegant Casa Granda in Santiago. Gran Caribe also manages several more modern hotels, such as the Habana Riviera in Havana and the Hotel Jagua in Cienfuegos, and well-equipped residences in seaside resorts such as the Hotel Internacional in Varadero and the Hotel Pelícano at Cayo Largo.

High standards are also guaranteed by the **Cubana-cán** and **Sol Meliá** chains, both of which have built hotels throughout Cuba. Cubanacán manages good hotels of its own and others affiliated to international

The foyer in the Hotel Meliá Cohiba, Varadero, seen from the glass lift

chains, including several good-value 3-star hotels, such as the Versalles in Santiago and the Faro Luna in Cienfuegos. The Sol Meliá chain manages the elegant Meliá Cohiba in Havana and the modern Hotel Santiago in Santiago de Cuba.

Gaviota, which specializes in ecological tourism (*see p246*), offers comfortable accommodation in the main coastal resorts, on the *cayos* and in mountain areas. Gaviota runs the only holiday village at Cayo Saetía.

The hotels forming the **Horizontes** chain are of a lower standard, but are still on an international level. **Islazul** hotels are generally inexpensive, and offer more basic levels of comfort.

Another quite different style is offered by **Habaguanex**, a Cuban company founded under the auspices of the Oficina del Historiador de la Ciudad in Havana, which restores old buildings in the Habana Vieja quarter, converting them into shops, cafés and hotels. Habaguanex hotels include historic buildings such as the Hostal Conde de Villanueva, a converted 17th-century mansion; the new San Miguel; the Hotel Ambos Mundos, a Hemingway favourite; and the Santa Isabel, in a splendid Colonial building facing the Plaza de Armas (*see p67*).

◁ **Interior of the historic Floridita bar-restaurant in Havana**

GRADING

CUBAN HOTELS are classified according to the international star system, from one star rising to five stars. However, visitors are likely to find that standards within a particular star rating can vary considerably. Some mid-range hotels may have been good quality in the 1950s, but have since become rundown and not brought into line with modern needs. One-star hotels are generally to be avoided; a better choice would be a private house.

The Meliá Cohiba in Havana, a five-star luxury hotel

PRICES

HOTEL RATES IN THE CAPITAL and in the more famous seaside resorts such as Cayo Largo, Varadero, Cayo Coco and Playa Guardalavaca, are higher than in the rest of the country and correspond more or less to international levels.

The terrace at the Casa Granda hotel in the heart of Santiago de Cuba

Whatever the star rating of a hotel, prices will be higher in peak season, which runs from Christmas to 1 April, and from the beginning of July to the end of August.

BOOKING

IT IS BEST TO BOOK accommodation well ahead of your visit through a travel agency in your home country to ensure that you will get a room and date to your liking. Your tour operator may also be able to offer special package deals that are rarely to be found in Cuba itself. In high season, in particular when there are special events such as Carnival in Santiago, or one of the many local and cultural festivals in Havana, it may be difficult to find a room.

Visitors taking part in trade events such as the Convención del Turismo (Tourism Fair), held in May, or the February Book Fair, will find there are special pricing agreements with hotels in Havana.

TIPPING

IT IS CUSTOMARY to leave a tip (propina) for the hotel staff at the end of your stay. The amount of the propina is at your discretion and will vary according to the type of hotel, how long you stay and the type and quality of service. It is, however, useful to remember that a tip in dollars may often amount to the equivalent of a month's salary in Cuban pesos (see p298).

A percentage of the tips is often donated to charities. The national fund for cancer research is one of the main causes to benefit in this way.

HOLIDAY VILLAGES

THESE ARE IDEAL for people who want a relaxing, sunny holiday by the beach or surrounded by unspoiled landscape, with comfortable rooms and all meals and facilities provided.

All-inclusive packages offer a complete deal, with lodging in bungalows or apartments with bathroom, phone, air conditioning and TV. The price typically includes breakfast, lunch and dinner (usually buffet), and all drinks. Plus, sports activities of all kinds (sailing, snorkelling, scuba diving, swimming, surfing) are provided. Other options include a snack bar and pool bar; games rooms; playgrounds and babysitting services; freshwater pools for children and adults; car rental service; shops and beach equipment. In some parts of Cuba, these all-inclusive holiday villages are the only hotel option available.

The pool and tennis courts at the Hotel Sol Club Palmeras in Varadero

The Hotel Moka, in the Sierra del Rosario reserve, a favourite with "eco-tourists"

CAMPING

BESIDES SOME VERY MODEST camping sites reserved for Cubans, there are other sites (*campismos*) run by **Cubamar Viajes**, located in or near nature reserves and along the coast. Despite being categorized as camping sites, accommodation is in fact in bungalows (*cabañas*). The sites also usually have a restaurant and a pool.

The quality of the *cabañas* varies, but they are usually simple and clean. However, this type of accommodation does not suit everyone. These camping sites often operate more like a holiday village, with daytime and evening recreational activities.

Casual tent-pitching or sleeping out on beaches is not permitted in Cuba.

SPECIALIST HOLIDAYS

MANY tour operators specializing in holidays in Cuba also offer specialist tours for those interested in a particular activity. Many all-inclusive resorts offer diving lessons for beginners, but qualified divers have a wider range of options. People planning more advanced diving need to provide proof of their qualifications and must take out fully comprehensive travel insurance. Many operators recommend that divers should be able to demonstrate a minimum of ten logged dives. Some dive sites such as María La Gorda (*see p142*) and Isla de la Juventud (*see p146*) require skill and experience.

Keen divers can stay in hotels and tourist villages near dive sites or in some of the marinas (particularly those belonging to the **Marinas Puertosol** chain). All-inclusive packages usually include the dives as well.

The best place to learn salsa is of course in Cuba, and UK-based **Dance Holidays** arranges all-inclusive holidays with salsa tuition by expert teachers and visits to the best dance venues.

Conservation-conscious holidays in unspoiled landscape are available from a few hotels that operate as ecological tourism centres. These are found in the Pinar

del Río area and in the Sierra del Rosario, near Marea del Portillo (in the Sierra Maestra) and Baracoa. Many centres also organize excursions, such as birdwatching trips.

There are also health farms, combining relaxation and medical or beauty treatments. The modern, comfortable clinics and beauty centres are run by well-trained staff. Health provision for foreign visitors is provided in these centres by **Servimed**, while accommodation is organized by **Cubanacán Turismo y Salud**.

The Gaviota and Horizontes chains also run a number of spa hotels; two of these are the Kurhotel at Topes de Collantes (*see p259*), and the Hotel Elguea at Corralillo (*see p254*).

A cabin in pinewoods in Las Terrazas village

DISABLED TRAVELLERS

ONLY THE MORE RECENTLY built hotels have rooms purpose-built for disabled people, including bathrooms with wheelchair access. Unfortunately, the majority of Cuban hotels are not equipped with such facilities. Nonetheless, in general hotel staff will do everything they can to be of help to disabled clients.

Accommodation in the María La Gorda holiday village, particularly popular with divers

PRIVATE ROOMS

Renting rooms in private homes *(casas particulares)* is a good arrangement for visitors who want to experience everyday Cuban life at first-hand and meet local people. Hosts will respect privacy, but you should be prepared to become involved in the family's everyday life. It will help to have a smattering of Spanish.

Besides single rooms, you can also rent small apartments. Sometimes you can even find very comfortable living quarters in historic buildings, particularly in old cities like Trinidad.

The proverbial Cuban hospitality makes this type of accommodation particularly pleasant: after all, living in a private home is the simplest and best way to feel part of the place. Another advantage is that the home owners and their families can provide ideas about what to see, where to eat and how to spend the evening.

If you are interested in this type of arrangement, it is best to get addresses from someone you know who has already done this. On the whole, avoid taking advice from strangers – above all, do not allow someone you have met casually on the street to take you to a private home, as he/she may simply be an unreliable "hustler". These people usually receive a commission of your room rent from the owners, which is added to the room price.

Interior of a private home in Gibara, in Holguín province

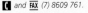

The sticker used for *casas particulares* licensed for rental

If you are pleased with the accommodation in a private home, ask the owners for recommended addresses in other places that you intend to visit: this should provide some guarantee of similar standards. Houses legally authorized to let out rooms can be recognized by the sticker on the door.

When you take up your room, the owners will request a passport or some identification, as they are obliged by law to register your personal data with the Immigration Police.

The taxes paid for room rental in the *casas particulares* are used by local authorities to build homes for young couples.

The amenities, cleanliness and charm of these homes will of course vary and there are no cut-and-dried standards. This type of accommodation is relatively new, and as yet there are no official lists of home owners offering rooms. Some information can be had by visiting: www.geocities.com/ Paris/Parc/6851/habana.htm.

DIRECTORY

HOTEL CHAINS

Cubanacán Hoteles
Marina Hemingway, Playa, Havana.
w www.cubanacan.cu
((7) 204 6316.
FAX (7) 204 6316.

Gaviota
Edificio La Marina, Ave. del Puerto 102, Havana.
w www.gaviota.cubaweb. cu/espannol/index.html
((7) 666 777.
FAX (7) 332 780.

Gran Caribe
Calle 7 no. 4210, e/42 y 44, Miramar, Havana.
w www.grancaribe.cu
((7) 204 0575, 204 0259.
FAX (7) 204 0238, 204 0565.

Habaguanex
Calle Oficios 110, e/ Lamparilla y Amargura, Havana.
w www.ohch.cu/f_turi. htm
(and FAX (7) 8609 761.

Horizontes
Calle 23 no.156, e/ N y O, Vedado, Havana.
w www.horizontes.hor.cu
((7) 334 090-042.
FAX (7) 334 596.

Islazul
Malecón y G, Vedado, Havana.
w www.islazul. cubaweb.cu
((7) 8325 152, 8320 571. FAX (7) 333 458

Sol Meliá
Ave. 5 no. 2008, Miramar, Havana.
w www.solmeliacuba.cu
((7) 204 0910.
FAX (7) 204 0912.

CAMPING

Cubamar Viajes
Calle 3e/ 12y Malécon, Vedado, Havana.
((7) 662 523, 662 524. FAX (7) 333 111.

SPECIALIST TOURISM

Dance Holidays
w www.danceholidays. com
((01206) 577 000 (UK).
FAX (01206) 570 057 (UK).

Marinas Puertosol
Calle 1 no. 3001, esq. 30, Miramar, Havana.
((7) 204 592 325.
FAX (7) 204 5928.

Servimed – Cubanacán Turismo y Salud
Ave. 43 no. 1418, esq.18, Miramar, Havana.
((7) 204 4811.
FAX (7) 204 1630.

Choosing a Hotel

THE HOTELS AND RESORTS in this guide have been selected across a wide price range for the quality of service, décor and location. The prices listed are those charged by the hotel, although discounts may be available through agencies, including those based in Cuba. The colour code indicates the area, and the map references refer to the Havana Street Finder (see pp118–23).

HAVANA

		NUMBER OF ROOMS	ALL-INCLUSIVE	CREDIT CARDS	SWIMMING POOL	RESTAURANT
LA HABANA VIEJA: *Hostal del Tejadillo*	$$$	32		▦		▦
Calle Tejadillo 12, esq. San Ignacio. **Map** 4 E2. 📞 (7) 8637 283. 🖷 (7) 8638 830. @ comercial@habaguanextejadillo.co.cu This small, extremely charming Colonial-style hotel opened recently. Spacious rooms with period furniture. Attractive foyer. 📺 ▤						
LA HABANA VIEJA: *Hostal Valencia*	$$$	12		▦		▦
Calle Oficios 53, esq. Obrapía. **Map** 4 E2. 📞 (7) 8671 037. 🖷 (7) 8605 628. @ reserva@habaguanexhvalencia.co.cu Intimate and welcoming, with Spanish architecture and décor and a lovely Colonial courtyard. The rooms are large and comfortable. 📺 ▤						
LA HABANA VIEJA: *Ambos Mundos*	$$$$	52		▦		▦
Calle Obispo 153, esq. Mercaderes. **Map** 4 E2. 📞 (7) 8609 530. 🖷 (7) 8609 532. @ diada@amundo.co.cu Dedicated to the memory of Hemingway, this hotel has a 1930s atmosphere. Room 511, the author's favourite, is now a small museum. Many rooms have a view of the sea. 📺 ▤ 🍽						
LA HABANA VIEJA: *El Comendador*	$$$$	14		▦		▦
Calle Obrapía, esq. Oficios. **Map** 4 E2. 📞 (7) 8671 037. 🖷 (7) 8605 628. @ reserva@habaguanexhvalencia.co.cu The 19th-century residence of a rich commander, this small and elegant hotel has Spanish décor and a Colonial atmosphere. The museum room has archaeological finds discovered in the cellar. 📺 ▤						
LA HABANA VIEJA: *Florida*	$$$$	25		▦		▦
Calle Obispo 252, esq. Cuba. **Map** 4 E2. 📞 (7) 8624 127. 🖷 (7) 8624 117. @ reserva@habaguanexhflorida.co.cu A restored 19th-century building with wrought-iron banisters, stained-glass windows and a covered Colonial courtyard. Spacious, tastefully furnished rooms. 📺 ▤ 🅿						
LA HABANA VIEJA: *Hostal Conde de Villanueva*	$$$$	9		▦		▦
Calle Mercaderes 202, esq. Lamparilla. **Map** 4 E2. 📞 (7) 8629 293. 🖷 (7) 8629 682. @ hconde@villanueva.ohch.cu A charming hotel in what was once the 18th-century residence of Conde de Villanueva (see p74). Facilities include a good restaurant, cigar shop and Smoking Club. 📺 ▤ 🍽						
LA HABANA VIEJA: *San Miguel*	$$$$	10		▦		
Calle Cuba 52, esq. Peña Pobre. **Map** 4 E1. 📞 (7) 8627 656. 🖷 (7) 8634 088. @ reserva@sanmiguel.ohch.cu A small, family-run hotel in a historic building. A bar on the ground floor serves good cocktails; upper floors have well-furnished rooms and views of the Castillo del Morro. 📺 ▤ 🅿 🍽						
LA HABANA VIEJA: *Santa Isabel*	$$$$$	27		▦		▦
Calle Baratillo 9, e/ Obispo y Narciso López (Plaza de Armas). **Map** 4 F2. 📞 (7) 8608 201. 🖷 (7) 8608 391. Luxury hotel in an elegant Colonial building facing Plaza de Armas (see p67), with a splendid courtyard, 19th-century furnishings, ten suites, modern facilities and excellent service. 📺 ▤ 🅿						
CENTRO HABANA AND PRADO: *Deauville*	$$$	144		▦	●	▦
Calle Galiano y Malecón. **Map** 3 C1. 📞 (7) 338 812. 🖷 (7) 338 148. Near the sea, a few blocks from La Habana Vieja, this blue, high-rise hotel is an unmistakable landmark. Bar with views, disco, car rental. 📺 ▤ 🅿						
CENTRO HABANA AND PRADO: *Inglaterra*	$$$$	83		▦		▦
Paseo de Martí (Prado) 416, e/ San Rafael y San Miguel. **Map** 4 D2. 📞 (7) 8608 594-7. 🖷 (7) 8608 254. @ comercial@gcingla.gca.tur.cu This recently restored historic hotel is a national monument (see p81). The Spanish-style foyer is elegant and the rooms very comfortable. Some have a balcony overlooking the Parque Central, but they can be noisy. 📺 ▤ 🅿						

		NUMBER OF ROOMS	ALL-INCLUSIVE	CREDIT CARDS	SWIMMING POOL	RESTAURANT

Average prices between low and high season per night in a double room, tax and service included (unless specified otherwise):
Ⓢ less than $25
ⓈⓈ $25–$40
ⓈⓈⓈ $40–$80
ⓈⓈⓈⓈ $80–$140
ⓈⓈⓈⓈⓈ more than $140

ALL-INCLUSIVE
When the term "all-inclusive" *(see p245)* is used, it means that the hotel or holiday village in question only offers this package deal. The price includes lodging, meals, drinks, recreational activities and other services.
CREDIT CARDS
VISA or MasterCard.
SWIMMING POOL
Unless specified otherwise, the pool is outdoors.
RESTAURANT
These are generally good in the quality hotels. If the restaurant is recommended, it is listed on pages 268–73.

CENTRO HABANA AND PRADO: *Plaza* ⓈⓈⓈⓈ | 188
Calle Ignacio Agramonte 267. **Map** 4 D2. 【 (7) 8608 583-89. FAX (7) 8608 592.
@ reserva@plaza.gca.tur.cu
This traditional hotel opened in 1909 *(see p81)*. Elegant Art Nouveau lounges. Good views from the top floor terrace. Piano bar, car rental. TV ▤ P Y

CENTRO HABANA AND PRADO: *Sevilla* ⓈⓈⓈⓈ | 188
Paseo de Martí (Prado) y Trocadero. **Map** 4 D2. 【 (7) 8608 560. FAX (7) 8608 582.
@ reserva@sevilla.gca.tur.cu
Historic Neo-Moorish hotel *(see p86)*, with spacious rooms. Excellent service. Sauna, fitness centre, bar-restaurant on terrace. TV ▤ P Y

CENTRO HABANA AND PRADO: *Hotel Telegrafo* ⓈⓈⓈⓈⓈ | 63
Paseo de Martí (Prado) 408 esq Neptuno. **Map** 4 D2.
【 (7) 8611 010. FAX (7) 8614 741. W hoteltelegrafo.co.cu
A clever mix of new and old, the recently opened (2001) Hotel Telegrafo has tastefully decorated and spacious rooms. Facilities include a good restauarant and a cyber café. TV ▤ P ♿

CENTRO HABANA AND PRADO: *Parque Central* ⓈⓈⓈⓈⓈ | 278
Calle Neptuno, e/ Paseo de Martí (Prado) y Zulueta (Parque Central). **Map** 4 D2.
【 (7) 8606 627-9. FAX (7) 8606 630. @ reservations@gtpc.cha.cyt.cu
Comparatively modern but not out of place in the square *(see p81)*. International levels of luxury and comfort. Business facilities. TV ▤ P ♿

VEDADO: *Capri* ⓈⓈⓈ | 215
Calle 21, e/ N y O. **Map** 2 F1. 【 (7) 333 747, 8320 511. FAX (7) 333 740.
Still has the atmosphere of the 1950s, when it was a favourite with wealthy Americans. Closed for restoration until late 2005. TV ▤ P

VEDADO: *Colina* ⓈⓈⓈ | 80
Calle L, e/ 27 y Jovellar. **Map** 2 F2. 【 (7) 334 071, 662 066. FAX (7) 334 104.
Situated near Havana university. A relaxed, informal atmosphere and good food in the restaurant. Snack bar. TV ▤ P

VEDADO: *Saint John's* @ jrecepci@stjohns.hor.tur.cu ⓈⓈⓈ | 94
Calle O n. 216, e/ 23 y 25. **Map** 2 F2. 【 (7) 333 740. FAX (7) 333 561.
Completely renovated, centrally located but quiet, with a small pool. A famous piano bar, the Pico Blanco *(see p281)*, is on the top floor. ▤ TV P

VEDADO: *Vedado* @ recep@vedado.hor.tur.cu ⓈⓈⓈ | 203
Calle O n. 244, e/ 23 y 25. **Map** 1 C1. 【 (7) 334 072. FAX (7) 334 186.
A comfortable, centrally located hotel in a modern eight-storey building. Little character, but the rooms are large and comfortable. ▤ TV

VEDADO: *Habana Riviera* ⓈⓈⓈⓈ | 352
Avenida Paseo y Malecón. **Map** 1 B2. 【 (7) 334 051. FAX (7) 333 739.
@ reserva@gcrivie.gca.tur.cu
A famous 1950s hotel right on the seafront. Some rooms have a breathtaking view of the sea. Spacious, elegant lobby with sculptures and furniture worthy of a museum. Large pool and gym. Car rental. ▤ TV P Y ♿

VEDADO: *Presidente* @ reservas@hpdte.gca.tur.cu ⓈⓈⓈⓈ | 160
Avenida de los Presidentes y Calzada. **Map** 1 C1. 【 (7) 551 801. FAX (7) 333 753.
A ten-storey building on an elegant, tree-lined avenue near the Malecón. Built in the early 1900s, it has been recently renovated, but has kept its 1930s décor and furnishings. ▤ TV

VEDADO: *Victoria* ⓈⓈⓈⓈ | 31
Calle 19 esq. M. **Map** 2 E1. 【 (7) 333 510. FAX (7) 333 109.
@ reserva@gcvicto.gca.cma.net
An elegant, secluded hotel with good facilities and first-class service. An oasis of peace in the middle of town. ▤ TV P

	Average prices between low and high season per night in a double room, tax and service included (unless specified otherwise): ⑤ less than $25 ⑤⑤ $25–$40 ⑤⑤⑤ $40–$80 ⑤⑤⑤⑤ $80–$140 ⑤⑤⑤⑤⑤ more than $140	**ALL-INCLUSIVE** When the term "all-inclusive" *(see p245)* is used, it means that the hotel or holiday village in question only offers this package deal. The price includes lodging, meals, drinks, recreational activities and other services. **CREDIT CARDS** VISA or MasterCard. **SWIMMING POOL** Unless specified otherwise, the pool is outdoors. **RESTAURANT** These are generally good in the quality hotels. If the restaurant is recommended, it is listed on pages 268–73.	NUMBER OF ROOMS	ALL-INCLUSIVE	CREDIT CARDS	SWIMMING POOL	RESTAURANT

VEDADO: *Habana Libre* ⑤⑤⑤⑤⑤ Calle L, e/ 23 y 25. **Map** 2 F2. **C** *(7) 334 011.* **FAX** *(7) 333 141, 662 177.* @ hotel@rllibre.tryp.cma.net One of the symbols of Havana *(see p98)*, with works by great Cuban artists: Amelia Peláez, Sosabravo and Portocarrero. Plus the famous Cabaret Turquino *(see p281)*. Spacious rooms, excellent service. 🖩 📺 **P** **Y**	574	■	●	■
VEDADO: *Meliá Cohiba* ⑤⑤⑤⑤⑤ Avenida Paseo, e/ 1ra. y 3ra. **Map** 1 B2. **C** *(7) 333 636.* **FAX** *(7) 334 555.* @ dep_res_mla@cohiba1.solmelia.cma.net The showpiece of the latest in hotel architecture, this towering hotel is a large-windowed, light marble tower overlooking the Malecón. The service is excellent. Fitness centre, sauna, business centre, shops, art gallery. The restaurants are also very good. 🖩 📺 **P** **&** **Y**	462	■	●	■
VEDADO: *Nacional* ⑤⑤⑤⑤⑤ Calle O, esq. 21. **Map** 2 F1. **C** *(7) 333 564-7.* **FAX** *(7) 335 054.* @ reserva@gcnacio.gca.tur.cu Havana's most prestigious hotel *(see p98)*, with lovely gardens, elegant 1930s lounges, comfortable rooms (some with period furniture) and 15 suites. It also has a good restaurant, a conference centre, sauna, exercise gym, tennis court and beauty centre. Car rental. 🖩 📺 **P** **Y**	464	■	●	■
GREATER HAVANA (COJÍMAR): *Panamericano Resort* ⑤⑤⑤ Calle A y Avenida Central. **C** *(7) 951 010.* **FAX** *(7) 953 913.* @ market@hpr.hor.tur.cu Close to the Villa Panamericana sports complex. There are two residential annexes and the place is popular with athletes, sports events organizers and sports lovers. 🖩 📺 **P**	81	■	●	■
GREATER HAVANA (KOHLY-PLAYA): *El Bosque* ⑤⑤⑤ Calle 28A, e/ Avenida 49A y 49C. **C** *(7) 204 9232.* **FAX** *(7) 204 5637.* @ reserva@bosque.gav.tur.cu This hotel in a leafy part of Havana is part of a holiday village that includes restaurants, bars and a swimming pool. The rooms are comfortable, light and very quiet. 🖩 📺 **P**	61	■		
GREATER HAVANA (KOHLY-PLAYA): *Kohly* ⑤⑤⑤ Avenida 49A y 36A. **C** *(7) 204 0240-2.* **FAX** *(7) 204 1733.* @ carp2@kohly.gav.cma.net A modern hotel in a quiet, leafy area. Facilities include tennis courts, a sauna, an exercise gym and a conference room. The rooms, with bamboo furniture, are large and comfortable. 🖩 📺 **P** **&**	136	■	●	■
GREATER HAVANA (MARINA HEMINGWAY): *Acuario* ⑤⑤⑤⑤ Residencial "Marina Hemingway", Calle 248 y Avenida 5. **C** *(7) 204 7628.* **FAX** *(7) 204 4379.* @ reserva@hvil.mh.cyt.cu All rooms have a balcony with a view of the sea or marina. Guests can use facilities in the Marina Hemingway nautical centre: deep-sea fishing, diving, water skiing, water-scooters. 🖩 📺 **P**	314	■	●	■
GREATER HAVANA (MARINA HEMINGWAY): *El Viejo y el Mar* ⑤⑤⑤⑤ Residencial "Marina Hemingway", Calle 248 y Avenida 5. **C** *(7) 204 6336.* **FAX** *(7) 204 6823.* @ reservas@vmar.mh.cyt.cu Consisting of a central hotel and two-storey *cabañas*, this hotel is inside the marina and ideal for lovers of deep-sea fishing, scuba diving and all kinds of nautical sports. 🖩 📺 **P**	186	■	●	■
GREATER HAVANA (MARINA HEMINGWAY): *Villa Paraíso* ⑤⑤⑤⑤ Residencial "Marina Hemingway", Calle 248 y Avenida 5. **C** *(7) 204 1150-6.* **FAX** *(7) 204 4379.* @ reserva@hvil.mh.cyt.cu A complex with a large swimming pool, 22 villas and 71 bungalows along the canals lined with yacht moorings. Guests can hire boats for fishing, snorkelling and scuba diving. 🖩 📺 **P** **&**	120	■	●	■

GREATER HAVANA (MIRAMAR): *Neptuno-Tritón* $ $ $ | 524

Avenida 3 y 70. ((7) 204 1606, 204 0245. FAX (7) 204 0042.
@ cobras@nep-tri.gca.tur.cu Two modern, luxury-class hotels by the sea
with comfortable, spacious rooms. Also on offer are sports facilities and
equipment, a seaside pool and car rental. ▤ TV P

GREATER HAVANA (MIRAMAR): *Bello Caribe* $ $ $ $ | 120

Calle 158, esq. 31. ((7) 336 487. FAX (7) 330 566.
@ gerente@bcaribe.cha.cyt.cu
A modern but cosy hotel, with a friendly atmosphere.
The Bello Caribe also has a club for children. ▤ TV P

GREATER HAVANA (MIRAMAR): *Chateau Miramar* $ $ $ $ | 50

Avenida 1, e/ 60 y 70. ((7) 204 1952-7. FAX (7) 204 0224.
@ reservas@chateau.cha.cyt.cu
Near the Palacio de las Convenciones and Pabexpo, where fairs
and trade shows are held, and suitable for business travellers. This
comfortable hotel has a diving school, as well as a seafront
swimming pool. ▤ TV P

GREATER HAVANA (MIRAMAR): *Comodoro* $ $ $ $ | 134

Avenida 3 y 84. ((7) 204 5551. FAX (7) 204 2028, 204 2089.
@ reservas@comodor.cha.cyt.cu
This sprawling complex close to the sea consists of a main hotel
building and 301 Mediterranean-style bungalows. Tennis courts,
a small private beach, as well as a disco. Cars for hire.
▤ TV P ♿

GREATER HAVANA (MIRAMAR): *Copacabana* $ $ $ $ | 168

Avenida 1, e/ 44 y 46. ((7) 204 0340. FAX (7) 204 2846.
@ comercio@copa.gca.cma.net
Situated near the sea and surrounded by greenery. A breakwater
creates a saltwater swimming pool. Organized diving tours,
water scooters for hire, a disco and car rental. ▤ TV P

GREATER HAVANA (MIRAMAR): *Novotel Miramar* $ $ $ $ | 427

Avenida 5 y 74. ((7) 204 3584. FAX (7) 204 3583.
@ miramar@miramar.gav.tur.cu
In the middle of a large tropical garden, this hotel combines modern and
Colonial décor and has tennis courts and a golf course. ▤ TV P

GREATER HAVANA (MIRAMAR): *Meliá Habana* $ $ $ $ $ | 409

Avenida 3, e/ 76 y 80. ((7) 204 8500. FAX (7) 204 8505, 204 3902.
@ depres@solmelia.habana.cma.net
An 11-storey new hotel near the coast. Almost all the rooms have
a balcony or terrace overlooking the sea. ▤ TV P ♿

GREATER HAVANA (PLAYAS DEL ESTE): *Club Atlántico* $ $ $ | 92

Avenida de las Terrazas 21, Santa María del Mar. ((7) 971 085.
A seaside hotel, run by Italians. The all-inclusive package includes all
kinds of services, including water sports, a sauna and a disco. A
conference centre is also at the guests' disposal. ▤ TV P

GREATER HAVANA (PLAYAS DEL ESTE): *El Mégano* $ $ $ $ | 83

Vía Blanca km 22,5, Santa María del Mar.
((7) 971 610, 971 356. FAX (7) 971 624.
@ vmegano@megano.hor.tur.cu
A modern, comfortable hotel with pleasant rooms facing the sea,
ideal for a holiday on the beach. Tennis court for guests, too.
▤ TV P ♿

GREATER HAVANA (PLAYAS DEL ESTE): *Sea Club Arenal* $ $ $ $ | 169

Laguna de Boca Ciega, Santa María del Mar.
((7) 971 272. FAX (7) 971 287.
Surrounded by the Itabo lagoon, near Santa María beach, this hotel
operates an all-inclusive package deal with special offers for families
with children. The rooms are comfortable and light. There is
a disco and car rental is available. ▤ TV P ♿

GREATER HAVANA (PLAYAS DEL ESTE): *Villa Los Pinos* $ $ $ $ | 70

Avenida de Las Terrazas 21, e/ 4 y 5, Santa María del Mar. ((7) 971 361.
FAX (7) 971 524. @ reserva@complejo.gca.tur.cu
The 70 charming and comfortable villas in this residence, some of which
have a private pool, are surrounded by greenery. ▤ TV P

		NUMBER OF ROOMS	ALL-INCLUSIVE	CREDIT CARDS	SWIMMING POOL	RESTAURANT

Average prices between low and high season per night in a double room, tax and service included (unless specified otherwise):
$ less than $25
$$ $25–$40
$$$ $40–$80
$$$$ $80–$140
$$$$$ more than $140

ALL-INCLUSIVE
When the term "all-inclusive" *(see p245)* is used, it means that the hotel or holiday village in question only offers this package deal. The price includes lodging, meals, drinks, recreational activities and other services.
CREDIT CARDS
VISA or MasterCard.
SWIMMING POOL
Unless specified otherwise, the pool is outdoors.
RESTAURANT
These are generally good in the quality hotels. If the restaurant is recommended, it is listed on pages 268–73.

Entry	Rooms	All-Incl.	Credit	Pool	Rest.
GREATER HAVANA (PLAYAS DEL ESTE): *Villa Tarará* $$$$ Vía Blanca km 12, Santa María del Mar. ((7) 971 510. FAX (7) 971 333. @ gerente@tarará.cha.cyt.cu Comprising 98 spacious and comfortable 1950s-style villas, this is a Servimed health centre *(see p295)*. Beauty and anti-stress treatments are on offer as well as various water sports activities. 🖃 TV P	348		■	●	■
GREATER HAVANA (PLAYAS DEL ESTE): *Villa Trópico* $$$$ Vía Blanca km 60, Jibacoa. ((692) 852 13. FAX (692) 852 08. This complex consists of several buildings by the sea. The management and cuisine are Italian. The all-inclusive price also covers many sports activities, including football and archery. 🖃 TV P	154	●	■	●	■
GREATER HAVANA (SIBONEY-PLAYA): *Spa La Pradera* $$$$ Calle 230 y 15. ((7) 337 484. FAX (7) 337 198-9. @ comercia@pradera.cha.cyt.cu Surrounded by vegetation, this spa has special offers for medical, dental and beauty treatment, and also has a rehabilitation therapy centre. The rooms are large, bright and cheerful. 🖃 TV P &	230		■	●	■

WESTERN CUBA

Entry	Rooms	All-Incl.	Credit	Pool	Rest.
CAYO LARGO DEL SUR: *Isla del Sur* $$$$ Cayo Largo del Sur, Archipiélago de los Canarreos. ((45) 248 113-18. FAX (45) 248 160. @ isla@isla.gca.tur.cu Located between Playa Lindamar and Playa Blanca, this hotel offers an all-inclusive package only. Sports facilities include squash, volleyball, horse riding and diving. The hotel is part of the modern and comfortable Isla del Sur chain. 🖃 TV P	58	●	■	●	■
CAYO LARGO DEL SUR: *Villa Coral* $$$$ Cayo Largo del Sur, Archipiélago de los Canarreos. ((45) 248 113-18. FAX (45) 248 160. @ isla@isla.gca.tur.cu Also known as *El Pueblito*, this all-inclusive complex consists of ten two-storey Colonial-style buildings with spacious, bright rooms overlooking the swimming pool. 🖃 TV P	60	●	■	●	■
CAYO LARGO DEL SUR: *Villa Lindamar* $$$$ Cayo Largo del Sur, Archipiélago de los Canarreos. ((45) 248 113-18. FAX (45) 248 160. @ isla@isla.gca.tur.cu An appealing holiday village comprising 63 bungalows with thatched roofs, surrounded by greenery. Cabins are only a few metres from the beach. 🖃 TV P	63	●	■	●	
CAYO LARGO DEL SUR: *Pelícano* $$$$ Cayo Largo del Sur. Archipiélago de los Canarreos. ((45) 248 333. FAX (45) 248 167. @ isla@isla.gca.tur.cu Six Mediterranean-style *cabañas* on Playa Lindamar *(see p148)*. Water sports centre, saltwater pool, and good baby-sitting service, all included in the price. 🖃 TV P	307	●	■	●	■
CAYO LARGO DEL SUR: *Villa Soledad* $$$$$ Cayo Largo del Sur, Archipiélago de los Canarreos. ((45) 248 113-118. FAX (45) 248 201. @ isla@isla.cls.tur.cu This complex consists of 24 bungalows or small two-story buildings facing the beach. Some rooms have good views and there is a safety deposit box in each one. Part of the Isla del Sur chain, this complex provides ideal accommodation for a relaxing holiday on the beach. Accommodation is all inclusive. 🖃 TV &	24	●	■	●	■

CAYO LEVISA: *Cayo Levisa* $$$ | 20
Costa Norte, La Palma. ((8) 6660 075.
The 20 bungalows on this small island off the north coast of the province of Pinar del Río are absolutely ideal for divers and water sports fans. The rooms are modern, comfortable and quiet. 🗐 📺 🅿

ISLA DE LA JUVENTUD: *El Colony* $$$$ | 77
Carretera de Siguanea km 41.5. ((46) 398 286. FAX (46) 398 420.
This hotel, which opened in the 1950s, consists of a main building and a few small villas close to the sea. It is very quiet, and the facilities for diving are the best in Cuba. B&B, half-board or full-board. 🗐 📺 🅿

PINAR DEL RÍO: *La Moka* $$$$ | 26
Autopista Habana-Pinar del Río km 51, Candelaria.
((82) 778 600. FAX (82) 778 506.
Rationalist architecture with a few Colonial elements, situated in the Las Terrazas rural community. The hotel has large, bright rooms and is set among luxuriant tropical vegetation. Tennis courts, mountain bikes for hire and excursions. 🗐 📺 🅿 ♿

VIÑALES: *Aguas Claras* $$ | 100
Carretera de Viñales km 7.5. ((82) 778 427. FAX (82) 778 426.
The bungalows, set in a lovely park near a river, are rustic but comfortable. *Fiestas campesinas*, colourful country festivals with food and dancing are laid on. Family atmosphere, good service, very reasonable prices. 🗐 🅿

VIÑALES: *La Ermita* $$$ | 62
Carretera de La Ermita km 2. ((8) 796 100. FAX (8) 796 091.
With a marvellous view of the Valle de Viñales, this hotel is ideal for nature lovers. Colonial furnishings. Organized horse riding, trekking and visits to the nearby caves. 🗐 📺 🅿

VIÑALES: *Los Jazmines* $$$ | 68
Carretera de Viñales km 25. ((8) 796 205. FAX (8) 796 215.
The rooms have bamboo furnishings and the swimming pool is in a lovely site on a terrace overlooking the Valle de Viñales. Horse riding, archery, bowls and volleyball. 🗐 📺 🅿

CENTRAL CUBA – WEST

CIENFUEGOS: *Rancho Luna* $$$ | 126
Carretera de Rancho Luna, Playa Rancho Luna.
((43) 548 012. FAX (43) 548 131.
On the shores of the Caribbean Sea, only 15 minutes by car from Cienfuegos international airport. Diving lessons are held in the large swimming pool. Car rental. 🗐 📺 🅿

CIENFUEGOS: *La Unión* $$$$ | 49
Calle 31, esq. 54. (& FAX (432) 551 020.
@ comercial@union.cfg.cyt.cu A complex of 19th-century buildings with typical Colonial architecture: large courtyard, stained-glass windows, wrought-iron grilles. Courteous service. Bar, conference centre, massage room, sauna, exercise gym and swimming pool with jacuzzi. 🗐 📺 🅿 ♿

CIENFUEGOS: *Mercure Jagua* $$$$ | 144
Calle 37 n. 1, Punta Gorda. ((432) 551 003. FAX (432) 551 245.
A recently restored large 1950s building on the picturesque bay of Cienfuegos. Comfortable rooms. Tennis court, car rental. 🗐 📺 🅿 ♿

GUAMÁ: *Guamá* $$$ | 44
Laguna del Tesoro, Gran Parque Natural Montemar (Matanzas).
((459) 5687.
This unusual accommodation is deep in the Zapata swamp *(see p162)*. Rustic wood-and-straw cabins, built to imitate pre-Columbian huts, perch on several small islands. Rooms are cosy and well-equipped. 🗐 📺 🅿

PLAYA GIRÓN: *Playa Girón* $$$$ | 197
Playa Girón, Gran Parque Natural Montemar, Península da Zapata (Matanzas).
((459) 4110. FAX (459) 4117.
@ reservas@pgiron.cyt.cu Located by the sea near the Zapata swamp and the mouth of the Bay of Pigs, this hotel has a Centro Internacional de Buceo, which organizes scuba diving excursions.
🗐 📺 🅿

For key to symbols, see back flap

> **Average prices** between low and high season per night in a double room, tax and service included (unless specified otherwise):
> $ less than $25
> $$ $25–$40
> $$$ $40–$80
> $$$$ $80–$140
> $$$$$ more than $140

ALL-INCLUSIVE
When the term "all-inclusive" *(see p245)* is used, it means that the hotel or holiday village in question only offers this package deal. The price includes lodging, meals, drinks, recreational activities and other services.
CREDIT CARDS
VISA or MasterCard.
SWIMMING POOL
Unless specified otherwise, the pool is outdoors.
RESTAURANT
These are generally good in the quality hotels. If the restaurant is recommended, it is listed on pages 268–73.

	NUMBER OF ROOMS	ALL-INCLUSIVE	CREDIT CARDS	SWIMMING POOL	RESTAURANT
SANTA CLARA (CORRALILLO): *Elguea* $$$ Corralillo, Via Clara. & FAX *(42) 208 072* A modern thermal spa hotel (in an area with sulphur hot springs), with comfortable rooms in large two-storey buildings, a normal and a special-diet restaurant, and medical assistance of every kind. Exercise gym, swimming pool with jacuzzi, sauna. ▤ 📺 🅿 ♿	42	■	●	■	
SANTA CLARA: *La Granjita* $$$ Carretera de Maleza km 2.5. *(42) 218 190-1.* FAX *(42) 218 149.* @ aloja@granjita.vcl.cyt.cu Located in an orange grove, this hotel is built to look like an Indian Taíno village. Organized excursions on horseback. ▤ 📺 🅿	75	■	●	■	
SANTA CLARA: *Los Caneyes* $$$ Avenida de los Eucaliptos y Circunvalación de Santa Clara. & FAX *(42) 218 140.* This complex includes circular cabins with conical roofs, much like the huts in the pre-Columbian Taíno villages. Mud baths, beauty treatments with fresh-fruit face masks. Car rental. ▤ 📺 🅿 ♿	95	■	●	■	
VARADERO: *Acuazul* $$$ Avenida 1, e/ 13 y 14. *(45) 667 132.* FAX *(45) 667 229.* @ cuentas@acua.hor.tur.cu Besides the comfortable hotel rooms and cosy studio flats, this modern and centrally located complex has apartments with two to seven rooms, some on the beach. Many evening activities and shows. ▤ 📺 🅿	78	■	●	■	
VARADERO: *Palma Real* $$$ Avenida 2, esq. 64. *(45) 614 555.* FAX *(45) 614 550.* @ jrecepcion@palmareal.hotetur.com A large complex consisting of the Siboney and Atabey hotels, with a shopping centre, sauna, tennis court and many bars and restaurants. It lies in a particularly lovely coastal area and offers rooms that are bright and comfortable, although somewhat plain. ▤ 📺 🅿 ♿	233	■	●	■	
VARADERO: *Dos Mares* $$$ Calle 53, esq. Avenida 1. *(45) 612 702.* FAX *(45) 667 499.* @ carpeta@dmares.hor.tur.cu A small, welcoming hotel in a charming Italianate building 150 m (490 ft) from the beach. Colonial décor, with dark wood and bamboo furniture. ▤ 📺 🅿	34	■	●		■
VARADERO: *Arenas Doradas* $$$$ Playa de Varadero km 17. *(45) 668 150.* FAX *(45) 668 159.* @ reserva@arenas.gca.cma.net Eleven two-storey buildings with pools for adults and children and jacuzzi. Guests can practise various sports, and take dancing and Spanish lessons, all included in the price. ▤ 📺 🅿	316	●	■	■	
VARADERO: *Beaches Varadero* $$$$ Carretera de las Morlas km 14.5. *(45) 668 470.* FAX *(45) 668 335.* @ reserva@beaches.var.cyt.cu Accommodation is in comfortable Junior Suites, reserved for guests over 16. Many sport and recreational activities included in the price. ▤ 📺 🅿	350	●	■	■	
VARADERO: *Brisas del Caribe* $$$$ Autopista Sur km 4. *(45) 668 030.* FAX *(45) 668 005.* @ ventas@bricar.var.cyt.cu This informal hotel offers a "super all-inclusive" package aimed at both couples and families with children over five. Tennis courts, exercise gym, pools with jacuzzis, shops, disco, and car rental. ▤ 📺 🅿	371	●	■	■	
VARADERO: *Cabañas del Sol* $$$ Avenida Las Américas. *(45) 667 038.* FAX *(45) 667 246.* Situated in one of the most beautiful parts of Varadero, these charming bungalows are part of the Hotel Internacional complex *(see below).* ▤ 📺	154	■	●	■	

VARADERO: *Club Med Varadero* $$$$ | 450
Autopista Sur km 11. (*(45) 668 288.* FAX *(45) 668 340.*
W www.clubmed.comThe only Club Méditerranée in Cuba. Only an all-inclusive
package is offered, with the efficient organization typical of the Club. The l
arge, comfortable rooms either face the sea or the swimming pool. The
service is very good. 📋 TV P &

VARADERO: *Club Playa de Oro* $$$$ | 385
Carretera de las Morlas km 12.5. (*(45) 668 566.* FAX *(45) 668 555.*
@ reservas@poro.gca.tur.cu With modern architecture and furnishings, this
hotel facesthe sea. The all-inclusive package includes a club
for children and a fitness centre. 📋 TV P &

VARADERO: *Club Tropical* $$$$ | 173
Avenida 1 y 21 y 22. (*(45) 613 915.* FAX *(45) 614 676.*
In the centre of Varadero, by a splendid beach. The spacious rooms are
in two-, three- or four-storey buildings, and many have a view of the sea.
Introductory diving courses, held in the round pool, are also included in
the price. 📋 TV P

VARADERO: *Cuatro Palmas* $$$$ | 309
Avenida 1, e/ 60 y 62. (*(45) 667 040.*
FAX *(45) 667 583.* @ reserva@gcpalho.gca.tur.cu
An elegant Spanish-style complex consisting of a three-storey Moorish-
style building overlooking the pool and two-storey villas, which are
situated a block away from the beach. 📋 TV P &

VARADERO: *Gran Hotel* $$$$ | 411
Carretera de Las Morlas km 11.5.
(*(45) 668 243.* FAX *(45) 668 202.* @ espcomercial@granhot.var.cyt.cu
One of the newest hotel complexes in Varadero,
suited to families with children of all ages. 📋 TV P &

VARADERO: *Hotel y Villas Kawama* $$$$ | 235
Calle O y Avenida 1, Reparto Kawama. (*(45) 614 416.* FAX *(45) 667 334.*
@ reserva@kawama.gca.tur.cu
A peaceful complex in a lush, green setting, offering an all-inclusive
package in the main hotel or residential hotel. A special feature
is the wide range of water sports on offer. 📋 TV P

VARADERO: *Internacional* $$$$ | 163
Avenida Las Américas. (*(45) 667 038-9.* FAX *(45) 667 246.*
@ reserva@gcinter.gca.tur.cu
Comfortable and traditional, built in the 1950s and recently restored, this
hotel has entertained illustrious guests. Besides all the services typical of
a large hotel, there are various bars and a famous cabaret. In front is a
large lawn, while behind it is a lovely private beach. 📋 TV P Y

VARADERO: *Las Morlas* $$$$ | 143
Avenida Las Américas, esq. A. (*(45) 667 230.* FAX *(45) 667 007.*
@ reserva@morlas.gca.cma.net
A Mediterranean-style complex offering water sports and outdoor
activities on the beach. Every room has a balcony facing the
swimming pool area, which is decorated with towers and
small bridges. Closed for renovation until early 2005. 📋 TV P &

VARADERO: *Sol Club Coral* $$$$ | 324
Avenida Las Américas, e/ H y K. (*(45) 667 240.* FAX *(45) 667 194.*
@ jefres@coral.solmelia.cma.net
Situated near the Plaza Américas shopping centre, this hotel has good
facilities, including a beer hall and an Italian restaurant. 📋 TV P

VARADERO: *Sol Club Las Sirenas* $$$$ | 309
Calle K, Reparto La Torre. (*(45) 668 070.* FAX *(45) 669 174.*
@ jefres@sirenas.solmelia.cma.net
An all-inclusive hotel with simple but functional rooms
as well as suites with jacuzzi tubs. 📋 TV P &

VARADERO: *Sol Club Palmeras* $$$$ | 607
Carretera de Las Morlas km 8.
(*(45) 667 009.* FAX *(45) 667 008.* @ depres@tetalme.solmelia.cma.net
The horseshoe-shaped main building curves around a swimming pool
with an island bar. There are numbers of bungalows. Excellent sport
and recreational activities. 📋 TV P &

For key to symbols, see back flap

Average prices between low and high season per night in a double room, tax and service included (unless specified otherwise): ⑤ less than $25 ⑤⑤ $25–$40 ⑤⑤⑤ $40–$80 ⑤⑤⑤⑤ $80–$140 ⑤⑤⑤⑤⑤ more than $140	**ALL-INCLUSIVE** When the term "all-inclusive" *(see p245)* is used, it means that the hotel or holiday village in question only offers this package deal. The price includes lodging, meals, drinks, recreational activities and other services. **CREDIT CARDS** VISA or MasterCard. **SWIMMING POOL** Unless specified otherwise, the pool is outdoors. **RESTAURANT** These are generally good in the quality hotels. If the restaurant is recommended, it is listed on pages 268–73.			

	NUMBER OF ROOMS	ALL-INCLUSIVE	CREDIT CARDS	SWIMMING POOL	RESTAURANT
VARADERO: *SuperClubs Puntarenas* ⑤⑤⑤⑤ Avenida Kawama Final. 📞 (45) 667 125. 📠 (45) 667 074, 668 391. @ reservas@riparad.gca.cma.net Two large modern buildings by the sea, with a large pool, a spectacular lobby on two levels and deluxe facilities: fitness centre, shops, sauna and art galleries. It is some distance from town but there is a desk for car and scooter rental. 🗎 📺 🅿	510	●	▦	●	▦
VARADERO: *SuperClub Varadero* ⑤⑤⑤⑤ Avenida Las Américas km 3. 📞 (45) 667 030-1. 📠 (45) 667 005. @ reservas@clubvar.var.cyt.cu This hotel facing the beach offers a "super all-inclusive" package. Known for the variety of its recreational activities and its excellent service. 🗎 📺 🅿	265	●	▦	●	▦
VARADERO: *Tortuga* ⑤⑤⑤⑤ Calle 7, Carretera Kawama. 📞 (45) 614 747. 📠 (45) 667 485. A hotel about 50 m (165 ft) from the beach, in an area with a number of nightclubs. Accommodation is in villas with very large and tastefully furnished rooms. Exercise gym, tennis court and archery area. 🗎 📺 🅿 ♿	273	●	▦	●	▦
VARADERO: *Turquesa* ⑤⑤⑤⑤ Carretera de Las Morlas km 12.5, Reparto Los Taínos. 📞 (45) 668 471. 📠 (45) 668 495. @ ventafrio@turquesa.gca.tur.cu A complex with comfortable bungalows, with all kinds of outdoor activities. Guests can have lunch on the beach. 🗎 📺 🅿 ♿	268	●	▦	●	▦
VARADERO: *Tuxpan* ⑤⑤⑤⑤ Avenida Las Américas km 4. 📞 (45) 667 560. 📠 (45) 667 561. @ reservas@tuxpan.var.cyt.cu Famous for its high-quality service and facilities, this hotel faces the beach and is ideal for water sports, all included in the price. 🗎 📺 🅿	233	●	▦	●	▦
VARADERO: *Villa Cuba Resort* ⑤⑤⑤⑤ Avenida Las Américas km 3, Reparto La Torre. 📞 (45) 668 280. 📠 (45) 668 282. @ reservas@vcuba.gca.tur.cu This pretty hotel is built on a rise by the beach. Guests can take beginners' lessons in diving, and hire bikes and mopeds. 🗎 📺 🅿 ♿	365	●	▦	●	▦
VARADERO: *Villas Punta Blanca* ⑤⑤⑤⑤ Reparto Kawama. 📞 (45) 667 105. 📠 (45) 667 588. @ reserva@pblanca.gca.tur.cu A hotel complex comprising a variety of buildings. The décor and furniture are often changed. Among the facilities are a tennis court, a discothèque and an exercise gym. There are two pools for adults, and one for children. 🗎 📺 🅿	269	●	▦	●	▦
VARADERO: *Arenas Blancas Resort* ⑤⑤⑤⑤⑤ Calle 64, e/ Avenida 1 y Autopista. 📞 (45) 614 450, 614 492. 📠 (45) 611 832. @ gere@arblcas.gca.tur.cu A few metres from the sea, this new hotel offers comfortable, well-equipped rooms. The all-inclusive package deal features "water safaris". 🗎 📺 🅿 ♿	358	●	▦	●	▦
VARADERO: *Barlovento* ⑤⑤⑤⑤⑤ Avenida 1, e/ 9 y 12. 📞 (45) 667 140. 📠 (45) 667 218. @ reserva@ibero.gca.tur.cu Centrally located, consisting of two- and three-storey buildings laid out around a huge swimming pool. Each of the spacious deluxe rooms has a balcony. The price includes many sports and recreational activities. 🗎 📺 🅿 ♿	276	●	▦	●	▦

VARADERO: *Bella Costa Resort* $$$$$ — 382
Avenida Las Américas km 3.5. ((45) 667 210. FAX (45) 667 174.
@ reservas@bcosta.var.cyt.cu
A seven-storey hotel a stone's throw from the golf course and from Villa Xanadú, which once belonged to the American millionaire Dupont *(see p159)*. It has a particularly lovely pool and is close to the beach.
目 TV P

VARADERO: *Hotel Barceló Solymar* $$$$$ — 525
Carretera Las Américas, km 3. ((45) 614 499. FAX (45) 668 798.
@ reserva@solymar.gca.tur.cu This modern complex was built in 2000 and is located not far from downtown. The accommodation is all inclusive and there are water sports and outdoor beach activities. 目 TV P &

VARADERO: *Meliá Las Américas* $$$$$ — 340
Carretera de las Morlas. ((45) 667 600. FAX (45) 667 625.
@ dep_res_mla@america.solmelia.cma.net
A four-storey luxury hotel near the sea with six pools and an adjacent golf course. Various different sports and recreational activities. 目 TV P

VARADERO: *Meliá Varadero* $$$$$ — 490
Autopista Sur km 7, Playa de las Américas. ((45) 667 013.
FAX (45) 667 012. @ dep_res_mla@melia.solmelia.cma.net
A luxury hotel with elegant yet practical rooms and suites, with a terrace or balcony overlooking the sea. The foyer is showy. 目 TV P &

VARADERO: *Paradisus Varadero* $$$$$ — 421
Punta Francés. ((45) 668 700. FAX (45) 668 705.
@ jefres@pvaradero.solmelia.cma.net
In the most verdant and peaceful part of the peninsula, this hotel has good water sports facilities. 目 TV P

CENTRAL CUBA – EAST

CAMAGÜEY: *Camagüey* $$$ — 142
Carretera Central km 4.5, Reparto Jayamá.
((32) 287 267. FAX (32) 287 180. @ comercial@hcamaguey.hor.tur.cu
A comfortable hotel just outside the city consisting of a large central building, six bungalows and a conference centre. The rooms are cosy and practical. Car rental and disco. 目 TV P

CAMAGÜEY: *Gran Hotel* $$$ — 72
Calle Maceo 67. ((32) 292 094. FAX (32) 293 933.
This five-storey hotel in the heart of town is old but the renovated rooms offer good value for money. There is a cabaret, and on the top floor is an elegant restaurant with a magnificent view of Camagüey. 目 TV P

CAYO COCO: *Cayo Coco* $$$$ — 965
Cayo Coco, Ciego de Ávila. ((33) 301 300.
FAX (33) 301 389. @ comer@club.tryp.cma.cu
A complex with two- or three-storey Neo-Colonial buildings. The rooms have balconies and terraces. The all-inclusive package is optional, and includes a varied programme of recreational activities and entertainment. 目 TV P &

CAYO COCO: *Meliá Cayo Coco* $$$$ — 250
Cayo Coco, Ciego de Ávila. ((33) 301 180. FAX (33) 301 195.
@ depres@smcoco2.solmelia.cma.net On the coast, about a kilometre from a coral reef, this hotel has excellent facilities, including a range of sporting activities. 目 TV P &

CAYO COCO: *Sol Club Cayo Coco* $$$$ — 270
Cayo Coco, Ciego de Ávila. ((33) 301 280. FAX (33) 301 285.
@ solclub.cayococo@smcoco1.solmelia.cma.net
In this new and well-equipped holiday village with spacious rooms guests can practise all kinds of sports, from football to bowls, golf and volleyball. The service is excellent. 目 TV P &

CAYO GUILLERMO: *Daiquirí* $$$$ — 312
Cayo Guillermo, Ciego de Ávila. ((33) 301 650. FAX (33) 301 645.
@ reserva@ibsdaiq.gca.tur.cu
A large hotel complex offering an all-inclusive deal. Seaside location, well-appointed rooms, multisports centre. 目 TV P

Average prices between low and high season per night in a double room, tax and service included (unless specified otherwise):

$ less than $25
$$ $25–$40
$$$ $40–$80
$$$$ $80–$140
$$$$$ more than $140

ALL-INCLUSIVE
When the term "all-inclusive" (see p245) is used, it means that the hotel or holiday village in question only offers this package deal. The price includes lodging, meals, drinks, recreational activities and other services.

CREDIT CARDS
VISA or MasterCard.

SWIMMING POOL
Unless specified otherwise, the pool is outdoors.

RESTAURANT
These are generally good in the quality hotels. If the restaurant is recommended, it is listed on pages 268–73.

	NUMBER OF ROOMS	ALL-INCLUSIVE	CREDIT CARDS	SWIMMING POOL	RESTAURANT
CAYO GUILLERMO: *Villa Cojímar* $$$$ Cayo Guillermo, Ciego de Ávila. ((33) 301 712. FAX (33) 301 724. @ aloja@cojimar.gca.cma.net A complex of Mediterranean-style bungalows with red tile roofs, and two-storey houses. The rooms are very comfortable and the service is excellent. This is a major water sports centre recommended for diving enthusiasts. Meals are included in the price. ▤ TV P	212		▦	●	▦
CAYO GUILLERMO: *Meliá Cayo Guillermo* $$$$$ Cayo Guillermo, Ciego de Ávila. ((33) 301 680. FAX (33) 301 684. The most luxurious and comfortable hotel on the *cayo*, with very large, well-appointed rooms, luxuriant gardens, elegant public areas and a great variety of sport and recreational activities. ▤ TV P	264		▦	●	▦
CAYO GUILLERMO: *Sol Club Cayo Guillermo* $$$$$ Cayo Guillermo, Ciego de Ávila. ((33) 301 760. FAX (33) 301 748. @ reserva@cguille.solmelia.cma.net A modern and self-contained village offering a variety of sport and recreational options. Large, light-filled rooms. ▤ TV P	270	●	▦	●	▦
LAS TUNAS: *Villa Covarrubias* $$$ Playa Covarrubias, Puerto Padre, Las Tunas. ((31) 555 30. FAX (31) 553 52. In an area off the beaten tourist track, this modern hotel complex offers comfortable rooms and excellent service. All water sports and evening entertainment provided. Meals are included in the price. ▤ TV P ♿	122	●	▦	●	▦
MORÓN: *Morón* $$$ Avenida Tarafa. ((335) 2230. FAX (335) 2131. @ hhmm@hmorón.cav.cyt.cu Near the coast and surrounded by lagoons, this is a good area for hunting and fishing. This hotel would suit people who love sports and outdoor pursuits. ▤ TV P	144		▦	●	▦
PLAYA ANCÓN: *Costasur* $$$ Playa María Aguilar. ((419) 6172. FAX (419) 6173. @ informatico@costasurhor.co.cu Besides the main building, this all-inclusive complex has some cottages with a view of the pool or the garden. Guests can play tennis, rent mopeds and go scuba diving. ▤ TV P	131		▦	●	▦
PLAYA ANCÓN (TRINIDAD): *Brisas Trinidad del Mar* $$$ Península Ancón. ((419) 6500, 6507. FAX (419) 6565. In a fine location on the peninsula of Ancón, this new hotel with a stupendous view of the sea and the mountain is a must for water sports enthusiasts. The all-inclusive package is optional. ▤ TV	241		▦	●	▦
PLAYA ANCÓN (TRINIDAD): *Hotel Ancón* $$$ Carretera de María Aguilar, Playa Ancón. ((419) 6120, 6129. FAX (419) 6121, 6151. @ reserva@ancon.gca.cma.net By a lovely beach, 12 km (7 miles) from town. This hotel offers a wide range of water sports. The all-inclusive package deal is optional. ▤ TV P	279		▦	●	▦
PLAYA SANTA LUCÍA (CAMAGÜEY): *Club Amigo Mayanabo* $$$ Playa Santa Lucía, Nuevitas. ((32) 336 369. FAX (32) 365 295. This hotel is surrounded by palms and is near a white sandy beach. The rooms are quite comfortable, and many overlook the sea. Ideal for water sports and scuba diving. ▤ TV	225	●	▦	●	▦
PLAYA SANTA LUCÍA (CAMAGÜEY): *Club Santa Lucía* $$$ Playa Santa Lucía, Nuevitas. ((32) 365 146. FAX (32) 365 153. @ aloja@clubst.stl.cyt.cu A stone's throw from the beach. Rooms and bungalows. Excellent service and facilities, all included in the price. ▤ TV P ♿	249	●	▦	●	▦

PLAYA SANTA LUCÍA (CAMAGÜEY): *Cuatro Vientos* $$$$ 412
Playa Santa Lucía, Nuevitas. (32) 336 317.
FAX (32) 336 255. @ aloja@cvientos.stl.cyt.cu
This beach-side holiday village is reminiscent of an Andalusian town.
The all-inclusive package includes lessons in Cuban dancing.
■ TV P

PLAYA SANTA LUCÍA (CAMAGÜEY): *Vita Club Caracol* $$$$ 150
Playa Santa Lucía. (32) 336 303. FAX (32) 365 307, 365 167.
@ aloja@caracol.stl.cyt.cu
One- and two-storey buildings laid out in the shape of a shell.
The all-inclusive package includes diving and lessons
in Spanish and Caribbean dancing. ■ TV P

SANCTI SPÍRITUS: *Rancho Hatuey* $$$ 74
Carretera Central km 384. (41) 283 15. FAX (41) 288 30. @ aloja@rhatuey.co.cu
A complex of bungalows on a hill, surrounded by luxuriant tropical
vegetation. Rustic furniture in functional, modern rooms.
The location is ideal for horse riding. ■ TV

TOPES DE COLLANTES: *Los Helechos* $$$ 82
Topes de Collantes, Sierra del Escambray. (42) 540 330.
Around 800 m (2,625 ft) above sea level, in the heart of the Sierra del
Escambray. The facilities – thermal pool, sauna, massages and steam
baths – make for a relaxing holiday. ■ TV P &

TOPES DE COLLANTES: *Kurhotel Escambray* $$$$ 210
Topes de Collantes, Sierra del Escambray.
(42) 540 288. FAX (42) 540 288. @ topescon@ip.etecsa.cu
An impressive eight-storey building on a hill, with simple, bright rooms.
A wide range of medical physiotherapy treatments, sport and recreational
activities are offered. There is also a conference room. ■ TV P &

TRINIDAD: *Las Cuevas* $$$ 112
Finca Santa Ana. (419) 6133. FAX (419) 6161. @ reservas@cuevas.co.cu
On a low hill, 1 km (0.6 mile) from town, this motel has one-storey, two-
family cottages and newer two-storey buildings. The spacious rooms
have rustic furniture and offer a splendid view of Trinidad and the sea.
Steps lead to the *Maravillosa* grotto. ■ TV P

EASTERN CUBA

BACONAO (SANTIAGO DE CUBA): *Motel Gran Piedra* $$ 22
Carretera La Gran Piedra km 14. (22) 686 147.
A complex of small buildings and bungalows in the Parque Nacional Gran
Piedra, 1200 m (3,935 ft) asl. Ideal for excursions and trekking. ■ TV P

BACONAO (SANTIAGO DE CUBA): *Club Valtur-Los Corales* $$$ 304
Carretera de Baconao, Playa Cazonal. (22) 356 122.
FAX (22) 356 116. @ reserva@carisol.scu.cyt.cu
A building with original Colonial architecture overlooking the
Caribbean Sea. There is a club for children and guests can go
scuba diving or horse riding. The rooms are quite cosy
and the service is efficient. ■ TV P

BACONAO (SANTIAGO DE CUBA): *Costa Morena* $$$ 115
Carretera de Baconao km 38.5, Siguá. & FAX (22) 356 135.
A few minutes by car from Santiago and the Parque Baconao, this
low-rise building has large, comfortable rooms, all facing the sea.
There are two swimming pools, one freshwater and the other
saltwater. An excellent base for trips around the province. ■ TV P

BARACOA: *El Castillo* $$$ 34
Calle Calixto García. (21) 45 164-6. FAX (21) 452 23.
This hotel is situated in a recently converted Spanish fortress
on top of a hill. From the viewpoint there are extraordinary
views over the city and the bay. The rooms have Colonial-style furniture.
■ TV P

BARACOA: *Porto Santo* $$$ 60
Carretera del Aeropuerto, Reparto Jaitesico.
(21) 45104. FAX (21) 45223. @ reserva@gaviota.gav.tur.cu
Just outside town, with a private beach with steps leading to
a tennis court. It is modern but has Colonial touches. ■ TV P

For key to symbols, see back flap

	NUMBER OF ROOMS	ALL-INCLUSIVE	CREDIT CARDS	SWIMMING POOL	RESTAURANT
Average prices between low and high season per night in a double room, tax and service included (unless specified otherwise): $ less than $25 $$ $25–$40 $$$ $40–$80 $$$$ $80–$140 $$$$$ more than $140 **ALL-INCLUSIVE** When the term "all-inclusive" *(see p245)* is used, it means that the hotel or holiday village in question only offers this package deal. The price includes lodging, meals, drinks, recreational activities and other services. **CREDIT CARDS** VISA or MasterCard. **SWIMMING POOL** Unless specified otherwise, the pool is outdoors. **RESTAURANT** These are generally good in the quality hotels. If the restaurant is recommended, it is listed on pages 268–73.					
CAIMANERA: *Caimanera I* $$$ Loma Norte, Caimanera. [(21) 99414. A new, austere building on the top of a hill; plain rooms with views of the American naval base at Guantánamo. The restaurant specializes in *caldo de jaiba* (a type of crab). ▤ TV P	19		▦	●	▦
CAYO SAETÍA: *Hacienda Cayo Saetía* $$$$ Cayo Saetía, Holguín. [(24) 969 00. FAX (24) 969 003. Ten rustic but comfortable cabins set in an ecological oasis, 65 per cent of which consists of woods and the rest of plains populated by zebras, antelopes and gazelles. ▤ TV P	12		▦		▦
HOLGUÍN: *Pernik* $$$ Avenida J. Dimitrov. [(24) 481 011, 481 667. FAX (24) 480 973. @ jreserva@pernik.holguin.inf.cu The best place to stay in Holguín: comfortable, with all amenities, even though it is on the plain side. The rooms are large and bright. ▤ TV P	200		▦	●	▦
PILÓN: *Farallón del Caribe* $$$$ Carretera Granma km 12,5. [(23) 597 047, 597 181. FAX (23) 597 080. On the southern edge of the Sierra Maestra. Besides the sports facilities and recreational activities, there is a splendid panoramic view of the mountains and the Marea del Portillo bay. ▤ TV P ⛅	140		▦	●	▦
PLAYA ESMERALDA (HOLGUÍN): *Sol Club Río de Luna* $$$$ Carretera Guardalavaca, Playa Esmeralda. [(24) 300 30. FAX (24) 300 65. @ jefres@luna.solmelia.cma.net A Spanish-style hotel in a 4-ha (10-acre) tropical garden. Rooms are elegant, all with balconies overlooking the sea. ▤ TV P ⛅	222	●	▦	●	▦
PLAYA ESMERALDA (HOLGUÍN): *Sol Río de Mares* $$$$ Carretera Guardalavaca, Playa Esmeralda. [(24) 300 60. FAX (24) 300 65. @ jefres@mares.solmelia.cma.net A recently built hotel. Functional rooms, each with a balcony. All-inclusive package with lively recreational activities including horse riding and water sports. Italian restaurant. ▤ TV P ⛅	242	●	▦	●	▦
PLAYA GUARDALAVACA (HOLGUÍN): *Club Amigo Guardalavaca* $$$ Playa Guardalavaca, Banes. [(24) 302 00. FAX (24) 302 21. A complex consisting of a number of buildings with spacious rooms, a disco, billiards and ping-pong. Organized horse riding excursions. The all-inclusive package is optional. ▤ TV P ⛅	234		▦	●	▦
PLAYA GUARDALAVACA (HOLGUÍN): *Delta Las Brisas* $$$ Playa Guardalavaca, Banes. [(24) 302 36. FAX (24) 304 18. @ reserva@brisas.gvc.cyt.cu Near the beach where Columbus first landed *(see p210)*. A vast, modern, efficiently organized hotel complex consisting of a hotel and a holiday village, with all kinds of sport and recreational activities, as well as areas for children. The all-inclusive package is optional. ▤ TV P ⛅	437		▦	●	▦
PLAYA GUARDALAVACA (HOLGUÍN): *Atlántico & Bungalows* $$$ Playa Guardalavaca, Banes. [(24) 301 80. FAX (24) 302 00. @ reserva@hatlan.gvc.cyt.cu The central section has rooms with a view of the sea or the garden, and there are various bungalows with a balcony and terrace. Among the facilities for guests are an exercise gym, massage and aerobics, all included in the price. ▤ TV P	233	●	▦	●	▦

PLAYA GUARDALAVACA (HOLGUÍN): *Meliá Río de Oro* $$$$ 300
Carretera Guardalavaca. **[** *(24) 300 90.*
FAX *(24) 300 95.* **@** depres@oro.solmelia.cma.net
In the heart of the Bahía Naranjo natural park, this luxury hotel has
both suites and extra-large suites. Tennis courts and a football pitch;
facilities for many other sports. Bicycles, mopeds
and cars for hire. ▤ TV P &

PLAYA PESQUERO (HOLGUÍN): *Costa Verde Beach Resort* $$$ 309
Playa Pesquero Nuevo, Rafael Freire. **[** *(24) 305 10-4.* **FAX** *(24) 305 15.*
@ jefrec@lteholguin.esehl.colombus.cu This recently built hotel is situated
behind a beautiful beach. The all-inclusive package deal offers many
activities. ▤ TV P &

SANTIAGO DE CUBA: *Las Américas* $$$ 70
Avenida Las Américas y General Cebreco. **[** *(22) 687 289.*
FAX *(22) 687 075.* **@** jcarpeta@hamerica.scu.cyt.cu
This modern, functional hotel is on one of the main avenues in town,
surrounded by parks and gardens. The rooms are comfortable though
not large, and the service is fairly good. ▤ TV P

SANTIAGO DE CUBA: *San Juan* $$$ 110
Carretera Siboney km 1.5.
[*(22) 687 200.* **FAX** *(22) 687 017.* **@** jcarpeta@sanjuan.scu.cyt.cu
On the hill of San Juan, in one of the most leafy parts of the city.
The complex has various two-storey buildings. Comfortable rooms,
a pool for children and adults, massage and disco. ▤ TV P

SANTIAGO DE CUBA: *Versalles* $$$ 61
Alturas de Versalles km 1.
[*(22) 691 016.* **FAX** *(22) 686 039.* **@** comercia@versall.scu.cyt.cu
A complex of typically tropical, low-rise buildings in
a leafy residential district east of town. The rooms
are large and comfortable and the service
is very good. ▤ TV P

SANTIAGO DE CUBA: *Villa Santiago* $$$ 47
Avenida Manduley 502, Reparto Vista Alegre.
[*(22) 641 368.* **FAX** *(22) 687 218.*
This accommodation consists of 13 apartments situated in a quiet
residential neighbourhood, not far from the town centre.
▤ TV P

SANTIAGO DE CUBA: *Casa Granda* $$$$ 58
Calle Heredia 201, e/ San Pedro y San Félix.
[*(22) 686 600.* **FAX** *(22) 686 035.* **@** reserva@casagran.gca.tur.cu
A lovely, white Neo-Classical-style building commissioned in 1912
by an Italian hotelier. The roof garden offers a magnificent view
of the city and bay. An atmospheric hotel with period
furniture, overlooking Parque Céspedes in the city centre.
▤ TV Y &

SANTIAGO DE CUBA: *Meliá Santiago de Cuba* $$$$$ 302
Avenida de Las Américas, esq. M.
[*(22) 687 070.* **FAX** *(22) 687 170.*
@ jefven@santiago.solmelia.cma.net
Built in the 1980s, this is one of the few examples of Cuban high-tech
architecture. The Pico Real bar provides a lovely view of the city.
▤ TV P

SIERRA MAESTRA: *Los Galeones Resort* $$$$ 34
Carretera Chivirico km 75, Chivirico. **[** *(22) 261 60.* **FAX** *(22) 532 22.*
@ galeones@smar.scu.cyt.cu
A Spanish-style building, in a lovely location on a hilltop overlooking a
grey sand beach. Large, comfortable rooms, sauna and pool. However,
children under 16 are not allowed. The price includes meals. ▤ TV P

SIERRA MAESTRA: *Hotel Sierra Mar* $$$$ 200
Carretera Chivirico km 60, Guamá. **[** *(22) 263 37.* **FAX** *(22) 290 07.*
@ sierramar@smar.scu.cyt.cu
Backed by the Sierra Maestra mountains but a stone's throw from the
Caribbean Sea. This hotel offers a "super all-inclusive" package deal,
which includes horse riding and diving lessons.
Special activities for children. ▤ TV P

For key to symbols, see back flap

WHERE TO EAT

IN TRADITIONAL Cuban cooking, rice and beans are the staples rather than bread, and the most common dishes are meat-based. Although Cuba is an island, fish and seafood are available regularly only in

The neon sign at the historic La Zaragozana restaurant

the top restaurants. Different influences can be seen in Cuban cooking and there are local variations, especially on the eastern side of Cuba. Food is rarely hot and spicy. Besides international dishes, local menus generally feature some specialities of *cocina criolla* (Creole cuisine; *see p264*). Places offering food range from state-run restaurants and hotel restaurants, which are usually comfortable and elegant, to informal *paladares* serving inexpensive home cooking. In Havana there are also Chinese and Arab restaurants, and pizzerias are everywhere. Vegetarian restaurants are non-existent.

RESTAURANTS AND CAFÉS

STATE-RUN RESTAURANTS have for years had a bad reputation. However, in recent years a great effort has been made to improve them (partly due to competition from private *paladares*). Now, standards in some cases, for example in branches of the **Palmares** chain run by Cubanacán, are very good.

Some of Havana's most delightful restaurants are housed in well-restored Colonial buildings with period furnishings. Many have a view or a garden of some kind. Live music is often performed and makes for a lively atmosphere.

The restaurants in luxury hotels are usually high-quality and feature international dishes along with a good wine list. As an alternative to formal, à la carte dining, many hotels offer buffets, which in Cuba are called *mesa sueca* (smorgasbord), where, for a fixed price, you can eat

The inviting Tocororo restaurant in Havana

anything from pasta to roast suckling pig with rice and black beans.

Some of Havana's most famous bars have a separately managed restaurant. Examples are the Bodeguita del Medio and El Floridita in Havana, and the Terraza Cojímar. These are open all day serving snacks and cocktails, and offer a full menu for lunch and dinner.

Dining out at La Campana de Toledo restaurant in Camagüey

PALADARES

THE CHEAPEST places offering Cuban cooking are called *paladares*. These are small private restaurants with a handful of tables, offering a fixed price or à la carte menu. Dishes are often simple – a limited range of ingredients is available – but can be surprisingly good. Since the Cuban government allowed its citizens to have family-run restaurants in their own homes, many *paladares* have opened and an equally large number have closed in a short time, too, which makes it difficult to make recommendations. It is best to get advice from other travellers, or to ask locals in the area.

However, be wary of people who accost you in the street and offer to show you a *paladar*: once there, your helpful guide will receive a commission from the proprietor... and your bill will cost a few dollars more. Furthermore, your new friend will probably also ask you to treat him to dinner!

In the *paladares* people usually drink cold beer with their food, but mineral water and soft drinks are also normally available. The price shown for a dish includes service and side dishes such as beans, salad and fried plantains or yucca.

Inside a typical *paladar*, which has traditional cuisine and live music

PRIVATE HOMES

IT OFTEN HAPPENS THAT private homes offering rooms to let *(see p247)* also provide main meals as well as breakfast. Since the food normally eaten by the home owners is plainer than the food offered to guests, you will be asked to let them know in advance whether you intend to eat in or out. In general, the standards of cleanliness in authorized private homes are good. The quality of the food varies quite a lot: you may be lucky and eat extremely well, feasting perhaps on fresh lobster or prawns.

SNACKS AND FAST FOOD

ALL KINDS OF SNACKS are widely available in Cuba. Virtually all *cafeterías*, inside and outside hotels, sell the classic Cuban sandwich, with cheese and ham, or hot dogs with mustard, ketchup and chips, to eat in or take away.

There is also an American-style fast food chain, **El Rápido**, where for a few dollars you can get fried chicken with a side dish of *papitas fritas* (chips), beer or *refresco* (soft drink). These places also offer *perritos calientes* (hot dogs), *hamburguesas* (hamburgers), pizza and ice cream.

People eat either at tables or at the counter. This chain is comparatively new and standards of hygiene are usually high.

Along the major roads and on the motorway you will find **Rumbos** kiosks – the equivalent of motorway cafés – which sell soft drinks, beer, fruit juice, pizza, ice cream and, sometimes, sandwiches. Some kiosks are set among trees, perfect for a relaxing stop in the shade.

The best ice cream is sold at the **Coppelia** parlours, which are found in many Cuban cities (the one in Havana is an institution, *see p98*). They are highly popular so be prepared to wait in a queue.

Lastly, you can buy food along the road from people who run small stalls in front of their homes. Food on offer may include pizza, sandwiches, fritters of corn or

Sign of the Coppelia ice cream chain

malanga (a local root vegetable), coconut sweets and peanut nougat. Around noon *cajitas*, cardboard boxes containing rice, beans, salad, pork or chicken, are served.

The same foods can be found on sale in the fruit and vegetable markets *(agros)* throughout the island. However, standards of hygiene may vary considerably *(see p294)*.

PAYING

IN MANY RESTAURANTS and *paladares*, expect to pay in US dollars, in cash. Only the better restaurants and hotels accept credit cards. At markets or on the road you can pay in Cuban *pesos*, although dollars would also be accepted (change will be given in *pesos*). Restaurant bills should include a tip; add more to show appreciation.

WHEN TO EAT

BREAKFAST *(desayuno)* is served from 6 or 7am and usually consists of a buffet offering fresh fruit, bread, butter, ham, cheese and eggs, yoghurt, milk, coffee and at times jam. Lunch is served from noon to 1:30pm, but many restaurants and *paladares* have adapted to tourists' needs and serve food well into the afternoon.

Dinner is eaten from 7 to 9pm. Don't expect to find a restaurant willing to serve you a meal after 10pm, except perhaps in Havana.

A branch of the fast-food chain, **El Rápido**, at Sancti Spíritus

What to Eat in Cuba

Traditional Cuban food, otherwise
known as *cocina criolla*, is a
mixture of Spanish, African and pre-
Columbian Indian influences. Local
produce such as tomatoes, sweetcorn,

**Guayaba
(guava) paste**

potatoes, yucca and bell peppers are used
together with other ingredients introduced
by the Galicians: pulses, pumpkin, cabbage, chicken,
and especially pork, which is eaten all year round and
is the most popular meat in Cuba. Then there are the
African vegetables: *malanga*, a root vegetable with a
very delicate flavour; *plátano vianda*, a variety of
plantain that is eaten cooked; and *quimbombó*, known
as okra or ladies' fingers, viscous when cooked.

White rice

**Fried
chicken**

**Chicharritas
(fried plantain)**

**Sliced
avocado**

**Congrí
(rice and
beans)**

Salad

Main dish: *this consists of* pollo frito, *chicken coated
with flour and fried in oil, served with salad,* congrí *and*
chicharritas. Congrí *(also known as* moros y cristianos*)
is white rice cooked with black beans and seasoned with
lard, bacon, onions, garlic, peppers, oregano and cumin.*
Chicharritas *are thin, crispy slices of plantain* (plátano vianda)
that are fried and served as a side dish with fish or meat.

Potaje *is a thick soup made
from black or red beans with
fried garlic, onion, pepper,
oregano, powdered cumin and
sometimes a lump of pork. It is
eaten with or without a bowl
of white rice.*

Ajiaco: *a minestrone with
all kinds of vegetables, pulses
and meat, a mix of various
culinary influences.*

**Viandas
(boiled root
vegetables)**

Arroz con pollo *is tasty stewed
chicken cooked together with
rice* (arroz) *and seasoned with*
bijol, *a saffron substitute. It is
rather like Spanish paella.*

Puerco asado *consists of pork
roasted either in an oven or on
a skewer and often served in a
chunk. Here, it is accompanied
by rice and black beans.*

Bistec de puerco *is lean
pork grilled over a hot flame
after being marinaded for
a few hours in lemon or
bitter orange juice.*

Camarones (*meaty Cuban prawns*) *may be served in different ways – stewed, boiled and garnished with mayonnaise, grilled or baked.*

Filete de pescado grillé *consists of a fillet of good fish such as grouper or bream, browned in the oven. It is a simple and delicate dish.*

Tostones *or* chatinos *are sliced plantains cooked in oil at a medium temperature, squashed and fried in boiling oil. Here they are served with potatoes.*

Enchilada de langosta *is a dish with lobster, which is first boiled and then cooked in a sauce consisting of tomatoes, peppers and other seasonal vegetables. Prawns may be used in the same recipe instead of lobster.*

Ensalada mixta (*mixed salad*) *can vary according to season: in winter, lettuce, tomatoes, white cabbage and, at times, beets; in summer, string beans, carrots, cucumbers and avocado.*

Papaya
(fruta bomba)

Pineapple
(piña)

Ensalada de frutas tropicales (*tropical fruit salad*) *is eaten by Cubans as an appetizer, while restaurants also serve it at the end of the meal, in keeping with European tradition.*

Mango

Banana
(plátano fruta)

Orange **(naranja)**

Dulce de coco con queso *is a dessert of cheese with coconut preserve, served together. The coconut is often replaced with a paste of* guayaba (*guava*), *a fruit that tastes much like quince.*

Fresh Fruit

Cubans grow a wide variety of exotic fruit, which is often eaten fresh for breakfast. Some kinds of fruit – such as papaya, mamey and mango – are also used to make delicious *batidos* (fruit shakes).

Papaya

Flan de huevos *is widely seen on Cuban menus. It is a typical Spanish dessert similar to crème caramel, but sweeter. It is made from milk and eggs.*

A papaya
batido

Banana

Pineapple

What to Drink in Cuba

A WIDE RANGE OF DRINKS, both alcoholic and non-alcoholic, is available in Cuba, although wine tends to be available only in restaurants and is almost always imported. Tap water is drinkable in many places but to avoid any health problems it is better to keep to bottled water. Visitors should be careful, too, about buying drinks such as fruit juice or fruit shakes from street or market stalls. In bars and cafés not up to international standards – especially in Eastern Cuba – avoid ice in drinks like cocktails. In such places stick to pre-packaged drinks, draught beer or rum.

Preparing refreshing *guarapo*, or sugar cane juice

BEER

B EER *(CERVEZA)* is the most widely seen and popular drink in Cuba. It is drunk very cold and at all hours of the day, as well as during meals. There are excellent bottled and canned Cuban lager beers, such as Cristal, Lagarto, Mayabe and Bucanero (the latter is also sold in a *fuerte* version, which is stronger and drier). A drink similar to beer is *malta*, a very sweet, fizzy malt-based drink that is popular with Cuban children. Beer is sometimes mixed with condensed milk to be used as an energizer and tonic.

Canned beer: Cristal (light) and Bucanero (strong)

PACKAGED SOFT DRINKS

S OFT DRINKS – lemon, orange and cola – called *refrescos*, either Cuban or imported, are sold canned, bottled or in cartons. The Tropical Island range of fruit juices is excellent. All kinds of fruits are used: mango, *guayaba* (guava), pineapple, apple, pear, orange, grapefruit, banana with orange, tropical cocktail, tamarind, peach and tomato. The most common brand of water sold, still *(sin gas)* or sparkling *(con gas)*, is Ciego Montero.

Tropical Island *guayaba* juice

HOT DRINKS

H OTEL BARS SERVE Italian espresso coffee or American coffee. The coffee served in private homes or sold on the streets is usually strong and has sugar already added. It is served in a tiny coffee cup. For a dash of milk, ask for a *cortado*; order a *café con leche* for a more milky coffee. *Sin azúcar* means "without sugar". Camomile tea *(manzanilla)* is also easy to find.

SPIRITS

T HE MOST WIDESPREAD AND POPULAR spirit in Cuba is, of course, rum. There are several different types *(see p75)*: the youngest – *silver dry* and *carta blanca* – are used in cocktails, while the aged rums (*carta oro*, five years old, and *añejos*, at least seven years old) are drunk neat. Besides Havana Club and Varadero, which are known worldwide, there are many other different brands of rum in Cuba. Among the best are Dos Marinos (known as "Paticruzado"), an amber-coloured rum with a well-rounded taste; Matusalém, an upmarket, aged rum from Santiago with a smooth flavour; and Mulata, which is very popular. A "poor relation" of rum is *aguardiente*, which is stronger and quite sour, and drunk mainly by locals. *Guayabita* is a speciality of Pinar del Río, made from rum and guava fruit *(see p137)*. A range of very sweet flavoured liqueurs (coconut, mint, banana and pineapple) is usually served with ice or in cocktails.

A bottle of aged rum

FRUIT SHAKES AND SQUASHES

T HE MOST COMMON FRUIT SQUASH is lemonade, made with lime, sugar, water and ice. More nutritious drinks are the *batidos*, which are shakes made from fresh fruit, often mango and papaya. Milk, sugar and *guanábana*, not an easy fruit to find, make a drink called *champola*. Coconut juice with ice is a delicious, refreshing drink. Another typical Cuban drink is *guarapo*, which is made by squeezing fresh sugar cane stalks with a special crusher. It makes for a refreshing and energizing drink, and is not as sweet as you may expect. Even so, to tone down the sweetness, Cubans add a few drops of lime or a dash of rum.

Coconut juice served in the shell

Cuban Cocktails

Cuba has been famous for its rum since the 1500s, although the rum the pirates loved so much was not the same as today's, but a bitter and highly alcoholic drink, at times sweetened with sugar and *hierba buena*, a variety of mint common in Latin America. This explosive mixture, jokingly called *draguecito* or "little dragon", is probably the ancestor of the *mojito*, one of the most famous Cuban cocktails. In the early 1900s a Cuban

Lime, used in all kinds of cocktails

engineer named Pagluchi and his American colleague Cox, while making an inspection near Santiago, mixed rum with sugar and lemon, and named the drink after the place they were in, Daiquirí. In the 1920s, during American Prohibition, Cuba, which had become an "off limits" paradise for drinkers, developed and refined these early cocktails and went on to create others. In parallel, the role of the professional barman *(cantinero)* acquired increasing importance.

Daiquirí frappé is served in a chilled cocktail glass. White rum is placed in an electric blender and mixed with one teaspoon of sugar, five drops of maraschino, lime juice and crushed ice. Hemingway liked to drink this cocktail at El Floridita (see p268).

Mojito comes in a highball glass. White cane sugar is mixed with lime juice and a crushed stem of mint. To this is added white rum, and the glass is then filled with sparkling mineral water and chopped ice and the drink is stirred. The "temple" of mojito is the Bodeguita del Medio (see p268).

Cuba Libre is made from rum and Coca-Cola mixed with ice and lime juice. The drink was supposedly invented by US soldiers who took part in the Cuban wars of independence (1898). The name, Free Cuba, comes from the nationalists' motto.

Havana Especial is made with pineapple juice, silver dry rum, a dash of maraschino and crushed ice, mixed and served in a tall, slim glass. This cocktail has a very delicate flavour.

THE *CANTINEROS'* CLUB

This club for professional barmen *(cantineros)* was founded in Havana in 1924 and sponsored by a group of Cuban distilleries and breweries. By the early 1930s the club had a central office on the Prado. The club's aims remain unchanged today: defence of the interests of its members, professional training for young people (who are required to learn the recipes for at least 100 cocktails), and English lessons. The club also currently promotes the Havana Club International Grand Prix.

The Bodeguita del Medio barman with a *mojito*

Canchánchara is made by the bar of the same name in Trinidad (see p178) with rum, lime, honey and water. It is served in an earthenware cup.

Choosing a Restaurant

THE RESTAURANTS in this guide have been selected for the quality of the food and good atmosphere. However, in some parts of Cuba there are no particularly recommendable eating places. Where this is the case, places have been suggested that offer at least good value. Alternatives are hotel restaurants *(see pp244–61)* and *paladares (see p263)*.

	CREDIT CARDS	CREOLE CUISINE	INTERNATIONAL CUISINE	OUTDOOR TABLES	LIVE MUSIC
HAVANA					
LA HABANA VIEJA: *El Santo Angel* ⑤ Calle Teniente Rey esq. San Ignacio. **Map** 4 E3. ▐ *(7) 8611 626.* Located in an 18th-century Colonial style building, with a charming court- yard and overlooking Plaza Vieja. International style food. 🍴 🔾 *lunch, dinner.*	▦		▦	●	▦
LA HABANA VIEJA: *Mirador De La Bahia* ⑤ Museo de Historia Naturel, Calle Obispo 61 e/ Oficios y Baratillo. **Map** 4 F2. ▐ *(7) 8613 652.* The fantastic views from this rooftop restaurant include the bay and the oldest part of the city. Cuban and international food are on offer here, as well as a range of light meals. 🍴 🔾 *lunch, dinner.*		●	▦	●	▦
LA HABANA VIEJA: *Bodeguita del Medio* ⑤⑤⑤ Calle Empedrado 207. **Map** 4 E2. ▐ *(7) 338 276.* **FAX** *(7) 338 857.* This famous restaurant *(see p65)* has a series of rooms and a pleasant roof terrace with wooden tables and rustic chairs. Typical Creole cuisine: *congrí, pollo frito, yuca* and *tostones.* 🍴 🔾 *lunch, dinner.* ▌ *all day.*	▦	●		●	▦
LA HABANA VIEJA: *Don Giovanni* ⑤⑤⑤ Calle Tacón 4. **Map** 4 E1. ▐ *(7) 8671 036.* The best-known Italian restaurant in Cuba is housed in a splendid Colonial building. Good food, with a varied wine list. 🍴 🔾 *lunch, dinner.*	▦			●	▦
LA HABANA VIEJA: *El Patio* ⑤⑤⑤ Calle San Ignacio 54, Plaza de la Catedral. **Map** 4 E2. ▐ *(7) 8671 035.* In a handsome Colonial building, with a leafy courtyard, and some tables overlooking Plaza de la Catedral, this old-established restaurant offers good Cuban and international cooking. 🍴 🔾 *lunch, dinner.* ▌ *all day.*	▦	●	▦	●	▦
LA HABANA VIEJA: *La Mina* ⑤⑤⑤ Calle Obispo 109, e/ Oficios y Mercaderes. **Map** 4 E2. ▐ *(7) 8620 216.* Tables are set out on the pavement as well as in the lovely Colonial courtyard. The menu, mostly Creole, is simple but varied and the service efficient. Live music. 🍴 🔾 *lunch, dinner.* ▌ *24 hours.*	▦	●		●	▦
LA HABANA VIEJA: *La Torre de Marfil* ⑤⑤⑤ Calle Mercaderes, e/ Obispo y Obrapía. **Map** 4 E2. ▐ *(7) 8671 038.* Elegant and traditional, with good Chinese food, including *arroz frito,* a one-course meal with fried rice, vegetables and an assortment of meats. Not much atmosphere, but good value. 🍴 🔾 *lunch, dinner.*	▦				
LA HABANA VIEJA: *La Zaragozana* ⑤⑤⑤ Calle Monserrate 352, e/ Obispo y Obrapía. **Map** 4 D2. ▐ *(7) 8671 040.* A historic Spanish restaurant specializing in *paella* and *tapas.* Good selection of wines. 🍴 🔾 *lunch, dinner.* ▌	▦		▦		▦
LA HABANA VIEJA: *El Floridita* ⑤⑤⑤⑤⑤ Calle Obispo 557, esq. Monserrate. **Map** 4 D2. ▐ *(7) 8671 300.* **FAX** *(7) 338 856.* The elegant Floridita is one of Cuba's best-known restaurants, made famous by Hemingway *(see p72).* House specialities: lobster and seafood. Good wine list and excellent cocktails. 🍴 🔾 *lunch, dinner.* ▌ *all day.*	▦		▦		▦
CENTRO HABANA AND PRADO: *A Prado y Neptuno* ⑤⑤ Calle Prado, esq. Neptuno. **Map** 4 D2. ▐ *(7) 8609 636.* Elegant restaurant-pizza parlour, run by Italians. The pizzas and pasta dishes are good quality. 🍴 🔾 *lunch, dinner.*	▦		▦		▦
VEDADO: *TV Café* ⑤ Edif Focsa, Calle 17. **Map** 1 B2. ▐ *(7) 334 499.* This modest restaurant is located in the lobby of the Focsa building, one of the most striking of modern Havana. It offers a number of inter- national and Creole dishes, and stays open until 2am. 🍴 🔾 *lunch, dinner.*		●	▦		

Price categories for a complete meal with beverages (excluding wine), including service:
$ less than $15
$$ $15–$20
$$$ $20–$25
$$$$ $25–$30
$$$$$ more than $30

CREDIT CARDS
VISA and MasterCard.
CREOLE CUISINE
Typical Cuban cooking (see pp264–5).
INTERNATIONAL CUISINE
European cuisine.
OUTDOOR TABLES
The option of eating on a terrace, or in a garden or courtyard.
LIVE MUSIC
Music is played to diners.

	CREDIT CARDS	CREOLE CUISINE	INTERNATIONAL CUISINE	OUTDOOR TABLES	LIVE MUSIC
VEDADO: *El Cedrano* $$$	■		■		
VEDADO: *La Casona de 17* $$$	■	●	■	●	■
VEDADO: *1830* $$$	■	●		●	■
VEDADO: *Monseigneur* $$$	■		■	●	■
GREATER HAVANA (EL CHICO): *La Rueda* $$	■	●			■
GREATER HAVANA (COJÍMAR): *La Terraza de Cojímar* $$$$	■		■		
GREATER HAVANA (CUBANACÁN): *Rancho Palco* $$$$	■	●	■	●	■
GREATER HAVANA (FLORES-PLAYA): *La Vicaria* $		●	■	●	
GREATER HAVANA (FLORES-PLAYA): *La Ferminia* $$$$	■	●	■	●	■
GREATER HAVANA (KOHLY-PLAYA): *Almendares* $$$	■	●	■		

VEDADO: *El Cedrano*
Hotel Meliá Cohiba. **Map** 2 E1. (7) 333 636.
The most flamboyant restaurant-buffet bar in Havana, with a wide selection of traditional dishes, as well as other staples such as cheese and fruit, and a variety of desserts. *breakfast, lunch, dinner.*

VEDADO: *La Casona de 17*
Calle 17 n. 60, e/ M y N. **Map** 2 E1. (7) 334 529.
Housed in a carefully restored early 1900s building with typical stained-glass windows, mosaics and paintings by contemporary artists. Good service. The speciality is *arroz* (paella) and barbeques. *lunch, dinner.*

VEDADO: *1830*
Malecón 1252, esq. 20. **Map** 1 A3. (7) 553 091-2.
Good service and a sophisticated setting with recently made, old-style furnishings. The cooking is good. *lunch, dinner.*

VEDADO: *Monseigneur*
Calle 21, esq. 0. **Map** 2 E1. (7) 8329 884.
A historic French-style establishment where the great Bola de ieve (see p28) performed in the 1950s and 1960s. Good service, stylish cooking. Great cocktails and atmosphere in the old bar. *lunch, dinner.*

GREATER HAVANA (EL CHICO): *La Rueda*
Calle 194, e/ 185 y 187, Wajay. (7) 558 738.
A simple, country-style restaurant with authentic Creole dishes (the speciality is goose). Simple décor. Live performances of Cuban country music. *lunch, dinner.*

GREATER HAVANA (COJÍMAR): *La Terraza de Cojímar*
Calle Real 161. (7) 939 486, 939 232.
This restaurant was Ernest Hemingway's favourite. There are lovely views of the bay. The menu features a fine selection of seafood specialities, including prawn and lobster cocktail and grouper. The bar is also a popular attraction. *lunch, dinner. all day.*

GREATER HAVANA (CUBANACÁN): *Rancho Palco*
Calle 140 esq. 19. (7) 203 5828.
Near the Palacio de las Convenciones and with a charming courtyard. This rustic but elegant restaurant offers high-quality food and service, looked after by one of the best Cuban chefs, who specializes in grilled meat and interesting appetizers. *lunch, dinner.*

GREATER HAVANA (FLORES-PLAYA): *La Vicaria*
Avenida 5, esq 180. (7) 339 100.
A restaurant-school for waiters and chefs, frequented more by locals than by visitors. The cuisine is mostly Creole and of good quality, and the service is, as you'd expect, attentive. *lunch, dinner.*

GREATER HAVANA (FLORES-PLAYA): *La Ferminia*
Avenida 5 n. 18207, e/ 182 y 184. (7) 336 786. **FAX** (7) 2720 655.
In a villa with a courtyard and garden, this formal restaurant has antique furniture and fine art. The cuisine and service are well up to international standards. Good wine list. *lunch, dinner. all day.*

GREATER HAVANA (KOHLY-PLAYA): *Almendares*
Calle 49C, esq. 28A. (7) 204 5162.
Located in the Club Almendares, in a leafy area of Havana. A wide-ranging international menu is offered as well as more traditional Cuban dishes. *lunch, dinner.*

	CREDIT CARDS	CREOLE CUISINE	INTERNATIONAL CUISINE	OUTDOOR TABLES	LIVE MUSIC

Price categories for a complete meal with beverages (excluding wine), including service:
$ less than $15
$$ $15–$20
$$$ $20–$25
$$$$ $25–$30
$$$$$ more than $30

CREDIT CARDS VISA and MasterCard.
CREOLE CUISINE Typical Cuban cooking (see pp264–5).
INTERNATIONAL CUISINE European cuisine.
OUTDOOR TABLES The option of eating on a terrace, or in a garden or courtyard.
LIVE MUSIC Music is played to diners.

GREATER HAVANA (MIRAMAR): *El Aljibe* $$$
Avenida 7, e/ 24 y 26. (7) 2041 583.
One of the best and most popular Cuban restaurants in Havana, frequented by diplomats and business people. Fixed price menu. The house speciality is barbecued *aljibe* chicken. lunch, dinner.
■ ●

GREATER HAVANA (MIRAMAR): *Don Cangrejo* $$$$
Avenida 1 n. 1606, e/ 16 y 18. (7) 204 4169.
This modern and elegant restaurant specializes in fish and seafood. Outside, the service is slower, but the prices are lower. Good wine list. lunch, dinner.
■   ■ ● ■

GREATER HAVANA (MIRAMAR): *La Cecilia* $$$$$
Avenida 5, e/ 110 y 112. (7) 204 1562.
One of Havana's best restaurants, with a welcoming atmosphere, a lovely garden and good service. There is also a cabaret. lunch, dinner.
■ ● ■ ● ■

GREATER HAVANA (MIRAMAR): *Tocororo* $$$$$
Calle 18, esq. 3, Miramar. (7) 204 2209.
A classy fish restaurant, considered one of the best in town, decorated with a mass of Art Nouveau lamps and fine art. International and Cuban food. Good wine list. lunch, dinner.
■ ● ■ ● ■

GREATER HAVANA (MORRO): *Bodegón de los Vinos* $$
Gran Parque Histórico Morro-Cabaña. Map 4 F1. (7) 8638 295.
Housed in an old building near the Castillo del Morro, this restaurant features simple, traditional dishes and a wide-ranging choice of wines. lunch, dinner.
■ ●   ● ■

GREATER HAVANA (MORRO): *Los XII Apóstoles* $$$
Gran Parque Histórico Morro-Cabaña. Map 4 F1. (7) 8638 295.
In a fine location at the foot of the Morro fortress, in converted garrison lodgings, offering stupendous panoramic views of the Malecón. Very good Creole cooking, and the late-night dancing can be entertaining too. lunch, dinner.
■ ●   ● ■

GREATER HAVANA (MORRO): *La Divina Pastora* $$$
Gran Parque Histórico Morro-Cabaña. Map 4 F1. (7) 8608 341.
This restaurant has a lovely waterside setting at the foot of the 18th-century Cabaña fortress. Excellent cooking, with the focus on fish and seafood. lunch, dinner.
■   ■ ● ■

GREATER HAVANA (PARQUE LENIN): *Las Ruinas* $$$
Calle 100 y Carretera de la Prensa. (7) 578 286.
In an unusual building incorporating the ruins of a sugar plantation house – a combination of old décor and modern architecture with stained-glass windows by René Portocarrero. A courtyard with luxuriant vegetation. Wide-ranging menu, quality food. lunch, dinner.
● ■ ●

WESTERN CUBA

ISLA DE LA JUVENTUD: *El Cochinito* $$
Calle 37, esq. 24, Nueva Gerona. (61) 228 09.
A classically simple Cuban restaurant featuring a menu of typical dishes, including roast pork (*puerco asado*) with fried plantain. lunch, dinner.
● ● ■

PINAR DEL RÍO: *Rumayor* $$
Carretera Viñales km 1. (82) 763 007.
With tables outdoors set among lush vegetation, this restaurant offers tasty, traditional dishes. The house speciality is smoked chicken (*pollo ahumado*). Stage shows in the evening. lunch, dinner.
● ● ■

VIÑALES: *Casa de don Tomás* $$
Calle Salvador Cisneros 140. [(8) 796 300.
Situated in a charming late 19th-century residence, the oldest in Viñales.
The house speciality is a kind of *paella*, called *delicias de don Tomás*,
with rice, lobster, fish, pork and sausage. ▤ ◘ *lunch, dinner.*

VIÑALES: *Cueva del Indio* $$
Carretera La Palma km 32. [(8) 796 280.
Next to the Cueva del Indio *(see p139)*. Indo-Cuban dishes such as *tortas*
(fritters) *de yuca* with chicken as well as Cuban dishes. ▤ ◘ *lunch.*

VIÑALES: *Mural de la Prehistoria* $$
Carretera El Moncada. [(8) 796 260.
Near the Mural de la Prehistoria *(see p138)*, with authentically Creole
dishes such as roast and smoked pork. ▤ ◘ *lunch.*

CENTRAL CUBA – WEST

CIENFUEGOS: *Café Cienfuegos* $
Calle 37 e/ 8 y 12. [(432) 512 891.
Located in the Club Cienguegos complex, this modest restaurant serves
creole and international cuisine and overlooks the ocean. ◘ *lunch, dinner.*

CIENFUEGOS: *Palacio del Valle* $$$
Calle 37, e/ O y 2. [(432) 551 226.
This restaurant, in the dazzling setting of the most famous building in town
(see p166), features good quality fish and seafood, including lobster. The
bar on the terrace has a splendid view of the bay. A pianist often plays.
▤ ◘ *lunch, dinner.* ▼ *all day.*

GUAMÁ: *Ranchón El Cocodrilo* $$
Guamá, Península de Zapata. *No phone.*
An unusual restaurant in the Parque Nacional di Montemar, the only
place in Cuba where you can try crocodile meat. ▤ ◘ *lunch, dinner.*

PLAYA GIRÓN: *Caleta Buena* $$$
Carretera Ciénaga de Zapata km 70. [(459) 5589.
Sample fish and seafood specialities while enjoying a magnificent
view of the Caribbean Sea. ▤ ◘ *lunch, dinner.*

SANTA CLARA: *Los Caneyes* $$
Avenida de los Eucaliptos, esq. Circunvalación. [(42) 218 140.
This restaurant in the hotel of the same name *(see p254)* has a tradition
of excellent chefs. Dinner à la carte and a very good buffet lunch.
The plantain mash *(fufú)* is the house special. ▤ ◘ *lunch, dinner.*

VARADERO: *Albacora* $$
Calle 59, Avenida Playa. [(45) 613 650.
An elegant restaurant, near the seafront. Prawns, lobster and good, freshly
grilled fish. ▤ ◘ *lunch, dinner.*

VARADERO: *El Bodegón Criollo* $$
Avenida de la Playa, esq. Calle 40. [(45) 667 784.
Simple, unadorned Cuban cuisine, based on meat and fresh grilled fish.
Decent service. ▤ ◘ *lunch, dinner.*

VARADERO: *La Barbacoa* $$
Calle 1, esq. 64. [(45) 667 795.
One of the smartest restaurants in Varadero. The grilled meat is
particularly delicious. ▤ ◘ *lunch, dinner.*

VARADERO: *La Casa de Al* $$
Carretera a Kawama final. [(45) 668 018 .
In the villa that once belonged to Al Capone, this restaurant specializes in
paella, but also offers good meat and prawns. ▤ ◘ *lunch, dinner.*

VARADERO: *Las Brasas* $$
Camino del Mar y 12. *No phone.*
Creole cooking is the hallmark of this restaurant, where the food,
especially pork, is barbecued. ▤ ◘ *lunch, dinner.*

VARADERO: *Méson La Campana* $$
Avenida 1, e/ 58 y 59. [(45) 667 224.
A friendly, rustic restaurant in the Parque Josone where you can enjoy tradi-
tional Creole dishes, simply cooked and presented. ▤ ◘ *lunch, dinner.*

For key to symbols, see back flap

	Price	CREDIT CARDS	CREOLE CUISINE	INTERNATIONAL CUISINE	OUTDOOR TABLES	LIVE MUSIC
VARADERO: *El Aljibe* Calle 36, esq. Avenida 1. (45) 614 021. A fixed price menu presents the best of Creole cuisine, especially chicken, prepared in a number of different ways. ◯ lunch, dinner.	$$$	■	●		■	●
VARADERO: *Antigüedades* Parque Josone, Avenida 1, esq. Calle 56. (45) 667 329. A small, sophisticated restaurant at the edge of a lovely park in the heart of Varadero. The menu includes fish. ▤ ◯ lunch, dinner.	$$$	■	●		●	
VARADERO: *El Galeón* Marina Gaviota, Varadero. No phone. Super fresh fish and seafood is served in this restaurant in a modern water sports centre. ▤ ◯ lunch, dinner.	$$$	■		■		
VARADERO: *La Fondue* Avenida 1, e/62 y 63. (45) 667 747. This restaurant offers an unusual menu featuring French-Swiss cuisine based on cheese fondue and beef. ▤ ◯ lunch, dinner.	$$$	■		■		
VARADERO: *Steak House Toro* Hotel Horizontes Club Tropical, Avenida 1, esq. Calle 25. (45) 667 145. This restaurant belongs to a restaurant chain specializing in beef and veal imported from Canada. The steak is delicious. ▤ ◯ lunch, dinner.	$$$	■		■		
VARADERO: *Las Américas* Mansion Xanadu, Autopista Sur km 8.5. (45) 667 750. Located in the former Dupont villa (see p159), this restaurant offers an upmarket menu of prawns, lobster and international cuisine. You can dine in the elegant rooms inside or in the arcade facing the beach, where prices are lower. ▤ ◯ lunch, dinner. ▼ all day.	$$$$$	■		■	●	■

CENTRAL CUBA – EAST

	Price	CREDIT CARDS	CREOLE CUISINE	INTERNATIONAL CUISINE	OUTDOOR TABLES	LIVE MUSIC
CAMAGÜEY: *La Campana de Toledo* Plaza San Juan de Dios 16. (322) 958 88. A lovely Colonial house with tables inside and in the courtyard. Good fish dishes and Creole specialities with meat from local livestock farms. ◯ lunch, dinner.	$		●		●	■
CAMAGÜEY: *Rancho-King* Carretera Santa Lucía. This country restaurant is housed in a former ranch where excursions on horseback and rodeos (see p199) are also organized. Creole food, with a strong emphasis on meat. ▤ ◯ lunch, dinner.	$$	■	●		●	■
PLAYA SANTA LUCÍA (CAMAGÜEY): *Las Brisas* Playa Santa Lucía. This is a good choice for those who want to try traditional food without travelling far from the beach. ▤ ◯ lunch, dinner.	$$	■	●		●	
PLAYA SANTA LUCÍA (CAMAGÜEY): *La Casa de la Langosta* Playa La Boca. This restaurant with a view of the sea offers a variety of lobster and shellfish dishes. ▤ ◯ lunch, dinner.	$$$	■		■	●	■
TRINIDAD: *Don Antonio* Calle Izquierdo 118, e/ Bolívar y Piro Guinart. (419) 6548. A good Creole restaurant that also offers fish dishes such as *filete de pescado Don Antonio*, the house speciality. ▤ ◯ lunch.	$$		●		●	■

TRINIDAD: *El Jigüe* $$
Calle Rubén Martínez Villena 69. [(419) 6476.
An elegant, Colonial-style restaurant in a quiet square near the town
centre *(see p185)*. The menu includes the house speciality, *pollo al Jigüe*.
☰ ○ *lunch, dinner.*

TRINIDAD: *Trinidad Colonial* $$$
Calle Maceo 402. [(419) 6473.
A restaurant in a handsome 18th-century building, Casa Bidegaray,
complete with courtyard. International menu. ○ *lunch, dinner.*

EASTERN CUBA

BACONAO: *Pedro El Cojo* $$$
Parque Baconao. *No phone.*
A well-known restaurant in the Parque Baconao, offering
traditional dishes such as spit-roast pork. ☰ ○ *lunch, dinner.*

BARACOA: *El Castillo* $$$
Hotel El Castillo, Calixto García, Loma El Paraíso. [(21) 451 64-6.
Local cuisine, with unusual dishes such as fish with coconut. Good
quality food and service, in a charming setting. ☰ ○ *lunch, dinner.*

BARACOA: *La Punta* $$$
Castillo de la Punta, Malecón. [(21) 452 24.
A historic restaurant in one of the city's fortresses, with a lovely view of
the bay. Offers decent traditional Creole cooking. ☰ ○ *lunch, dinner.*

CAYO BARIAY (HOLGUÍN): *Las Carabelas de Colón* $$$
Cayo Bariay.
This small restaurant with a lovely view over the sea offers
fish and shellfish specialities. ☰ ○ *lunch, dinner.*

HOLGUÍN: *Taberna de Pancho* $$
Avenida Jorge Dimitrov. [(24) 481 868, 481 158.
Good local sausage and salami, accompanied by beer produced
in the nearby Mayabe brewery. ☰ ○ *lunch, dinner.*

PLAYA GUARDALAVACA (HOLGUÍN): *El Cayuelo* $$$
Playa Guardalavaca.
This small restaurant by the beach specializes in Creole cuisine and
arroz a la marinera (seafood paella). ☰ ○ *lunch, dinner.*

SANTIAGO DE CUBA: *El Morro* $$
Carretera del Morro km 9. [(22) 691 576.
A welcoming, unpretentious place on a clifftop near El Morro castle, with a
terrace overlooking the sea. Tasty food and courteous service.
☰ ○ *lunch, dinner.*

SANTIAGO DE CUBA: *La Fondita* $$
Avenida de las Américas, esq. General Cebreco. [(22) 642 011, 687 163.
Located in Las Americas hotel, this restaurant serves traditional Creole
dishes in an country style salon setting. ☰ ○ *lunch, dinner.*

SANTIAGO DE CUBA: *La Taberna de Dolores* $$$
Calle Aguilera y Reloj. [(22) 623 913.
In a historic building facing Plaza de Dolores, in the centre of Santiago.
Good Cuban cooking: chicken with bitter orange sauce and garlic, ham,
and oven-roasted pork. ☰ ○ *lunch, dinner.*

SANTIAGO DE CUBA: *Santiago 1900* $$$
Calle San Basilio, esq. Carneceria. [(22) 623 507.
Situated in the former residence of the Bacardi family, this famous
restaurant is run by the local cookery school. Cuban and international
dishes. There is a bar in the inside courtyard. ☰ ○ *lunch, dinner.* ☒ *all day.*

SANTIAGO DE CUBA: *El Cayo* $$$
Cayo Granma. [(22) 690 109.
In the fascinating setting of Cayo Granma, in Santiago bay.
Excellent fish dishes. ☰ ○ *lunch, dinner.*

SANTIAGO DE CUBA: *Zun Zun* $$$
Ave. Manduley 159. [(22) 641 528.
A sophisticated restaurant featuring traditional Cuban dishes with a new
twist and elaborate international dishes. ☰ ○ *lunch, dinner.*

For key to symbols, see back flap

SHOPS AND MARKETS

TOURISTS DO most of their shopping in state-run dollar shops, often in the hotels. However, the legalization of limited private enterprise has given a boost to the handicrafts and food markets *(mercados agropecuarios)*. Until a few years ago there wasn't much to buy, but now an improving range of souvenirs is available. All the same, Cuba is

Hand-made cigars on display for customers

not the place to look for designer outlets. State-run shops offer goods at fixed prices, which tend to be on the high side, whereas market prices are lower and may be negotiable. Cigars of guaranteed quality are sold only in specialist shops and in hard currency shops. Be very wary of buying cigars – or anything else for that matter – on the black market.

Handicrafts for sale at La Rampa market in Havana *(see p98)*

OPENING HOURS

OPENING HOURS in Cuba are erratic but as a guideline, food shops and *tiendas* (dollar shops) are open 10am–7pm in the summer and 9am–6pm in the winter, while small shops open 9am–6pm all year round. On Sundays, shops close at 1pm. The fruit and vegetable markets are open on Sunday mornings, closed on Mondays, then open Tuesday to Friday from 8am to around 6pm. Fast food chains – El Rápido, Di Tú, Burgui, and Rumbos *(see p263)* – are open 24 hours a day.

HOW TO PAY

MOST TOURISTS will not use the local currency, the *peso (see p299)*, at all during their stay. Most goods that tourists want to buy, from rum to CDs, are only available in hard currency shops (most of which accept credit cards). In the food markets, the locals use mainly *pesos* but stall holders will happily accept dollars (change may be in

pesos). To buy *pesos*, go to one of the bureaux de change, called CADECA, found in most city centres and often near the entrance to major food markets.

WHERE TO GO

IN THE CITIES and tourist resorts, *tiendas* and supermarkets sell everything from cosmetics and clothes to tinned food, but do not carry the range of items seen in European supermarkets. Tourist resorts and larger towns often have shops

The logo of a popular *tiendas* chain

specializing in clothes (though not designer ranges). Tourist *tiendas*, especially in hotels, sell T-shirts printed with Cuban images including the inevitable portraits of Che, as well as *guayaberas*, typical Caribbean cotton shirts.

In the El Rápido and Rumbos *(see p263)* chains, and in the Fotoservice shops where film is sold and processed, visitors can buy soft drinks, rum, biscuits, sweets, butter and milk, as well as small household utensils and articles normally found in perfume shops.

Fresh fruit, vegetables and fresh meat are to be found only in the food markets.

SPECIALIST SHOPS

CIGARS SHOULD BE purchased either in the *tiendas* in hotels or at the airport, or in the specialist shops, often known as **La Casa del Habano**, which sell cigars direct from the cigar factories (and which may, in fact, be attached to a factory), and keep them at the right temperature and humidity level. It is best not to buy cigars from people

An outlet of the hard-currency Tiendas Panamericanas chain

on the street, as they are almost inevitably fakes made by machine, rather than hand-made, or are badly preserved or bear signs of faulty work-manship. In addition, you will not receive an official purchase receipt, needed to take goods out of the country.

Branches of the **ARTex** chain stock a good selection of CDs, records and cassettes. Another well-stocked music store is **Longina**, in Calle Obispo, Habana Vieja. Note that recordings of local music may not be available outside Cuba.

Paintings, sculpture and prints in the art galleries and in the *tiendas* of the Fondo de Bienes Culturales are sold with official authenticity certificates, which will be needed for export.

La Casa del Habano

Real Fábrica de Tabacos Partagás, Havana.
[(7) 338 060.
Ave 1, esq. 64, Varadero.
[(45) 667 843.
Shopping Center Marina Hemingway, Havana.
[(7) 204 6772.

Tienda ARTex

Ave. L esq. 23, Havana. **[** (7) 553 162. Calle 18, n. 509, Miramar, Havana. **[** (7) 241 212.

HANDICRAFTS

C UBA DOES NOT HAVE a long tradition of producing handicrafts. Today, however, market stalls are found every-where, selling all sorts of

A squash stand in the Mercado de Cuatro Caminos, Havana

things from wood carvings and ceramics to embroidery, papier mâché objects and musical instruments.

In Havana there is a daily handicrafts market behind the Castillo de la Real Fuerza and a second-hand book market in Plaza de Armas *(see p69)*.

Shelves with cigars in a Casa del Habano

There is also a market on La Rampa in Vedado.

The market in Trinidad, near the central square, is a good place to look for embroidered linen and cotton. Crafts are also sold in state-run shops, in the Ferias de Artesanía and in the Galerías de Arte throughout the island.

MARKETS

T HE FRUIT AND VEGETABLE markets *(mercados agropecuarios)* in Cuba are lively and entertaining places to stroll around. Stalls sell fresh fruit and vegetables, pork and sausages, sweets, traditional food and flowers.

In Havana, the most central food market is in the Barrio Chino *(see p90)*, but the largest and most famous is the Mercado de Cuatro Caminos, south of the centre at Máximo Gómez (Monte) 256. The market is housed in a building constructed in 1922 and originally occupied by stalls selling Chinese food. It takes up a whole block.

Today the market extends out into nearby streets and includes stalls selling every-thing from meat to dried fruit. There are also cheap restaurants and stalls selling fritters, fruit shakes and juice.

Mercado de Cuatro Caminos

Máximo Gómez (Monte) 256, e/ Arroyo (Manglar and Matadero), Havana. ◯ *Tue–Sat, Sun am.*

A SOUVENIR IN FRONT OF THE CAPITOLIO

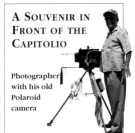
Photographer with his old Polaroid camera

In front of the Capitolio *(see pp82–3)* in Havana, visitors can have their picture taken with an original 1930s Polaroid camera, for one dollar. The photos develop immediately and the resulting picture, in black and white, looks just like a convincingly old photograph.

Embroidered table linen at the Trinidad market

What to Buy in Cuba

APART FROM THE FAMOUS Cuban cigars and excellent rum, there are many other good things to buy in Cuba: gold and silver jewellery, and hand-crafted objects made from local materials: wood, straw, papier mâché, shells, seeds, terracotta and glass. Cuban musical instruments are also popular choices. There are also toiletries and pharmaceutical products that are to be found nowhere else in the world, on sale in the international pharmacies and duty-free shops in the airport, where you can also buy books, video cassettes and CDs.

Dancing rag dolls

Rum
This classic brand of rum can be bought all over Cuba. Bottles are also sold in boxes (especially at the airport) to make them easier to transport.

Bauza
Cigars that do not meet the rigorous standards of the cigar-makers are labelled Bauza. However, they are still of very good quality. They are sold at authorized outlets at very reasonable prices.

A box of Vegas Robaina cigars

CIGARS
Packaged in elegant cedar boxes, Cuban cigars make a luxury gift *(see pp30–31)*. Make sure that the box has the branded label *"hecho in Cuba totalmente a mano"* (totally hand-made in Cuba), the official government seal, and the "Habanos" band. If they do not, they are not genuine.

Local Handicrafts
Raw material from the Caribbean (bamboo, shells and seeds) is used to make rustic household objects such as sonajeros, decorative wall hangings, and pretty, colourful necklaces.

A seed necklace

A seed and shell necklace

Musical Instruments
Many traditional Cuban musical instruments (see p29) such as claves, bongos, maracas, güiro, *and* tumbadora *drums are made by craftsmen. They are sold in music stores and markets. Some, such as guitars, can be made to order.*

Bongos

Hats and Baskets
Banana leaves and other plant fibres are used to weave typical hats and baskets of various shapes and sizes: an affordable, classic souvenir.

BLACK CORAL

Although the famous black coral from Cuban reefs makes delightful jewellery (earrings, rings, necklaces and pendants), bear in mind that conservation groups are anxious to discourage the plundering of fragile reefs. Authentic black coral commands high prices. Cheaper "black coral" pendants sold in handicrafts markets are unlikely to be genuine.

A black coral necklace

Silver and coral earrings and pendants

A cedar-wood cigar box

PAPIER MÂCHÉ

The *papier mâché* technique is a recent introduction to Cuba. It is used to produce masks, models, knick-knacks and toys. These articles are always painted in bright, decorative colours.

A mask representing the sun

Doll

Model vintage cars

African-style figures

WOOD

Cedar and rosewood are used to make small wooden figures that often draw inspiration from African tradition. Carved cedarwood cigar boxes always display elegant craftsmanship. Wooden objects can also be found on sale in the Galerías de Arte.

PERFUMES AND MEDICINES

The Suchel Camacho company produces very good perfumes, including spicy Coral Negro, flower-scented Mariposa and elegant Alicia Alonso, as well as quality face and body creams, at reasonable prices. The pharmaceutical sector is also in the avant-garde: PPG, an anti-cholesterol drug obtained from sugar cane, is also good for arteriosclerosis; shark cartilage strengthens bones in children and older people; and spirulina is a food supplement derived from algae. Excellent honey, with royal jelly and propolis (bee-glue), is also available.

Naïf Paintings
The Galerías de Arte sell naïf paintings of Afro-Caribbean inspiration depicting landscapes and views of Colonial towns, or Afro-Cuban divinities.

Eau de toilette

Moisturizing cream

ENTERTAINMENT IN CUBA

THE POSSIBILITIES for lively entertainment are diverse in a country where there is tremendous love of music and dancing and theatrical display. Ballet, theatre, concerts, festivals and sporting activities are in full swing all year round, in venues of every scale. Any street corner may easily be turned into an improvised dance floor with just the

An Afro-Cuban dancer in Santiago

help of a cassette recorder, and there are numerous discos everywhere, both indoors and outdoors. In Havana and all the other major cities there are theatres and concert spaces, and even in the smaller towns you will find a Casa de la Cultura or Casa de la Trova, where you can go along to listen to often high-quality live music or watch dance performances.

INFORMATION

AIRPORTS, hotels and travel agencies all distribute information brochures free of charge. These list the addresses of nightclubs and other venues, hotels, restaurants, and useful phone numbers. *Bienvenidos a Cuba* is a small guide with information on the most important shows and cultural events. It is available at Havana's José Martí airport. For full information regarding cinema, theatres and night-clubs in the capital, free copies of the weekly *Cartelera* can be found in the lobbies of the main hotels in Havana.

Visitors can also tune in to the local radio stations for information. Radio Taíno is especially useful for visitors as broadcasts are in Spanish and English. There is also a television channel for tourists, but this can only be viewed in the international 4- and 5-star hotels.

BUYING TICKETS

SOME FESTIVALS, such as the one dedicated to ballet in Havana, draw large crowds of people. In order to avoid long queues for such events, visitors can purchase tickets by going to the tourist agencies in the hotels, or by contacting the **Agencia Paradiso**, an agency which specializes in cultural tourism.

For cabaret shows at the world-famous Tropicana clubs in Havana and Santiago, on the other hand, tickets can be obtained at the reception desk of any hotel.

THEATRE

THEATRE PRODUCTIONS in Cuba have a long and illustrious tradition. The main cities offer both mainstream and experimental theatre. Some companies, such as the Teatro Cabildo at Santiago and El Público in Havana, have their own permanent sites.

Rehearsing a play at the Teatro Sauto in Matanzas *(see p154)*

The Yara, one of the largest cinemas in Havana

CINEMA

CUBANS ADORE the cinema, a form of entertainment that virtually everybody can afford, because ticket prices are so low. There are almost 200 cinemas in Havana, which screen Cuban and international films.

Cuba has its own thriving cinema industry, among the most active and forward-looking in the Americas. An annual Festival Internacional del Cine Latinoamericano, a major international film festival (Dec), is organized by ICAIC, which presides over the activities of the "seventh art" in Cuba *(see p27)*.

POPULAR MUSIC

CUBAN POPULAR MUSIC covers a broad range of styles including rumba, *guaguancó*, *danzón*, salsa, cha-cha-cha, *son*, bolero and *punto guajiro* *(see pp28–9)*. Live music is performed in a variety of places: on the streets, in Casas de la Música, Casas de la Cultura and Casas de la

A traditional *son* band performing in a Trinidad street

DIRECTORY

TICKET AGENCIES

Agencia Paradiso
Calle 19 n. 560, esq. C, Vedado,
Havana. **Map** 2 D3.
C *(7) 8326 928, 8329 538.* **FAX**
(7) 333 921.
@ paradis@tutcult.get.tur.cu

Trova, as well as in the many restaurants and bars that feature live music, such as La Mina in Havana, and La Canchánchara in Trinidad.

A Tropicana dancer in a typically exotic costume

CASAS DE LA TROVA

THE TRADITIONAL and intimate Casas de la Trova are clubs where people can listen to live music, dance or just relax over a cocktail. First opened in 1959 in almost all Cuban provincial capitals, these were originally places where older musicians, interpreters of traditional *trova*, could perform and educate younger people in their musical skills. Today, some Casas de la Trova also organize lectures, conferences and exhibitions, thus maintaining their original spirit as keepers of tradition.

In some places, such as in Santiago and Trinidad, Casas de la Trova are more geared to tourists, with a bar offering different Cuban cocktails, and a shop selling cassettes, CDs, books and souvenirs (for dollars). Whatever the style, Casas de la Trova continue to be popular with Cubans of all ages.

NIGHTCLUBS, CABARETS AND DISCOTHÈQUES

MOST TOURIST RESORTS in Cuba have several clubs which stay open until late. Customers pay in dollars, so don't expect to find a broad cross-section of Cuban society. Cabarets are exotic and colourful, with music and extravagantly dressed dancers in sequins and feathers. The most famous are the Tropicana clubs in Havana and Santiago.

Keen dancers can choose from the many discos in the hotels and holiday villages. Discos take place even in small provincial towns – often open air. They accept *pesos*, though tourists may have to pay in dollars. Hotels are a good source of information.

CHILDREN

AQUARIUMS put on shows featuring dolphins, which children love, and Cuba also has plenty of playgrounds. All year round, plays and puppet shows are performed. Holiday villages provide safe play areas for small children, as well as shallow swimming pools.

CULTURAL TOURS

A RANGE OF WEEK-LONG theme holiday packages is available from **Agencia Paradiso** in Havana. The cost includes accommodation in a 4-star hotel, lunch and dinner in typical Cuban restaurants, transport and specialist guides, free entrance to museums and theatres, meetings with Cuban artists, and visits to schools and specialist educational centres.

The *"Panorama de las Artes Plásticas en Cuba"* programme focuses on the museums and art galleries in Havana, while *"Paraíso Cultural"*, *"Nuestra Gente"* and *"Cuba: un paraíso para descubrir"* are cultural tours of the rest of the island. Cuba has a strong tradition in figurative arts, and the many art galleries encourage and feature young artists. Silk-screen prints and lithographs can often be found at low prices.

Interior of the Casa de la Trova in Trinidad

Entertainment in Havana

THE LIVELY, PLEASURE-LOVING capital of Cuba can offer entertainment to suit the varying needs of visitors of all ages. Theatres, cinemas and concert halls are active all year round. Havana has the biggest and best night-clubs in the country – the top salsa bands draw the liveliest crowds, but all kinds of music are on offer, from jazz to bolero. Dancers can enjoy themselves until dawn in the discos, while those who prefer less energetic entertainment can investigate the neighbourhood cultural centres.

Ballet Nacional de Cuba ballet dancers

THEATRES

THE MOST IMPORTANT and active theatres in Havana, a city that hosts a famous Festival Internacional del Teatro every two years, are almost all located in the Vedado quarter.

The **Teatro Nacional de Cuba**, a complex with several auditoriums *(see p102)*, often hosts major international companies. The **Teatro Hubert de Blanck** specializes in contemporary drama, while the **Julio A Mella** has a more varied programme. The **Trianon** and **El Sótano** are committed to presenting experimental theatre. The **Café Teatro Brecht** opens only at weekends to a limited audience.

A theatre offering something quite different is the **Guiñol**, which is active all year with puppet theatre for children.

CLASSICAL MUSIC AND OPERA

THERE ARE TWO music "shrines" in Havana. The **Teatro Amadeo Roldán**, which was recently restored after a fire, is the home of the national symphony orchestra. The **Gran Teatro de La Habana** *(see p82)*, which has excellent acoustics, hosts opera and other productions.

The lovely **Basílica de San Francisco de Asís** *(see p74)* is an atmospheric venue for concerts of choral and chamber music. Almost all of these are performed by the Camerata Romeu, the only Cuban orchestra to specialize in this musical genre.

BALLET

CLASSICAL DANCE is popular in Cuba thanks to the promotion and training activities of the **Ballet Nacional de Cuba**, which was founded by Alicia Alonso, the international ballet star. This institution organizes an annual ballet festival for participants from all over the world and promotes specialist courses for foreign dancers. Performances take place in the Gran Teatro de La Habana.

ROCK AND JAZZ

AMONG THE MUSICAL genres imported from the US – besides rock, which is played and danced to in the **Patio de María** in Havana – jazz is the one that stands out. Cuban jazz, using local rhythms and instruments, is now popular the world over. An annual jazz festival is held in Havana, during which bands play in different venues around the city. Among the best of these is the **La Zorra y el Cuervo Jazz Club**.

POPULAR MUSIC

EXCELLENT CONCERTS are held at the **Casa de la Música** in Miramar, a club which first opened in 1994 with an inaugural concert by the jazz pianist Chucho Valdés. The **Casa de la Trova** tends to host mainly bands playing *son* and bolero.

In Havana visitors can also see displays of Cuban dance. The most important company in this field is the **Conjunto Folklórico Nacional**, which organizes a rumba show every Saturday, as well as lessons for Cubans and foreigners. Dance weekends are also held in the gardens of **UNEAC**, the Cuban National Union of Writers and Artists. Rumba and Afro-Cuban dances can also be seen at the **Casa de la Cultura de La Habana Vieja**.

NIGHTCLUBS

SOME NIGHTCLUBS in Havana, such as the **Café Cantante** in the Teatro Nacional and the **Café Habana** in the Meliá Cohiba hotel, which alternate music with comic acts, are comparatively new; others, such as the **El Gato Tuerto** or **El Pico Blanco** – famous as homes of the blend of Cuban and North American music called *feeling* – have a long tradition. Fans of the bolero should head for the **Dos Gardenias**. **La Maison** is a sophisticated club featuring fashion shows with live music.

Among the best discos are the **Macumba** in the city centre, and the **Disco Show** at the Marina Hemingway. For cabaret, the **Tropicana** *(see*

A production by the Conjunto Folklórico Nacional

Dancers at the Tropicana in Havana

p109) puts on the most famous nightclub show, while the hotel shows include the **Cabaret Parisien** at the Nacional, the **Cabaret Salón Rojo** (the bolero paradise), at the Capri, and the **Cabaret**

Discoteca Turquino at the Habana Libre. All these shows feature grandiose choreography, with lavish costumes and legendary dancers.

CULTURAL CENTRES

AMONG THE CULTURAL programmes offered by the Paradiso agency *(see p279)*, one is entirely dedicated to museums and art in Havana. The *"Encuentro con la música"* (encounter with music) presents a week of music in Havana.

Visitors interested in Cuban culture can also visit major

cultural centres such as the **Casa de las Américas** *(see p100)*, which has a very good library, a well-stocked book shop and a fine art gallery.

Another centre is the **Casa de la Cultura de Plaza**, which organizes music and poetry festivals. High-level cultural events are also held at the **Fundación Alejo Carpentier**, dedicated to the work of the great Cuban writer, and the **Fundación Fernando Ortiz**, which specializes in Afro-Cuban studies.

The premises of the **Asociación Cultural Yoruba**, which is dedicated to African-derived religions, has a library, halls for art exhibits and lectures.

DIRECTORY

THEATRES

Café Teatro Brecht
Calle Línea, esq I. **Map**
2 D1. (7) 8329 359.

El Sótano
Calle K, e/ 25 y 27. **Map**
2 E2. (7) 8320 630.

Guiñol
Calle M, e/ 17 y 19. **Map**
2 E1. (7) 8326 262.

Hubert de Blanck
C/ Calzada, e/ A y B. **Map**
1 B2. (7) 8301 011.

Julio A Mella
C/ Línea 657, e/ A y B. **Map**
1 C2. (7) 8338 696.

Nacional de Cuba
Calle Paseo y 39. **Map**
2 E5. (7) 8796 011.

Trianon
Calle Línea y Paseo. **Map**
1 C2. (7) 8309 648.

CLASSICAL MUSIC AND OPERA

Basílica de San Francisco de Asís
Calle Oficios, e/ Amargura y Brasil. **Map** 4 F3.
(7) 8629 683.

Gran Teatro de La Habana
Paseo de Martí (Prado) y San Rafael. **Map** 4 D2.
(7) 8629 473.
@ bit@cth.cult.cu

Teatro Amadeo Roldán
Calle Calzada, e/ D y E.
Map 1 C1.
(7) 8324 521.

BALLET

Ballet Nacional de Cuba
Calle Calzada 510, e/ D y E.
Map 1 C1.
(7) 552 945.

ROCK AND JAZZ

La Zorra y el Cuervo Jazz Club
Calle 23 n. 155. **Map**
2 E2. (7) 662 402.

Patio de María
Calle 37, e/ Paseo y 2. **Map**
2 D5. (7) 8810 722.

POPULAR MUSIC

Casa de la Cultura de La Habana Vieja
Calle Aguiar 509, e/ Amargura y Brasil. **Map**
4 E3. (7) 8634 860.

Casa de la Música
Calle 20 n. 3308, Miramar.
(7) 204 0447.

Casa de la Trova
Calle San Lázaro 661. **Map**
3 B2. (7) 8793 373.

Conjunto Folklórico Nacional
Calle 4 n. 103, e/ Calzada
y 5. **Map** 1 B2. (7)
8334 560.

UNEAC
Calle H, esq. 17. **Map**
2 D2. (7) 553 113.

NIGHTCLUBS

Cabaret Discoteca Turquino
Hotel Habana Libre, level
25, Calle 23 y N. **Map**
2 F2. (7) 334 011.

Cabaret Parisien
Hotel Nacional,
Calle 21 y O. **Map** 2 F1.
(7) 333 564.

Cabaret Salón Rojo
Hotel Capri, Calle 21,
e/ N y O. **Map** 2 F1.
(7) 333 747.

Café Cantante
Teatro Nacional de Cuba,
Paseo y 39. **Map** 2 E5.
(7) 8796 011.

Café Habana
Hotel Meliá Cohiba, Calle
Paseo, e/ 1 y 3. **Map** 1 B2.
(7) 333 636.

Disco Show
Ave 5 y 248, Santa Fe,
Marina Hemingway.
(7) 2041 150.

Dos Gardenias
Complejo Dos Gardenias,
Calle 7 y 26, Playa.
(7) 2042 353.

El Gato Tuerto
Calle O, e/ 17 y 19.
Map 2 F1.
(7) 662 224.

El Pico Blanco
Hotel St John's, Calle O, e/
23 y 25. **Map** 2 F2.
(7) 333 740.

La Maison
Calle 16 n. 701, Miramar.
(7) 2041 543.

Macumba
Complejo La Giraldilla, La
Coronela. (7) 330 568.

Tropicana
Calle 72, e/ 41 y 45,
Marianao.
(7) 2671 717.

CULTURAL CENTRES

Asociación Cultural Yoruba
Paseo de Martí 615. **Map**
4 D2. (7) 8635 953.

Casa de las Américas
Calle 3 y G. **Map** 1 C2.
(7) 552 706.

Casa de la Cultura de Plaza
Calle Calzada y 8.**Map** 1
B2. (7) 8312 023.

Fundación Alejo Carpentier
Calle Empedrado 215 e/
Cuba y San Ignacio.
Map 4 E2.
(7) 8610 506.

Fundación Fernando Ortiz
Calle L 160, esq. 27. **Map**
2 F2. (7) 8324 334.

Entertainment: Beyond Havana

Dancers at the
Museo del
Carnaval, Santiago

THE PROVINCES OFFER as much variety in the way of entertainment as Havana. In Cuba's small towns old traditions have generally been preserved and the cultural life is more rural, but in the towns along the coast all forms of modern entertainment prevail. The lively city of Santiago has a wide range of venues and clubs with music, dance, theatre and stage shows.

Music and dancing at the Casa de la Tradición in Santiago de Cuba

THEATRES

SANTIAGO is a city with an active theatre life. There are several experimental companies which for years have boldly sought new forms of expression. These can be seen at the **El Mambí** theatre or the **Van Troi/Cabildo Teatral Santiago** hall. The **José Martí** theatre is more traditional. The modern and prestigious **José María Heredia** theatre is particularly active during the Fiesta del Fuego in June *(see p35)*.

BALLET

HIGH-LEVEL CLASSICAL dance productions, performed by the Ballet de Camagüey, are held at the **Teatro Principal de Camagüey**.

POPULAR MUSIC

YOU CAN LISTEN to "música popular" in Casas de la Música located all around the island. The **Casa de la Música de Trinidad** hosts concerts by local groups and splendid masked balls by the

Conjunto Folklórico de Trinidad, which also performs Bantu and Yoruba dances outside Cuba.

Santiago is the home of the **Ballet Folklórico Cotumba**, whose rehearsals, held from Tuesday to Sunday, are open to the public, and the **Conjunto Folklórico de Oriente**. In the courtyard of the **Museo del Carnaval** *(see p225)* the public is welcome at rehearsals of folk groups preparing for Carnival: Afro-Cuban dances and songs are performed in costume. Do not miss the evening training

sessions in the various *focos culturales* from Tuesday to Friday. One of them, the **Cabildo Carabalí Izuama**, rehearses Carnival songs derived from African musical traditions, while in the **Tumba Francesa** *foco cultural*, founded by Haitian slaves in the late 1700s, 18th-century dances are accompanied by Bantu musical instruments.

CASAS DE LA TROVA

THE MOST IMPORTANT Casas de la Trova are in **Santiago**, home of *son*, and **Trinidad**, where the classical tradition of the *trova* prevails. The *trova* at **Bayamo** has a faster rhythm, and stronger Afro-Caribbean overtones, while **Holguín** as well as **Camagüey** focus more on melodic tunes.

In some towns traditional Casas de la Trova activities are held in the Casas de la Cultura: in **Baracoa** and **Sancti Spíritus**, for example, they put on performances by *repentistas* (improvisers). The Casa de la Cultura in **Pinar del Río** hosts performers of *punto guajiro*, country-style music centred around improvisation.

A less touristy alternative to the Casa de la Trova is the **Casa de la Tradición** in Santiago, a good place to see up-and-coming local groups.

NIGHTCLUBS

IF YOU LIKE CABARET, besides the **Tropicana Santiago**, which has the same glorious tradition as the Tropicana in Havana, there is **La Cueva**

A show at La Cueva del Pirata, a disco-cabaret in Varadero

del Pirata at Varadero, where shows are held in an atmospheric natural cave.

Among the discos, most of them are based in the resorts. Some of the better ones to try include **La Rumba**, **El Kastillito Club** and **La Patana** in Varadero, and the **La Maison** disco in Santiago de Cuba.

These are large, modern discos, featuring loud music (almost always salsa and Latin), neon lighting, and simple decor. The entry fee is in dollars and is usually quite expensive, and therefore the majority of the clients are foreigners. However, there is usually a sprinkling of young Cuban people.

CULTURAL CENTRES

THE CASA DE LA CULTURA is an institution in every Cuban city. These cultural centres foster various forms of artistic expression: the figurative arts, poetry and music. Trinidad and Santiago are the most active cities culturally.

In Santiago, those interested in anthropology and religions can visit the **Centro Africano Fernando Ortiz**, dedicated to the African influence in Cuba, and the **Casa del Caribe**, which organizes an annual Caribbean Cultural Festival.

The Casa de la Cultura in Trinidad: an art gallery by day and dance hall in the evening

UNEAC (National Writers and Artists' Union), with branches in a number of cities, puts on exhibitions, conferences and concerts. The Santiago branch is very active and hosts cultural debates, art shows and music shows, as well as poetry readings.

DIRECTORY

THEATRES

El Mambí
Calle Bartolomé Masó 303, Santiago de Cuba.

José Maria Heredia
Ave. las Américas, Santiago de Cuba.
(22) 620 510.

José Martí
Calle Santa Tomas 313, Santiago de Cuba.
(22) 620 507.

Van Troi/ Cabildo Teatral Santiago
Calle Saco 415, Santiago de Cuba.

BALLET

Teatro Principal de Camagüey
Calle Padre Valencia 64, Camagüey.
(32) 293 048.

POPULAR MUSIC

Ballet Folklórico Cotumba
Calle Saco 170, Santiago de Cuba.
(22) 620 922.

Cabildo Carabalí Izuama
Calle Pío Rosado, e/ San Mateo y San Antonio.

Casa de la Música de Trinidad
Calle Zerquera 407.
(419) 6622.

Conjunto Folklórico de Oriente
Calle Hartmann 407, Santiago de Cuba.

Museo del Carnaval
Calle Heredia 303, esq. Carniceria, Santiago de Cuba.
(22) 626 955.

Tumba Francesa
Calle Los Maceos 501, Santiago de Cuba.

CASAS DE LA TROVA

Baracoa
Calle Maceo 149.

Casa de la Cultura
Calle Maceo, e/ País y Maraví.
(21) 42349.

Bayamo
Calle Maceo y Martí.

Camagüey
Calle Cisneros y Martí.
(32) 291 357.

Holguín
Parque Calixto García.

Pinar del Río
Casa de la Cultura
Calle Martí.

Sancti Spíritus
Calle Máximo Gómez.

Casa de la Cultura
Calle Cervantes 11.
(41) 237 72.

Santiago
Calle Heredia 208.
(22) 633 496.

Casa de la Tradición
Calle Rabí, Tivolí quarter.
(22) 653 892.

Trinidad
Plazuela de Segarte.
(419) 4308.

NIGHTCLUBS

Cueva del Pirata
Autopista Sur km 11, Varadero.
(45) 667 751.

El Kastillito Club
Ave. Playa y Calle 49, Varadero.
(45) 613 888.

La Maison
Ave. Manduley 52, esq. 1, Vista Alegre, Santiago de Cuba.
(22) 643 265.

La Patana
Canal de Kawama, Varadero.
(45) 619 971.

La Rumba
Ave. Las Américas, km 4, Varadero.
(45) 668 210.

Tropicana Santiago
Autopista Nacional, km 1.5, Santiago de Cuba.
(22) 643 268, 643 036, 643 610.

CULTURAL CENTRES

Casa del Caribe
Calle 13 n. 154, Santiago de Cuba.
(22) 642 285.

Centro Africano Fernando Ortiz
Ave. Manduley 106, Vista Alegre, Santiago de Cuba.
(22) 642 487.

UNEAC
Calle Heredia 266, Santiago de Cuba.
(22) 653 465.

Spectator Sports

After the revolution, the government abolished professional sports and invested large amounts of money in physical education and amateur sports, and as a result some outstandingly successful sportsmen and women have emerged. Baseball and boxing are by far the most popular sports (baseball is virtually a national obsession), but volleyball, basketball, football and athletics are also widely practised. Major sporting events are held in Havana and televised throughout the island.

The Cuban national women's volleyball team in action

INFORMATION AND TICKETS

It is both easy and cheap to go to a baseball game; in fact, tickets cost only a few Cuban *pesos*, which is less than a dollar. Tickets can be purchased directly at the stadium box office just before the game.

The major stadiums have specially reserved seating areas for foreign spectators.

MULTI-PURPOSE SPORTS ARENAS

A new stadium, the **Estadio Panamericano** sports complex, was built in the Habana del Este quarter of the capital for the 1991 Pan-American Games. It is now a major venue for football and athletics. Cuba has produced some great athletes, including Javier Sotomayor, Ana Fidelia Quirot and Ivan Pedroso (see p17). The centre also has pools for swimming competitions, water polo and synchronized swimming, tennis courts and a velodrome.

The **Sala Polivalente Ramón Fonst** in Centro Habana specializes in volleyball and basketball, while the **Coliseo de la Ciudad**

Deportiva in the Boyeros district hosts national and international volleyball, basketball, boxing and fencing matches.

BASEBALL

This is the national sport. It has been a passion here for over a century, and today's teams are world-class. The first baseball stadium in Havana was built in 1881 and the first amateur championship was held in 1905. The official baseball season is from November to March, and games are played on Tuesday, Wednesday and Thursday at 8pm, on Saturdays at 1:30 and 8pm and on Sundays at 1:30pm.

Watching a game is fun; many families attend and there is always a good atmosphere. Games are played in the **Estadio Latinoamericano**, inaugurated in 1946, which has a seating capacity of 55,000.

BOXING

Cuba has won several Olympic boxing titles. The founder of the modern school of boxing is Alcides Sagarra, a trainer who has

been active in the profession since 1960, producing such greats as Teófilo Stevenson, the Olympic heavyweight champion, who has since set up his own school.

At the annual Girardo Córdova Cardín tournament, expert boxers fight against emerging ones; this is part of the selection procedure for the Equipo Cuba, one of the best boxing teams in the world.

Fights can be seen at the **Sala Kid Chocolate**, located opposite the Capitolio in Centro Habana.

DIRECTORY

MULTI-PURPOSE SPORTS ARENAS

Coliseo de la Ciudad Deportiva
Ave. de Rancho Boyeros y Vía Blanca, Havana.
(7) 577 047, 545 020.

Estadio Panamericano
Carretera de Cojímar, km 1.5.
(7) 954 140.

Sala Polivalente Ramón Fonst
Ave. Rancho Boyeros y Bruzón, Havana. **Map** 2 E4.
(7) 8820 000.

BASEBALL

Estadio Latinoamericano
Calle Zequeira 312, El Cerro, Havana.
(7) 8706 526.

BOXING

Sala Kid Chocolate
Paseo de Martí (Prado) y Brasil, Havana. **Map** 4 D3.
(7) 8628 634.

Cuba's national baseball team during a game

Outdoor Activities

The logo of Cubadeportes

The varied Cuban landscape allows for a wide range of outdoor activities. Facilities for a variety of water sports along the coast are increasingly good, particularly in the north, and mountain ranges and nature parks have just as much to offer. Tourist centres are equipped with exercise gyms, swimming pools and tennis courts, and also organize trekking and horse riding excursions. For athletes and fitness fanatics who want to stay in good shape, the state-run Cubadeportes organization makes it possible to experience Cuban sports at first-hand by arranging meetings with local athletes and the provision of special courses.

Beach volleyball at a tourist village on Cayo Largo

DIVING

With 5,746 km (3,570 miles) of coastline and over 4,000 small islands, Cuba is one of the supreme places in the Caribbean for diving enthusiasts. The crystal-clear water (with a temperature ranging from 23–30° C, 70–85° F) and variety of sea beds in particular make the Cuban sea a paradise for scuba divers at any time of year. Thanks to the coral reef and numerous offshore islands (cayos), there are no strong currents along the coast and the horizontal visibility under water is hardly ever less than 40 m (130 ft).

There is an abundance of sites along the coral reef for both wall and platform dives. Besides all kinds of coral, on the sea bed divers can see gorgonian fans and sponges, multicoloured fish (see p143), tarpons, barracuda, sea turtles, large lobsters, beautiful anemones, and perhaps even sharks. A family of pelagic sharks lives in the Boca de Nuevitas (near Playa Santa Lucía), and the area can be visited with the guides and

instructors from the **Shark's Friends** diving centre.

There are also fascinating shipwrecks to explore. In the past the island's bays were used as refuges for pirate galleons, and in some areas, such as Playa Santa Lucía, divers can still see anchors and cannons – relics of 19th-century and even more recent ships – lying on the sea floor. Underwater tunnels and grottoes add to the attractions.

The development in tourism has triggered the opening of new diving centres and the updating of existing ones. As a result, virtually every resort has at least one centre. Scuba centres have all the latest facilities as well as trained international-level instructors, and offer courses for all levels of ability. Some, such as the Hotel Colony on Isla de la Juventud (see p146), also have decompression chambers. Divers can hire all the equipment they need on site; however, it is advisable

to bring along indispensable items such as a depth gauge and a knife. Underwater photographers are advised to bring spare film and batteries, as these items may be in scarce supply.

The most important diving centres (centros de buceo) are **El Colony** on Isla de la Juventud (best suited to experienced divers), the **Centro de Buceo María La Gorda**, **Carisub** in Havana, **Acua** at Varadero, and the **Centro de Buceo Jardines del Rey** at Cayo Guillermo. It is possible to dive from the shore at Playa Santa Lucía and Playa Girón, two other prime dive sites.

The Jardines de la Reina islands are also wonderful places to dive, although they can only be reached by sea, and still have no tourist facilities to speak of: only a rather plain "floating hotel". Cruise yachts take scuba divers to sites with unspoiled sea floors, where sea turtles can be seen.

For information concerning diving in general, contact **Cubanacán Nautica**.

SURFING AND WINDSURFING

At the main seaside resorts (Varadero, Guardalavaca, Cayo Largo, Cayo Coco and Marea del Portillo) conditions are ideal for surfing and windsurfing, and at the larger holiday villages all the necessary equipment can be hired.

A scuba diver exploring a shipwreck off the Playa Santa Lucía (see p202)

Enjoying the sea on a catamaran hired from a tourist marina

SAILING AND MOTORBOATS

THANKS TO ITS POSITION at the entrance to the Gulf of Mexico, Cuba makes an ideal stopping-off point for yachts and sailing boats. The tourist marinas, many of which belong to the **Marinas Puertosol** chain *(see p246)*, provide a series of facilities and services, including motorboats and catamarans for hire and yacht excursions.

Most sailing is done around the Archipiélago de los Canarreos, south of the mainland. The best season for sailing is from December to April, because the climate is mild, the winds are not too strong, and storms infrequent. However, Cuba is surrounded by generally tranquil waters, and there are plenty of bays if shelter is needed.

FISHING

FISHING ENTHUSIASTS will be in their element in Cuba. The northwestern coast is marvellous for deep-sea fishing, where the catch might include swordfish, tuna or mackerel, while fish such as tarpon can be caught off the southern coast.

Fishing is often one of the many activities provided by marinas and holiday villages. Holidays tailor-made for fishermen are organized by the **Havanatur Pesca y Caza** company.

In May, the Marina Hemingway *(see p133)* is the venue for the Ernest Hemingway International Marlin Fishing Tournament, a competition reserved for expert marlin fishermen. The original rules were established by the American author, who had a passion for deep-sea fishing.

The freshwater lakes and rivers around the island are very good for trout fishing.

TENNIS AND GOLF

ALMOST ALL THE HOLIDAY villages and large hotel complexes have tennis courts. Non-residents usually make use of them by paying a fee.

The island also has two good golf courses: the nine-hole **Club de Golf Habana** and the 18-hole **Club de Golf Las Américas** at Varadero.

The sport is increasingly popular and there are plans to lay out even more golf courses in the main tourist resorts in the near future.

CYCLING

TOURING THE ISLAND by bicycle is an excellent way to enjoy the landscape and meet local people. The bicycles offered for rent to tourists (by larger hotels and most holiday villages) are of better quality than those the locals have to use. Cycling is not usually dangerous, particularly outside the towns where traffic is light. Beware, however, of potholes in the road. Fortunately, there are plenty of roadside workshops *(talleres)*, where repairs can be carried out.

Bikes should always be locked or left in supervised places (thefts are common), and remember to wear a helmet. Mountain bikes are best for rough terrain.

Hikers on a path near Topes de Collantes *(see p187)*

HIKING, EXCURSIONS AND BIRDWATCHING

TREKKING ON HORSEBACK is another very enjoyable way to see the Cuban landscape. In Havana the only horse riding centre is in Parque Lenin *(see p116)*, but hotels in the main resorts, eco-tourist centres and camping sites can provide horses as well as organized excursions. Both experienced and inexperienced riders are catered for.

Until recently, the only opportunities for hiking – either with official guides or on well-marked trails – were in the areas of Viñales, Topes de Collantes and Sierra Maestra (from Alto de Naranjo to Las Cuevas). However, in

Varadero's golf course, close to the sea

recent years eco-tourist principles have been spreading to all parts of Cuba and programmes have been devised to cater for a wider range of interests, such as speleology, botany and bird-watching. The Península de Zapata *(see pp160–63)* is a particularly good area for birders, since the marshland

ecosystem is a haven for hundreds of different bird species. Migratory birds may also be seen in season.

For information, contact **Gaviota Tours** and **Ecotur**; the latter organization oversees the upkeep and improvement of the trails, and also arranges nature tours and programmes.

HUNTING

C UBANS ENJOY THE THRILL of hunting and the island has a number of hunting reserves *(cotos de caza)*, where people are allowed to hunt birds and small animals within rigorously defined limits and under the supervision of the forest rangers. The reserves are usually sited near lagoons, lakes or cays, and hunting is for wild duck, snipe, guinea fowl and pigeons, among other birds. In general, it is possible to hire all the equipment needed for hunting at these reserves, although prices can be high. The hunting season is from the end of October until the middle of March.

Cuba has no specialist hunting trip agencies, but **Havanatur Pesca y Caza** offers some organized holidays that include an element of hunting.

Horse riding among the *mogotes* in the Valle de Viñales

DIRECTORY

INFORMATION

Cubadeportes SA
Calle 20 n. 710, e/ 7 y 9, Playa, Havana. **Map** 1 A4.
(7) 2040 945.
FAX (7) 2041 914.

DIVING

Acua
Ave Kawama 201, e/ 2 y 3, Varadero.
(45) 668 063.

Carisub
Ave 5, esq. 258, Santa Fe, Playa, Havana.
(7) 204 6342.

Centro de Buceo Jardines del Rey
Villa Cojímar, Cayo Guillermo.
(33) 301 738.

Centro de Buceo María La Gorda
La Bajada.
(82) 778 131.

Cubanacán Nautica
Calle 184 n. 123, Reparto Flores, Havana.
(7) 336 675.
FAX (7) 337 520.

El Colony
Carretera de Siguanea, km 41, Isla de la Juventud.
(46) 398 181.
FAX (46) 398 420.

Shark's Friends
Hotel Cuatro Vientos, Playa Santa Lucía, Camagüey.
(32) 336 317.
FAX (32) 336 255.

SAILING AND MOTORBOATS

Marea del Portillo
Marea del Portillo, Pilón.
(23) 597 195.

Marina Cayo Coco-Guillermo
Cayo Coco, Archipiélago Jardines del Rey.
(33) 301 738 .
FAX (33) 301 738.

Marina Cayo Largo
Cayo Largo.
(45) 248 384.

Marina Chapelin
Carretera de las Morlas, km 21, Varadero.
(45) 667 550.

Marina Guardalavaca
Playa Guardalavaca, Holguín.
(24) 301 85.

Marina Hemingway
Ave. 5 y 248, Santa Fe, Playa, Havana.
(7) 2041 150.

Marina Internacional Vita
Bahía de Vita, Holguín.
(24) 304 45.

Marina Santa Lucía
Playa Santa Lucía, Camagüey. (32) 336 317.

Marina Santiago
Ave. 1, Punta Gorda, Santiago de Cuba.
(226) 691 446.

Marina Tarará
Vía Blanca km. 18, Playa Tarará, Havana.
(7) 971 462.

Marina Trinidad
Carretera María Aguilar, Playa Ancón.
(419) 6205.

Marina Varadero
Carretera de las Morlas km 21, Varadero.
(45) 667 755.

FISHING AND HUNTING

Havanatur Pesca y Caza
Edificio Sierra Maestra,

Calle 1, e/ 0 y 2, Playa, Havana.
(7) 203 9783.

GOLF

Club de Golf Habana
Carretera de Vento km 8, Capdevila.
(7) 338 919.
FAX (7) 338 820.

Club de Golf Las Américas
Ave. Las Américas, Varadero.
(45) 667 788.
FAX (45) 668 180.

TREKKING AND BIRDWATCHING

Ecotur
Ave Boyeros 116 esq. Santa Catalina, Havana.
(7) 8310 707.
FAX (7) 8317 575.

Gaviota Tours
Edificio La Marina, level 3, Ave del Puerto 102 e/ Jústiz y Obrapía, Havana. **Map** 4 F2.
(7) 666 777.
FAX (7) 332 780.

SURVIVAL
GUIDE

PRACTICAL INFORMATION

IN THE LAST 20 YEARS Cuba has made great strides in the field of tourism and can now provide visitors with modern, international-level facilities. It is now possible for tourists to move about much more easily on the island, although advance planning is still essential, especially as regards transport around the island. An effective approach is to contact one of the many travel agencies in Cuba, which may have their own offices or be based in the major hotels. The latter also func-

Logo of the Cuban
Tourist Board

tion as tourist offices, providing practical information and often a booking service. However, although Cuban tourist operators are very good, visitors still need to be adaptable and flexible. The pace of life here is slow, as is the bureaucracy, so be prepared to waste a certain amount of time when trying to get things done. Whatever happens, try and remain optimistic. With a bit of patience and a lot of perseverance *"todo se resuelve"*, as they say in Cuba: a solution can always be found.

One of the Playas del Este at Havana, crowded with tourists and locals

WHEN TO GO

APART FROM September to November, prime hurricane months, and July and August, when the torrid heat can make touring quite tiring (unless you spend your entire holiday at the seaside), any time of year is good for a visit to Cuba. It is possible to relax on the beach all year round, thanks to the mild climate.

The best period for visits is December to March, when there are more cultural events and the climate is warm without being unbearable.

VISAS AND PASSPORTS

TO ENTER CUBA, European travellers must have a valid passport, a return ticket and a visa *(tarjeta de turista)* issued by a Cuban consulate, or the travel agency or the airline you bought your ticket from. This

visa is a yellow piece of paper which you have to fill in with your personal data and the name of the place where you are planning to stay. Visas are valid for one month and can be extended for another 30 days: in Havana, go to the **Main Immigration Office**. In other cities, you must go to the local Dirección Provincial de Inmigración. If, however, you are going to Cuba on business or to work as a journalist, you should apply to the Cuban embassy or consulate in your home country well in advance for a special visa.

For US-passport holders, special regulations apply *(see p300)*.

Main Immigration Office
Calle 20 e/ Ave 3 y 5,
Miramar, Havana.

CUSTOMS INFORMATION

BESIDES THEIR PERSONAL belongings, tourists are allowed to take into Cuba new or used objects whose overall value is no more than $250, plus 10 kg (22 lb) of medicines in their original packaging. Small appliances such as electric razors are allowed, but not objects such as telephone apparatus or fax machines. It is forbidden to import fresh food such as fruit and plants of any kind, as well as explosives, drugs, and pornographic material. Hunters with firearms must present their permits at customs.

If you intend to take more than 50 cigars out of the country you must be able to produce a receipt declaring their purchase at a state-run shop; their value must not exceed $2,000. If you take out more than 50 you may well need to pay duty when you get home. Visitors can take no more than four bottles of rum or liqueur out of the country.

In order to export works of art that are part of the national heritage, you must have

**Brochure
illustrating customs
regulations**

◁ View of Calle Enramada in Santiago de Cuba

official authorization from the Registro Nacional de Bienes Culturales del Ministerio de la Cultura.

Avoid purchasing items made from endangered species such as tortoiseshell, or bags or belts made from non-farmed reptile skins. These are covered under the Convention on International Trade in Endangered Species (CITES). The import and export of vaccinated domestic animals is allowed.

Rum for sale in a *tienda*, four per person for export

LANGUAGES

THE OFFICIAL LANGUAGE in Cuba is Castilian Spanish, which is spoken with a distinctive local inflection and vocabulary (*see p326*).

English is spoken fairly widely in Havana and in the main hotels and resorts.

FORMS OF GREETING

THE MOST COMMON greeting in Cuba is a kiss on the cheek, while shaking hands is common among men only in formal circumstances. It is polite to use proper titles when speaking to Cubans – *señor, señora, señorita, doctor, ingeniero* (engineer) and *profesor*. The word *compañero* (comrade) is not used as much as it once was and in any case is used only among Cubans, or at the very most with foreigners who are part of volunteer organizations on the island.

WHAT TO WEAR

THE MOST SUITABLE CLOTHING for tourists is light and generally casual attire. In the winter a cotton or woollen sweater is useful in the evening, and may be useful at other times of year in places with air conditioning. A waterproof may come in handy all year round because of the tropical showers. Sunhats are recommended to protect the skin from the burning sun.

Two tourists in casual summer clothes

Except for evenings out at cabarets and nightclubs, there is usually no need for evening dress. However, Cubans do appreciate elegance and cleanliness. For a formal meeting or interview, men should not wear shorts or T-shirts, but trousers and a light shirt instead; and women should wear a dress or a skirt and blouse, but nothing too revealing.

LOCAL CUSTOMS

CUBA IS A TOLERANT country but attitudes are still rather conservative. Nudism and topless sunbathing are not allowed on most beaches; and men with earrings or men and women with body piercing and tattoos may provoke raised eyebrows.

Despite the macho traditions in Cuba, the taboo concerning homosexuality has virtually disappeared, provided that common sense and modesty are respected.

Cuban men feel virtually obliged to pay compliments to women passing by on the street: it is almost a form of chivalry, a ritual, even if it is not always expressed with good taste. In any case, these kinds of comments should not be misinterpreted; no reaction is seriously expected, or at the very most a smile. Women travelling alone should not experience problems, although they may be obliged to deal with frequent offers of assistance from men. The best way to put an end to undesired flirtation without offending is simply to say that you are married.

HITCH-HIKING

THE LACK OF FUEL and consequent scarcity of public transport in recent years has forced Cubans to resort to hitch-hiking (*pedir botella*) both in town and in the country. Everyone hitch-hikes, young and old, but it is never completely reliable. Students sometimes have to walk for miles and miles to get to their schools.

If you are driving a car, remember that picking up hitch-hikers is very much appreciated by Cubans, is generally not dangerous, and can provide an excellent opportunity to make friends. Cubans always pick up their fellow countrymen, but if they offer a foreigner a ride they may be fined by police unless they have a permit.

Hitch-hiking, often the only alternative to walking on a country road

Jineterismo

The tourist boom and the economic crisis have given rise to a particular form of prostitution known as *jineterismo*, which consists of living off foreign tourists, not only through prostitution proper, but also by selling counterfeit goods (especially cigars), finding rooms for rent or *paladares* and receiving a commission from the owners. The *jinetera* (*jinetero* if male) accosts the tourist, and initiates a relationship that may last a night or several days. Sometimes the aim is not just to make money, but also to get an invitation to go abroad.

At first this social phenomenon was underestimated, but now the Cuban authorities are trying to limit its spread with severe measures, not against tourists but against Cubans acting in this way. To avoid difficult situations, be wary of "chance" meetings, above all outside hotels or in discos.

This mainly affects Havana and cities and resorts popular with tourists. Cubans are very friendly people so don't dismiss everyone as a *jinetero*.

Cuban Law

Foreign visitors may find it useful to know that in Cuba camping and sleeping in sleeping bags on the beach, or in areas not specifically used as a camping site, is strictly forbidden.

Cannabis may be offered on the street or outside a disco, but purchasing even a tiny amount of marijuana is illegal and could lead to immediate expulsion from the country.

Plaque at entrance to the Colonial Art Museum, Sancti Spíritus

Tourist brochures and maps published by Ediciones GEO

Tourist Information

In all the hotels there are state-run tourist bureaus, such as Rumbos, offering basic information, ticket booking and trips. Maps, guides and brochures are also available at the Infotur offices in airports and major cities. The Cuban publisher Ediciones GEO produces particularly good maps.

Disabled Travellers

Only major airports, hotels and restaurants have wheelchair access for the disabled. However, a programme is under way to gradually add such facilities in airports and stations, public buildings, museums, offices and streets.

Opening Hours

Normal working hours on weekdays are from 8am to 5:30pm, while banks open at 8am and close at 3pm.

Museum opening hours vary, but in general they are from around 10am to 5pm, while on Sunday museums are open only half a day. Museum hours can be unpredictable, so if a visit is important to you, it is best to telephone ahead.

An entry fee is always charged at museums. Children pay half-price, Cubans pay in national *pesos* and tourists in dollars. On average, the entrance fee is $1–3. The same amount may be charged for permission to take photos in museums.

Electrical Adaptors

Electric current in Cuba is 110 volts AC (same as in US), so for European-type appliances and plugs you will need a voltage converter and an electric adaptor plug. Many recently built hotels also have 220-volt AC current.

Cuban Time

Cuba is five hours behind Greenwich Mean Time (GMT), like the US east coast, and in the summer there is daylight saving time, exactly as in Europe.

DIRECTORY

EMBASSIES

United Kingdom
Calle 34 No. 702–4, esq. Ave. 7, Miramar, Playa, Havana.
(7) 2041 771, 2041 049.
FAX (7) 2048 104.

Canada
Calle 30 No. 518, esq. Ave. 7, Miramar, Playa, Havana.
(7) 2042 516.
FAX (7) 2042 044.

USA
Special Interest Section, Calle Calzada, esq. L, Vedado, Havana. **Map** 2 E1.
(7) 333 551-4.
FAX (7) 333 700.

TOURIST BUREAU

Ministry of Tourism
Calle 19 No. 710 e/ Paseo y A, Vedado, Havana. **Map** 1 C3.
w www.cubatravel.cu
(7) 334 323.
FAX (7) 330 546.

WEBSITES

General
w www.cuba.com
w www.dtcuba.com
w www.cubaupdate.org
w www.gocubaplus.com

Cuban Culture
w www.cubanculture.com
w www.afrocubaweb.com
w www.orishanet.com

In Spanish
w www.cubatravel.cu
w www.cubaweb.cu

Personal Security

A traffic policeman

COMPARED WITH ANY OTHER PART OF North, Central or South America, Cuba is a peaceful and safe place to travel in. However, in recent years, the great development of tourism, combined with the economic crisis, has triggered an increase in petty crime, especially in Havana and Santiago. Although the situation is under control, it is wise to take a few precautions: leave your valuables, documents and money in the hotel safe; never carry a large amount of money with you; do not wear showy jewellery; and keep an eye on your camera. If you have a hired car, it is always advisable to park near hotels or in pay car parks if possible, and do not leave any belongings open to view in the car.

CUBAN POLICE AND THE FIRE BRIGADE

POLICEMEN IN CUBA are usually polite and willing to help tourists. The officials who check passports in the airports, who belong to the Inmigración y Extranjería and wear green military uniforms, do their job slowly and with what might be considered excessive meticulousness, but problems are not common. Expect problems if you have not organized a place to stay, if only for the first few days. Tourists' luggage is often not checked, but it is best to adhere to the customs regulations to be on the safe side.

The policemen of the PNR (Policía Nacional Revolucionaria) wear blue trousers and a light blue shirt. Their role is to maintain public order, and they seldom stop foreigners. In some tourist areas such as Varadero and La Habana Vieja, you may see policemen in dark blue uniforms; they belong to a special corps that was created expressly to protect

A fire engine at Matanzas

tourists from pickpockets and to check the documents of suspicious individuals. They speak some English and can also provide information.

Different uniforms are worn by the traffic policemen *(policía de tránsito)* and firemen *(bomberos)*.

Guards from the relatively new SECSA organization provide security for banks and *tiendas* and also see to transporting valuables.

The telephone number for emergencies varies from province to province.

Road sign indicating a dangerous stretch of road

ROAD SAFETY

THERE ARE NOT that many cars in Cuba, even though traffic is increasing. While driving in the cities, watch out for cyclists, who do not always observe traffic regulations. The greatest potential dangers while travelling on roads and motorways through the countryside *(see p305)* are the animals grazing on the side of the road and the railway crossings without gates. The road surface is often bumpy, with sometimes deep potholes, so speeds should be kept down.

When it rains for several days in a row, the roads may easily become flooded.

THEFT AND LOST PROPERTY

TO REPORT THE LOSS or theft of personal documents and belongings, either find a policeman, who should take you to the nearest police station, or ask for directions. Once there, be prepared for a long wait to make your report.

NATURAL DISASTERS

THE GREATEST NATURAL DANGER in Cuba is the possibility of being caught in a hurricane. The autumn months are when hurricanes are most likely, but in practice they occur mostly in October. Nowadays hurricanes are forecast well in advance, leaving plenty of time for adequate security measures, so the risk involved should not be that great. Should a hurricane occur, visitors should follow the instructions given by hotel staff. You will probably be told to wait in the hotel until it passes, and asked to keep well away from windows.

DIRECTORY

EMERGENCY NUMBERS

Ambulance
Havana C (7) 405 093.
Santiago C (22) 626 485.

Police
Havana C 106.
Santiago C 106.

Fire Brigade
Havana C 105.
Santiago C 105.

Health and Medical Matters

A pharmacy sign

Thanks to the good health services, and the absence of most tropical diseases, a trip to Cuba should pose no unusual health risks. All the international hotels have a doctor on 24-hour call, and the first visit, as well as first-aid service, is free of charge. However, owing to the present economic difficulties in the country and the embargo, everyday pharmaceutical items are in very short supply. Normal pharmacies are rarely well stocked with medicines, and the well-supplied *farmacias internacionales* – international pharmacies which charge in dollars – are not found in every town. It is best to bring your own supply of usual medicine – pain relievers, fever reducers, antibiotics and stomach treatments – as well as strong sunscreens and insect repellents.

A Cuban ambulance

VACCINATIONS

No vaccinations or inoculations are required for visits to Cuba. Remarkably, almost all tropical diseases have been eliminated, and it is quite safe to travel around the entire island.

Malaria has also gone, thanks to a successful eradication campaign. There are restrictive sanitary regulations only for those arriving from countries in which yellow fever and cholera are endemic diseases.

MEDICAL TREATMENT

Cuban public health care is excellent, free of charge, and superior to that offered in any other Latin American country, though it has been put under severe pressure by the US embargo.

The national service is reserved for Cuban citizens. Foreign visitors are treated in international clinics or in public hospitals, where they will have to pay for treatment in dollars. On the plus side, they are given more comfortable rooms.

PHARMACIES

The national pharmacies are not well stocked and generally reserved for Cubans. Medicines are sold only upon presentation of a prescription. In these pharmacies foreigners can only purchase medicines made from natural ingredients, including syrups, tinctures and vegetable essences, which are made on the premises. They are excellent, effective and cost virtually nothing (they can be paid for in *pesos*). On the other hand, the international pharmacies, which are located in Havana and a few tourist resorts, stock various medicines that can be bought with or without a prescription, as well as over-the-counter products (sanitary pads, ear plugs, ointments for fungal infections and sunburn and so on) that cannot be found in the common *tiendas*.

PUBLIC WCs

In Cuba public toilets are hard to find, and they are often dirty and without water. There is no such thing as toilet paper, except in the bathrooms in restaurants, hotels, luxury nightclubs and airports, so it is wise to carry a good supply with you.

ILLNESSES

Summer colds are quite common in Cuba, often caused by the contrast between the heat of outside and the chilly air in hotels and so on, where air conditioning is on maximum. It is a good idea to carry a light sweater or jacket for these occasions.

Asthma sufferers may find that the humid climate could trigger an attack; visitors to Cuba with respiratory problems should always carry their usual medicine and an inhaler with them. All the hospitals and *policlínicos* (the neighbourhood outpatient clinics) are well-equipped for these problems.

Entrance to the historic Taquechel pharmacy in Havana *(see p72)*

Wearing a hat and using sunscreen to avoid burns and heatstroke

Another fairly common nuisance in Cuba is diarrhoea, or worse, dysentery. This can generally be prevented by always drinking bottled water, or water that has been purified with tablets; another useful precaution is to avoid food and drinks sold on the street. It may be best to avoid ice in cocktails as well.

All these measures should also be enough to ward off giardiasis, a disease caused by a parasite that attacks the intestine and causes dysentery, nausea, fatigue and weight loss.

Rare cases of yellow fever and dengue fever may occur in the summer in the marshy zones of Eastern Cuba (although in practice few tourists visit these areas). However, since these two diseases are spread by mosquitoes, it is advisable to use plenty of insect repellent when planning to tour marshy areas.

A bottle of Ciego Montero mineral water

PROTECTION FROM THE SUN

THE SUN in Cuba is very strong and protection is necessary, especially in July and August. Wear a hat, whether in town or in the countryside, and use a strong sun lotion with a high screen factor. It is also advisable to drink a lot of water to prevent dehydration. High humidity and heat may cause heatstroke, with symptoms of thirst, nausea, fever, and dizziness. If this occurs, keep up fluid intake and take cold baths.

INSECTS

MOSQUITOES are the main irritant in Cuba (and can cause disease). In swampy or lagoon areas, such as the Zapata swamp, pay particular attention to applying insect repellent, cover up in the evening and sleep with the fan or air conditioning on.

DIRECTORY

EMERGENCY NUMBERS

Ambulance and First Aid
Havana [C] (7) 405 093.
Santiago [C] (22) 626 485.

INTERNATIONAL HOSPITALS AND CLINICS

Havana
Ospedale Cira García,
Calle 20 n. 4101,
esq. 43, Miramar, Havana.
[C] (7) 2042 811, 2040 330.

Santiago de Cuba
Ave Raul Pujol y Calle 10.
[C] (22) 642 589.

Varadero
Calle 60 y 1.
[C] (45) 667 711.

INTERNATIONAL PHARMACIES

Farmacia Internacional Biotop
Calle 7 n. 2603, esq. 26,
Miramar, Havana.
[C] (7) 2047 980.

Farmacia Internacional Habana Libre
Hotel Habana Libre, Ave. L,
e/ 23 y 25, Vedado, Havana.
Map 2 E2. [C] (7) 554 593.

HEALTH TOURISM

Servimed – Cubanacán Turismo y Salud
Ave 43 n. 1418, esq. 18,
Miramar, Havana.
[C] (7) 2047 218 .

HEALTH TOURISM

Thanks to its favourable climate, Cuba has long been regarded as an effective sanatorium, popular with an international clientele. By the 19th century, the first hotels had been built near springs of therapeutic mineral water. Beside the spas, there are now international clinics which provide general medical care and also specialize in anti-stress and skin treatments, as well as hospitals for the rehabilitation of alcoholics and drug addicts. These centres are located throughout the country and are in great demand: the waiting lists are not long, the prices are competitive, and the results are good. They are run by the state-run **Servimed** organization, part of the Cubanacán group.

Dermatological treatment in one of the specialist clinics

Communications

T HE TELEPHONE IS BY FAR the most widespread system of communication in Cuba. Unlike the postal service, which is not all that efficient, the telephone network run by ETECSA has improved considerably. Today there are new public telephones that work with pre-paid phone cards. The use of e-mail is spreading, if mainly in business. Cuba also has two national television channels and several national, regional and municipal radio stations. Many hotels have a satellite dish and broadcast a TV channel especially for tourists. The leading daily newspaper is *Granma*, while the weekly *Granma Internacional* is printed in various languages. *Business Tips on Cuba* is a business monthly on investments in Cuba.

An unusual letter box

HOW TO USE A PUBLIC TELEPHONE

1 Lift the receiver and wait for the dialling tone. The display will ask the user to insert a telephone card *(inserte su tarjeta)* in the slot above the receiver.

2 Once you have inserted the telephone card, the display will show how much credit remains on the card.

3 Dial the number you want to call. While you are dialling, the number you are calling will appear on the display. The readout will also say how much credit remains on the phone card.

Telephone cards

4 After the call is finished, place the receiver back on the hook. The phone card will be returned from the slot automatically. If the card expires while you are phoning, the connection will be interrupted and you will have to phone again.

DIALLING CODES

- Directory inquiries 113
- If you want to make a long-distance telephone call via the operator, dial 00.
- To make a reverse charge (collect) international telephone call via the operator, dial 09.
- To dial long-distance within Cuba from a phone card public telephone, add 0 in front of the area code.
- To make a direct-dial international telephone call from a public telephone with a phone card, dial 119, and from a hotel 88, followed by the country code (Australia 61; Ireland 353; New Zealand 64; UK 44; USA and Canada 1), the area code and then the local telephone number.

TELEPHONE NUMBERS

I F YOU ARE CALLING from abroad, dial the international access code of your country (eg 00 in the UK), followed by the Cuba country code (53), the local area code, and lastly the local phone number you want to reach. The local area codes, which may have one, two or three digits, are given in brackets in front of all phone numbers listed in this guide. For local calls, there is no need to dial the area code. The number of digits of local numbers varies, since the phone network system is in the process of being updated.

5 centavos

20 centavos

Coins used for phoning

PUBLIC TELEPHONES

T HROUGHOUT THE COUNTRY there has been an increase in the number of new public telephones, which can be used to make direct-dial international calls without the help of the operator. Magnetic telephone cards *(tarjetas telefónicas)* can be purchased at hotels, post offices, *tiendas* and ETECSA telephone centres for $10, $20 and $50.

There are also coin-operated telephones which take *pesos*. For a local call you must insert at least a five *centavos* coin (also known as *"medio"*), or one for 20 *centavos* *("peseta")* to talk for a few minutes.

Local, long-distance and international calls can also be made from hotels. This is certainly the easiest way, since the operator does everything for you, but it is also the most expensive.

PRIVATE TELEPHONES

T HE ONLY DIRECT-DIAL calls that can be made from private telephones are local ones, while long-distance and international calls must be made through an operator. Calls to foreign countries are always reverse charge, unless you use an ETECSA telephone with a contract specifying payment in dollars. This type of telephone can be found in hotels, in travel agencies, in some public offices, and in the homes of foreigners who work in Cuba, rarely in Cubans' private homes.

POSTAL SERVICE

THE CUBAN POSTAL SERVICE is slow, but is generally no worse than in any other Latin American country. For letters and postcards, use the stamps *(sellos)* that can be purchased in dollars in the hotels or in *pesos* in the post offices *(oficinas de correo)*. Whatever the postage, letters take a long time to arrive, although it may help a little to post mail in the *oficinas de correo* postboxes.

The safest, and comparatively the fastest, way to post documents, letters or parcels that are important or urgent, is via international courier services: **DHL**, **Cubapost**, or **Cubapack Internacional SA**.

Entrance to a post office *(oficina de correo)* in Havana

ADDRESSES

IN CUBA THE STREET NUMBER, preceded by "N." or "#", comes after the name of the street or square, followed by *"esq."* (*esquina* = corner) and the name of the cross street, or by *"e/"* (*entre* = between) and the name of two streets *(see p118)*. This is followed by the number of the apartment, if it has one, or by *"altos"* (first floor) or *"bajos"* (ground floor) if it is a private house, followed by the name of the *"reparto"* (quarter) or district, and then by the locality.

A crowded news-stand in Pinar del Río

RADIO AND TELEVISION

THERE ARE TWO CUBAN television channels. *Tele-Rebelde* specializes in news and sports programmes, and is on the air on weekdays from 7–11pm, Saturday 5–11pm, and Sunday 10am–11pm. *CubaVisión* broadcasts films, soap operas and documentaries (weekdays 6:30–11pm, Saturday 5pm–1:30am and Sunday noon–11pm). Before the national programmes begin, space is given over to local TV stations such as *Tele Turquino* in Santiago de Cuba or *Tele Cubanacán* in Santa Clara.

There is also a tourist channel which can be viewed in hotels. *Canal del Sol* features mainly films and sports programmes (7–9am and 2pm–2am).

A good radio station is *Radio Taíno*, with music and information in English and Spanish (1180 AM in Havana and 1100 AM in Varadero). *Radio Rebelde* has news, music and sports; *Radio Habana Cuba* broadcasts for an overseas audience; and *Radio Reloj* broadcasts news 24 hours a day.

NEWSPAPERS AND PERIODICALS

THE DAILY NEWSPAPER with the widest circulation is *Granma*, the official organ of the Cuban Communist Party, which also publishes a weekly version for foreigners, *Granma Internacional.* There are also several provincial

Masthead of the daily *Granma*

dailies: *Trabajadores* (Monday to Saturday only) and *Tribuna de La Habana* in Havana; *Guerrillero* in Pinar del Río; *Girón* in Matanzas; *5 de Septiembre* in Cienfuegos; *Adelante* in Camagüey; *Ahora* in Holguín; *Sierra Maestra* in Santiago de Cuba; and *Victoria* in Isla de la Juventud.

Among Cuba's magazines are *Bohemia*, a cultural weekly, and a periodical for investors and foreign tourists, *Business Tips on Cuba*, which is printed in several languages.

INTERNET AND FAX

E-MAIL IS USED increasingly in Cuba, mainly in offices, while surfing the Internet is still limited to the "privileged few". You can log onto the Web at the **Cyber Café** in the Capitolio, Havana.

Fax services are available in all the international post offices in the large cities and major hotels, as well as in the **Centro de la Prensa Internacional**, centrally located on Calle 23, near Hotel Nacional, in the Vedado district of Havana.

DIRECTORY

COURIER SERVICE

Cubapack Internacional SA
Calle 22 n. 4115, e/ 41 y 47, Playa, Havana. 🄲 *(7) 2042 817.*

Cubapost
Calle 21 n. 1009, e/ 10 y 12, Vedado, Havana. **Map** 1 B4.
🄲 *(7) 8319 825.*

DHL
Calle 26, esq. 1, Playa, Havana.
🄲 *(7) 2040 998.*

INTERNET AND FAX

Centro de la Prensa Internacional
Calle 23 e/ O y N, Vedado, Havana. **Map** 2 F2.
🄲 *(7) 8320 526.*

Cyber Café
Capitolio, Paseo de Martí (Prado), Havana. **Map** 4 D3.

Banking and Local Currency

Cuba's currency is the national *peso*, but in tourist resorts all pricing is done in US dollars. Tourists can buy and pay for everything in dollars, although they can choose to use the national *pesos* to pay, for example, for local bus fares. Confusingly, a currency known as the convertible *peso*, which has the same value as the US dollar, also circulates. Although all banks accept major world currencies, it is sensible to arrive in Cuba with dollars you have purchased in your own country (as cash or travellers' cheques – although American Express travellers' cheques are not always accepted). Remember that credit cards issued by banks in the US (including American Express) are not accepted anywhere in Cuba.

BANKS AND BUREAUX DE CHANGE

Among the banks that carry out transactions with foreign countries are the international **Banco Nacional de Cuba** (BNC) and **Banco Financiero Internacional** (BFI) and the national Banco Popular de Ahorro. All of these have branches throughout the country – and some even have branches in hotels.

Banks are usually open from 8am to 3pm from Monday to Friday, although these hours are extended by some branches in Havana and the main holiday areas. In the provincial capitals and tourist resorts, some exchange offices are open 24 hours a day. In addition to cashing travellers' cheques, money can also be withdrawn using a credit card (Visa or MasterCard), but not with

The logo of the Banco Financiero Internacional

Automated Teller Machine (ATM) cards. In practice, many tourists end up cashing their travellers' cheques at their hotel reception, but the commission is higher (4 per cent) than that charged by the banks (2 or 3 per cent). Travellers' cheques can also be used for direct payment.

There is also a chain of bureaux de change, known as CADECA, often located near *tiendas* or markets, and these are the best places to buy local *pesos*. In order to receive a bank transfer or make a request for one via telegraphic money order, apply to the main offices of the Banco Nacional de Cuba or the Banco Financiero Internacional in Havana.

CREDIT CARDS

All hotels and many restaurants and *tiendas* frequented by tourists (ie which charge in dollars) accept non-US credit cards. If there is a problem using a credit card, contact the **Centro de Tarjetas de Crédito** in Havana.

However, it is always wise to carry a certain amount of cash with you, as it will be needed for tips and making small purchases, paying for meals and drinks and so on.

The handsome Neo-Classical façade of a bank in Santa Clara

CURRENCY

The dual economy of the *peso* and the dollar has provoked its own social consequences. Cubans who work in the tourist sector are paid in dollars and therefore earn good salaries compared with people working in other sectors. Visitors have to pay for almost everything in dollars, even for meals in *paladares (see p262)*. The *pesos convertibles* (convertible), issued to reduce the flow of US currency in circulation, can be used in the same way as dollars. One dollar is worth one *peso convertible* and about 26 national *pesos*.

Coins

There are 100 centavos (cents) to a national peso. The Cuban coins are 1 centavo ("kilo"), 2 centavos, 5 centavos ("medio", used for phone calls), 10 centavos, 20 centavos ("peseta", used for phone calls), 25 centavos; and 1 and 3 pesos (the latter bears Che Guevara's portrait).

3 pesos

1 peso

25 centavos

10 centavos

5 centavos

1 centavo

Bank Notes

Cuban bank notes come in units of 1, 3, 5, 10, 20, 50 and 100 pesos. Each of these has a different colour. Twenty pesos correspond to one US dollar and one peso convertible (also worth one dollar): be careful not to confuse the bank notes.

5 pesos

10 pesos

20 pesos

Convertible Pesos

Bank notes of the peso convertible circulate in units of 1, 3, 5, 10, 20, 50 and 100 pesos. The coins, bearing the word "Intur", come in units of 5, 10, 25, 50 cents and 1 peso. These pesos convertibles are equivalent in value to US dollars but are worthless outside Cuba.

1 peso convertible (= 1 US dollar)

10 pesos convertibles (= 10 US dollars)

10 centavos

25 centavos

TRAVEL INFORMATION

THE MAJORITY OF FOREIGN TOURISTS arrive in Cuba by aeroplane. Charter and regular scheduled flights arrive from Europe, Canada, Central and South America, and there are even some special flights from the US. The internal connections within Cuba are good, and there is at least one airport in every province; 9 are international and 21 domestic. Taxis are available at the airport for hotel transfers, if these have not been previously arranged, or cars may be hired (driving is the most efficient way of getting around Cuba). From José Martí airport in Havana, a modern coach service, part of the Vaivén company line, provides a link with the city centre. On Cayo Largo, one of Cuba's most well-known island resorts, there is an airport with international links, and Isla de la Juventud is linked to the rest of Cuba by a domestic airport as well as by ferries and hydrofoils.

Logo of Cuba's national airline

ARRIVING BY AIR

CUBA IS CONNECTED to Europe and the rest of the world by flights operated by several major airlines, with scheduled and charter flights.

Most arrivals from Britain are charter flights; scheduled direct flights from London to Havana are rare. British Airways flights from Gatwick to Havana, via Kingston, Jamaica, cease in July 2002. **Monarch Airlines** offers flight-only deals from Gatwick to Holguín and Varadero, as well as package holidays, as do **Airtours** and **JMC Holidays**. The Cuban national airline is Cubana de Aviación, but they have currently no flights from the UK to Havana.

Most scheduled routes from Britain involve a stopover in a third country. **Air France** flights depart from Heathrow and other UK airports to

Entrance to the José Martí airport in Havana

Havana via Paris. **Iberia** flights (from London and Manchester) go via Madrid in Spain and **Air Jamaica** flies from Heathrow via Montego Bay or Kingston in Jamaica.

In Canada, regular Cubana flights go from Toronto and Montreal. Cubana also operates flights from Cancún and Mexico City.

US TRAVELLERS

AMERICAN LAW MEANS that it is illegal for US-passport holders to travel to Cuba as tourists or on business, but it is possible to apply for a licence from the **US Treasury Department**. These can be given for religious or humanitarian interest trips, to freelance

CITY	AIRPORT	ℹ INFORMATION	DISTANCE FROM CITY OR TOURIST CENTRE
Havana	José Martí	(7) 335 777	Town centre: 25 km (15 miles)
Varadero	Juan Gualberto Gómez	(45) 613 016	Town centre: 6 km (4 miles)
Cayo Largo del Sur	Vilo Acuña	(45) 248 205	*(in the middle of the cay)*
Camagüey	Ignacio Agramonte	(322) 610 10	Town centre: 9 km (5.5 miles)
Holguín	Frank País	(24) 462 512	Town centre: 13 km (8 miles)
Santiago de Cuba	Antonio Maceo	(22) 692 314	Town centre: 5 km (3 miles)
Manzanillo	Sierra Maestra	(23) 530 19	Town centre: 8 km (5 miles)
Ciego de Ávila	Máximo Gómez	(33) 309 155	Cayo Coco: 80 km (50 miles)
Cienfuegos	Jaime González	(432) 552 047	Town centre: 5 km (3 miles)

journalists (full-time journalists need no specific licence), and to students whose university has applied for a licence. Regulations tend to change, so check the current situation.

The **Center for Cuban Studies** has its own licence and can therefore arrange group and individual travel for US-passport holders of the above categories and also provides updates and advice.

Some US travellers choose to go without a licence, flying via Mexico, Canada or the Caribbean. These trips cannot be arranged through US travel agents, and it is vital to avoid having your passport stamped by the Cuban authorities.

Aeropuerto Internacional José Martí-La Habana Terminal Internacional

Sign for the international terminal at Havana airport

AIRPORTS

CUBA HAS 9 international and 21 domestic airports. The main international airport is José Martí, 18 km (11 miles) south of Havana. This modern and reasonably efficient airport is the main arrival point for international flights to Cuba. Charter flights land at Terminal II, scheduled flights at Terminal III, while Terminal I is reserved for domestic flights.

Most of the other international airports (other than in Havana) are for charter flights for tourists en route to holiday resorts. Of these, Varadero is the busiest.

ARRIVING BY SEA

BECAUSE OF the US embargo, Cuba is not connected to North and South America by ferries, and few cruise ships dock here. But private yachts are welcome at Cuba's many harbours, including Marina Hemingway in Havana (special rules applies for US passport holders – see above). The following documents are needed: the passports of all those on board, the ownership documents, the name and registration number of the boat, and the customs document (*zarpe*) issued at the last port the ship called at.

The *Cruising Guide to Cuba* by Simon Charles is a good source of information.

ORGANIZED TOURS AND PACKAGE HOLIDAYS

AIR FARES VARY depending on the airline and time of year. Fares tend to be higher at peak periods, that is in July and August and at Christmas and Easter. The best value is often to buy a package including charter flights from a tour operator; your travel agent can help you decide which is the most suitable for your needs. There are usually reductions for children under 12 years.

From the UK, charter flights are available to Cuba from both Gatwick and Manchester.

Mainstream UK tour operators include **Airtours**, **Cosmos Holidays** and **JMC Holidays**. Specialist operators, who can help independent travellers plan a tailor-made visit, include **Captivating Cuba**, **Havanatur**, **Journey Latin America** and **Regent Holidays**. **Dance Holidays** (*see pp246–7*) offers arrangements including music and dance tuition.

Special interest holidays, especially those involving diving, water sports and salsa are particularly popular, and eco-tourism is also a developing area (*see p246*).

An aeroplane landing at Cayo Largo, an international holiday resort

DIRECTORY

AIRLINES

Airtours
📞 01706-240 033 (UK);
0870-241 2567 (reservations).

Air France
🖥 www.airfrance.com
📞 0845-084 5111 (UK).

Air Jamaica
🖥 www.airjamaica.com
📞 020-8570 7999 (UK).

Iberia
🖥 www.iberiaairlines.co.uk
📞 0845-601 2854 (UK).

Monarch Airlines
📞 01582-400 000 (UK).

US TRAVELLERS

Center for Cuban Studies
🖥 www.cubaupdate.org
📞 (212) 242-0559 (US).

US Treasury Department
🖥 www.treas.gov/ofac
📞 (202) 622-2480 (US).

TOUR OPERATORS

Captivating Cuba
🖥 www.captivating-cuba.co.uk
📞 0870-887 0123 (UK).

Cosmos Holidays
🖥 www.cosmos-holidays.co.uk
📞 0870-909 6299 (UK).

The Cuba Experience
🖥 www.theholidayplace.co.uk
📞 020-7431 0670 (UK).

Havanatur UK
📞 01707-646 463 (UK).

JMC Holidays
🖥 www.jmc.com
📞 0870-607 5086 (UK).

Journey Latin America
🖥 www.journeylatinamerica.co.uk
📞 020-8747 8315 (UK).

Regent Holidays
📞 0117-921 1711 (UK).

Scuba en Cuba
🖥 www.scuba-en-cuba.com
📞 01895-624 100 (UK).

South American Experience
🖥 www.southamericanexperience.co.uk
📞 020-7976 5511 (UK).

Getting Around Cuba

IF YOUR TIME IS LIMITED, the best way to get around the island is without doubt by aeroplane, because this is the only really fast means of transport in Cuba. The network of domestic flights is good and connections are made via Cubana de Aviación and Aerocaribbean airlines. Trains are much cheaper, but they are also much slower. Tourist coach services, on the other hand, have greatly improved. They are becoming more numerous and comfortable and provide services to all the tourist resorts and provincial capitals.

Nueva Gerona national airport, Isla de la Juventud

BOOKING AND CHECK-IN FOR DOMESTIC FLIGHTS

THERE ARE FLIGHTS from Havana to the following destinations: Baracoa, Bayamo, Camagüey, Cayo Coco, Cayo Largo, Ciego de Ávila, Cienfuegos, Guantánamo, Holguín, Las Tunas, Manzanillo, Moa, Nueva Gerona, Playa Santa Lucía, Santa Clara and Santiago de Cuba.

It is not necessary to go in person to the **Cubana de Aviación** or **Aerocaribbean** airline offices to book a domestic flight; any travel agency will contact these

airlines for you and make your reservation without any extra charge. However, bear in mind that you should book early, especially for flights in high season. Check-in is 60 minutes before take-off, and the maximum luggage weight allowance is 20 kg (44 lbs).

Domestic flights cost about twice as much as trains or coaches, but if you book one together with an international flight with Cubana, there is a saving of 25 per cent. Children under two travel free

of charge, and young people under 18 pay 33 per cent of the normal fare.

The aeroplanes are not always new, and the service may lack frills, but the staff are experienced and reliable.

SHIPS AND FERRIES

IF TIME IS NOT AN ISSUE, it is possible to travel to Isla de la Juventud by sea rather than by air. Departure is from the port of Batabanó, on the southern coast of Havana province, 60 km (37 miles) from the capital. There are two options: a three-deck ferry boat that makes the trip in six hours (on Tuesday, Wednesday, Friday and Sunday only) or an express hydrofoil, which does the journey in only two hours in a regular daily service from 10am to 4pm. Tickets can be bought at the quay and there is no need to book ahead of time.

A recent development is a daily service between Varadero and Havana in elegant catamarans that belong to the Dodero Argentine shipping line and are run by Cubanacán. The catamarans depart in the morning from Marina Chapelín, in Varadero, and dock at the cruise ship terminal in Havana; the return trip is in the late afternoon. The trip takes two and a half hours and cruising speed is 35 knots. This air-conditioned ship has a seating capacity of 380, and facilities include a solarium.

A Cubana de Aviación plane for domestic flights

A *lanchita*, a waterbus connecting the various towns around the bay of Havana

In the cities of Havana, Santiago and Cienfuegos, you can also find waterbuses or ferries called *lanchas* or *lanchitas*, which operate around their respective bays, linking towns or providing a crossing to the opposite side.

Small ferries connect the coast north of Pinar del Río with Cayo Levisa.

TRAINS

Cuba has 4,881 km (3,030 miles) of public railway lines, serving all the provincial capitals. In recent years the service has been extended and slightly improved, although the carriages are by no means modern and clean. Refreshments may not be available, so take supplies.

There is at least one train per day on each of the main lines, but do not count on it arriving on time.

The trains known as "*especiales*", which cover long-distance routes such as Havana-Santiago, have air conditioning (though it may not always function as it should), reclinable seats, and a refreshment service.

Information on timetables and tickets (tourists have to pay in dollars) can be obtained in Havana railway station at the **Ferrotur** offices. An alternative is the LADIS agency, which also sells tickets for long journeys.

The advantage in travelling by train is that it is almost always possible to find a seat without booking in advance, even in high season. If you have time, patience and are on a tight budget, railway travel can be a very pleasant and sociable way of travelling around Cuba.

A minibus for tourists

Façade of the railway station in Morón

COACH SERVICES

The modern coaches operated by the **Víazul** company provide transport to the main cities and towns and tourist resorts in Cuba. They connect Havana with Santiago (passing through Santa Clara, Ciego de Ávila, Camagüey, Las Tunas, Holguín and Bayamo), Varadero, Trinidad and Viñales. There is also a direct service between Varadero and Trinidad.

On the positive side, Viazul coaches are very comfortable and arrive on time – the disadvantage is that, at least on the stretch between Havana and Santiago, the frequent intermediate stops in all the provincial capitals make for rather a long journey. The seats can be reclined (a little), and there are toilets and a minibar for passengers. The air conditioning is always turned on full, so that if you do decide to use this means of transport, always carry a sweater or jacket.

Travel agencies also supply hotels with minibus shuttle services to take guests to nearby tourist resorts.

DIRECTORY

AEROCARIBBEAN

Havana
Calle 23 n. 113, Vedado.
Map 2 F2. ▐ *(7) 8797 524.*

CUBANA DE AVIACIÓN

Camagüey
Calle República 400.
▐ *(322) 913 38, 921 56.*

Holguín
Calle Libertad, esq. Martí.
▐ *(24) 464 148, 464 149.*

Havana
Calle 23, e/ P e Infanta, Vedado.
Map 2 F1. ▐ *(7) 334 446.*

Santiago de Cuba
Calle Enramada esq. San Pedro.
▐ *(22) 651 578.*

Varadero
Ave 1ra e/ 54 y 55.
▐ *(45) 611 823-5.*

FERROTUR

Havana
Estación Central de Ferrocarriles,
Egido y Arsenal. **Map** 4 E4.
▐ *(7) 8614 259.*

VÍAZUL

Havana Main Office
Ave 26 y Zoológico, Nuevo
Vedado. ▐ *(7) 8811 413.*
FAX *(7) 666 092.*

Varadero
Calle 36 y Autopista.
▐ *(45) 614 886.*

Santiago de Cuba
Ave de los Libertadores,
esq. Yarayó.
▐ *(22) 628 484.*

A Víazul line coach

Travelling by Car

THE BEST way to see a lot of Cuba's hinterland is to travel by car. With a car it is possible to discover places and scenery that it would be difficult to see on an organized tour, and even more so if you travel by air. It is best to plan an itinerary and stopovers in advance, and a good road map is essential. A few precautions should be taken. Keep speed down and always park in supervised car parks. In summer, because of the heat, it is advisable to travel early in the morning. You will see many people hitch-hiking on the road; you are not obliged to pick them up, but it is a normal way of life in Cuba and the lift will be appreciated *(see p291)*.

Example of a new road sign seen outside cities

A lorry picking up hitch-hikers on the Autopista Nacional (motorway)

THE HIGHWAY CODE

IN CUBA TRAFFIC DRIVES on the right. The speed limits for cars are 20 km/h (12 mph) in parking areas, 40 km/h (25 mph) near schools, 50 km/h (30 mph) in town, 60 km/h (37 mph) on dirt roads and in tunnels, 90 km/h (55 mph) on asphalt roads and 100 km/h (62 mph) on the motorway.

Every so often on the *Autopista* (motorway) you will see signs telling you to reduce your speed to around 50 km/h: do not ignore these instructions, as they are often followed by road blocks. In general, the police are quite tolerant with tourists, but speeding may invalidate car hire insurance.

In town, headlights should be kept dipped. Seat belts are only fitted in the more recent models of car. Their use is not compulsory, but is recommended.

The road signs are the usual international ones, but there are also others on the country roads that warn drivers they are approaching a junction or a stretch of dangerous road *(see p293)*.

THE ROAD NETWORK

THE CARRETERA CENTRAL is an old, narrow and not particularly comfortable road linking Pinar del Río to Guantánamo, via all the provincial capitals. The only motorway in Cuba is the Autopista Nacional, or "Ocho Vías"; it goes from Pinar del Río to Jatibonico, near Sancti Spíritus (the Holguín–Santiago de Cuba stretch is under construction) and is toll-free. It is in good condition but should be used as if it were an ordinary road, without

exceeding the speed limit, because every so often the road is crossed by unmarked railway lines or you may come across wandering animals.

The worst roads, with potholes and bumps, are found in Eastern Cuba, but the surfaces of city streets are by no means perfect either.

PETROL

FUEL IS distributed through the many Servi-Cupet service stations throughout the island. They sell petrol for dollars and many are open 24 hours a day. However, there are fewer stations outside the towns, so it is best to keep the tank topped up, just in case.

Ask the car hire company for a free copy of an *automapa*, which shows where the Servi-Cupet service stations are located across the island.

ROAD MAPS

A GOOD ROAD MAP is essential. *Tiendas* and the book shops in hotels and elsewhere sell good road maps which are published by Ediciones GEO.

Maps and brochures are also distributed free of charge in travel agencies and by the car hire companies.

A hire car at a Servi-Cupet service station

NUMBER PLATES

Cuban car number plates come in different colours, indicating the type of ownership. Above the number is a word indicating the category of the vehicle: *"estatal"* means it belongs to a state-run organization, *"particular"* means it is a private car, *"turismo"* is used for cars rented by tourists and *"empresa"* for joint venture companies.

Official plate

Private plate

Tourist plate

ROAD SAFETY

THE MOST SERIOUS DANGER on Cuban roads is posed, in fact, by slow vehicles: carts and carriages, tractors and cyclists tend to occupy the middle of the road, and before overtaking them it is a good idea to sound the horn.

It is also a good rule of thumb to sound the horn before making a sharp turn or when passing a lorry (they often do not have rear-view mirrors).

It is forbidden to keep your car lights on during the day, unless there is heavy fog. It is advisable not to drive outside town at night unless absolutely necessary, because of poor visibility. Roads are not lit and you may run

into animals, pedestrians and even cyclists, whose bicycles are rarely equipped with front lights and rear reflectors.

At any time of day, take extra care after rainy weather, because road surfaces may become flooded *(see p293)*. In mountain areas there may be some danger of falling rocks.

Tourists on a scooter

CAR HIRE

IN ORDER TO HIRE a car in Cuba visitors must have a valid driver's licence from their own country or an international licence, be over 21 years of age, and have a valid passport to show to the car rental company. The main agencies are **Transautos**, **Havanautos**, **Cubacar** and **Vía Rent a Car**. The first two companies have a number of branch offices in hotels throughout the island and in Servi-Cupet service stations, so that they are able to provide a good network of support, while the other two have offices only in the main cities.

Cars can be picked up and dropped off at most of the airports, but it is advisable to book them well in advance, especially in high season, when the smaller and cheaper models are very much in demand. Payment is made in advance, and you must either leave a cash deposit (which is refunded) or leave an imprint of your credit card. A car may be dropped off at a different

office from the one where it was hired, but there will be a high charge. A penalty will also have to be paid if the contract for car hire is lost.

There are two kinds of optional insurance for hire cars. Plan A covers accidents but not theft, and Plan B covers all risks except for loss of a tyre.

In the event of an accident you must obtain a copy of the police report, which should then be handed over to the car hire company.

For exploring certain parts of the island, including the extreme west and far east, it may be best to hire a four-wheel drive (off-roader) to negotiate the pitted roads.

Larger groups of visitors might prefer to rent a minibus from **Cubamar**, **Cubanacán** or **Transgaviota**. It is also possible to hire scooters.

(see p293)

DIRECTORY

CAR HIRE

Cubacar (Cubanacán)
Calle 1ra. 16401, Miramar, Havana. ⟨**C**⟩ *(7) 332 277.*

Havanautos (Havanatur)
Calle 1 e/ 0 y 2, Miramar, Havana. ⟨**C**⟩ *(7) 203 9833.*

Transautos
Calle 1ra e/ 26 y 28, Miramar, Havana. ⟨**C**⟩ *(7) 204 7644.*
Booking and breakdown: (7) 204 4057.

Vía Rent a Car (Gaviota)
Calle 47 e/ 34 y 41 dep. Kohly, Playa. ⟨**C**⟩ *(7) 2043 606.*
FAX *(7) 2044 455.*

MINIBUS HIRE

Cubacar
Calle 164 esq. 1ra, Reparto Flores, Havana.
⟨**C**⟩ *(7) 332 277.*

Micar
Calle 110 e/ 5 y 3, Playa Habana, Havana. ⟨**C**⟩ *(7) 2042 444.*

Transtur
Calle 1ra esq. 26, Playa Habana, Havana. ⟨**C**⟩ *(7) 2045 532.*

A hired four-wheel drive: a good choice of vehicle for the road conditions in Cuba

Getting Around Havana

IN HAVANA, ROAD TRAFFIC is on the increase but is still nowhere near the levels of a normal European or American city. Unfortunately, getting about using public transport can be a major undertaking, and the same holds true for the other cities on the island. On the other hand, there are plenty of taxis as well as the new *cocotaxis*, which offer a safe and fast way of getting around town. In Habana Vieja and Centro Habana, the most pleasant way to explore is to stay on foot.

Traffic around the Capitolio: rickshaws, vintage cars and a *camello*

WALKING IN HAVANA

HAVANA IS AN IMMENSE city and every district *(municipio)* extends for miles. However, if you are staying in the city centre (the area described on pages 56–105) then it should be quite feasible to do a lot of exploring on foot. Besides, walking along the Malecón seaside promenade, or through the tree-lined streets in the Vedado quarter, or the old Colonial section of town, is a very pleasant occupation. Visitors have the chance to discover hidden corners and details of buildings that would not be noticed in a car.

The best places for hailing taxis are the main arteries such as Calle 23 in Vedado. Should you get lost, ask a local passer-by for help; Cubans are usually very courteous and helpful with foreign tourists.

BUS SERVICES

TRAVELLING BY BUS IN the city can be something of an adventure. Be prepared to devote plenty of time and patience to each journey. The ability to speak a little Spanish will help, and be sure to make a note of the number of the bus you have to take as well as its route, because there are no route maps at the bus stops to indicate the various stops. At any bus stop you must generally ask who is the last (*último*, or *última*) in line for the *ruta* (destination) you want. There is a queue, even though you may not be aware of it, which will re-form in an organized way once the bus arrives.

Passengers get on at the front of the bus, where the conductor pays the fare in small change, always and only in national *pesos*. The cost is very low (less than a *peso*), but you don't get much in return: there may not be many seats, the buses are almost always very crowded, and the heat can often be suffocating.

Allow plenty of time to get off, because passengers tend to block the exit door. Hold wallets and bags close to deter pickpockets.

As well as the normal buses, there are vehicles called *ciclobus*, which also carry bicycles, and *camellos*, a kind of lorry and trailer used for longer routes. They have plenty of room but are nonetheless very uncomfortable. They were a substitute for an underground railway that was planned in the late 1980s, but never built because of the economic crisis.

A comfortable public transport system paid for in dollars has not yet been built. At present the main dollar service is offered by Vaivén minibuses, which link the airport to the city centre, stopping at the main hotels. Fares are cheap and there is air conditioning.

Ciclobuses, carrying people and bicycles around the city

TAXIS

CERTAINLY THE SAFEST and most comfortable way of getting about in Havana is by taxi. There are many cars bearing the word TAXI, but not all of them are authorized to pick up tourists. Official taxis can be recognized easily because they are new and

A *camello* or "camel" bus, so-called by the locals because of its shape

well-kept, comfortable, and almost always have air conditioning. Avoid illegal taxis, which have no accident insurance and may often be more expensive. The taxi companies are **Transgaviota**, **Ok Taxi**, **Turistaxi**, **Fénix**, **Habanataxi**, **Transtur** and **Panataxi** (the cheapest).

Taxis can be summoned by phone or hailed in the street. Taxi ranks are found in front of hotels, at the airport and in the following two places in Habana Vieja: by Plaza de Armas behind el Templete, at the corner of Avenida del Puerto, and in Parque Central at the corner of Calle Empedrado and Tacón.

A state-owned taxi, the best way to get from one district to another

COCOTAXIS

A N ORIGINAL means of transport exclusively for tourists is the *cocotaxi*, an egg-shaped yellow scooter that can carry two passengers as well as the driver. It costs more or less the same as a taxi, but has no meter and the driver does not give receipts. It is very useful for short rides. Besides Havana, *cocotaxis* are now used in almost all Cuban cities. In Trinidad, for example, they shuttle from the city to Playa Ancón.

HORSE-DRAWN VEHICLES

I N HABANA VIEJA it is possible to go on an enjoyable sightseeing tour in horse-drawn carriages – perfectly restored old carts or Colonial-

style carriages, quite unlike those used by Cubans outside of town. These horse-drawn vehicles are not exactly cheap, but can be a romantic and picturesque way of moving around the city.

The carriage and gig rank is located in the square between Calle Empedrado and Calle Tacón, at one end of the handicrafts market.

The *cocotaxi*, an unusual three-seater scooter for tourists

RICKSHAWS

A MORE environmentally friendly but slower alternative to taxis is to use a rickshaw, or bicitaxi, as they are known in Cuba. These are used by Cubans and tourists for short rides in the centre.

They circulate mostly in Habana Vieja, or can be found outside hotel entrances.

DRIVING IN HAVANA

P EOPLE WHO ARE USED TO heavy traffic in big cities will not find driving in Havana too difficult. But it is important to stay alert at all times and watch out for the many cyclists, pedestrians and even dogs, which often run free in the streets. Keep speeds low in order to be able to spot and avoid the many potholes and bumps. The road signs and markings are reasonably good.

In the city centre there are two tunnels. One passes under the Almendares river, connecting Vedado and Miramar (see p109). The other, which begins in Plaza Mártires del 71, behind the Castillo de la Punta, takes you rapidly to the other side of the bay and the Morro and Cabaña fortresses (see pp110–11). The latter is especially useful for those heading for the beaches in Habana del Este (see p113). The alternative is the long, winding port road, though it is easy to get lost.

DIRECTORY

TAXIS

Fénix
(7) 8639 580, 8622 526, 8639 720.

Habanataxi
(7) 539 086.

Ok Taxi
(7) 204 1446, 204 9518.

Panataxi
(7) 555 555.

Transgaviota
(7) 666 777.

Transtur
(7) 553 990.

Turistaxi
(7) 8776 666.

A horse-drawn carriage in Calle Obispo, Habana Vieja

General Index

Acknowledgments

FABIO RATTI EDITORIA would like to thank the following staff at Dorling Kindersley:

MAP CO-ORDINATOR
Dave Pugh.

DTP MANAGER
Jason Little.

MANAGING EDITOR
Anna Streiffert.

MANAGING ART EDITOR
Jane Ewart.

DIRECTOR OF PUBLISHING, TRAVEL GUIDES
Gillian Allan.

PUBLISHER
Douglas Amrine.

DORLING KINDERSLEY would like to thank all those whose contribution and assistance have made the preparation of this book possible.

MAIN CONTRIBUTOR
IRINA BAJINI, a scholar who specializes in Hispanic-American languages and literature, lives in Milan and Havana. Among her publications are a conversation handbook, a Cuban-Italian dictionary published by Vallardi, and a book on the santería religion: *Il dio delle onde, del fuoco, del vento* (The God of the Waves, Fire and Wind), published by Sperling&Kupfer. She has also translated a number of Cuban books.

OTHER CONTRIBUTORS
ALEJANDRO ALONSO, an expert in Cuban art, is a journalist and critic who has published essays and curated exhibitions in Cuba and abroad. The former deputy director of the Museo de Bellas Artes, Alonso now heads the Museo Nacional de la Cerámica (National Ceramics Museum) in Havana, which he founded in 1990.

MIGUEL ANGEL CASTRO MACHADO, the second *historiador de la ciudad* of Baracoa, teaches Hispanic-American literature at the University of Santiago de Cuba.

ANDREA G MOLINARI is executive director of Lauda Air Italia airline and a passionate smoker of, and expert on, Cuban cigars. He is the author of *Sigaro. La guida per l'apprendista fumatore di sigari cubani* (Cigars. A Guide for Newcomers to Cuban Cigar Smoking), published by IdeaLibri.

MARCO OLIVA is a diving instructor and an expert on diving in the Caribbean. He holds various specialist licences, including those for underwater photography, scuba-diving on wrecks, and marine biology.

FRANCESCA PIANA, a journalist and specialist on Latin America, has written numerous travel articles as well as guides to Greece, Mexico, Ecuador and Chile for the Touring Club.

EDITORIAL AND DESIGN ASSISTANCE
Alejandro Alonso, Walfrido La O (Academia de la Historia de Cuba, Havana), Juan Romero Marcos.
For Dorling Kindersley: Monica Allende, Conrad van Dyk, Kathryn Lane, Naomi Peck, Marisa Renzullo, Mary Scott.

PROOF READER
Stewart J. Wild.

SPECIAL THANKS
Archivo fotográfico e histórico de La Habana; Archivo ICAIC; Laura Arrighi (Lauda Air Italia); Bárbara Atorresagasti; Sandro Bajini; Freddy L Cámara; Casa de África, Havana; Aleida Castellanos (Havanatur Italia); Pedro Contreras (Centro de Desarrollo de las Artes Visuales, Havana); Vittoria Cumini (Tocororo restaurant, Milan); Juan Carlos and José Arturo de Dios Lorente; Alfredo Díaz (Tocororo restaurant, Milan); Mariano Fernández Arias (Gaviota); Cecilia Infante (José Martí publishers, Havana); Jardín Botánico del Parque Lenin; Lien La O Bouzán; Manuel Martínez Gomez ("Bohemia" archives); Adrian Adán Gonzalez (Tocororo restaurant, Milan); Guillerma López; Chiara Maretti (Lauda Air Italia); Stefano Mariotti; François Missen; Annachiara Montefusco (Cubanacán Italia); Jorge A Morente Padrón (Archipiélago); Orencio Nardo García (Museo de la Revolución); Eduardo Núñez (Publicitur); Mariacarla Nebuloni; Oficina del Historiador de la Ciudad, Havana; Sullen Olivé Monteagudo (Arcoiris); Angelo Parravicini (Lauda Air Italia); Milagros Pérez (Havanatur Italia); Alicia Pérez Casanova (Horizontes); Josefina Pichardo (Centro de Información y Documentación Turísticas); Richard Pierce; Poder Popular de Isla de la Juventud; Carla Provvedini (Ufficio Turistico di Cuba, Milan); Quinta de los Molinos, Havana; Gianluca Ragni (Gran Caribe); Celia Estela Rojas (Museo de las Parrandas de Remedios); Federica Romagnoli; Aniet Venereo (Archipiélago); Yoraida Santiesteban Vaillant; Lucia Zaccagni.

The Publisher would like to thank Andrea G Molinari in particular for the enthusiasm and willingness with which he supported the preparation of this guide.

PICTURE SOURCES
Geocuba, Havana; Habanos SA.

REPRODUCTION RIGHTS
The Publisher would like to thank all the museums, hotels, restaurants, shops and other sights of interest for their kind assistance and authorization to photograph their premises.

SPECIALLY COMMISSIONED PHOTOS
Dishes and drinks: Paolo Pulga, courtesy of the Tocororo restaurant, Corsico (Milan).

PICTURE CREDITS
key: t = top; tl = top left; tlc = top left centre; tc = top centre; trc = top right centre; tr = top right; tra = top right above; cla = centre left above; ca = centre above; cra = centre right above; cl = centre left; c = centre; cr = centre right; cla = centre left above; crb = centre right below; cb = centre below; bl = bottom left; br = bottom right; b = bottom; bc = bottom centre; bcl = bottom centre left; bcr = bottom centre right; (d) = detail.

Every effort has been made to trace the copyright holders. The publisher apologizes for any unintentional omissions and would be pleased, in such cases, to add an acknowledgment in future editions. The publisher would like to thank all the individuals, local bodies and associations and photographic agencies for permission to reproduce their photographs.

ALEJANDRO ALONSO, Havana: 93cl, 95c.

ARCHIVIO MONDADORI, Milan: Andrea and Antonella Ferrari 149t.

ARCHIVIO RADAMÉS GIRO, Havana: 28br, 28bl.

PIERFRANCO ARGENTIERO, Somma Lombardo: 30bl (all the photos), 31br, 31b, 276cla, 276clb.

MARCO BIAGIOTTI, Perugia: 17bl, 25cl, 87t, 91c, 110c, 128, 135c, 135clb.

CASA DE ÁFRICA, Havana: 9 (insert), 40bl, 42–3c, 42cl, 42bl, 73b.

CENTRO DOCUMENTAZIONE MONDADORI, Milan: 46tr, 47bl, 49tr, 49tl, 52b, 87br, 114cl, 114cr, 114b, 117bl, 163b.

CENTRO HISTORICO DE LA CIUDAD DE LA HABANA, Havana: 26c, 26br, 27tr, 40, 41, 43t, 44, 45, 46bl, 47b, 48tr, 48b, 49bl, 50cl, 59b, 147cl, 215t.

GIANFRANCO CISINI, Milan: 57bl, 80tr, 111br, 161b, 169tl, 170c, 171t, 172t, 184c, 217clb, 227c.

RAUL CORRALES, Havana: 50–51c.

CUBANACAN, Milan: A Cozzi 295b.

MARTINO FAGIUOLI, Modena: 22cra, 22clb, 32tr, 32bl, 32br, 33br, 51tl, 86cr, 178tr, 216b, 220c, 221tl, 221tr, 221c, 222tl, 223b, 222br, 224tl, 225 cla, 225c, 225br, 229tl, 229b, 230c, 231c, 232t, 232b, 238c, 238b, 239t, 239b, 306t.

FARABOLAFOTO, Milan: 49cr, 50tr, 51tr, 52tr, 53bl, 57tl, 66cl.

PAOLO GONZATO, Milan: 12tl, 16c, 18crb *(aura tiñosa)*, 18crb (ox), 27c, 28tr, 29tr *(claves)*, 29tr *(güiro)*, 32–3c, 33br, 33b, 53cb, 75br (all the photos), 126br, 151, 156t, 159t, 168t, 168b, 169cb, 169bl, 169br, 174, 176b, 178tl, 178clb, 180tl, 180tr, 180c, 184cra, 184clb, 184crb, 184b, 185t, 187bl, 188b, 190c, 197b, 208tl, 208tl, 209t, 216t, 227t, 230t, 232c, 244b, 264tl, 266cr, 267clb, 274t, 276tl, 276tr, 276clb, 277tl, 277b (all the photos), 279t, 283, 292t, 294c, 304t, 304b, 305cl (all the photos), 306c, 307t.

GRAZIA GUERRESCHI, Milan: 21ad, 21bd, 37as.

HOTEL HABANA LIBRE, Havana: Sven Creutzmann 244t.

ICAIC, Havana: 25bl, 27bl, 27br, 37b.

IMAGE BANK, Milan: 19 clb (flamingo), L Abreu 5t, 211b, C Ansaloni 152b, 161ca, 162tr, 162b, G Bandieri, 58cra, A Cavalli 14c, 16t, 19tra, 21bd, 21bl, 53br, 54–5, 58cla, 59tr, 59cr, 67tl, 81c, 81br, 88t, 102tl, 113br, 116t, 130c, 148c, 149c, 150, 153t, 166b, 172c, 173tr, 178cl, 181t, 188t, 189t, 194tl, 212tl, 230b, 234c, 235t, 245c, 290c, 277cl; M Everton 286b; GW Faint 281t; L King 295t; A Mihich 286t; A Pistoleri 19cra, 140–41, 144b, 146c, 207b, 231b, 240t, 241t; GA Rossi 4b, 12, 18tr, 18cra, 33tr, 57tr, 58br, 61t, 65b, 66b, 72tr, 72cr, 75cb, 85ca, 85b, 87bl, 96, 105b, 110t, 111b, 115tr, 115b, 126cr, 127tl, 129, 148t, 148b, 152t, 158t, 159b, 164c, 175, 194c, 228t, 229c, 245b, 262t, 262c, 285ca, 301b; E Vergani 113t, 161c.

STEFANO MARIOTTI, Milan: 30br.

CUBAN MINISTRY OF TOURISM, Havana: 278cr, 280t.

MUSEO NACIONAL DE BELLAS ARTES, Havana: 24, 25tr, 25cr, 38, 92, 93, 94, 95.

PAOLO NEGRI, Milan: 80cla, 80b, 144tl, 144c, 146b, 266t, 267b, 276br.

MARCO OLIVA, Milan: 75cla, 89c, 130b, 132b, 133tr, 133c, 133b, 134t, 134bl, 142t, 143 (all the photos), 146t, 169tr 187t, 203b, 228c, 246c, 246b, 285b.

OLYMPIA, Milan: 17cr, 53t, 64b, 284t, 284b.

PRENSA LATINA, Havana: 26tr, 28bc, 29tl, 29bl, 29bc, 36c, 47tr, 50bl, 51br, 51bl, 52c, 167b, 198c, 234b, 280b.

LAURA RECORDATI, Milan: 118t, 118b, 263c.

LUCIO ROSSI, Milan: 3, 16b, 18tl, 18cla, 18clb (woodpecker), 18clb *(cartacuba)*, 18bl, 19tl, 19 trb, 19clb *(gavilán)*, 19crb *(zunzuncito)*, 19crb (lizard), 19bl, 19 br, 20ca, 20cb, 21tl, 23br, 33cra, 34t, 35tr, 59cl, 69b, 72tl, 72b, 87crb, 98cl, 109b, 114t, 127tr, 127b, 132tr, 132c, 135tl, 138t, 138c, 139t, 142c, 142b, 149b, 160tl, 160tr, 160bl (all photos), 161tl, 162tl, 163t, 163c, 176t, 188c, 189b (all photos), 193t, 193c, 193b, 194tr, 194b, 195c, 195b, 205, 206b, 214b, 216c, 217t, 218tr, 220tr, 225t, 225cra, 226b, 233c, 233b, 235b, 236–7, 238tl, 238tr, 240t, 240c, 241c, 241b, 244c, 245t, 246t, 263t, 278b, 287, 293b, 297t, 307b.

ALBERTO SALAZAR, Havana: 29c.

STUDIO FALLETTI, Milan: 31tr, 31cla, 31cr, 31clb, 134cr, 135tr, 135crb.

Cover: all the photos were commissioned except for PAOLO GONZATO F/C cb (Chevrolet); IMAGE BANK F/C r (musical trio); PIERFRANCO ARGENTIERO F/C bc (cigars); SOUTH AMERICAN PICTURES: Rolando Pujol spine, b (mosaic); B/C (Church of San Francisco de Asís in Trinidad).

All other images © Dorling Kindersley. For further information see:

www.dkimages.com

Phrase Book

The Spanish spoken in Cuba is basically the same as the Castilian used in Spain. Among the grammatical variations, visitors should be aware that in Cuba the second person plural is hardly ever used: in place of *vosotros*, people use the pronoun *Ustedes*; consequently they conjugate the verb in the third person plural. As in all of Latin America, here too the "z" is pronounced like the "s", and an "s" followed by a consonant or at the end of a word is aspirate. Some Indian, African and English words are commonly used in present-day Cuban Spanish. This basic phrase book includes common phrases and words, and particular attention has been paid to typically Cuban idioms and words.

CUBAN TERMS

apagón: black-out, power cut
babalawo: a priest of Afro-Cuban religion
bohío: a traditional rural house with palm leaf roof
carro: car
casa de la trova: a club where traditional music is played
batey: village around the sugar factory
cayo: small island
central: a sugar plant
chama: child
criollo: Creole (of Spanish descent born in Cuba)
divisas: (slang) dollars
guagua: bus
guajiro: farmer
guarapo: sugar cane juice
guayabera: men's traditional cotton shirt
ingenio: sugar factory complex
jama: food, meal
eva: woman
jinetera: prostitute, or female hustler
jinetero: male person hustling tourists
libreta: rations book
mogote: cone-shaped hill
moneda nacional: pesos ("national currency")
moros y cristianos: rice & black beans ("Moors and Christians")
orisha: santería religion divinity
paladar: privately-owned restaurant
puro: authentic Cuban cigar
santero: santería priest
tabaco: mediocre quality cigar
tambor: Afro-Cuban religion musical feast
tienda: shop that only accepts dollars
trago: alcoholic drink
tunas: prickly pear
zafra: sugar cane harvest

For food, drinks and fruit, see also pp164-7

EMERGENCIES

Help!	**¡socorro!**
Stop!	**¡pare!**
Call a doctor	**Llamen un médico**
Call an ambulance	**Llamen a una ambulancia**
Police!	**¡policía!**
I've been robbed	**Me robaron**

COMMUNICATION ESSENTIALS

Yes	**sí**
No	**no**
Please	**por favor**
Pardon me	**perdone**
Excuse me	**disculpe**
I'm sorry	**lo siento**
Thanks	**gracias**
Hello!	**¡buenas!**
Good day	**buenos días**
Good afternoon	**buenas tardes**
Good evening	**buenas noches**
Night	**noche**

Morning	**mañana**
Tomorrow	**mañana**
Yesterday	**ayer**
Here	**acá**
How?	**¿cómo?**
When?	**¿cuándo?**
Where?	**¿dónde?**
Why?	**¿por qué?**
How are you?	**¿qué tal?**
It's a pleasure!	**¡mucho gusto!**
Goodbye, so long	**hasta luego/chau**

USEFUL PHRASES

That's fine	**está bien/ocá**
Fine!	**¡qué bien!**
How long?	**¿Cuánto falta?**
Do you speak a little English?	**¿Habla un poco de inglés?**
I don't understand	**No entiendo**
Could you speak more slowly?	**¿Puede hablar más despacio?**
I agree/OK	**de acuerdo/ocá**
Certainly!	**¡Claro que sí!**
Let's go!	**¡Vámonos!**

USEFUL WORDS

Large	**grande**
Small	**pequeño**
Hot	**caliente**
Cold	**frío**
Good	**bueno**
Bad	**malo**
So-so	**más o menos**
Mediocre	**regular**
Sufficient	**suficiente**
Well/fine	**bien**
Open	**abierto**
Closed	**cerrado**
Full	**lleno**
Empty	**vacío**
Right	**derecha**
Left	**izquierda**
Straight	**recto**
Under	**debajo**
Over	**arriba**
Quickly, soon /early	**pronto/temprano**
Late	**tarde**
Now	**ahora**
Soon	**ahorita**
More	**más**
Less	**menos**
Little	**poco**
Much	**mucho/muy**
Too much	**demasiado**
In front of	**delante**
Behind	**detrás**
First floor	**primer piso**
Ground floor	**planta baja**
Lift	**elevador**
Bathroom	**servicios**
Women	**mujeres**
Men	**hombres**
Toilet paper	**papel sanitario**
Camera	**cámara**
Roll of film	**rollo**
Batteries	**baterías**
Cell battery	**pilas**
Passport	**pasaporte**
Visa; tourist card	**visa; tarjeta turistica**

HEALTH

I don't feel well	**Me siento mal**
I have a stomach ache headache	**Me duele el estómago la cabeza**
He/she is ill	**Está enfermo/a**
I need to rest	**Necesito decansar**
Drug store	**farmacia**

POST OFFICE AND BANK

Bank	**banco**
I'm looking for a bureau de change	**Busco una Cadeca**
What is the dollar rate?	**¿A cómo está el dolar?**
I want to send a letter	**Quiero enviar una carta**
Postcard	**postal tarjeta**
Stamp	**sello**
Draw out money	**sacar dinero**

SHOPPING

How much is it?	**¿Cuánto cuesta?**
What time do you open/close?	**¿A qué hora abre/ cierra?**
May I pay with a credit card?	**¿Puedo pagar con tarjeta de crédito?**

SIGHTSEEING

Avenue	**avenida**
Beach	**playa**
Castle, fortress	**castillo**
Cathedral	**catedral**
Church	**iglesia**
District	**barrio**
Garden	**jardín**
Guide	**guía**
House	**casa**
Map	**mapa**
Motorway	**autopista**
Museum	**museo**
Park	**parque**
Road	**carretera**
Square, plaza	**plaza/parque**
Street	**calle, callejón**
Town hall	**Ayuntamiento**
Tourist bureau	**buró de turismo**

TRANSPORT

When does it leave?	**¿A qué hora sale?**
Could you call a taxi for me?	**¿Me puede llamar un taxi?**
Airport	**aeropuerto**
Train station	**estación de ferrocarriles**
Bus station	**terminal de autobús**
Customs	**aduana**
Port of embarkation	**puerta de embarque**
Boarding pass	**tarjeta de embarque**
Car hire	**alquiler de carros**
Bicycle	**bicicleta**
Rate	**tarifa**
Insurance	**seguro**
Petrol/gas station	**estación de gasolina**
Garage	**garage**
I have a flat tyre	**Ponché una goma**

Staying in a Hotel

Single room/ double	**habitación sencilla/ doble**
Shower	**ducha**
Bathtub	**bañera**
Balcony	**balcón, terraza**
I want to be awakened at...	**Necesito que me despierten a las...**
Warm water/ cold	**agua caliente/ fría**
Soap	**jabón**
Towel	**toalla**
Key	**llave**

Eating Out

What is there to eat?	**¿Qué hay para comer?**
The bill, please	**la cuenta, por favor**
Glass	**vaso**
Cutlery	**cubiertos**
I would like some water	**Quisiera un poco de agua**
Have you got wine?	**¿Tienen vino?**
The beer is not cold enough	**La cerveza no está bien fría**
Breakfast	**desayuno**
Lunch	**almuerzo**
Dinner	**comida**
Raw	**crudo**
Cooked	**cocido**

Menu Decoder

aceite	oil
agua mineral	mineral water
aguacate	avocado
ajo	garlic
arroz	rice
asado	roasted
atún	tuna
azúcar	sugar
bacalao	cod
café	coffee
camarones	prawns
carne	meat
congrí	rice with beans and onions
cerveza	beer
dulce	sweet, dessert

ensalada	salad
fruta	fruit
fruta bomba	papaya
helado	ice cream
huevo	egg
jugo	fruit juice
langosta	lobster
leche	milk
marisco	seafood
mantequilla	butter
pan	bread
papas	potatoes
postre	dessert
pescado	fish
plátano	banana
pollo	chicken
potaje/sopa	soup
puerco	pork
queso	cheese
refresco	drink
sal	salt
salsa	sauce
té	tea
vinagre	vinegar

Time

Minute	**minuto**
Hour	**hora**
Half-hour	**media hora**
Quarter of an hour	**un cuarto**
Monday	**lunes**
Tuesday	**martes**
Wednesday	**miércoles**
Thursday	**jueves**
Friday	**viernes**
Saturday	**sábado**
Sunday	**domingo**
January	**enero**
February	**febrero**
March	**marzo**
April	**abril**
May	**mayo**
June	**junio**
July	**julio**
August	**agosto**
September	**setiembre**
October	**octubre**
November	**noviembre**
December	**diciembre**

Numbers

0	**cero**
1	**uno**
2	**dos**
3	**tres**
4	**cuatro**
5	**cinco**
6	**seis**
7	**siete**
8	**ocho**
9	**nueve**
10	**diez**
11	**once**
12	**doce**
12	**trece**
14	**catorce**
15	**quince**
16	**dieciséis**
17	**diecisiete**
18	**dieciocho**
19	**diecinueve**
20	**veinte**
30	**treinta**
40	**cuarenta**
50	**cincuenta**
60	**sesenta**
70	**setenta**
80	**ochenta**
90	**noventa**
100	**cien**
500	**quinientos**
1000	**mil**
first	**primero/a**
second	**segundo/a**
third	**tercero/a**
fourth	**cuarto/a**
fifth	**quinto/a**
sixth	**sexto/a**
seventh	**séptimo/a**
eight	**octavo/a**
ninth	**noveno/a**
tenth	**décimo/a**